SPIRITUAL TEACHINGS OF THE PROPHET

SPIRITUAL TEACHINGS OF THE PROPHET

by
Tayeb Chourief

Translated by
Edin Q. Lohja

Edited by
Fatima Jane Casewit

FONS VITAE

First published in 2011 by
Fons Vitae
49 Mockingbird Valley Drive
Louisville, KY 40207
http://www.fonsvitae.com
Email: fonsvitaeky@aol.com

Library of Congress Control Number: 2011943606
ISBN 978-1891785-85-6

Printed in Canada

Table of Contents

Author's Note

This collection deals exclusively with the spiritual teachings contained in the *Ḥadīth*. It presupposes a sufficient knowledge of the life of the Prophet ﷺ (*sīrah nabawiyya*)[1] and a certain familiarity with different aspects of his *Sunna*.[2]

There exists a distinction between the moral teachings consisting of a set of injunctions aimed at the realization of good conduct in diverse situations, and spiritual teachings seeking inner perfection through knowledge and spiritual wayfaring. Only the spiritual teachings of the Prophet ﷺ will be dealt with here.[3]

---

1. Besides the celebrated and voluminous work *al-Sīrah al-Nabawiyya* by Ibn Hishām (d. 218/833), there are shorter and more recent biographies like Ṣafy al-Raḥmān al-Mubārakafūrī's *al-Raḥīq al-Makhtūm* ("The Sealed Nectar", in numerous editions). The best biography in English remains Martin Lings' *Muhammad, His Life Based on the Earliest Sources*, in several editions.
2. Al-Nawawī's (d. 676/1277) collection of *ḥadīth Riyāḍ al-Ṣāliḥīn* ("Gardens of the Righteous") addresses in a rather complete fashion the rituals and ethics, while remaining accessible.
3. The contemporary scholar Muḥammad al-Ghazzālī (d. 1417/1996) has devoted a special collection to the moral teachings of the Prophet, entitled *Khuluq al-Muslim* (Damascus: Dār al-Qalam, 1416/1996). This work has been translated into French as *L'Ethique du Musulman* (Paris: Al Qalam, 2000).

Editor's Note

It has been an honor to edit this work. Attempting to capture the essence and spirit of these blessed Prophetic sayings specific to spiritual growth and wayfaring through translation between three languages has been a formidable task for all those who have been involved in producing the English version of this precious volume. To this end, several critical editorial decisions have had to be made. It was decided to use, throughout the book, the Arabic term *ḥadīth*, which is the singular form of the noun meaning "Prophetic saying" rather than interchange it with its plural form *aḥādīth*, which could cause confusion for readers not familiar with Arabic and detract from the content of the Prophetic sayings and commentaries.

"Man" or "men" is used in its original theological meaning, i. e. "a being composed of a body and a soul or spirit"[1] and includes both genders, the general meaning being "humankind." Arabic has specific terms which refer to human beings as such (*insān* is one example) and do not distinguish between genders.

We arc indebted to the translator, Edin Lohja, for his ardor and stamina in integrating editing suggestions, following the long process of translation. We are also very grateful to Elena Lloyd-Sidle and Omar Ahmadouchi for their valuable contributions and insights during the editing process. On behalf of the entire team that produced this English version, special thanks are due to Dr. Kenneth Honerkamp of the Department of Religion at the University of Georgia at Athens for combing through the text during the final days before going to press.

1. The American Heritage Dictionary, p. 761, Houghton Mifflin Company, Boston 1985

List of Abbreviations

'Awn al-Ma'būd, Shams al-Ḥaqq al-'Aẓīm al-Ābādī, *'Awn al-Ma'būd* [commentary of Abū Dāwūd's *Sunan*], ed. Muḥammad 'Abd al-Muḥsin, Medina: 1968.

Bayān: 'Alī Jum'a, *al-Bayān limā yashghal al-adhhān*, Cairo: al-Muqaṭṭam, 2005.

Crisis: René Guénon, *The Crisis of the Modern World*, Alger: Bouchène, 1990.

Dhû l-Nûn: Ibn al-'Arabī, *La Vie merveilleuse de Dhû l-Nûn al-Misrî* [translation of *Kawkab*; text edited with *The Sufis of Andalusia*].

E.I. (2): *Encyclopedia of Islam*, second edition, E. J. Brill, Leiden.

Echoes: Frithjof Schuon, *Echoes of Perennial Wisdom*, Bloomington: World Wisdom, 2002.

Écrits: Abd al-Kader, *Écrits spirituels* [translation of *Kitāb al-mawāqif* of Amīr 'Abd al-Qādir], Paris: Seuil, 1982.

Enseignement: al-Junayd, *Enseignement spiritual. Traités, lettres, oraisons et sentences*, tr. from Arabic and presented by Roger Deladrière, Sindbad, 1983.

Extinction: Ibn al-'Arabī, *Le Livre de l'extinction dans la contemplation*, tr., presented and commented by Michel Vâlsan, éd. de l'Œuvre, 1984.

Eye: Frithjof Schuon, *Eye of the Heart: Metaphysics, Cosmology, Spiritual Life,* Bloomington: World Wisdom, 1997.

Face: Frithjof Schuon, *In the Face of the Absolute*, Bloomington: World Wisdom, 1994.

Fayḍ al-Qadīr: al-Munāwī, *Fayḍ al-Qadīr fī sharḥ al-Jāmi' al-ṣaghīr*, Beirut: Dār al-ma'rifa, 1972.

Form: Frithjof Schuon, *Form and Substance in the Religions*, Bloomington: World Wisdom, 2002.

Fut: Ibn al-'Arabī, *al-Futūḥāt al-Makkiyya*, Cairo: Būlāq, 1329 H. OH refers to the critical edition by Osman Yahya.

Haltes: 'Abd al-Kader, *Le Livre des Haltes* [partial translation of *Kitāb al-mawāqif* by Amīr 'Abd al-Qādir], éd. Alif, 1996.

Ḥikam: Ibn 'Aṭā' Allāh, *al-Ḥikam al-'Atā'iyya*, ed. Paul Nwiya, in *Ibn 'Aṭā' Allāh et la Naissance de la Confrérie Šaḏilite*, éd. Dar el-Machreq, 1990.

Ibrīz: 'Abd al-'Azīz al-Dabbāgh, with comments gathered by Ibn al-Mubārāk al-Lamtī, critical edition by Muḥammad 'Adnān al-Shammā', Damascus, 1984.

Insights: René Guénon, *Insights into Islamic Esoterism and Taoism*, tr. Samuel D. Fohr, New York: Sophia Perennis, 2003.

Introduction: Titus Burckhardt, *Introduction to Sufi Doctrines*, tr. Samuel D. Fohr, Sophia Perennis.

Iḥyā': al-Ghazzālī, *Iḥyā' 'Ulūm al-Dīn*, ed. Badawī Ṭabbāna, Cairo, 1957.
Kawkab: Ibn al-'Arabī, *el-Kawkab al-durrī fī manāqib Dhī'l-Nūn al-Miṣrī*, Beirut: Dār al-Kutub al-'ilmiyya, 2005.
Khiḍriyya: 'Abd al-Wahhāb al-Sha'rānī, *al-Mīzān al-Khiḍriyya*, Beirut: Dār al-kutub al-'ilmiyya, 1999.
Latā'if: Ibn 'Aṭā' Allāh, *Latā'if al-Minan*, Beirut: Dār al-kutub al-'ilmiyya, 1998.
Le Soufi: Jean-Louis Michon, *Le Soufi Marocain Aḥmad Ibn 'Ajība et son Mi'rāj*, éd. Vrin, 1973.
Lettres: Partial translation of *Rasā'il* of Shaykh Darqāwī, by M. Chabry, under the title *Lettres sur la Voie Spirituelle*, éd. La Caravane, 2003.
Letters of a Sufi Master: partial translation of *Rasā'il*, by Titus Burckhardt, Louisville: Fons Vitae, 1998.
Lettre ouverte: Translation of Shaykh al-'Alawī's *Qawl*, by M. Chabry, under the title *Lettre Ouverte a Celui qui Critique le Soufisme*, éd. La Caravane, 2001.
Luma': Abū Naṣr al-Sarrāj, *Kitāb al-Luma'*, ed. and tr. by S. de Laugier de Beaurecueil as *Les Étapes des Itinerants vers Dieu*, éd. I.F.A.O., 1962.
Maqṣad: al-Ghazzālī, *al-Maqṣad al-asnā*, verified and edited by F. A. Shehadi, Beirut: Dār al-mashrik, 1982.
Mawāqif: Yūsuf Khaṭṭār, *al-Mawsū'a al-Yūsufiyya fī Bayān Adillat al-Ṣūfiyya*, Damascus, 1999.
Mishkāt: al-Ghazzālī, *Mishkāt al-anwār*, critical edition by Samīḥ Daghīm, Beirut: Dār al-Fikr al-lubnānī, 1994.
Mi'rāj: Ibn 'Ajība, *Mi'rāj al-Tashawwuf ilā Ḥaqā'iq al-Taṣawwuf*, in *Silsila nūrāniyya*, Maktabat al-Rashād, 1997.
Minaḥ: Aḥmad al-'Alawī, *al-Minaḥ al-Quddūsiyya*, Beirut: Dār Ibn Zaydūn, 1986.
Munqidh: al-Ghazzālī, *al-Munqidh min al-Ḍalāl*, French translation with Arabic text, by Farid Jabre, Beirut, 1969.
Océan: Michel Chodkiewicz, *Un Océan sans Savage*, éd. du Seuil, 1992.
Patience: Tayeb Chouiref, *Le Livre de la Patience*, éd. La Ruche, 2001.
Perspectives: Frithjof Schuon, *Spiritual Perspectives and Human Facts*, London: Faber and Faber, 1955.
Qaṣd: Ibn 'Aṭā' Allāh, *al-Qaṣd al-Mujarrad fī Ma'rifat al-Ism al-Mufrad*, Cairo, n.d.
Qawl: Aḥmad al-'Alawī, *al-Qawl al-Ma'rūf liman ankara al-Taṣawwuf*, Mostaganem, 1367 H.
Rasā'il: al-'Arabī al-Darqāwī, *Bushūr al-Hidāya fī Madhhab al-Ṣūfiyya: al-Rasā'il al-Darqāwiyya*, Beirut: Dār al-kutub al-'ilmiyya, 2003.
Reign: René Guénon, *The Reign of Quantity and the Signs of the Times*, tr. Lord Northbourne, New York: Sophia Perennis, 2004.

Risāla: 'Abd al-Karīm al-Qushayrī, *al-Risāla al-Qushayriyya fī 'ilm al-Taṣawwuf*, Beirut: Dār al-jīl, n.d.

Soufis: Ibn al-'Arabī, *Les Soufis d'Andalousie*, tr. and presented by R. W. J. Austin, French version by Gérard Lecomte, éd. Albin Michel, 1995.

Stations: Frithjof Schuon, *Stations of Wisdom*, Bloomington: World Wisdom, 1995.

Sufi Saint: Martin Lings, *A Sufi Saint of the Twentieth Century*, Cambridge: Islamic Texts Society, 1993.

Sufism: Frithjof Schuon, *Sufism, Veil and Quintessence*, Bloomington: World Wisdom, 2007.

Tabernacle: al-Ghazzālī, *Le Tabernacle des Lumières*, tr. and intr. by Roger Deladrière, éd. du Seuil, 1981.

Tāj: al-Junayd, *Tāj al-'Ārifīn*, texts collected by Su'ād al-Ḥakīm, Cairo: Dār al-Shurūq, 2004.

Sufi Path of Knowledge: William Chittick, *The Sufi Path of Knowledge* Albany: State University of New York Press, 1989

Understanding Islam: Frithjof Schuon, *Understanding Islam*, tr. London: Allen & Unwin, 1963.

What is Sufism?: Martin Lings, *What is Sufism?* Cambridge: Islamic Texts Society, 1995.

Introduction

There are several terms in Arabic referring to the teachings of the Prophet ﷺ. The term *ḥadīth* (utterance, narrative) refers to a tradition going back to the Prophet ﷺ and reporting his actions (*fi'l*), his words (*qawl*), his explicit or implicit approvals (*taqrīr*), or his traits (*ṣifāt, shamā'il*). The word *khabar* (lit. information, news) sometimes refers to a tradition of the Prophet ﷺ, and at other times to a tradition of the Companions (*ṣaḥāba*) or the Followers (*tābi'ūn*), depending on the authors. As for the term *athar* (lit. trace, vestige), it usually refers to a tradition of the Companions or the Followers.

The *Ḥadīth* literature therefore seeks to record what has appropriately been called the *sunna* of the Prophet ﷺ, or the wont of the Prophet ﷺ. However, during the first three Islamic centuries, the terms *ḥadīth* and *sunna* retained specific connotations: "The former is the initially orally transmitted and later written registration of, among other things, the revered practice of the pious forebears, with at their head the Prophet ﷺ and the earliest Muslims, while the latter is an abstraction which encompasses the revered practice of anyone of the past, although despised or indifferent practices are also occasionally referred to with the term."[1] It would seem that the Umayyad caliph 'Umar ibn 'Abd al-'Azīz was the first to isolate the *sunna* of the Prophet ﷺ from other *sunna*s.[2]

****

It is known that, in the early period, the Prophet ﷺ had forbidden his Companions from gathering the *Ḥadīth* in writing, in order to give priority to the Qur'ān and avoid any interference with the Revealed Book: "Do not transcribe anything from me except the Qur'ān. May whoever transcribes anything from me perish!"[3]

In order to have an idea of what the conditions of the transmission of oral teachings from the Prophet ﷺ may have been, it might be useful to recall the point made by M. Hamidullah regarding this issue: "It goes without saying that it is humanly impossible to record *everything* that someone says, does, and approves. At the beginning of Islam, for several years, there were only a handful of Muslims who were persecuted to the point of being prevented from freely meeting the Prophet ﷺ. Furthermore, most of them were illiterate."[4] These factors explain why we possess so few written

1. G. H. Juynboll, *E. I.* (2), art. *Sunna*.
2. *Ibid.*
3. Related by Abū Sa'īd al-Khudrī, as quoted by Aḥmad ibn Ḥanbal.
4. El-Bokhari, *Les traditions islamiques*, Association culturelle islamique, série nº 5, p. V, Paris, 1981.

documents going back to the Meccan period: "There are written narrations concerning the Prophet ﷺ from the Meccan period, but no systematic collection of *ḥadīth* took place then. The religious persecution by the pagan Meccans may be partially responsible for this."[5]

The Medinite period, which saw the birth and organization of the first "City-State" of Islam, was favorable to the development of writing. "During the Medinite period of the life of the Prophet ﷺ, the task of transcribing letters and of carrying out official correspondence grew continually, due to the exigencies of the administration of State and other political needs. [. . .] One should not be surprised that, later on, the number of secretaries increased greatly and that a regular body of secretariat was given the task to devote itself exclusively to the official correspondence of the Holy Prophet ﷺ"[6] These elements led M. Hamidullah to the following conclusion: " . . . to skeptically declare that nothing was put to writing during the life of the Holy Prophet ﷺ would mean to rely as proof on a suspicion pushed to the extreme, to the point of absurdity."[7]

The *Ḥadīth* were gathered and transmitted in an oral tradition, until the Prophet ﷺ, considering that the Qur'ān was sufficiently known and widespread, authorized 'Abd Allāh ibn 'Amr al-'Āṣ, amongst other Companions, to put them into writing. The latter relates the following anecdote: "The Prophet ﷺ gave me permission to note anything I wished from his words, which surprised me, and we had the following dialogue:

> May I write everything that I hear you say?
> Indeed, yes!
> Whether you are content or angry?
> Certainly, for I say nothing but the truth, whatever my disposition [might be]!"[8]

This authorization of the Prophet ﷺ enabled 'Abd Allāh ibn'Amr to be considered the most knowledgable companion on the Prophetic traditions. From the notes he accumulated, he composed a book which he named *Ṣaḥīfa Ṣādiqa*. According to some witnesses this work brought together a thousand *ḥadīth*.[9] The collection of *Ḥadīth* began during the first century of

5. *Ibid.*
6. *Ṣaḥīfa*, § 25.
7. *Ibid.*, § 28.
8. Muhammad Hamidullah, "La Rédaction du Hadith aux Premiers Temps de l'Islam", *Le Musulman*, nº 17, (1991), p. 14.
9. *Ibid.* Hence, Hamidullah deems that one can still have an idea about the contents of this work: "We must be grateful to Ibn Ḥanbal for having seemingly incorporated the totality of this work of 'Abdullāh ibn 'Amr into his invaluable and voluminous *Musnad*, under the chapter "'Abdullāh ibn 'Amr ibn al-'Āṣ," which compensates for the loss of the original to a certain degree. As we shall later see, he did the same for the *Ṣaḥīfah* of Hammām." *Ṣaḥīfah* § 51.

the *Hijra.*[10] As an example, let us mention Anas ibn Mālik (d. 93/711), another Companion who was part of the Prophet's close circle of Companions in Medina and who recorded numerous *ḥadīth* in writing, despite his young age. This young boy, who knew how to read and write, was assigned by his parents to serve the Prophet ﷺ, a duty which he fulfilled day and night for ten years.[11] Anas lived for many years after the Prophet's death, and one of his disciples, Sa'īd ibn Hilāl, witnessed the teachings transmitted by him: "After we became numerous—an alternate reading: after we greatly insisted—Anas brought out notebooks (*majāll*) for us from a safe which he possessed, and he said, 'This is what I have heard from the Prophet ﷺ; I wrote it all down and then showed it to him.'"[12]

The specialist historian of *ḥadīth* James Robson, while confessing to not understanding why certain *ḥadīth* mention a prohibition against recording the teachings of the Prophet ﷺ, nonetheless recognizes the existence of small collections of *ḥadīth* from the earliest days of Islam:

> Whatever may be the justification for the opinion according to which recording *ḥadīth* was prohibited, even early on there were persons who took notes for their personal use, and these notes constituted the basis for the more extensive books which saw the light of day. Amongst these men, one can mention 'Urwa ibn al-Zubayr (d. 94/712 or 99/717) from Medina, who reportedly transmitted numerous traditions from his aunt 'Ā'isha, and Muḥammad ibn Muslim ibn Shihāb al-Zuhrī (d. 124/741) who settled in Syria and was one of the most largely quoted authorities. Mention is also made of *ṣaḥīfa*s (scrolls) on which certain Companions of the Prophet ﷺ would write down traditions.[13]

This is how written collections of *Ḥadīth* appeared during the lifetime of the Prophet ﷺ. Nonetheless, this was not done without hesitation, and it is well known that the first caliphs were particularly cautious in this domain. Thus, Ibn Shihāb al-Zuhrī[14] relates from 'Urwa ibn al-Zubayr that 'Umar ibn al-Khaṭṭāb had thought of putting the *Ḥadīth* to writing. For this, he consulted a number of Companions, most of whom shared his view. But 'Umar was overtaken by his conscience and suspended his decision for

10. Contrary to what has been claimed by I. Goldziher. His important work, *Muhammedanische Studien*, which appeared in 1890, remained for a long time the principal reference for the subject of *Ḥadīth* studies in Western languages. This work has been translated into French by Léon Bercher: *Études sur la tradition islamique*, Paris 1952. On Goldziher's concepts and their refutal, see M. M. Azami's *Studies in Early Hadith Literature*, American Trust Publications, 1992, pp. 8-27.
11. Cf. *ḥadīth* 168.
12. "La rédaction du Hadith aux premiers temps de l'Islam" cited on p. 15.
13. E.I. (2): art. HADĪTH.
14. On this important figure and his role in *Ḥadīth* transmission, see *Early Hadith*, pp. 88-93, and especially pp. 278-92.

a month. At the end of this period, he gathered the Companions and told them: "I have spoken to you about putting the traditions to writing, but I remembered what the People of the Book (*ahl al-kitāb*) did before you. Having written down matters other than the Sacred Book, they started to occupy themselves with them and neglected the Book that God had sent to them. That is why I shall not mix anything with the Qur'ān."[15] Similarly, it is related that Abū Bakr, the first Caliph, had undertaken the writing of a collection of *ḥadīth* by bringing together what he knew himself and what had been related to him by other Companions. According to Hamidullah, "It was perhaps on the request of his learned and eminent daughter 'Ā'isha, widow of the Prophet ﷺ (who knew how to read but could not write, and whose thirst for various sciences, jurisprudence, medicine, history, arithmetic, poetry, etc., was insatiable), that Abū Bakr handed his notebook to her, only to take it back the next day, saying: 'I could not sleep because of my conscience, as there are narrations which I kept from my friends; maybe the words therein are not those used by the Prophet ﷺ. Then, he immediately destroyed this work.'"[16]

One can easily understand the caution the Companions showed when one considers how immense the *Ḥadīth* literature had grown. Indeed, Hamidullah estimates that "the 'scholars' of the earliest days, the Companions of the Prophet ﷺ, are reckoned in the hundreds of thousands; and, according to a classical expert, more than one hundred thousand of them have left us at least one *ḥadīth* about their master, Muḥammad."[17] In another study,[18] Hamidullah specifies that indeed, at the end of the Meccan period, there were more or less five hundred converts, and that it is admitted that 140,000 pilgrims witnessed the farewell sermon (*khuṭbat al-wada'*) delivered by the Prophet ﷺ three months before his death. This explains why there were so many Companions who related one or more *ḥadīth*.

Concerning the written records of the *Ḥadīth*, modern scholars have been able to establish that about fifty Companions had composed small collections.[19] Apart from those already mentioned, the main ones amongst them are:

Sa'd ibn 'Ubāda (d. 15/636)
'Abd Allāh ibn Mas'ūd (d. 32/652)
'Alī ibn Abī Ṭālib (d. 40/661)
Mughīra ibn Shu'ba (d. 50/670)

15. Malake Abiad, "Règles et méthods de transmission du Ḥadīth", *Le Musulman*, nº 1, January-March 1991, p. 21.

16. El-Bokhari, *Les Traditions islamiques*, *op. cit.*, p. viii.

17. "La rédaction du Hadith aux premiers temps de l'Islam", p. 13.

18. El-Bokhari, *Les Traditions islamiques*, p. v.

19. On this subject, readers will benefit from M. M. Azami's work *Studies in Early Hadith Literature*, pp. 34-60.

Samura ibn Jundub (d. 59/678)
Jābir ibn ʻAbd Allāh (d. 78/697)
ʻAbd Allāh ibn Abī Awfā (d. 86/705)

Let us add to this list Abū Hurayra (d. 58/677), who related several thousand *ḥadīth*[20] without writing them down himself, and who had a disciple called Hammām ibn Munabbih (d. 101/719), who wrote a *ṣaḥīfa*[21] (scroll) containing 138 *ḥadīth*.[22]

In addition, about fifty Companions are known to have outlived the Prophet ﷺ by 50 or more years. Amongst them we could mention:

Abū al-Ṭufayl (d. 110/728)
Hirmās ibn Ziyād (d. 102/720)
Maḥmūd ibn al-Rabīʻ (d. 99/717)
Wāthila ibn al-Asqaʻ (d. 83/702)

The latter, even though he did not put the *ḥadīth* to writing himself, held circles of learning in Damascus, where he related Prophetic traditions, which people would write down as he dictated. Also, there were numerous Companions who migrated to different regions of the caliphate: Egypt, Syria, Mesopotamia, and so on.

Very early on, probably from the first century, fabricated traditions appeared and were forged for different motives. Although there were sometimes pious exaggerations seeking to uplift the believers, there were also interest-driven falsehoods during times of dogmatic or political quarrels. All of this contributed to sensing the need to control and verify the reports and narrations going back to the Prophet ﷺ. This is how many disciplines, brought together under the title *ʻulūm al-ḥadīth*, the *Ḥadīth* sciences, were born. Amongst these disciplines, *asmā' al-rijāl* was devoted to the knowledge of the transmitters of *ḥadīth*: comprised of some 100,000 brief biographies. A set of criteria was established to determine if a transmitter was trustworthy or not. These criteria can be summed up as righteousness (*ʻadāla*) and reliability (*ḍabṭ*). Righteousness includes the following aspects: being Muslim, having reached puberty, having discernment, and being exempt from any depravity. As for reliability, it excludes deficient memory, gross mistakes, and distraction. All these criteria gave rise to the discipline which received the name *jarḥ wa taʻdīl*. The first works in this domain were *al-Tārīkh al-kabīr* by al-Bukhārī (d. 256/870), *al-Jarḥ wa*

20. The largest number of *ḥadīth*, almost 3500, were reported by this Companion.

21. According to M. M. Azami, this term is synonymous with *nuskha* (lit. copy) and he quotes al-Dhahabī who uses the term for the *ṣaḥīfa* of Hammām.

22. This collection was found and published by Muḥammad Hamidullah under the title "Aqdam ta'tīf fī-l-Ḥadīth al-nabawī, Ṣaḥīfat Hammām ibn Munabbih wa makānatuhā fī ta'rīkh ʻilm al-Ḥadīth," *Majallat al-Majmaʻ al-ʻilmī al-ʻarabī* (R.A.A.D.), 28, (1953). We shall return again to this important collection.

al-ta'dīl by Ibn Abī Ḥātim (d. 327/938) and Ibn Ḥibbān's (d. 354/965) *al-Thiqāt*.

The non-Arabs, who became integrated as "clients" (*mawālī*) into the Caliphate, very often played a relatively important role in the transmission of *Ḥadīth*: "In its entirety, the *Ḥadīth* literature owes a lot to the *mawālī*, the foreign 'clients' of the Arab families or tribes, who occupied an important place in the drawing up and development of transmission."[23]

The effort of putting the *Ḥadīth* into writing brought about a relatively strong circulation of "collected scrolls" of *ḥadīth* in the second century of the Hijra. Thus, A. L. de Prémare speaks of ". . . a veritable circulation of writings from all genres in the Arabia of the seventh and eighth centuries, and a relatively common usage of writing in general."[24]

Amongst the *mawālī*, we must mention the eminent role of Nāfi' (d. 117/735 or 120/738), an emancipated slave of 'Abd Allāh ibn 'Umar (d. 74/693). Under the dictation of the latter, this very learned man wrote down the *Ḥadīth*. He spent thirty years under the supervision of Ibn 'Umar, to whom the following saying is attributed: "The presence of Nāfi' amongst us is truly a great blessing from God."[25] It is related that Nāfi' dictated *ḥadīth* to his students and that he asked them to bring their notes to him for verification of their contents.[26]

Another Follower who would play a firsthand role in the history of the written transmission of the *Ḥadīth* was Hammām ibn Munabbih (d. 101/719), the author of the famous *ṣaḥīfa* bearing his name. This student of Abū Hurayra—who likewise hailed from Yemen—recorded 138 *ḥadīth* in a collection which has fortunately reached us. The discovered manuscript of the *Ṣaḥīfa* can be verified by comparing it with the text which is included in the *Musnad* of Aḥmad ibn Ḥanbal. Here are the conclusions reached by M. Hamidullah after studying the contents of this *Ṣaḥīfa*: "After meticulously comparing and collating it, one obtains the proof that the later compilers, Ibn Ḥanbal, al-al-Bukhārī, Muslim, etc. . . . did not change a word, not even an iota, and they did not touch the general sense of the tradition of the Prophet ﷺ. Every *ḥadīth* of the *Ṣaḥīfat Hammam* is not only found *verbatim* in the six canonical books of *ḥadīth* (*al-Ṣiḥāḥ al-sittah*) where they

23. A. L. de Prémare, "Comme il est écrit" - l'histoire d'un texte, *Studia Islamica*, n° 70 (1989), p. 42.

24. *Ibid.*, p. 47.

25. Ibn Ḥajar, *Tahdhīb al-tahdhīb*, c.f. M. Hamidullah, *Ṣaḥīfa*, § 70.

26. *Early Hadith*, p. 96. In this work, M. M. Azami has published the manuscript of a collection of Nāfi' containing 127 *ḥadīth*. This manuscript is from the *Ẓahiriyya* of Damascus: *Majmū'* 105, folio 135-149. On Nāfi', see also *E. I.* (2) art. NĀFI', where G.H.A. Juynboll goes so far as to question the historical existence of this *mawlā*. Harald Motzki refuted this thesis of Juynboll at length: "Quo vadis Hadiṯ-Forschung?", *Der Islam*, 1996, vol. 73, no. 1, pp. 40-80; no. 2, pp. 193-231.

are related on the authority of Abū Hurayra, but also the meaning of each of these sayings of the Prophet ﷺ is found expressed on the authority of other Companions of the Prophet ﷺ. Thus, a complete proof is supplied establishing [the fact] that the attribution of these *ḥadīth* to the Holy Prophet ﷺ is neither fictitious nor baseless. For example, *ḥadīth* 56 of this collection [of Hammam] is found in the *Ṣaḥīḥ* of al-al-Bukhārī as related by Anas, and number 124 as related by ʻAbd Allāh ibn ʻUmar . . . "[27]

We should also mention the role played by the Caliph ʻUmar ibn ʻAbd al-ʻAzīz (d. 101/720) in the recording of the *Ḥadīth*. He sent a missive to Qāḍī Abū Bakr ibn Ḥazm al-Anṣārī (d. 117/735) enjoining him to gather the collections of *Ḥadīth*: "Start compiling the traditions of the Prophet ﷺ ﷺ, for I fear they will get progressively lost."[28] He made the same demand to Zuhrī, who then compiled a collection.

Amongst the writings which saw the light of day, we also possess the *Jāmiʻ* of Maʻmar ibn Rāshid[29] (d. 153/770), a student of Hammām; and the *Muṣannaf* of ʻAbd al-Razzāq al-Ṣanʻānī[30] (d. 211/826), a student of Maʻmar. ʻAbd al-Razzāq was the teacher of the famous Aḥmad ibn Ḥanbal who in turn was one of the masters of al-Bukhārī. The preservation of all these documents, as well as the analysis of their contents, argue for the seriousness of critical work carried out during the transmission of the *Ḥadīth*: "In the presence of these documents, it would be nothing but childish to suggest that, in order to compose his work, al-Bukhārī had either assembled the folklore of his age or completely invented his narrations of the Prophet ﷺ, attributing them to the earlier sources in an uninterrupted chain. Indeed, one finds the same reports in the same unaltered terms from the *Ṣaḥīfah* of Abū Hurayra to the *Ṣaḥīḥ* of al-Bukhārī, whose authenticity is proven by the fortunate discovery of the early sources."[31]

Western critique has severely judged the collecting of the *Ḥadīth*, and although it is true that there exist *ḥadīth* which are completely invented—which Muslim scholarship calls *aḥādīth mawḍūʻa*—there is only one particular orientalist school which comes to some quite extreme conclusions.

Titus Burckhardt (Ibrāhīm ʻIzz al-Dīn) summarizes the assumptions which lead certain orientalists to almost reject the authenticity of the corpus of *Ḥadīth*: "Certain 'specialists,' in judging the authenticity of the *ḥadīth* of the Prophet ﷺ, suppose that they can establish the following criteria,

---

27. *Ṣaḥīfa*, § 87.

28. Mentioned by Imam Mālik in his *Muwaṭṭa'*. One of the reasons why this Qāḍī was chosen for this important work of compilation was that his aunt ʻAmra was the disciple of ʻĀ'isha.

29. On this *muḥaddith*, see *Early Hadith*, p. 148.

30. Published in Beirut (1972).

31. M. Hamidullah, "La rédaction du Hadith aux premiers temps de l'Islam", *Le Musulman*, no. 17, (1991) p. 16.

disregarding thirteen centuries of Muslim scholarship:

> (1) If some *ḥadīth* can be interpreted as favoring some particular group or school, this means it has certainly been invented. If, for instance, a *ḥadīth* is in favor of the spiritual life, then the Sufis invented it. If, on the contrary, it provides an argument for literalists hostile to spirituality, then the literalists fabricated it.
>
> (2) The more complete the chain of intermediaries indicated by traditionalists, the greater the chance that the particular *ḥadīth* is false because, they say, the need for proof grows in proportion to the lapse of time. Such arguments are truly diabolical for, taken as a whole, they amount to this reasoning: if you bring me no proof it is because you are wrong, but if you do bring proof it means you need it and so again you are wrong. How can these orientalists believe that countless Muslim learned men—men who feared God and hell—could have deliberately fabricated sayings of the Prophet ﷺ? It would lead one to suppose poor intentions to be the most natural thing in the world, were it not that 'specialists' have almost no feeling for psychological incompatibilities."[32]

Muslim scholarship took care to avoid the inclusion of fabricated *ḥadīth* into the teachings of the Prophet ﷺ. This is how Marwān ibn Muḥammad al-Tatarī (d. 210/825), an important traditionalist from Damascus, summarizes the qualities of one whose *ḥadīth* may be accepted: "There are three indispensable qualities for the traditionalist: sincerity (*al-ṣidq*), an excellent memory, and the exactitude of his writings." The absence of rigor in collecting *Ḥadīth* sufficed for discrediting a traditionalist. Regarding this matter, Sulaymān ibn Mūsā (d. 115/733) said: "One comes across three kinds of students next to the scholar: some write down everything they hear from him, others listen without writing, and yet others apply a choice to what they hear, and they put it into writing. The latter are the best." This is why Ibn 'Amr al-Awzā'ī (d. 158/774) would ask his students to submit to him what they had written under his dictating. He would review the *ḥadīth*, eventually correcting them, and finally authorize his students to relate them on his authority.

However, let us specify that the transmission of *ḥadīth* was not always done "to the letter" but "in meaning." This explains the existence of multiple variations for a single *ḥadīth*: "Taking the opportunity of a visit by Wāthila ibn al-Asqa' to Ḥims, a man from the village asked him: 'Relate to us a tradition as you heard it from the mouth of the Prophet ﷺ, without adding or omitting anything.' The Companion answered him angrily: 'You have plenty of copies of the Qur'ān at your disposal, which you leaf through every day, and it happens that you make mistakes in reciting it. How can you ask me to relate a tradition which I have only heard once from the Prophet ﷺ, without adding or omitting anything? The important thing is to give the meaning of the tradi-

32. *Introduction aux doctrines ésotériques de l'Islam*, éd. Dervy, 1985, p. 55.

tion.' Abū al-Dardā', the master of Sham, would do the same. While relating a *ḥadīth*, he would add: 'That is more or less it; it has this meaning.'"[33]

Jacques Berque, on the other hand, analyzes the methodological drift of certain orientalists in the following terms: "Transferring the long-dismissed historicism of Biblical and New Testament studies onto Islam, a healthy rigor is sometimes pushed to peremptory rejection. Thus Caetani arrives at 'the pessimistic conclusion that we cannot find anything true on Muḥammad in the Tradition, and we may rule out as apocryphal all the traditional materials that we possess.' Historical anthropology has since explored traditional cultures with much less pretension. In Africa, for example, it has learned to investigate the oral sources to the point of sometimes drawing centuries-long restitutions from them. With C. Sanders Pierce we have learned the role of the 'iconic,' that is, of the social semantics of images in certain civilizations. And above all, we no longer consider with disregard the rules of those methodologies, the only fault of which is to disconcert us."[34]

It is appropriate, however, to add that the thesis of I. Goldziher and of Caetani has survived in the works of Joseph Schacht and James Robson, and that they received a new version in the writings of G. H. A. Juynboll. Thus, in his work *The Origins of Muhammadan Jurisprudence* (Oxford, 1950), J. Schacht acknowledges his debt to the works of Goldziher and states that he confirms the latter's conclusions: "This book not only confirms the conclusions reached by Goldziher, but it goes even further on certain points: a great number of *ḥadīth* found in the classical as well as in the other collections started circulating only after the time of Shāfi'ī. The first original collection of *ḥadīth* dates from the second century, contrary to slightly earlier *ḥadīth* related by the Companions and by other authorities."[35] And G. H. A. Juynboll, having been unable to ignore the refutations made to the preceding thesis, expresses himself more cautiously while still claiming the heritage of Goldziher: "However, since the conclusions of Goldziher and Schacht in their works, as well as the more recent studies that have shed new light on these conclusions, the questions of chronology from the origin and/or authority relative to these generalizations probably do not fail to intrigue most Western readers, for whom the presence in a canonical collection of a tradition attributed to the Prophet ﷺ does not necessarily imply that this attribution is historically founded."[36]

Juynboll's method consists in analyzing the different chains of transmission of a *ḥadīth* (*isnād*) in order to highlight the "common link."[37] According

33. Malake Abiad, pp. 21-22.

34. Tabarî, *La Chronique, Histoire des prophètes et des rois* (Actes Sud: 2001), p. 19.

35. p. 4.

36. "Some Isnād—Analytical Methods illustrated on the basis of several sayings demeaning to women from *Ḥadīth* Literature," *Al-Qanṭara*, X, 1989, p. 343.

37. Cf. his work *Muslim Tradition*, Cambridge University Press, 1983, pp. 206-17.

to this method initially introduced by Joseph Schacht,[38] if one notices that all the *isnād* (chains of transmission) include, at a certain stage, a common transmitter, one must identify him as the inventor of the *ḥadīth*. Nevertheless, Juynboll recognized that what has reached us from the earliest period of Islam must be considered by and large as true: "I realize that it is difficult to admit that these ancient narrations can be considered as historically true, or that the details of each of these narrations can be considered as real facts. But I maintain that, over all, all of these narrations offer an almost reliable description of a period of history which has been minutely studied."[39]

In a recent and richly documented work, A. L. de Prémare seems to seek a merging of the classical Muslim critique of the *Ḥadīth* with the work of the orientalists into the same perspective, and he openly claims to be the representative of I. Goldziher: "It has long been known, even in Muslim circles of the past and of today, that the traditions of *Ḥadīth* are for the most part apocryphal. [. . .] This fact, long well-known to Muslim scholars, was particularly highlighted in modern Western scholarship from the 1890's onwards by Ignaz Goldziher."[40] However, after a few lines, this expert on early Islam denies any impartiality and objectivity to the effort of Muslim scholars for establishing the chains of transmission: "these *isnād* are often those that licensed Muslim clerics have selected, validated or invalidated, in function of their own criteria and in order to serve their own vision of the facts."[41]

The reductionism and "disregard for rules" called into question by Jacques Berque coincide with a mentality which has been best described by Frithjof Schuon ('Īsā Nūr al-Dīn) on several occasions in his rich and profound written works:

> One of the most vexing aberrations of our era is the 'historical method' with its 'close criticism' of documents and its systematic contempt for all sources connected either with miraculous acts or even with exceptional coincidences. When one denies the supernatural it is imprudent to hold forth on matters to which it alone gives a meaning, or to busy oneself with the psychology of those who accept it.
>
> Critics who deny the supernatural are applying to things which *a priori* elude them a logic that is both artificial and meticulous. What is evident appears to them as 'naive'; they substitute for intelligence a sort of icy cunning that feeds on negation and paradox.[42]

Authors who defend the legitimacy of the traditional point of view on

38. Cf. *The Origins of Muhammadan Jurisprudence,* Oxford, Clarendon Press, 1950, pp. 170-175.
39. *Ibid.*, pp. 6-7.
40. *Les Fondations de l'Islam*, Seuil, 2002, p. 22.
41. *Ibid.*, p. 27.
42. *Perspectives*, pp. 20-21.

the transmission of *Ḥadīth* emphasize its crucial role in the homogeneity and harmony within the religious and spiritual life in Islam. S. H. Nasr does not hesitate to make the following remarks: "The danger inherent in this criticism of the *Ḥadīth* lies in decreasing its value in the eyes of those Muslims who, having come under the sway of its arguments, accept the fatally dangerous conclusion that the body of *Ḥadīth* are not the sayings of the Prophet ﷺ and therefore do not carry his authority. In this way, one of the foundations of Divine Law and a vital source of guidance for the spiritual life is destroyed. It is as if the whole foundation were pulled out from underneath the structure of Islam. What would be left in such a case would be the Quran, which, being the Word of God, is too sublime to interpret and decipher without the aid of the Prophet ﷺ."[43] Underlying the intrusion into the Muslim world of ideas which he is about to denounce, S. H. Nasr adds: "There are few problems that call for as immediate action on the part of the Muslim community as a response by qualified, traditional Muslim authorities in scientific—but not 'scientistic'—terms to the charges brought against *Ḥadīth* literature by modern Western critics, who have now also found a few disciples amongst Muslims. They have found a few followers of Muslim background who have left the traditional point of view and have become enamored by the apparently scientific method of the critics which only hides an *a priori* presumption no Muslim can accept, namely the negation of the heavenly origin of the Quranic revelation and the actual prophetic power and function of the Prophet ﷺ."[44]

In a seminal article, Wael B. Hallaq assesses the modern studies on the authenticity of *Ḥadīth* and distinguishes three attitudes regarding this question[45]: those representing the conclusions of Schacht, like John Wansbrough and Michael Cook, those who, on the contrary, attach themselves to their rebuttal such as Nabia Abbott, Fuat Sezgin, M. Azami, Gregor Schoeler and Johan Fück, and finally, those who seek a middle and original way, such as Harald Motzki and Fazlur Rahman, amongst others. There is little doubt that for Wael B. Hallaq, the question of the authenticity of *Ḥadīth* is but a pseudo-problem, and he considers that traditional Muslim scholarship has furnished satisfying answers, provided that one makes the effort to study it. He has thus been led to analyze the notions of *khabar wāḥid* and of *khabar mutawātir*,[46] pointing out that Western scholarship has been little interested in such fundamental notions.

Finally, that which gives meaning to the emergence of the science of

43. *Ideals and Realities of Islam*, Cambridge: Islamic Texts Society, 2001, p. 98.

44. *Ibid.*, p. 100.

45. "The Authenticity of Prophetic *Ḥadīth*: A Pseudo-problem", *Studia Islamica*, 1999, pp. 75-90.

46. A *ḥadīth* transmitted by several persons, whose minimum number is often required by Muslim scholars to be ten.

Ḥadīth—and which at the same time is its foundation and native mold—is the extraordinary genealogical memory amongst Arabs, even before the rise of Islam: "Whatever may be the way in which the Muslim science of *Ḥadīth* was born and died off for the Arabs, it was centered upon the genealogical memory of groups, which is critical in its own way. In fact, this critique has been exercised and is still exercised within Islam, even on the subject of the Prophet ﷺ's biography, to the point that a contemporary author could call into question the *Sīrah* of Ibn Hisham . . . True, this reductionism is compensated for by the research of Mr. Hamidullah, for example, who has very recently found some written records of documents pertaining to the prophetic mission and basically confirming the traditions already considered as certain."[47]

Muslim scholarship has therefore come to propose an extremely precise classification of the different degrees of acceptability of a *ḥadīth*. Below we give the definition of the two categories concerning the *ḥadīth* quoted in this collection:

الصحيح ما اتصل سنده بنقل العدل الضابط عن مثله إلى

منتهاه من غير شذوذ ولا علة.

An authenticated[48] (*ṣaḥīḥ*) *ḥadīth* is one that has a known chain of transmitters, and each transmitter is both righteous (*'adl*) and reliable (*ḍābiṭ*), without there being any marginality (*shudhūdh*)[49] or flaw (*'illa*)[50] in the chain.

الحسن ما اتصل سنده بنقل العدل الذي خف ضبطه عن

مثله إلى منتهاه من غير شذوذ ولا علة.

A validated (*ḥasan*) *ḥadīth* is one that has a chain of transmission which is continuous until its end, and every transmitter is righteous but not necessarily completely reliable. Its chain must also not include any marginality or defect.[51]

---

47. Jacques Berque, *op. cit.*, pp. 19-20.

48. The criteria for the authenticity of a *ḥadīth* may vary significantly amongst different authors. Thus, al-Suyūṭī considers that al-Ḥākim confers the status of *ṣaḥīḥ* too easily at times.

49. This term refers in the science of *Ḥadīth* to the contrast with an even more reliable source.

50. *'Illa* has to be understood as a flaw which is difficult to detect, due to the good faith in the perfection of the chain of transmission. That is the case, for example, of a complete and uninterrupted chain which quotes successively two persons who could not have possibly met.

51. This definition is based on that of Ibn Ḥajar al-'Asqalānī (d. 852/1449). The above definitions were taken from Maḥmūd al-Taḥḥān's *Taysīr musṭalaḥ al-*

While noticing a common vision of the different positions of classical Islam on the problem of verification of the *ḥadīth*, one cannot overlook a very particular mode of verification: the verification by unveiling (*al-taṣḥīḥ bi'l-kashf*). With regards to this, Ibn al-'Arabī affirms that a *ḥadīth* whose chain is weak may very well prove to be authentic: the person to whom an unveiling has been given will know through the "eye of certainty" (*'ayn al-yaqīn*) that the *ḥadīth* under question is authentic.[52] This was an often defended idea, and three centuries later, the celebrated Ibn Ḥajar Haythamī (d. 974/1566) issued a *fatwa* on the verification of a *ḥadīth* by way of unveiling: "This is indeed possible, and it is amongst the graces bestowed to the saints (*karāmāt al-awliyā'*) as confirmed by al-Ghazzālī, Bārazī, al-Tāj al-Subkī, al-'Afīf al-Yāfi'ī amongst the Shāfi'īs, and Qurṭūbī and Ibn Abī Jamra for the Mālikīs. It is related that a saint attended a session directed by a jurist (*faqīh*). While the latter was citing a *ḥadīth*, the saint interrupted him: 'This *ḥadīth* is false (*bāṭil*).' The jurist then asked him, 'Where did you get that?' and the saint replied: 'The Prophet ﷺ is here and he is standing before you! He says that he never uttered these words!' At that moment, the jurist had an unveiling and saw the Prophet ﷺ."[53]

At this point, one could ask why a book on the spiritual teachings of the Prophet ﷺ is needed.

The traditional biographies (*kutub al-sīrah*) naturally emphasize thc incidental aspects of the life of the Prophet ﷺ, and they do not deal directly with his teachings. They transmit an outward vision of his mission and pass in silence over that which ultimately constitutes the heart of his teachings: knowledge of the self and inner reform. Moreover, the *Ḥadīth* literature is extremely vast; several thousands of *ḥadīth* are scattered throughout a great number of collections. This makes difficult the prospect of creating a clear idea about the spiritual teachings of the Prophet ﷺ. Let us also add that the oldest Sufi works that have reached us do not always quote the *ḥadīth* that could support the doctrinal expositions they contain, and this has sometimes been a point of reproach from the partisans of a literalist Islam. The cases of certain great spokesmen of Muslim spirituality such as Abū Ḥāmid al-Ghazzālī (d. 505/1111) and especially Ibn al-'Arabī (d. 638/1240) different. Their expositions are in fact for the most part based on or illustrated by the Qur'ān and *Ḥadīth*—especially in their major works: *Iḥyā' 'ulūm al-dīn* and *al-Futūḥāt al-makkiyya*, respectively.

Regarding the first of these two works, it has been claimed that al-Ghazzālī was not always rigorous in citing *ḥadīth*, with the more or less declared intention of disparaging this work. Let us point out first of all that the *Iḥyā'* contains more than 4000 *ḥadīth*, three fourths of which are either sound (*aḥādīth*

ḥadīth, Riyad, 1996.

52. C.f. *Fut.*, II, p. 358 [O.Y].

53. *Al-Fatāwā al-Ḥadīthiyya*, pp. 211-12, Dār al-Fikr, n.d.

ḥasana) or authentic (*aḥādīth ṣaḥīḥa*). Furthermore, the great majority of the *Ḥadīth* specialists are unanimous in affirming that quoting *ḥadīth* whose chain of transmission is weak (*isnād ḍa'īf*) is perfectly acceptable, not when establishing a legal ruling (*ḥukm shar'ī*), but when enjoining the purification of the soul and inviting to virtue (*targhīb wa tarhīb*).[54] This being said, one has to take the work of al-Ḥāfidh al-'Irāqī (d. 806/1403) on the verification of the *ḥadīth* found in the *Iḥyā'*[55] with some reservation, because he is satisfied with a critique of their chains without any effort to find well authenticated *ḥadīth* enunciating the same truths. In this regard, al-Murtaḍā al-Zabīdī (d. 1205/1791) in his monumental commentary of the *Iḥyā'*, *Itḥāf al-sādat al-muttaqīn*[56] was careful to review the work of al-Ḥāfiẓ al-'Irāqī, often finding well identified *ḥadīth* having the same meaning as those with problematic chains. Let us add that the *ḥadīth* whose chains are not firmly established comprise less than a quarter of all the *ḥadīth* found in the *Iḥyā'*.

As for the teachings of Ibn al-'Arabī, in spite of the boldness and liberal expressions he manifests, they are indissolubly linked to the Qur'ān and the *Ḥadīth* for both doctrinal and spiritual reasons which he himself explains in several instances.[57]

Besides the lexicographic clarifications and some circumstantial remarks, the reader will find, above all, in these *ḥadīth* commentaries quotes from great spiritual masters of Islam. These quotations are clearly not the only ones which could have clarified the *ḥadīth* of this collection, but the selection had to be kept to a manageable size.

The great spokespersons of Muslim spirituality have strongly emphasized the importance of meditating upon the *Ḥadīth*. Thus, al-Junayd (d. 298/911), widely called "master of the mystics" (*sayyid al-ṭā'ifa*) declared without any ambiguity that

"علمنا مضبوط بالكتاب والسنة ومن لم يحفظ القرآن و لم
يكتب الحديث و لم يتفقه لا يقتدى به."[1]

"Our science is rooted in the Book and the Prophetic tradition, and whoever is not amongst those who have memorized the Qur'ān, recorded the *Ḥadīth*

54. Nonetheless, there are those who do not accept the use of "very weak" (*ḍa'īf jiddan*) *ḥadīth*.

55. His work on the verification of the chains of *ḥadīth* is nowadays published in the notes of all the editions of the *Iḥyā'*.

56. This work has appeared in numerous editions. It has recently been published in 14 volumes by Dār al-kutub al-'ilmiyya, Beirut, 2005.

57. On this subject, see the introduction of our book *Le Mahdī et ses Conseillers*, éd. Mille et une lumières, 2006, pp. 16-18.

and mastered the sciences of *fiqh*, must not be followed."[58]

Nevertheless, the importance of the prophetic *Sunna* stressed by al-Junayd is not to be interpreted in a literal sense; it is clearly a matter of spiritual understanding for him. It is precisely this spiritual comprehension which is evoked by the *ḥadīth* distinguishing between the *ḥāmil fiqh* (bearer of knowledge) and the *faqīh* (the man of understanding): "May God fill with rewards the person who, having heard one of my words, memorizes it in order to transmit it to someone else. Indeed, it may be that someone transmits a deep knowledge (*fiqh*) to another who has been gifted with greater intelligence. And certainly, it can happen that a 'bearer of knowledge' may not be gifted with intelligence!"[59]

It is hardly necessary to specify that the two hundred and thirty four *ḥadīth* of this collection do not claim to exhaust the spiritual teachings of the Prophet ﷺ,[60] but they do offer, we believe, an adequate picture of them, quite distanced from prejudices that have unfortunately become common.

The aim of this anthology is to introduce readers to wisdom flowing from an oral tradition, and to help them revise what they know or what they believe they know about Islam and its Prophet ﷺ.

The commentaries of the spiritual masters testify to their inspiration (*ilhām*) and their long meditation upon the *ḥadīth*, thus bringing to light numerous aspects which would remain in the dark without their teachings. This is why the present collection cannot be an introduction to the understanding of *Ḥadīth*, of which many already exist. It is rather a guide for meditation and deepening of understanding of the message of the last Messenger of God.

At a time when everything and its opposite is being said about Islam and its founder, it is more urgent than ever to offer readers—be they Muslim or not—the opportunity for a more direct contact with what remains a living source of wisdom, and which, for more than a billion people, embodies human perfection:

> *Verily in the Messenger of God ye have a good example for him who looketh unto God and the Last Day, and remembereth God much.* (Qur'ān, XXXIII:21)

---

58. *Tāj*, p. 173.

59. Cf. *ḥadīth* 72.

60. All the traditions quoted in this collection have been either authenticated (*ṣaḥīḥ*) or validated (*ḥasan*) by al-Suyūṭī or by the author citing them.

SPIRITUAL TEACHINGS OF THE PROPHET

The Virtues: فضائل الأخلاق

Ḥadīth 1

عن ابن عمرو : "إِنَّ مِنْ أَحَبِّكُمْ إِلَيَّ أَحْسَنُكُمْ أَخْلاقاً."

(رواه البخاري. حديث صحيح)

Narrated Ibn ʻAmr: "Verily, the ones I prefer the most amongst you are those who are the noblest in character."

(Quoted by al-Bukhārī. Authenticated *ḥadīth*.)

Ḥadīth 2

عن أبي هريرة : "إِنَّما بُعِثْتُ لِأُتَمِّمَ مَكارِمَ ٱلأَخْلاقِ."

(رواه الإمام مالك. حديث صحيح)

Narrated Abū Hurayra: "Verily, I have been sent to perfect nobility of character."

(Quoted by Imām Mālik. Authenticated *ḥadīth*.)

Commentary

The Arabic term *innamā* at the beginning of the second *ḥadīth* stresses the exclusive character of the prophetic mission: the unique goal of the *Sunna* of the Prophet ﷺ is to offer the spiritual means for the purification of the soul until the soul rediscovers the beauty inherent in its creation: the primordial nature (*fiṭra*) of man which everyone carries within. According to the words of al-Ghazzālī, religion contains all the "means for curing the ills of the heart."

al-Ghazzālī

Nobility of character is an attribute of the master of the messengers, and also that which is most precious amongst the qualities realized by the sincere ones (*ṣiḍḍīqūn*). It is doubtless an important part of religion. It is the fruit obtained by men and women of piety (*muttaqūn*) through their inner struggle (*mujāhada*), and by devout servants (*mutaʻabbidūn*) through their spiritual exertion (*riyāḍa*).

Baseness of character is a violent poison, which leads to clear perdition and vilifies man, distancing him from the nearness of the Lord of the worlds. It imprisons man in the devil's net and constitutes an open door towards "the fire which devours the depths." [. . .]

Thus, knowing the means for curing the ills of the heart is a necessity for those who are disposed to them—even greater than that of knowing the means for curing the illnesses of the body—as no heart is immune from illness. [. . .]

God the Exalted has said to His beloved Prophet ﷺ: *And lo, thou art of a tremendous character*[1] and when 'Ā'isha was asked about the Prophet ﷺ, she replied: "His character was of the Qur'ān." . . . On the other hand, the Prophet ﷺ said: "I have been sent to perfect nobility of character."

(*Iḥyā'*, III, pp. 47-8)

1. LXVIII: 4

Ḥadīth 3

عن سهل بن سعد : "إِنَّ ٱللهَ كَرِيمٌ يُحِبُّ ٱلكَرَمَ وَيُحِبُّ مَعالِي ٱلأَخْلاقِ وَيَكْرَهُ سَفْسافَها."

(رواه الطبراني. حديث صحيح)

Narrated Sahl ibn Sa'd: "Verily, God is generous and loves generosity: He loves nobility of character and detests baseness."

(Quoted by al-Ṭabarānī. Authenticated *ḥadīth*.)

Commentary

The virtues must not be considered solely from the moral point of view or their social benefit, because they constitute above all a reflection of the Divine qualities within man. Although the theological perspective adheres to morals and social benefits as seen from a point of view of merit and reward, spirituality encompasses all these elements into a path of knowledge of God and of man. This is why the *ḥadīth* links God's generosity with the generosity of His servant. This distinction between the moral point of view and the ontological perspective to which we alluded is expressed by al-Ghazzālī through the contrasting of the "fruits" of nobility of character with its "reality."

al-Ghazzālī

Know that many have spoken about what nobility of character is. However, they have not expounded on its reality but on the fruits it bears. Al-Ḥasan [al-Baṣrī] has said: "Nobility of character is to have a relaxed face, to be generous and to abstain from food." [. . .]

Nobility of character is a disposition (*hay'a*) deeply rooted in the soul. When it manifests itself, praiseworthy actions are accomplished with ease and without any need of effort. Thus, if the inner disposition of an individual leads him to acting with beauty—both from the point of view of the intellect and that of the sacred Law—one can speak of nobility of character.

We have spoken about [this] disposition as being deeply rooted in the soul, because he who manifests generosity only occasionally and for outward motives is not characterized by generosity (*sakhā'*). Likewise, we have considered it a condition that praiseworthy actions be performed with ease, because the person who must make a great effort to make a gift, or to keep silent while in anger, is not characterized by generosity or forbearance.

(*Iḥyā'*, III, pp. 51-52)

Frithjof Schuon (‘Īsā Nūr al-Dīn)

The virtues, when they are realized to their very limit—as far as their universal and Divine prototypes—coincide with metaphysical truths: to be humble, charitable and truthful in a quasi “absolute” manner—which is impossible outside truth—is to “know”; it is assuredly impossible to know in an absolute manner without being humble, charitable and truthful. Truth is necessary for the perfection of virtue, just as virtue is needed for the perfection of truth.

(*Perspectives*, p. 98)

Ḥadīth 4

عن عثمان ابن عفان : "إِنَّ لِلّهِ تَعالَى مِئَةَ خُلُقٍ وَسَبْعَةَ عَشَرَ مَنْ أَتاهُ بِخُلُقٍ مِنْها دَخَلَ ٱلْجَنَّة."

(رواه الحكيم. حديث حسن)

Narrated 'Uthmān ibn 'Affān: "Verily, God Most High possesses one hundred and seventeen attributes: the person who assumes one of these attributes [through the corresponding virtue] will enter Paradise."

(Quoted by al-Ḥakīm. Validated *ḥadīth*.)

Commentary

The commentaries given for this *ḥadīth* teach us the immense importance of virtues in the spiritual life. A virtue limited to the moral or the social plane cannot prevent the risk of hypocrisy, and one may not understand how it can become the cause of salvation, as affirmed by the *ḥadīth*. Indeed, outward generosity sometimes coexists with self-sufficiency and a pride which readily hide themselves behind charitable motives. Inversely, when a virtue is of a spiritual nature, it will lead the whole being of the person in whom it is actualized, towards the essence of the virtue. Virtues of a spiritual nature are Divine qualities.

Thus, he who truly realizes a virtue necessarily realizes "something" from all the virtues.

al-Munāwī

God has manifested the attributes mentioned in this *ḥadīth* for His servants and through His power. He has placed them in His treasures, and has distributed them amongst His servants in accordance with the degree that each of them occupies in His eyes. Thus, certain persons may realize one attribute, some others five, ten . . .

When God wishes the best for His servants, He bestows upon them the realization of these attributes. Inversely, when He does not bestow His grace upon a servant, the servant will not possess any virtue and will assume the attributes of Satan. According to Ibn al-'Arabī, al-Junayd was once asked about gnosis and the gnostics, and his reply was: "Water assumes the color of its container." He meant that the gnostic has dressed himself in the attributes of God to the point of being none other than Him, without, however, being Him!

(*Fayḍ al-Qadīr*, *ḥadīth* no. 2364).

Titus Burckhardt (Ibrāhīm ‘Izz al-Dīn)

Virtue is a qualitative form of the will. To speak of a form is to speak of an intelligible essence. Spiritual virtue is centered on its own essence and is a Divine Quality. This means that spiritual virtue implies a kind of knowledge. According to Aḥmad ibn al-‘Arif, spiritual virtue is distinguished from virtue in the ordinary sense by being pure of any individual interest. If virtue implies a renunciation, that renunciation is not made to obtain some later recompense, for it bears its fruit within itself, fruit of knowledge and beauty. Spiritual virtue is neither a mere negation of natural instincts—asceticism is only the very smallest step to such virtue—nor yet, of course, is it merely a psychic sublimation. It is born of a presentiment of the Divine Reality which underlies all objects of desire—noble passion is nearer to virtue than is anguish—and this presentiment is in itself a sort of "natural grace" which is a compensation for the sacrificial aspect of virtue. Later, the progressive unfolding and flowering of this presentiment is answered by an ever more direct irradiation of the Divine Quality of which virtue in man is the trace, and, inversely, virtue grows in proportion as its Divine model is revealed.

(*Introduction*, pp. 118-19)

Ḥadīth 5

عن أبي هريرة : "إِذا قاتَلَ أَحَدُكُمْ أخاهُ فَلْيَجْتَنِبِ ٱلوَجْهَ فَإِنَّ ٱللهَ خَلَقَ آدَمَ عَلَى صُورَتِه."

(رواه مسلم. حديث صحيح)

Narrated Abū Hurayra: "When one of you is fighting his fellow man, he must not hit him on the face, because God created Adam in His image."

(Quoted by Muslim. Authenticated *ḥadīth*.)

Commentary

This enigmatic *ḥadīth* has given rise to numerous commentaries and has been quoted abundantly by the spiritual masters. In his celebrated commentary of the collection of Muslim, al-Nawawī reminds us that many scholars have refrained from commenting upon this *ḥadīth*, contenting themselves with saying: "We believe in what its words convey while recalling that they should not be taken literally (*ẓāhiruhā ghayru murād*). These words have such meaning as befits them (*ma'nā yalīqu bihā*). This position is that of the majority of the Predecessors (*salaf*), and the most cautious one as well." Al-Ghazzālī also interprets this "resemblance" as a correspondence (*munāsaba*) and emphasizes that this *ḥadīth* is inconceivable for ordinary understanding. This correspondence is linked to the mystery of the Spirit and can only be approached by one who has received an inner opening at the end of the spiritual path.

al-Ghazzālī

All love is born from a correspondence (*munāsaba*), and this is what generates the love of God Most High. It is not a question of inner correspondence without any relationship to outward forms. Among the inner correspondences there are those that can be used in writing and those that cannot. They should be left hidden until they are uncovered by the travelers on the Path (*sālikūn*), if the latter remain faithful to their conditions. That which can be used in this domain is the proximity between the servant and the Lord at the level of the Divine attributes, from which man should be inspired and which he must assume. That is why it has been said: "Assume the Divine Qualities." This pertains to the acquisition of noble character traits which are none other than Divine qualities: knowledge, kindness, beneficence, and benevolence . . .

As for the specific correspondence, which is not permissible to put into writing, it concerns that which characterizes man as such, which is what the verse, *They are asking thee concerning the Spirit. Say: The Spirit is by command of my Lord, and of knowledge ye have been vouchsafed but little*[2] alludes to. God clearly indicates through this verse that the Spirit exceeds the comprehension capacities of creatures. Even more direct is the verse, *So, when I have made him and have breathed into him of My Spirit . . .* [3] This, then, is the reason to the prostration of the angels [to Adam]. The verse *We have set thee as a vicegerent (khalīfa) on the earth*[4] alludes to this specific correspondence without which Adam would not have been the vicegerent of God on earth. The same is true for the *ḥadīth*: "Verily, God created man according to His image." Unfortunately, some persons with limited understanding think that there is no other form apart from the outward appearance perceivable by the senses. This is why they fall into anthropomorphism by attributing a body and an external form to God. Highly exalted is the Lord of the worlds above that which the ignorant ones ascribe to Him! Another allusion to this specific correspondence is the word of God to Moses: "I was sick and thou didst not visit Me." Moses replied, "Lord, how is this so?" God said to him, "My servant so-and-so was sick and thou didst not visit him; had thou visited him, thou wouldst have found Me beside him." This correspondence is apparent only to one who practices supererogatory acts of worship (*nawāfil*) with perseverance, besides the obligatory ones (*farā'iḍ*), as the Most-High has said: "My servant does not cease to approach Me with supererogatory acts of worship until I love him. And when I love him, I am his Hearing with which he hears, his Sight with which he sees, his tongue with which he speaks . . . "

One must know how to control the pen in such matters . . .

(*Iḥyā'*, IV, pp. 298-9)

2. XVII: 85.
3. XV: 30.
4. XXXVIII: 26

Ḥadīth 6

عن ابن عمر : "الرَّاحِمُونَ يَرْحَمُهُمُ ٱلرَّحْمانُ تَبارَكَ وَتَعالَى. اِرْحَمُوا مَنْ فِي ٱلأَرْضِ يَرْحَمْكُمْ مَنْ فِي ٱلسَّماءِ."

(رواه الحاكم. حديث صحيح)

Narrated Ibn ʿUmar: "The All-Merciful—exalted be He—shall bestow His mercy upon those who show mercy. Be merciful towards the created beings on earth and He who is in Heaven shall bestow His mercy upon you."

(Quoted by al-Ḥākim. Authenticated *ḥadīth.*)

Commentary

This *ḥadīth* is amongst the many exhortations to assume the Divine attributes. Divine mercy (*raḥma*) must radiate within man and be offered to others in the form of generosity, forbearance, and forgiveness.

Ḥadīth 7

عن أبي هريرة : "أَفْضَلُ ٱلأَعْمالِ بَعْدَ ٱلإيـمانِ بِٱللهِ ٱلتَوَدُّدُ إِلَى ٱلنَّاسِ."

(رواه الطبراني. حديث حسن)

Narrated Abū Hurayra: "The best deed after belief in God is benevolent love towards people."

(Quoted by al-Ṭabarānī, Validated *ḥadīth*)

Ḥadīth 8

عن عائشة : "عَلَيْكَ بِٱلرِّفْقِ، وَإِيَّاكَ وَٱلعُنْفَ وَٱلفُحْشَ."

(رواه البخاري. حديث صحيح)

Narrated 'Ā'isha: "You must practice benevolence and guard against being violent or indecent."

(Quoted by al-Bukhārī. Authenticated *ḥadīth*.)

Commentary

There are numerous *ḥadīth* stressing the fundamental quality of benevolence (*rifq*), which implies the absence of any willingness to harm, in any way whatsoever. According to al-Ghazzālī, showing benevolence and clemency (*al-naẓar bi'l-raḥma*) towards the person who practices sin—whose scope remains individual and does not spread to the community—is a sign of humility (*tawāḍu'*). Inversely, the use of violence (*'unf*) is a form of oppression (*zajr*).

al-Ghazzālī

Sins, such as the consumption of alcohol or abandoning a religious duty, the consequences of which are limited to the person committing it, are less grave [than sins whose consequences extend to the rest of the community]. If one witnesses such a sin, one must put an end to it immediately. . . . As for the use of harshness or of softness towards the sinner, the opinions of the scholars differ. The most just is to consider the intention of the sinner. In this situation more than in any other, it has to be remembered that actions are only judged according to their intentions. In any case, benevolence and a merciful record towards creatures are expressions of humility. Inversely, violence and the rejection of others are considered oppression against them. In this domain, one has to ask one's heart.

(*Iḥyā'*, II, pp. 167-68)

Ḥadīth 9

عن معقل بن يسار :"أَفْضَلُ ٱلإيـمانِ ٱلصَّبْرُ وَٱلسَّماحة."

(رواه الديلمي. حديث صحيح)

Narrated Ma'qal ibn Yasār: "The best faith is that which is accompanied with patience and forbearance."

(Quoted by al-Daylamī. Authenticated *ḥadīth*.)

Commentary

The two important virtues of patience before trials and forbearance towards the other are presented in this very brief and holistic *ḥadīth* as keys for achieving the most sublime faith. Other *ḥadīth* give more details concerning the relationship between faith and these virtues.[5]

5. On this subject, see *ḥadīth* 29.

Ḥadīth 10

عن أبي هريرة : "أَحِبُّوا ٱلفُقَراءَ وَجالِسُوهُمْ، وَأَحِبَّ ٱلعَرَبَ مِنْ قَلْبِكَ، وَلْيَرُدَّكَ عَنِ ٱلنَّاسِ ما تَعْلَمُ مِنْ نَفسِكَ."

(رواه الحاكم. حديث صحيح)

Narrated Abū Hurayra: "Love the poor and visit them. Love the Arabs with all your heart, and guard what you know about yourself from the compliments of people."

(Quoted by al-Ḥākim. Authenticated *ḥadīth*.)

Commentary

As often in the hadith corpus, when different attitudes mentioned successively in a same ḥadīth do not seem to be related to each other, one can find an inner link that unites them and gives them meaning.

Loving the poor is a sign of detachment of worldly values from social and material accomplishment, in addition to the altruistic and charitable aspect of this attitude. To love the poor and to visit them is therefore a way to affirm—and also to prove through actions—that success in this world is not an end in itself for the believer.

To love the Arabs means to love the linguistic and cultural form in which the Revelation and the Prophetic message were expressed. To love the form of a religion does not necessarily mean to demonstrate literalism. Ideally, it is a matter of realizing that without the "sacred form" which religions assume, it would be difficult for a large number of souls to escape the tyranny of the world and of the ego. This is why the *ḥadīth* ends with a warning against the ego, which uses all sorts of strategies so as not to see itself for what it is in its "wretched interior." Self-esteem is, amongst other things, particularly sought by the ego, even if this seeking sometimes uses roundabout means and takes on very indirect aspects. The believers have to learn to substitute the eyes of others, which inevitably includes some tyranny, with God's "eyes," the only liberating ones there are.

The inner link uniting the different spiritual teachings of this *ḥadīth* is the purification of the ego and the acquisition of the virtues. As a consequence, this *ḥadīth* also insists on that which contributes to the realization of the virtues.

Frithjof Schuon ('Īsā Nūr al-Dīn)

When we speak of the "Arab soul," we are not unaware that it was relatively diverse from pre-Islamic times in the sense that religious indifferentism was characteristic of the Arabs of the Center and the North, whereas those of the South were distinguished by a rather contemplative temperament; but they were homogeneous as regards their qualities of nobility. The "Arab miracle"—the lightning-like expansion of Islam and the glories of medieval Islamic civilization—presupposes and includes a spirit of magnanimity whose roots are plunged in the pre-Islamic Bedouin mentality, and which—whatever the falsifiers of history may say—contributed to the almost unprecedented phenomenon of the tolerance of the Muslim conquerors of the early centuries, when the Arab influence was predominant in Islam. Bedouin magnanimity consisted essentially in "virility" (*muruwwa*)—in the sense of the Latin word *virtus*—and in "chivalry" (*futuwwa*), which comprised above all courage, generosity, and hospitality; the most precious, the most fragile and the most specifically Arab feature—in the context of the Middle East—being the virtue of generosity.

(*Sufism*, pp. 80-81)

Ḥadīth 11

عن محجن بن الأدرع : "خَيْرُ دِينِكُمْ أَيْسَرُهُ."

(رواه الطبراني. حديث صحيح)

Narrated Maḥjan ibn al-Adra‘: "The best [thing] about your religion is its simplicity."

(Quoted by al-Ṭabarānī. Authenticated *ḥadīth.*)

Ḥadīth 12

عن محجن بن الأدرع : "إِنَّ ٱللَّهَ تَعالَى رَضِيَ لِهَٰذِهِ ٱلأُمَّةِ ٱليُسْرَ وَكَرِهَ لَها ٱلعُسْرَ."

(رواه الطبراني. حديث صحيح)

Narrated Maḥjan ibn al-Adra‘: "Verily, God—exalted be He—has decreed simplicity for this community and He detests difficulty for it."

(Quoted by al-Ṭabarānī. Authenticated *ḥadīth.*)

Commentary

Spiritual and religious life must not be complicated to the point of becoming unbearable, and it is not by making things difficult that one progresses on the Path to God. In fact, the spiritual masters in general have a tendency to invite their disciples to reach the essential in their practices and to avoid any excess of zeal which could imprison them in a false ego-centered inwardness. Of course, the ease mentioned in the *ḥadīth* does not mean seeking the least effort, but a quest for the qualitative and not the quantitative. On this subject Ibn al-‘Arabī quotes the phrase of Abū Su‘ūd ibn al-Shibl, the companion of ‘Abd al-Qādir al-Jilānī:

كان يقول : ما هو (التصوف) إلا الصلوات الخمس وانتظار الموت .

Sufism is but five prayers and awaiting death.[6]

6. *Fut.* I, p. 188. After quoting this saying, Ibn al-‘Arabī notes: "There is an immense science in this."

Shaykh al-Darqāwī

If you wish your path to be shortened in order to attain realization (*taḥqīq*) swiftly, hold fast to the obligatory acts of worship (*wājibāt*) and to what is particularly recommended concerning voluntary observances (*nawāfil*); learn outer knowledge (*al-'ilm al-ẓāhir*) as is indispensable for worshipping God, but do not linger on it, since you are not required to study this deeply. What has to be deepened is inner knowledge. Furthermore, disobey your [carnal] soul and you will see marvels!

(*Rasā'il*, letter 2, p. 33)

Ḥadīth 13

عن ابن عباس : "قيل لرسول ٱللهِ ﷺ : "أَيُّ ٱلأَدْيانِ أَحَبُّ إِلَى ٱللهِ ؟" قالَ : "ٱلْحَنِيفيَّةُ ٱلسَّمْحَةُ."

(رواه الإمام أحمد. حديث صحيح)

Narrated Ibn 'Abbās: "The Messenger of God ﷺ was asked, 'Which religion is the dearest to God?' He replied, 'indulgent primordial monotheism.'"

(Quoted by Aḥmad ibn Ḥanbal. Authenticated *ḥadīth*.)

Ḥadīth 14

عن عائشة : "قالَ رَسُولُ ٱللهِ يَوَمَئِذٍ لَتَعْلَمُ ٱليَهُودُ أَنَّ فِي دِينِنا فُسْحَةً إِنِّي أُرْسِلْتُ بِٱلْحَنِيفيَّةِ ٱلسَّمْحَةِ."

(رواه الإمام أحمد. حديث صحيح)

Narrated 'Ā'isha: "The Messenger of God ﷺ said one day: 'The Jews must know that I have been sent with indulgent primordial monotheism.'"

(Quoted by Aḥmad ibn Ḥanbal. Authenticated *ḥadīth*).

Commentary

In the Qur'ān and the *Ḥadīth*, the term *ḥanīf* denotes the monotheism of Abraham, Islam being the return to this simple and essential monotheism: *And they say: Be Jews or Christians, then ye will be rightly guided. Say (unto them, O Muḥammad): Nay, but (we follow) the religion of Abraham, the upright, and he was not of the polytheists.*[7]

This relationship is then underlined by the formulae of *tashahhud* concluding every ritual prayer: *Allāhumma ṣalli 'alā sayyidinā Muḥammad wa 'alā āli sayyidinā Muḥammad kamā ṣallayta 'alā sayyidinā Ibrāhīm wa 'alā āli sayyidinā Ibrāhīm* . . . (My God, bless our Lord Muḥammad and the Household of Muḥammad, as Thou hast blessed our Lord Abraham and the Household of Abraham . . .)

Frithjof Schuon ('Īsā Nūr al-Dīn)

Integral Monotheism comprises two distinct lines of descent, one Israelite

7. II: 135.

and the other Ishmaelite; now whereas in the Israelite line Abraham is, so to speak, renewed or replaced by Moses—the Sinaitic Revelation being like a second beginning of Monotheism—Abraham continues to remain the unique and primordial Revealer for the sons of Ishmael. The Sinaitic miracle called for the Messianic or Christly miracle: it is Christ who, from a certain point of view, closes the Mosaic line and concludes the Bible, gloriously and irrevocably. But this cycle, extending from Moses to Jesus, or from Sinai to the Ascension, does not comprise the whole of Monotheism: the Ishmaelite, and still Abrahamic, line was situated outside this cycle and in a way remained open; it called in its turn for a glorious completion, not Sinaitic and Christly in character, but Abrahamic and Muḥammadan, and, in a certain sense, "nomadic" and "of the desert."

Abraham existed before Moses; consequently Muḥammad had to appear after Jesus; the "miraculous cycle" extending from Sinai to Christ is as though encompassed—temporally speaking—by a parallel cycle of a very different kind, one that in a more marked degree bears the imprint of the monotheistic Truth alone, with all the absoluteness and saving power inherent in its nature, and one that is irradiated by primordial simplicity and "Platonic" transcendence; Islam and Abrahamism are basically religions of nomads without history, scorched by the ever present and ever eternal Divine Sun. In the face of this Sun, man is nothing: that the Caliph 'Umar should conquer a part of the ancient world or that the Prophet ﷺ should milk his goat amounts to more or less the same thing; that is to say there is no "human greatness" in the profane and titanesque sense, and thus no humanism to give rise to vain glories; the only greatness admitted is the lasting one of sanctity, and this belongs to God.

(*Form*, pp. 85-86)

Ḥadīth 15

عن معاذ بن جبل : "أَخْلِصْ دِينَكَ يَكْفِكَ ٱلقَلِيلُ مِنَ ٱلعَمَلِ."

(رواه الحاكم. حديث صحيح)

Narrated Mu'ādh ibn Jabal: "Be completely sincere in your religion and a few good deeds will suffice you."

(Quoted by al-Ḥākim. Authenticated *ḥadīth.*)

Commentary

The term *ikhlāṣ* is difficult to render into English, as it has no exact equivalent. It implies purity of intention and sincere commitment to serving God.

Complete sincerity is the attitude of perfect inner conformity to the Truth: it is pure receptivity before God. Human nature outside of any spiritual wayfaring is woven with forgetfulness (*ghafla*). Being a spiritual station (*maqām*), total sincerity is in principle permanent and pervades all aspects of life for the person who has realized it. This is why "few works suffice", as in reality all actions acquire a spiritual dimension. The Qur'ān remarks regarding this subject:

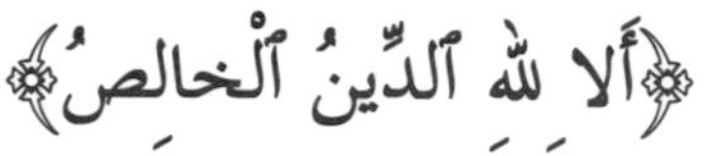

Is it not to God (alone) that sincere devotion is due?[8]

al-Junayd

Complete sincerity implies that the intention be devoted solely to God and that its aspiration (*qaṣd*) is focused perfectly on Him; and this sincerity takes place through the attentive presence of the soul to the origin of things and the clear vision of inner changes (*talwīn*) that can occur. This is how a sincere man accepts in himself what conforms to his aspiration towards God, and this is how he rejects the manifestations of his ego and the influences of the Enemy. This requires the extinction of all individual consideration, and the constant attention to Divine grace. A completely sincere man finds his happiness in the awareness that he is a receiver of Divine favor, which renders him indifferent to the criticism of men. Similarly, he experiences aversion to being praised, fearing that this will harm his spiritual integrity. Thus, one no longer notices the opinion of creatures as soon as the spiritual states intervene. But this is known only to the conscience of the

8. XXXIX:3

completely sincere, and necessarily escapes others.

(*Tāj*, p. 258).

Ibn 'Ajība

Complete sincerity consists in freeing one's behavior before God from all worldly preoccupation, so that God becomes the only goal of our worship, or in clearing the heart from all that is not the Lord.

Complete sincerity of the common people consists in acting without worrying about being seen by others. Complete sincerity of the [spiritual] elite is acting without asking for any reward, neither in this world nor in the next. Complete sincerity of the elect amongst the elite is to not attribute to oneself either might or strength, and to forget all otherness in order to consider only the One, so that every act is by God, from God, and for God.

(*Mi'rāj*, pp. 15-16)

Ḥadīth 16

عن عائشة : "إِذا كَثُرَتْ ذُنوبُ ٱلعَبْدِ فَلَمْ يَكُنْ لَهُ مِنَ ٱلعَمَلِ ما يُكَفِّرُها ابْتَلاهُ ٱللهُ بِٱلْحَزَنِ لِيُكَفِّرَها عَنْهُ."

(رواه الإمام أحمد. حديث حسن)

Narrated 'Ā'isha: "When the sins of the servant become numerous and he has no more good actions to compensate them, God tries him with sadness in order to purify him."

(Quoted by Aḥmad ibn Ḥanbal. Validated *ḥadīth.*)

Commentary

The sadness mentioned in this *ḥadīth* must not be taken in the sense of nostalgia, like the one that is mentioned in the *ḥadīth* which states that God loves the "saddened hearts".[9] Rather, it involves an inner unease and a profound discomfort felt by the believer, which have an expiatory value for him provided the believer understands that this distress is an aid for the realization of spiritual poverty (*faqr*), and that therefore it draws him near to God.

Ibn 'Aṭā' Allāh

The best of your moments is the one wherein you witness the existence of your profound indigence (*fāqa*) and, through it, you are brought back to your [inner] lowliness (*dhilla*).

Sometimes you will find more benefit in states of indigence than you find in fasting or ritual prayer.

(*Ḥikam*, no. 92 and no. 163)

9. Cf. Ḥadīth 45 and Ḥadīth 130.

The Here-Below: الدنيا

Ḥadīth 17

عن عائشة : "الدُّنْيا دارُ مَنْ لا دارَ لَهُ وَمالُ مَنْ لا مالَ لَهُ وَلَها يَجْمَعُ مَنْ لا عَقْلَ لَهُ."

(رواه الإمام أحمد. حديث صحيح)

Narrated 'Ā'isha: "This world is the dwelling-place for he who has none, and its wealth belongs to he who possesses none: only those lacking in intelligence amass in this world."

(Quoted by Aḥmad ibn Ḥanbal. Authenticated *ḥadīth*).

Commentary

Shaykh al-Darqāwī

Assuredly, when men of the elect, such as our master and his like, humble themselves outwardly and of their own accord, God raises them up both inwardly and outwardly. Therefore, they are in perpetual joy. However, ordinary men do the opposite in seeking to show strength outwardly. God then abases them inwardly and outwardly, which is why they are constantly unhappy.

Our master was content with his knowledge of God and he was perfectly indifferent to whether he would become famous or remain unknown. He had regard only for his relationship with God and had no care for the praise or blame of others.

(*Rasā'il*, letter 82)

Ḥadīth 18

عن ابن عباس : "الدُّنْيَا حَرَامٌ عَلَى أَهْلِ ٱلآخِرَةِ، وَٱلآخِرَةُ
حَرَامٌ عَلَى أَهْلِ ٱلدُّنْيَا، وَٱلدُّنْيَا وَٱلآخِرَةُ حَرَامٌ عَلَى أَهْلِ
ٱللَّهِ."

(رواه الديلمي. حديث حسن)

Narrated Ibn 'Abbās: "This world (*dunyā*) is forbidden for the people of the Hereafter; the Hereafter is forbidden for the people of this world; and both this world and the Hereafter are forbidden for the folk of God."

(Quoted by al-Daylamī. Validated *ḥadīth*.)

Commentary

This *ḥadīth* exposes very clearly a distinction which is addressed and developed by the spiritual masters. Thus, the category denoted by the term "people of the Hereafter" in this *ḥadīth* includes two categories: al-'āmma (the common folk from amongst the believers) and al-khāṣṣa (the elite). The latter degree includes ascetics (*zuhhād*) and devout worshippers ('*ubbād*), that is, those who live their faith with a neediness and a fervor greater than those of the 'āmma. As for the "folk of God," they are generally denoted by the expression khāṣṣat al-khāṣṣa (the elite of the elite) or by the term 'ārifūn bi-Llāh (knowers through God or gnostics). Contrary to a widespread idea—including certain Sufi circles—true Islamic esoterism is not represented by al-khāṣṣa whose path is a fervent exoterism, but by the khāṣṣat al-khāṣṣa whose path is that of metaphysical realization through Knowledge or Gnosis.[10] The latter path must sometimes be hidden, even from persons claiming to belong to spiritual paths of Islam. Considered from any aspect, this is no less paradoxical. As an example, it is known that certain sages discouraged their disciples from reading Ibn al-'Arabī, in order not to disturb the simplicity of their understanding, especially in matters of the profession of creed ('aqīda). Such disciples in fact only follow a path of the khāṣṣa, regardless of the true grandeur of their master, whom they often only know indirectly.

Amīr 'Abd al-Qādir

This *ḥadīth* tells us: "Whoever shows satisfaction with his good actions and is grieved by his sins is not but a believer."

This tradition was reported by al-Tirmidhī. Its formulation has an ex-

---

10. Corresponding here to *ma'rifa*, from the same root as '*ārif* (gnostic).

clusive character: The Prophet ﷺ attributes faith only to those befitting this description. Others would be either disbelievers who treat faith like falsehood, or contemplative gnostics who have been veiled and for whom the unseen (*ghayb*) has become the object of contemplation. The term "believer" applies only metaphorically to them. Therefore, the definition of "believer" in this *ḥadīth* points completely elsewhere. Such a person therefore confirms the news which the Legislator has brought to us concerning that which is normally hidden from us, attributing to the servants in particular the actions which emanate from them, as it would seem at first . . .

The gnostic is the person to whom God has unveiled Reality as it is, so much so that knowing himself he knows his Lord. As for the gnostic, he is neither satisfied with his good actions nor grieved by his sins. Were he predestined to slay a thousand prophets he would not be affected and would experience no sadness—even if the killer must, of course, acquit himself of the blood. And were the function of the Supreme Pole to be announced to him, this would still not affect him, nor would it cause him any joy. In fact, as a Gnostic, he knows that he has no part in the command, and if he confirms—as does every simple believer—the teachings of the Legislator regarding that which escapes the senses, he still surpasses it to the extent that that which was hidden has become for him an object of contemplation. This is why the gnostic attributes to himself neither good nor evil action, if that is not what is attributed to him by the Law by virtue of a wisdom known only to God or to an elite chosen by God whom He has made the depository of this wisdom.

The Law contains both the kernel and the shell, whereas the Truth (*ḥaqīqa*) contains only the kernel!

(*Mawāqif*, no 79)

Ḥadīth 19

عن أبي هريرة : "إِنَّ ٱلدُّنْيا مَلْعُونةٌ، مَلْعُونٌ ما فِيها إِلاَّ ذِكْرَ ٱللهِ وَما وَالاهُ، وَعالِماً أَوْ مُتَعَلِّماً."

(رواه الترمذي. حديث حسن)

Narrated Abū Hurayra: "This world and everything in it is cursed, except the invocation of God, and that which aideth thereto, along with the master and the disciple."

(Quoted by al-Tirmidhī. Validated *ḥadīth*.)

Ḥadīth 20

عن أبي الدرداء : "الدُّنْيا مَلْعُونةٌ، مَلْعُونٌ ما فِيها إِلاَّ ما ٱبْتُغِيَ بِهِ وَجْهُ ٱللهِ عَزَّ وَجَلَّ."

(رواه الطبراني. حديث صحيح)

Narrated Abū al-Dardā': "This world and everything in it is cursed, except what is done for the sake of God, the Exalted."

(Quoted by al-Ṭabarānī. Authenticated *ḥadīth*)

Commentary

What meaning ought one give to these words? Does creation not possess any positive aspect?

One must note that these *ḥadīth* do not concern Creation in its totality, but solely the here-below (*dunyā*), which is the framework wherein the terrestrial life of man takes place. This terrestrial abode is not accursed for what it is but only to the extent that the human soul gets lost in it. Driven by ego-centered desires, the soul sinks into multiplicity and forgets its celestial homeland. Thus, it can even go so far as to completely reject faith and spirituality.

The very direct expression of these *ḥadīth* aims at bringing the soul out of its slumber and to firmly invite it to beware of the seduction of immediate pleasures. It must be stressed that the two spiritual means laid out by these *ḥadīth* are the invocation and the master-disciple relationship.

Shaykh al-Darqāwī

O disciple, one who does not turn away from this world—as the Prophet ﷺ did—while it tries to seduce him, is amongst the deluded ones (*maghrūrūn*), or even the people of perdition (*hālikūn*). How else could it be when such a person has exchanged the Tradition (*sunna*) for innovation? May God protect us! The Prophet ﷺ turned away from this world even though the latter was offered to him, because he knew how harmful it was for us.

(*Rasā'il*, letter 64, p. 80)

Ḥasan al-Baṣrī

Protect yourself from this world with all your attention, for it resembles a venomous snake: smooth to touch but deadly! Turn away from all that enchants you in it during the short time you will spend in its company. Abandon the worries it arouses in you since you know that it is ephemeral and that you will be separated from it. Stand firmly before the world's trials for the bliss that shall soon be yours . . .

Every time the worldly man feels secure in one of this world's pleasures, it throws him into some difficulty . . .

Even if God Most High had not warned us of the dangers of the here-below through the parables of the Qur'ān, its nature would suffice to awaken the man who is plunged in slumber and forgetfulness.

(Letter to caliph 'Umar ibn 'Abd al-'Azīz, *Ḥilyāt al-awliyā'*, II, pp. 135-136)

Ḥadīth 21

عن أبي هريرة : "لا يَزالُ قَلْبُ ٱلكَبيرِ شابّاً فِي ٱثْنَتَيْن : فِي حُبِّ ٱلدُّنْيا وَطُولِ ٱلأَمَل."

(رواه البخاري. حديث صحيح)

Narrated Abū Hurayra: "The heart of an old man remains young with respect to two things: the love of the here-below and long-term expectations."
(Quoted by al-Bukhārī. Authenticated *ḥadīth*.)

Commentary

Ideally, old age should be the age of wisdom and detachment from passions. The dispersion and ardor of youth should be followed by contemplation and serenity of mature age. Unfortunately, this is not always what happens. Although it is true that desires related more directly to the body diminish for biological reasons, this is not the case with the purely psychic attachments of the ego. Attachment to earthly life and a lack of awareness of the ephemeral nature of things does not diminish except through a veritable spiritual wayfaring, a path of inner purification and a surpassing of illusions.

Shaykh al-Darqāwī

Behold what happened to me when I decided to quit the here-below and turn myself completely to my Lord: It would suffice for me to look at someone, with the intention of making him go from heedlessness (*ghafla*) to the remembrance of God (*dhikr*), for that person's spiritual state to change instantly, in conformity to my will! That was neither a choice on my part nor on that person's part; rather it was the choice of God and of the realization of His command. When I would turn myself to the here-below and pay attention to it, my station which—by God—was similar to that of the Friend of God Abū Madyan, would be taken away from me! I would become as I was at the time of heedlessness. Nay, even worse! *So learn a lesson, o ye who have eyes!*[11] Thankfully, it was too difficult for me to give in to this world and I obtained nothing, due to the blessing of the spiritual master to whom I was attached.

I met two aged men who were at the point of reaching the end of the Path but the world showed itself to them, pulling them back to it. However, God rescued them, before they were seduced, as both of them were able to escape from it and to abandon it, thanks also to the blessing of the spiritual master to whom we were attached.

---

11. LIX: 2

I also knew another old man very well whom the here-below succeeded in getting hold of, and who died in that state. His spiritual master was not alive, and yet I do not think that he was worthy of taking a deceased person as master. [. . .]

No one can pretend to be a master when entering any discipline, *a fortiori*, when this is the spiritual Path. On this matter, the masters say: "He who has no master, has Satan for his master."

Whoever pretends to become a spiritual master turns away from the door and meets a wall. If we were still entirely faithful to the teachings of the Messenger of God ﷺ and if our hearts and our limbs did not oppose those teachings on any matter, we could effectively claim to be spiritual masters. But we have changed and altered these teachings so much that our hearts and our limbs have become hardened. This is why we are inwardly impure! How can we pretend to be spiritual masters? This can be claimed only by a proud man, an ignorant man, or someone who is complacent with his ego.

(*Rasā'il*, letter 17, pp. 51-52)

Ḥadīth 22

عن أبي الدرداء: "حُبُّكَ ٱلشَّيْءَ يُعْمِي وَيُصِمُّ."

(رواه أبو داود. حديث حسن)

Narrated Abū al-Dardā': "Love of things renders one blind and deaf."
(Quoted by Abū Dāwūd. Validated *ḥadīth*)

Ḥadīth 23

عن ابن عباس : "إِيَّاكُمْ وَٱلْهَوَىَ فَإِنَّ ٱلْهَوَىَ يُصِمُّ وَيُعْمِي."

(رواه السيوطي. حديث صحيح)

Narrated Ibn 'Abbās: "Beware of caprice (*hawā*) for it renders one deaf and blind."
(Quoted by al-Suyūṭī. Authenticated *ḥadīth*.)

Commentary

On reading these *ḥadīth* without a commentary, one question inevitably comes to mind: how is it that we cannot see and hear because of our caprices? To what extent does Reality escape us because of our attachment to created things?

Shaykh al-Darqāwī

One day our master remarked during a conversation: "If you contemplate Him in everything, His contemplation will prevent you from seeing anything else. How can the existence of a thing appear to you, when it is He who bestows existence on everything? How can something be when He is the Unique without any partner? If you relate the ephemeral to the Eternal, the ephemeral will disappear and only the Eternal will remain. When the Qualities of the Beloved manifest themselves, the veil and the veiled disappear. When the lights of contemplation show themselves, the ascetic and that which he renounces become extinct."
(*Rasā'il*, letter 82, p. 104)

Ḥadīth 24

عن ابن عمر : "أَخَذَ رَسُولُ ٱللهِ ﷺ بِمَنْكِبِي فَقَالَ : "كُنْ فِي ٱلدُّنْيَا كَأَنَّكَ غَرِيبٌ أَوْ عَابِرُ سَبِيلٍ."

(رواه البخاري. حديث صحيح)

Narrated Ibn ʿUmar: "The Messenger of God ﷺ took me by the shoulder and said: 'Be unto this world like a stranger or a passenger."

(Quoted by al-Bukhārī. Authenticated *ḥadīth*)

Commentary

Detachment and necessary withdrawal from ephemeral things are only possible when one remembers the transitory character of earthly life. Ibn ʿUmar's comment on this *ḥadīth* is the following: "When evening comes, do not await the morning, and when the morning comes do not await the evening. Benefit from health before illness intervenes in your life, and from your life before death seizes you."

Ḥadīth 25

عن أنس بن مالك : "إِذا أَحَبَّ ٱللهُ قَوْماً ٱبْتَلاهُمْ."

(رواه الطبراني. حديث صحيح)

Narrated Anas ibn Mālik: "When God loves a people, He afflicts them with trials."

(Quoted by al-Ṭabarānī. Authenticated *ḥadīth*.)

Ḥadīth 26

عن أبي سعيد الخدري : "أَنَّهُ قالَ :"يا رَسُولَ ٱللهِ مَنْ أَشَدُّ ٱلنَّاسِ بَلاءً ؟" قالَ : "الأَنْبياء." قالَ : "ثُمَّ مَنْ ؟" قالَ : "العُلَماء." قالَ : "ثُمَّ مَنْ ؟" قالَ : "الصَّالِحُون."

(رواه الحاكم. حديث صحيح)

Narrated Abū Sa'īd al-Khudrī:

I asked: O Messenger of God, which people are tried the most?
The prophets.
And after them?
The scholars.
And then?
The virtuous.

(Quoted by al-Ḥākim. Authenticated *ḥadīth*)

Commentary

This *ḥadīth* establishes a hierarchy in trials, proportional to the spiritual station of the believer. After the prophets come the people of knowledge who are denoted by a term which has become common nowadays, namely *'ulamā'*. At the time of the Prophet, however, this term obviously did not refer to the intellectual class of theologians and jurists, but to people who had received an inner light, which inclined them to knowledge. *Be wary of God and He will teach you.*[12]

Shaykh al-Darqāwī

It is inevitable that the folk of knowledge and the folk of love will be at-

12. II: 282

tacked by someone seeking to harm them: *Such has been the course of God that has indeed run before, and ye shall not find a change in God's course.*[13] The Friends of God have therefore had to be subjected to great injustices: some of them were imprisoned, others were whipped, others were chastised in public, and still others were even killed. On this subject, the death of the spiritual pole 'Abd al-Salām ibn Mashīsh and that of Sīdī al-Ḥallāj are perfect examples. This was the case also with the Companions and the prophets, because the Most High has said: *And with how many a prophet have there been a number of devoted men who fought (beside him). They never lost heart for aught that befell them in the way of God, nor did they weaken, nor were they brought low. God loveth the steadfast.*[14]

We consider the injustices that the Prophets underwent greater than those that were met by the Companions, just as the latter were tried more severely than the other Friends of God. Indeed, trials are proportionate to the spiritual station (*maqām*) as indicated by the words of the best of creation: "The people who are tried the most are the Prophets, then the Friends of God, and then those who resemble them the most." But—by God—that does not mean that He abandons them or neglects them; quite the opposite, this is proof of a grace that He bestows upon them! It is a favor, a benefit and a great gift from God to them.

(*Rasā'il*, letter 134, p. 148)

13. XLVIII: 23
14. III: 146

Ḥadīth 27

عن ابن عباس : "لَيْسَ بِمُؤْمِنٍ مُسْتَكْمِلِ ٱلإيمانِ مَنْ لَمْ يَعُدَّ ٱلبَلاءَ نِعْمَةً وَٱلرَّخاءَ مُصِيبَةً."

(رواه الطبراني. حديث صحيح)

Narrated Ibn 'Abbās: "Whoever does not consider trial as a blessing and ease as a misfortune is not amongst the accomplished believers."

(Quoted by al-Ṭabarānī. Authenticated *ḥadīth*.)

Commentary

According to this *ḥadīth*, faith is only completely realized by the person who considers every event which he is forced to undergo from the viewpoint of spiritual progression. In this perspective, a trial will be experienced as a blessing because it allows a victory over the ego, when undergone along the Path. The trial is then accepted without rancor—and, amongst the Friends of God, with a certain joy—even though it is difficult to live through it every day. The Qur'ān addresses the believers regarding this matter in the following terms:

﴿أَحَسِبَ ٱلنَّاسُ أَنْ يُتْرَكُوا أَنْ يَقُولُو آمَنَّا وَهُمْ لا يُفْتَنُونَ﴾

Do men think that they be left on saying, 'We believe' and not be tried?[15]

Ibn al-'Arabī

Nūna Fāṭima lived in Seville. When I met her, she was already ninety-six years old and feeding on leftovers that people placed at the doorsteps of their houses. Despite her very old age and the small amount of food she ate, I was almost ashamed to look at her face as it was rosy and fresh. Her personal surah was the Fātiḥa. She told me once, "I have been given the Fātiḥa. It is at my disposal for anything I wish to do." [. . .]

She entered the Path when she was still a young girl living with her father. [Then] she married an honest man whom God afflicted with leprosy. She served him for twenty-four years, after which he died. When she was hungry and she could find neither leftovers nor alms on her street, she would be content and would thank God for His favor since He subjected her to the trials that He inflicts upon the prophets and the saints. Then she

15. XXIX: 2.

would say, "O Lord, how can I deserve this high position: that Thou treatest me like Thou treatest Thy friends?"

(*Soufis*, pp. 139-140)

Ḥadīth 28

عن ابن عمر : "مَنْ أَحَبَّ دُنياهُ أَضَرَّ بآخِرَتِه وَمَنْ أَحَبَّ آخِرَتَهُ أَضَرَّ بِدُنْياهُ، فَآثِرُوا ما يَبْقَى عَلى ما يَفْنَى."

(رواه الترمذي. حديث صحيح)

Narrated Ibn 'Umar: "Whoever loves the life of this world will suffer in the Hereafter and whoever loves the Hereafter will suffer in this world. Therefore, prefer that which endures to what is evanescent."

(Quoted by al-Tirmidhī. Authenticated *ḥadīth*.)

Commentary

From the way it is constructed, this *ḥadīth* clearly shows the incompatibility between this world and the next. But incompatibility does not mean absolute opposition: it is not a question of rejecting the life of this world but of being aware of the incommensurability between the here-below and the Hereafter. This awareness must be expressed through a "preference" given to the heavenly abode any time that an alternative presents itself. But in order to realize this attitude, one has to "know" the reality of the here-below: one has to grasp its evanescence existentially and not just mentally. This is why the Qur'ān chastises those who only know it superficially:

﴿يَعْلَمُونَ ظاهِراً مِنَ ٱلْحَياةِ ٱلدُّنْيا وَهُمْ عَنِ ٱلآخِرَةِ هُمْ غافِلُونَ﴾

They know the outward life of this world, but of the hereafter they are heedless.[16]

Ibn 'Aṭā' Allāh

O Thou Who makes lights shine in the heart of Thy friends, and Who removed from the heart of Thy friends all that is other-than-Thou; O Thou Who was their Intimate before having made them strangers to the world, and who guided them until Thy signs were manifested to them: what has he found who lost Thee, and what has he lost who found Thee? Deceived is he who prefers another to Thee! Nothing but desolation will he find who wishes to turn elsewhere from Thee.

(*Munājāt*, no. 26)

---

16. XXX: 7.

Ḥadīth 29

عن أبي الدرداء : "إِنَّ لِكُلِّ شَيْءٍ حَقِيقَةً وَما بَلَغَ عَبْدٌ حَقِيقَةَ ٱلإِيـمانِ حَتَّى يَعْلَمَ أَنَّ ما أَصابَهُ لَمْ يَكُنْ لِيُخْطِئَهُ وَما أَخْطَأَهُ لَمْ يَكُنْ لِيُصِيبَهُ."

(رواه الإمام أحمد. حديث حسن)

Narrated Abū al-Dardā': "Verily, every thing has a reality: the servant does not attain the reality of faith without understanding that that which has befallen him was inevitable and that which he did not go through could not befall him."

(Quoted by Aḥmad ibn Ḥanbal. Authenticated *ḥadīth*.)

Commentary

This *ḥadīth* emphasizes the reality (*ḥaqīqa*) of faith. The term *ḥaqīqa* here stresses the fact that it does not suffice to recognize the existence of God, and not even to submit to His injunctions in order for man to realize faith in his heart. The Qur'ān rejects the claim of persons who, despite having shortly entered Islam, claim to possess faith:

﴿قالَتِ ٱلأَعْرابُ آمَنَّا قُلْ لَمْ تُؤْمِنُوا وَلَـٰكِنْ قُولُوا أَسْلَمْنا وَلَمَّا يَدْخُلِ ٱلإِيـمانُ فِي قُلُوبِكُمْ﴾

The wandering Arabs say: We believe. Say (unto them, O Muḥammad): Ye believe not, but rather say "We submit," for the faith hath not yet entered into your hearts.[17]

The *ḥadīth* therefore emphasizes that one can be a Muslim without having realized completely what faith is. The father of 'Āmir ibn Sa'd relates a *ḥadīth* confirming the distinction between *islām* (submission) and *īmān* (faith): "The Messenger of God ﷺ distributed some goods amongst (a group of) people while I was sitting there but he left out a man whom I thought the best of the lot. I asked, 'O Messenger of God! Why have you left out that person? By God, I regard him as a man of faith (*mu'min*).' The Prophet ﷺ commented: 'Or is he merely a Muslim?' I remained quiet for a while, but could not help repeating my question because of what I knew about him. Then the Prophet ﷺ said, 'O Sa'd! I give to a person while an-

17. XLIX: 14.

other is dearer to me, for fear that he might be thrown on his face in the Fire by God.'" (Quoted by al-Bukhārī)[18]

Faith is therefore recognized through certain signs, and according to al-Ghazzālī patience (*ṣabr*) and gratitude (*shukr*) are its two halves. This is the reason why he treats these two virtues in the same chapter of the *Iḥyā'*.[19]

al-Ghazzālī

The two halves of faith are patience and gratitude as reported in the Prophetic traditions. They are amongst the Attributes of God the Most High, and His Names, as He is called the Patient (*al-Ṣabūr*) and the Thankful (*al-Shakūr*). To ignore the reality of patience and the reality of thankfulness is to ignore the two halves of faith. Moreover, it amounts to negating two of the Attributes of the Most Merciful.

There is no way to approach God without faith. Indeed, how can one conceive of advancing along the path of faith without knowing what faith is and what one must believe in?

Those who are interested in faith and neglect the knowledge of patience and of thankfulness will be prevented from grasping what faith is and what one must believe in. Thus, there is a great need to explain and clarify the two halves of faith.

(*Iḥyā'*, IV, pp. 59-60)

When faith becomes stable and the conviction of reaching a blissful end is reinforced, patience becomes easy. For this reason, God the Exalted has said, *As for him who giveth and is dutiful (toward God) and believeth in goodness (al-ḥusnā); Surely We will ease his way unto the state of ease (al-yusrā).*[20]

This aspect of patience is comparable to a fighter's physical superiority. A strong man is capable of knocking down a weak adversary very easily, in a fight in which he finds neither difficulty nor fatigue. The fighter is

---

18. Arabic text of complete *ḥadīth*:

[3] عن عامر بن سعد، عن أبيه : "قَسَّمَ رَسُولُ ٱللهِ صَلَّى ٱللهُ عَلَيْهِ وَسَلَّمَ قسْماً. فَقُلْتُ : يا رَسُولَ ٱللهِ ! أَعْطِ فُلاناً فَإِنَّهُ مُؤْمِن. فَقالَ ٱلنَّبِيُّ صَلَّى ٱللهُ عَلَيْهِ وَسَلَّمَ "أَوْ مُسْلِمٌ" أَقُولُها ثَلاثاً وَيُرَدِّدُها عَلَيَّ ثَلاثاً "أَوْ مُسْلِمٌ" ثُمَّ قَالَ "إِنِّي لَأُعْطِي ٱلرَّجُلَ وَغَيْرُهُ أَحَبُّ إِلَيَّ مِنْهُ مَخافةً أَنْ يَكُبَّهُ ٱللهُ فِي ٱلنَّار". (رواه البخاري)

19. Cf. *Iḥyā'*, IV, Chapter 2.
20. XCII: 5-7

strengthened by exertion, intensive effort and sweat.

This is what the struggle between the religious tendency and the passionate tendency should be like, for in reality, it is a struggle between "the armies of the angels" and "the armies of the devils." As long as concupiscent desires are subdued and brought to heel, and the religious tendency prevails, continuous patience becomes easy and one reaches the station of satisfaction (*maqām al-riḍā*), as we shall see in the *Kitāb al-riḍā*.[21]

This station is higher than that of patience, and this is why the Prophet ﷺ has said: "Worship God and be satisfied; if you cannot accomplish this, then be patient towards what is unpleasant to you, for in this there is a great deal of good."[22]

According to an *'ārif*,[23] patience has three degrees. The first consists in abandoning concupiscent desire, which is the degree of the repented servants (*tā'ibīn*). The second consists in being satisfied with the Divine decree, and this is the degree of the ascetics (*zāhidīn*). The third is love of all that God the Sovereign Lord does, and this is the degree of the sincere ones (*ṣiddīqīn*). In the *Book of Love* we shall demonstrate that this station is higher than that of satisfaction.

(*Iḥyā'*, IV, p. 67)

---

21. Cf. *Iḥyā'*, IV, Chapter 6.
22. Quoted by al-Tirmidhī as narrated by Ibn 'Abbās.
23. That is, he who possesses a knowledge that comes to him directly from God, hence the expression *'ārif bi-Llāh*. The term "gnostic" and "gnosis" are often used as translations of *'ārif* and *'irfān* respectively.

Ḥadīth 30

عن أبي سعيد : "مَنْ لَمْ يَشْكُرِ ٱلنَّاسَ لَمْ يَشْكُرِ ٱللَّهَ."

(رواه الإمام أحمد. حديث صحيح)

Narrated Abū Sa'īd: "Whoever is not grateful to people is not grateful to God."

(Quoted by Aḥmad ibn Ḥanbal. Authenticated *ḥadīth*.)

Commentary

al-Ghazzālī

Whoever receives a gift must thank the giver, supplicate God for him and praise him. In doing so, he will retain in his consciousness that the giver is an intermediary (*wāsiṭa*) whom God has chosen as a means for bestowing a blessing upon him. And yet, the "means" is due a certain consideration for having been chosen by God as an instrument. This does not prevent the blessing from being viewed as coming from God—exalted be He. Regarding this, the Prophet ﷺ said: "Whoever is not grateful to people is not grateful to God." God Himself praises certain servants for their actions even though He is their Creator and the capacity to act comes from Him. That is why He has said: *How excellent a slave! Surely he was ever returning (to Us).*[24]

(*Iḥyā'*, I, pp. 223-224)

24. XXXVIII: 44

Ḥadīth 31

عن أبي الدرداء : "أُعْبُدِ ٱللهَ كَأَنَّكَ تَراهُ وَعُدَّ نَفْسَكَ مِنَ ٱلْمَوْتَى وَإِيَّاكَ وَدَعْوَةَ ٱلْمَظْلُومِ."

(رواه الطبراني. حديث حسن)

Narrated Abū al-Dardā': "Worship God as if you see Him, and count your ego amongst the dead, and beware of the supplication of the oppressed."
(Quoted by al-Ṭabarānī. Validated *ḥadīth*.)

Commentary

Spiritual wayfaring consists in dying to one's ego—an essential concept in spiritual training—which is often indicated by the term *fanā'* in the mystical texts. Literally this term means "extinction". However, this attitude is meaningful only within the framework of seeking spiritual excellence (*iḥsān*) mentioned at the beginning of this *ḥadīth*: in order to see God everywhere, one must not see oneself anymore. Extinction must be followed by subsistence (*baqā'*), which is an inner rebirth followed by the illumination of the heart:

﴿أَوَمَنْ كانَ مَيْتاً فَأَحْيَيْناهُ وَجَعَلْنا لَهُ نُوراً يَمْشِي بِهِ فِي ٱلنَّاسِ كَمَنْ مَثَلُهُ فِي ٱلظُّلُماتِ لَيْسَ بِخارِجٍ مِنْها﴾

Can he who was dead, to whom We gave life and a Light whereby he can walk amongst men, be like him who is in the depths of darkness, from which he can never come out? Thus to those without Faith their own deeds seem pleasing.[25]

al-Qushayrī

Whoever accomplishes the extinction of his concupiscent desires realizes subsistence in sincerity belonging to the state of the believer; whoever detaches himself from the world in his heart will extinguish in himself all passionate desires. Whoever purifies his character will extinguish jealousy, hatred, avarice, greed, anger, pride and all the other maladies of the soul from his heart . . .

When one removes the illusion of multiplicity, one's being realizes subsistence through the Divine Attributes. Whoever is dominated by the Truth to the point of no longer seeing the creatures in their limitations, has

25. VI: 122

realized extinction before creatures and subsistence in the Truth . . .

Regarding extinction, God the Exalted has said: *And when they saw him they exalted him and cut their hands, exclaiming: God is Blameless! This is not a human being. This is none other than some gracious angel.*[26] This anecdote evokes the rapture of one creature before another; how then must be the rapture of the contemplator of God? Should one be astonished at him who no longer possesses an ordinary awareness of his individuality and that of others?

(*Risāla*, pp. 67-68)

26. XII: 31

Supplication: الدعاء

Ḥadīth 32

عن علي : "الدُّعاءُ سِلاحُ ٱلْمُؤْمِنِ وَعِمادُ ٱلدِّينِ وَنُورُ ٱلسَّماواتِ وَٱلأَرْضِ."

(رواه الحاكم. حديث صحيح)

Narrated 'Alī: "Supplication is the weapon of the man of faith, the mainstay of religion, and the light of the heavens and the earth."

(Quoted by al-Ḥākim. Authenticated *ḥadīth*.)

Commentary

Supplication (*du'ā'*) is a pillar of religion inasmuch as the latter seeks to "re-bind" man to God. This is precisely what supplication does as a spontaneous prayer; it is a free petition which the believer addresses to his Lord. Canonical prayer (*ṣalāt*) also realizes a bond with God, but of an altogether different nature, because the requests pronounced in it by the believer are those formulated by Revelation. In the canonical prayer, it is man as such who addresses God, whereas in supplication the individual opens his heart to God and confesses his needs and personal difficulties. This is why supplication permits the believer to overcome a good number of inner obstacles and tensions. In this sense, it is the weapon of the believer, through which he can defeat his inner enemies.

al-Qushayrī

The Most High has said: *Supplicate your Lord humbly and secretly.*[27] *Supplicate Me and I will respond to you.*[28] *The Messenger of God* ﷺ has said: "Supplication is the heart of worship . . . "

Abū 'Abd Allāh al-Makānisī relates this anecdote: "I was with al-Junayd when a woman came begging to him: 'Supplicate God for me because my son is lost.' Al-Junayd replied, 'Go and be patient.' The woman left and she returned after a while to ask him the same. Al-Junayd replied in the same way: 'Go and be patient.' To each new visit from this woman, al-Junayd replied, 'Go and be patient.' One day, she told him: 'My patience

27. VII: 55.
28. XL: 60.

has been completely exhausted.' At that, al-Junayd told her: 'If it is truly as you say, return home, for your son shall be given back to you.' She obeyed and later on returned to thank him, and asked him, 'How did you know that my son had returned?' He replied: 'The Most High has said: *Does He not answer the distressed who call on Him and relieve their suffering? . . .* '"[29]

Ja'far al-Ṣādiq was asked: "Why are our supplications not answered?" He replied: "Because you do not know the One you are supplicating."

(*Risāla*, pp. 264-267)

29. XXVII: 62.

Ḥadīth 33

عن ابن عمر : "إِذا فُتِحَ عَلى ٱلعَبْدِ ٱلدُّعاءُ فَلْيَدْعُ رَبَّهُ فَإِنَّ ٱللهَ يَسْتَجِيبُ لَه."

(رواه الترمذي. حديث حسن)

Narrated Ibn 'Umar: "When the servant is given a spiritual opening during a supplication, he should pray to his Lord, for then he shall be answered."

(Quoted by al-Tirmidhī. Validated *ḥadīth*.)

Commentary

When the servant opens himself to his Lord presenting his heart to Him without any swerving or reservation, his demand is "heard" and answered. The friend (*walī*) of God is he who has received the gift of having his supplications answered through his bond with God. This gift cannot be received without certain minimal conditions which can be summarized in view of the sacred Law and purity of intention. Thus, after showing the path of sanctity, the famous *ḥadīth al-walī*[30] affirms that the petitions of God's friend are answered, which results precisely from the purity of his bond with God.

Beyond the conditions mentioned in the *ḥadīth*, the spiritual masters point out that a human being's profound indigence (*fāqa*) can serve as an opening to the Divine Generosity.

Shaykh al-Darqāwī

The noble Shaykh Ibn 'Aṭā' Allāh has said in his *Ḥikam*, "The best of your moments is the one wherein you witness the existence of your indigence (*fāqa*) and, through which you are brought back to your [inner] lowliness (*dhilla*)."[31] "Sometimes you will find more benefit in states of neediness than you find in fasting or ritual prayer."[32] The state of profound distress is none other than the intensity of need (*shiddat al-iḥtiyāj*). Yet, the master of our master, Sīdī al-'Arabī ibn 'Abd Allāh called it the distress of "elicitation" because it elicits the one experiencing it to turn to his Lord. And our master used to say, "If people knew the great number of secrets and benefits that indigence brings in itself, they would have no need but to have need." He also used to say, "Intense neediness serves as God's supreme Name (*ism al-a'ẓam*)."

(*Rasā'il*, letter 105; *Lettres d'un maitre*, pp. 132-133)

30. Cf. no. 197.
31. Cf. *Ḥikam* no. 92.
32. Cf. *Ḥikam* no. 163.

Ḥadīth 34

عن أبي أسامة : "إنَّ لله تعالى مَلَكاً مُوَكَّلاً بِمَنْ يَقُولُ : "يا أَرْحَمَ ٱلرَّاحِمِينَ". فَمَنْ قالَها ثَلاثاً قال لَهُ ٱلْمَلَكُ : "إنَّ أَرْحَمَ ٱلرَّاحِمِينَ قَدْ أَقْبَلَ عَلَيْكَ فَسَلْ."

(رواه الحاكم. حديث صحيح)

Narrated Abū Usāma: "Verily, God possesses an angel dedicated to those who supplicate by saying, 'O Most Merciful of the merciful.' To whomever repeats this three times in his supplication the angel says, 'Indeed, the Most Merciful of the merciful is before you, therefore ask!'"

(Quoted by al-Ḥākim. Authenticated *ḥadīth.*)

Commentary

Supplicating God through the expression "O Most Merciful of the merciful" implies an awareness that turning to God amounts to opening oneself to the Merciful. Such a supplication must be motivated, according to al-Ghazzālī, by the awareness that the believer has concerning his limitations and of his fundamental neediness *vis-à-vis* God.

al-Ghazzālī

Mercy requires a being on which it can be exercised (*marḥūm*). Yet, such a being is necessarily in need. [. . .] Divine Mercy is perfect in the sense that it responds to every needy being which addresses itself to Mercy. It is universal to the extent that it is poured onto those who deserve it and those who do not.

(*Maqṣad*, p. 65)

Perhaps you will say: "How is one to understand the fact that God is both All-Merciful (*Raḥīm*) and Most Merciful of the merciful (*arḥam al-rāḥimīn*)? Indeed, when a merciful person sees an afflicted or a wronged being, subjected to chastising or to grave illness, he hastens to relieve it from pain as much as he can. And yet, God has the power to end every trial, to dispel all poverty, to make all illness disappear, and every evil cease. Unfortunately the world is brimming with illnesses, trials and afflictions. God could stop them all, and yet He leaves His servants prey to misfortunes and afflictions."

Our reply is that it often happens that a mother refuses to subject her child to bloodletting due to her sentimental weakness, whereas the lucid father subjects him to the operation by force. The ignorant will think that here the mother is merciful and the father is not; the intelligent one knows that the father's behavior is an expression of his tenderness (*'aṭf*) and of his real compassion (*tamām shafaqatih*) towards his child. In reality, the mother acts as an enemy, under the cover of affection, for a passing suffering in face of a great benefit is not an evil, but a greater good.

The All-Merciful wants beyond any shadow of a doubt the best for His servant. However, there is no evil which does not contain a good. If evil is removed, the good that it contains and to which it leads also disappears, resulting in an even greater evil.

(*Maqṣad*, pp. 67-68)

Ḥadīth 35

عن أبي هريرة : "ٱدْعُوا ٱللّٰهَ وَأَنْتُمْ مُوقِنُونَ بِٱلإجابة،
وَٱعْلَمُوا أَنَّ ٱللّٰهَ لا يَسْتَجِيبُ دُعاءً مِنْ قَلْبٍ غافِلٍ لاهٍ."

(رواه الحاكم. حديث صحيح)

Narrated Abū Hurayra: "Supplicate God with the certitude that He will answer you. Know that God does not answer the supplication uttered with a distracted and inattentive heart."

(Quoted by al-Ḥākim. Authenticated *ḥadīth*.)

Commentary

The distracted (*ghāfil*) and inattentive (*lāhin*) heart is the one is dispersed in multiple preoccupations and worries, and which therefore has great difficulty remaining in contemplation. And yet, the awareness of God's presence and the certainty that He will answer supplications allows one to escape the hold of worries and self-propagating thoughts (*khawāṭir*).

al-Ghazzālī

Know that your heart is comparable to a house with many entrances: different inner states (*aḥwāl*) penetrate it from each entrance . . .

Various impressions enter the heart at every moment, both from the outside—through the five senses, and from the inside—through imagination (*khayāl*): passionate desire, anger . . . , and the character shaped by the person's tendencies [. . .]. All these causes constantly generate changes and impressions in the heart.

The most common products of the heart are called self-propagating thoughts (*khawāṭir*), by which I mean the thoughts and the memories which are born in the heart, the former being created entities and the latter reminiscences. [. . .]

In order to free oneself from these self-propagating thoughts, one has to shut the outer doors of the heart which are the five senses, and their inner doors which are the desires and the ties to the here-below. The solitude of an obscure room shuts the door of the senses, and the breaking of the interpersonal and material attachments reduces the inner openings of the heart. However, the door of the memories will remain open. The only way to shut it is to be absorbed in the invocation (*dhikr*) of God.

(*Iḥyā'*, III, pp. 25-29)

The Heart: القلب

Ḥadīth 36

عن أنس بن مالك : "إِنَّ فِي ٱلْجَسَدِ مُضْغَةً إِذا صَلُحَتْ صَلُحَ لَها سائِرُ ٱلْجَسَدِ، وَإِذا فَسَدَتْ فَسَدَ لَها سائِرُ ٱلْجَسَدِ، أَلا وَهِيَ ٱلْقَلْبُ."

(رواه البخاري. حديث صحيح)

Narrated Anas ibn Mālik: "There is a piece of flesh in the body; if it is purified the whole body becomes pure but if it gets spoilt the whole body becomes spoilt, and that is none other than the heart."

(Quoted by al-Bukhārī. Authenticated *ḥadīth*.)

Commentary

In order to clarify the meaning of this *ḥadīth*, one has to answer the following two questions: How can the heart, which at first sight is a physical organ, reform or corrupt the entire body? To what extent can a "piece of flesh" (*muḍgha*) be the seat of faith and the organ of spiritual perception, as affirmed by the Qur'ān? This is, in fact, what numerous verses of the Holy Book state, amongst which are the following:

﴿فَإِنَّها لا تَعْمَى ٱلأَبْصارُ وَلٰكِنْ تَعْمَى ٱلْقُلوبُ ٱلَّتِي فِي ٱلصُّدُورِ﴾

For indeed it is not the eyes that grow blind, but it is the hearts, which are within the bosoms, that grow blind.[33]

﴿إِنَّما ٱلْمُؤْمِنُونَ ٱلَّذِينَ إِذا ذُكِرَ ٱللهُ وَجِلَتْ قُلُوبُهُمْ﴾

They only are (true) believers whose hearts feel fear when God is mentioned[34]

33. XXII: 46.
34. VIII: 2.

Martin Lings (Abū Bakr Sirāj al-Dīn)

The Qur'ān says: *It is not the eyes that are blind but the hearts.* This shows—and it would be strange if it were otherwise—that the Qur'ānic perspective agrees with that of the whole ancient world, both of East and of West, in attributing vision to the heart and in using this word to indicate not only the bodily organ of that name but also what this corporeal centre gives access to, namely the centre of the soul, which itself is the gateway to a higher "heart," namely the Spirit. Thus "heart" is often to be found as a synonym of "intellect," not in the sense in which this word is misused today but in the full sense of the Latin *intellectus*, that is, the faculty which perceives the Transcendent.

In virtue of being the centre of the body, the heart may be said to transcend the rest of the body, although substantially it consists of the same flesh and blood. In other words, while the body as a whole is "horizontal" in the sense that it is limited to its own plane of existence, the heart has, in addition, a certain "verticality" for being the lower end of the "vertical" axis which passes from the Divinity Itself through the centres of all the degrees of the Universe.[35] . . . It is in virtue of this interconnection, through which the centres are as it were merged into one, that the bodily heart receives Life from the Divinity (according to Sufi doctrine all Life is Divine) and flood the body with Life. In the opposite direction the bodily heart may serve as a focal point for the concentration of all the powers of the soul in its aspiration towards the Infinite, and examples of this methodic practice are to be found in most forms of mysticism and perhaps in all.

(*What is Sufism?*, pp. 48-49).

35. This is the reason why the heart is the "seat of the vision of God". C.f. *ḥadīth* 42.

Ḥadīth 37

عن ابن مسعود : "لا يَدْخُلُ ٱلْجَنَّةَ مَنْ كانَ فِي قَلْبِهِ ذَرَّةٌ مِنَ ٱلْكِبْر. قِيلَ : إِنَّ ٱلرَّجُلَ يُحِبُّ أَنْ يَكُونَ ثَوْبُهُ حَسَناً وَنعلُهُ حَسَنَة. قالَ : إِنَّ ٱللّٰهَ جَميلٌ يُحِبُّ ٱلْجَمال. الكِبْرُ بَطَرُ ٱلْحَقِّ وَغَمْطُ ٱلنَّاس."

(رواه مسلم. حديث صحيح)

Narrated Ibn Mas'ūd: "'He in whose heart there is the weight of a mustard seed of pride shall not enter Paradise.' A person said: 'Verily a person loves his dress to be fine, and his shoes to be fine.' (The Prophet) remarked: 'Verily, God is Beautiful and He loves Beauty. Pride is disdain for the truth, and contempt for people.'"

(Quoted by Muslim. Authenticated *ḥadīth.*)

Commentary

If the slightest presence of pride in the heart suffices to corrupt it, it is because this vice is of a different nature from other inner defects. It prevents all Divine light from entering the heart. That is the reason why al-Ghazzālī considers it as the veil (*ḥijāb*) *par excellence*. One must nevertheless distinguish between pride and self-respect, which results from dignity and nobility (*karam*). Although the Qur'ān condemns pride very severely, it also recognizes the dignity of man:

﴿ وَلَقَدْ كَرَّمْنا بَنِي آدَمَ ﴾

Verily We have honored the children of Adam.[36]

Commenting upon this verse, Ibn 'Abbās specified that it alludes to the gift of intelligence. Yet, the organ of spiritual knowledge is the heart, as pointed out by al-Bukhārī, who uses this formula in his *Ṣaḥīḥ*: "Knowledge is in the heart (*al-ma'rifa fi'l-qalb*)."[37] In order to emphasize the central role of the heart in the spiritual life and to justify the perdition of those who let vices enter therein, al-Bukhārī quotes this verse:

36. XVII: 70.
37. Īmān 11.

﴿وَلَٰكِن يُؤَاخِذُكُم بِمَا كَسَبَتْ قُلُوبُكُمْ﴾

But He will take you to task for that which your hearts have earned.[38]

al-Ghazzālī

In order for one to become proud, there has to exist a being towards whom this is done (*mutakabbar 'alayhi*) and there have to exist [illusory] motives for doing so (*mutakkabar bihi*). This is precisely where pride differs from vanity (*'ujb*) which does not imply the taking into consideration of another. [. . .]

Pride is an extremely dangerous vice into which even people possessing certain spirituality have managed to fall: few righteous slaves, ascetics, and scholars have known how to avoid it. What can be said then about the common people?

How can one be surprised at the dangerous character of this vice when the Prophet ﷺ has said, *Whoever has an atom's weight of pride in his heart shall not enter Paradise*? If this vice deprives one of Paradise, it is because it makes the believer lose all the virtues (*akhlāq*). Now, it is the virtues that are the gates to Paradise.

(*Iḥyā'*, III, pp. 334-335)

Frithjof Schuon ('Īsā Nūr al-Dīn)

Pride consists in taking ourselves for what we are not and disparaging others. Self-respect is knowing what one is and not allowing oneself to be humbled. Self-respect does not prevent a man from humbling himself before that which surpasses him; it is far from being the opposite of true humility, whatever the more superficial moralists may say.

Modesty may be a quality or a defect according to whether it springs from veracity or weakness. But even in the latter case it is nearer to virtue than vice, for weakness is worth more than presumption.

According to St. Augustine, "the other vices are attached to evil, in order that it may be done; pride alone is attached to the good, in order that it may perish." According to Boethius, "all the other vices flee from God; pride alone rises up against Him."

Spiritually speaking, pride consists in attributing to oneself what is due to God. It poisons and kills every value, for as soon as a good is claimed in its cause and in its essence by man, it is transmuted into evil: it espouses the limitations of the creature and engenders limitations in its turn. Pride appropriates to itself the Divine gift and then strangles it. A good vivifies insofar as it comes from God—not in so far as it is usurped by man.

Man deems himself good even before God, who is Perfection, and when he forces himself to recognize his wretchedness, he still deems himself good on account of this effort.

(*Perspectives*, pp. 262-64)

38. II: 225.

Ḥadīth 38

عن أبو أمامة الباهلي : "أَخَذَ بِيَدِي رَسُولُ ٱللهِ ﷺ فَقَالَ
لِي : يا أَبا أُمامة إِنَّ مِنَ ٱلْمُؤْمِنِينَ مَنْ يَلِينُ لِي قَلْبُه."

(رواه الإمام أحمد. حديث صحيح)

Narrated Abū Umāma al-Bāhilī: "The Messenger of God ﷺ took me by the hand and said to me: 'O Abū Umāma, there are believers whose hearts are softened for me.'"

(Quoted by Aḥmad ibn Ḥanbal. Authenticated *ḥadīth*.)

Commentary

Love of the Prophet ﷺ is an integral part of faith as certain *ḥadīth* show. The presence of love of the Prophet ﷺ in the hearts softens them: the Arabic term *layn* is the opposite of *qaswa,* meaning hardness. The latter is described by God as forgetfulness and denial of God.[39] To love the Prophet ﷺ is in reality to love our *fiṭra*, the original nature of man; it is therefore to love the virtues that he personifies and which the believer must actualize within him/herself.

Frithjof Schuon ('Īsā Nūr al-Dīn)

Love of the Prophet ﷺ constitutes a fundamental element in Islamic spirituality . . . Muslims see in the Prophet ﷺ the prototype and model of the virtues which constitute the theomorphism of man and the beauty and equilibrium of the Universe, and which are so many keys or paths towards liberating Unity—this is why they love him and imitate him even in the very smallest details of daily life. The Prophet, like Islam as a whole, is as it were a heavenly mold ready to receive the influx of the intelligence and will of the believer and one wherein even effort becomes a kind of supernatural repose.

(*Understanding Islam*, p. 112)

39. Cf. II: 74 and VI: 43.

Ḥadīth 39

عن أبي هريرة : "أَنَّ رَجُلاً شَكَا إِلَى رَسُولِ ٱللهِ ﷺ قَسْوَةَ قَلْبِهِ فقالَ لَهُ : إِنْ أَرَدْتَ تَلْيِينَ قَلْبِكَ فَأَطْعِمِ ٱلْمِسْكِينَ وَٱمْسَحْ رَأْسَ ٱلْيَتِيمِ."

(رواه الإمام أحمد. حديث حسن)

Narrated Abū Hurayra: "A man came to complain to the Messenger of God ﷺ about the hardness of his heart and [the Prophet] replied to him, 'If you want your heart to become soft, feed the poor and take care of the orphan.'"

(Quoted by Aḥmad ibn Ḥanbal. Validated *ḥadīth.*)

Commentary

Hardness of heart is always related to egocentrism in its different forms. Reducing the effect of the ego on the heart is certainly a way of giving of oneself. This *ḥadīth* mentions a means of giving of oneself as a possibility amongst others: generosity towards the most underprivileged.

al-Ghazzālī

Whoever hopes to acquire the virtue of generosity must learn to give away everything he possesses. He should devote himself to this and exert himself relentlessly in fighting against his ego in this path until his generosity becomes natural. Then he will have become generous . . . In this domain, the ideal is that the act of giving become pleasant.

(*Iḥyā'*, III, 56)

Ḥadīth 40

عن أبي هريرة : "لا تُكْثِرُوا ٱلضَّحِكَ فَإِنَّ كَثْرَةَ ٱلضَّحِكِ تُمِيتُ ٱلْقَلْبَ."

(رواه ابن ماجه. حديث صحيح)

Narrated Abū Hurayra: "Do not laugh much, for too much laughing kills the heart."

(Quoted by Ibn Mājah. Authenticated *ḥadīth*)

Commentary

According to the spiritual masters, death of the heart is the dispersion into worldliness and the hardening resulting from this dispersion. The heart then loses its spiritual sensibility and looks for immediate pleasures, which will be crude or subtle depending on its tendencies.

al-Ghazzālī

Know that what is forbidden in relation to laughing and jesting is to devote oneself continuously (*mudāwamma*) and excessively (*ifrāṭ*) to it. Giving oneself to it continuously is forbidden because this leads to being completely distracted by play and frivolity. In itself, playing is permitted, but to devote oneself to it ceaselessly is blameworthy (*maḍmūm*). As for jesting in excess, it leads to excessive laughing. Now, too much laughing kills the heart, and can even ruin it. This excess makes one also lose all tenure and all dignity. Apart from these cases, joking is not blameworthy, as is shown by this saying of the Prophet ﷺ: "Certainly, it happens that I joke, but [in doing so] I tell nothing but the truth." Indeed, he was capable of joking by saying nothing but the truth, but most people seek to produce laughter by all possible means when they joke. Regarding this, the Prophet ﷺ said: "Verily, man can amuse his entourage with words that will carry him to the bottom of Hell!"

'Umar [ibn al-Khaṭṭāb] said, "Whoever laughs much ends up losing his dignity and whoever jests much is no longer taken seriously: whoever gives himself too much to something ends up being known as such. Whoever speaks too much says too much nonsense; whoever speaks too much nonsense loses his modesty (*ḥayā'*); whoever has no modesty has no shame (*wara'*); whoever has no more shame sees his heart dying because too much laughing is a sign of forgetting the Hereafter. On this matter, the Prophet ﷺ said: 'If you knew what I know, you would laugh less and weep more.'"

(*Iḥyā'*, III, p. 124)

Ḥadīth 41

عن عمر بن الخطاب : "أَنَّهُ خَرَجَ يَوْماً إِلَى مَسْجِدِ رَسُولِ ٱللهِ ﷺ، فَوَجَدَ مُعَاذَ بْنَ جَبَلٍ قَاعِداً عِنْدَ قَبْرِ النَّبِيِّ ﷺ يَبْكِي. فَقَالَ : مَا يُبْكِيكَ ؟ قَالَ : يُبْكِينِي شَيْءٌ سَمِعْتُهُ مِنْ رَسُولِ ٱللهِ ﷺ. سَمِعْتُ رَسُولَ ٱللهِ ﷺ يَقُولُ إِنَّ يَسِيرَ الرِّيَاءِ شِرْكٌ. وَإِنَّ مَنْ عَادى لِلَّهِ وَلِيّاً، فَقَدْ بَارَزَ ٱللهَ بِالْمُحَارَبَةِ. إِنَّ ٱللهَ يُحِبُّ ٱلأَبْرَارَ ٱلأَتْقِيَاءَ ٱلأَخْفِيَاءَ ٱلَّذِينَ إِذَا غَابُوا لَمْ يُفْتَقَدُوا وَإِنْ حَضَرُوا لَمْ يُعْرَفُوا قُلُوبُهُمْ مَصَابِيحُ ٱلْهُدَى يَخْرُجُونَ مِنْ كُلِّ غَبْرَاءَ مُظْلِمَةٍ."

(رواه الحاكم. حديث صحيح)

Narrated ‘Umar ibn al-Khaṭṭāb: “One day while I was entering the Mosque of the Prophet ﷺ, I saw Mu‘ādh ibn Jabal crying by the tomb of the Prophet ﷺ, and I asked him: ‘Why are you crying?’ He said: ‘Because of some things I have heard from the Messenger of God ﷺ. I heard him say: The smallest ostentation (*riyā’*) is association (*shirk*); being hostile to one of God’s friends amounts to declaring war on Him; verily, God loves the virtuous, the pious and the obscure: those who are not missed when gone, and who are not noticed when present. Their hearts are lanterns of guidance, and they live in poor places sheltered from looks.’”

(Quoted by al-Ḥākim. Authenticated *ḥadīth*.)

Commentary

In this *ḥadīth* the expression “God loves the virtuous, the pious and the obscure people” denotes as saints those who have a function of spiritual guidance. This is emphasized by the fact that it describes their hearts as being lanterns of guidance (*maṣābīḥ al-hudā*). These lanterns are the “means of approach” (*wasīla*) to the guidance mentioned in the following verse of the Qur’ān, quoted by Amīr ‘Abd al-Qādir in his *mawqif* translated below:

﴿يا أَيُّها ٱلَّذِينَ آمَنُوا ٱتَّقُوا ٱللَّهَ وَٱبْتَغُوا إِلَيْهِ ٱلْوَسِيلَةَ وَجاهِدُوا فِي سَبِيلِ ٱللَّهِ لَعَلَّكُمْ تُفْلِحُونَ﴾

O ye who believe! Be wary of God, and seek the means of approach unto Him, and strive in His way in order that ye may succeed.[40]

Thus, it is by visiting such persons, and through their example and teachings, that the aspirant will be able to find the path leading him from his inner darkness towards the Divine light.

Amīr ʿAbd al-Qādir

This verse is a signpost on the course of the spiritual Path which leads to gnosis.

Firstly, God orders the believers to be wary of God (*taqwā Llāh*). This corresponds to what we call the "station of repentance" (*maqām al-tawba*) which is the basis for any progress on the Path, and the key for the attainment of the "station of realization" (*maqām al-taḥqīq*). Whoever is given the station of repentance will be given the attainment of the goal, and whoever is refused this station will be refused the attainment of the goal [i.e. union]. As a spiritual master has said, "Those who do not reach the goal (*wuṣūl*) have in fact not respected the principles (*uṣūl*)."

God then tells us: *seek the means of approach unto Him*, that is, after having mastered the station of repentance within you, conforming to all its conditions, look for the means of approach. This means is none other than the spiritual master whose initiatic lineage (*nisba*)[41] is without defects, who truly knows the Path, and the human limitations (*ʿilal*) which are an obstacle, as well as the maladies that prevent the attainment of gnosis (*al-ʿilm bi-Llāh*). He must also possess knowledge for curing souls and balancing temperaments, and he must know how to provide the appropriate remedy. The Folk of God unanimously state that, in the path to gnosis, a "means of approach"—that is, a spiritual master—is indispensable. Bookish knowledge does not provide such a means, even more so since there will be inspirations (*wāridāt*), flashes of theophanies (*bawāriq al-tajalliyāt*), and spiritual events (*wāqiʿāt*); therefore, it becomes necessary to explain to the disciple what has to be accepted or rejected, what is healthy and what is vicious in all that. On the other hand, at the beginning of the Path, the

40. V: 35.

41. This lineage is represented by the chain of spiritual masters (*silsila*) transmitting, from one generation to the next, the Muḥammadan grace (*al-baraka al-muḥammadiyyah*). This transmission often takes the form of an initiatory pact (*mubāyaʿa*) as the one performed by the Prophet ﷺ through the pact of Ḥudaybiyya, mentioned in the Qurʾān (cf. XLVIII: 10 and 18).

disciple may satisfy himself with books which deal with pious behavior and the spiritual struggle in its most general sense.

(*Mawāqif*, no. 197)

Ḥadīth 42

عن أبي هريرة : "إِنَّ ٱللَّهَ تَعالَى لا يَنْظُرُ إِلى صُوَرِكُمْ وَأَمْوالِكُمْ، وَلكِنْ إِنَّما يَنْظُرُ إِلَى قُلُوبِكُمْ وَأَعْمالِكُمْ."

(رواه مسلم. حديث صحيح)

Narrated Abū Hurayra: "Verily God does not look at your appearance and your wealth but He looks at your heart and at your deeds."

(Quoted by Muslim. Authenticated *ḥadīth*)

Commentary

This *ḥadīth* clarifies in a certain way *ḥadīth* 11 which emphasizes the refusal of every unnecessary complication in religion, and the return to the essential. The right intention—which seeks God and His pleasure—is an orientation of the heart, and that is why this *ḥadīth* starts by stating that God does not pay attention to the outward. As for the inward, it pertains to the life of the heart, which is precisely whence actions should flow.

al-Ghazzālī

The Prophet ﷺ has said, "Verily God does not look at your appearance and your wealth but He looks at your heart and your deeds." If God looks only at the heart, this is because it is the place where intentions are formed. [. . .]

Know that the terms "intention" (*niyya*), "will" (*irāda*), and "goal" (*qaṣd*) have one and the same meaning. They refer to an inner state and to a characteristic of the heart which is based on two things: knowledge and action. Knowledge precedes actions because it is the root (*aṣl*) and the necessary condition (*sharṭ*); action follows knowledge because it is the fruit and application (*far'*) of knowledge. It is so because every action—by which I mean both movement and rest—proceeds from a choice. Therefore, in order for an action to take place, three things are required: knowledge, will, and potentiality (*qudra*). In reality, man only wills what he knows; knowledge is therefore necessary [for the action to take place]. By will, one must understand the heart's impetus towards that which is perceived as conforming to the suggested goal, be it a long term one or not. Man has been created in such a way that certain things are suitable and conform to his goal, and others are not. Therefore he has to strive for what befits him and repel what hinders him. It is therefore necessary for him to be able to perceive the beneficial (*nāfi'*) and the harmful (*muḍirr*), in order to incline towards the first and escape from the second. Indeed, whoever cannot perceive food and does not know it cannot obtain it, and whoever does not perceive the fire cannot avoid it. This is why God created guidance and gnosis. He assigned two channels to these gifts: the external senses and the internal senses, but this is not our subject here.

(*Iḥyā'*, IV, pp. 351-354)

Ḥadīth 43

عن أبي سعيد الخدري : "القُلُوبُ أَرْبَعَة : قَلْبٌ أَجْرَدُ فيه مِثْلَ ٱلسِّراجِ يَزْهَرُ وَقَلْبٌ أَغْلَفُ مَرْبُوطٌ عَلَى غلافه وَقَلْبٌ مَنْكُوسٌ وَقَلْبٌ مُصْفَح. فَأَمَّا ٱلقَلْبُ ٱلأَجْرَدُ فَقَلْبُ ٱلْمُؤْمِنِ سراجُهُ فيه نُورُهُ وَأَمَّا ٱلقَلْبُ ٱلأَغْلَفُ فَقَلْبُ ٱلكافِرِ وَأَمَّا ٱلقَلْبُ ٱلْمَنْكُوسُ فَقَلْبُ ٱلْمُنافِقِ عَرَفَ ثُمَّ أَنْكَرَ وَأَمَّا ٱلقَلْبُ ٱلْمُصْفَحُ فَقَلْبٌ فيه إِيْمانٌ وَنفاقٌ وَمَثَلُ ٱلإِيْمانِ فيه كَمَثَلِ ٱلبُقْلَة يَمُدُّها ٱلْماءُ ٱلطَّيِّبُ وَمَثَلُ ٱلنِّفاقِ كَمَثَلِ ٱلقَرْحة يَمُدُّها ٱلقَيْحُ وَٱلدَّمُ فَأَيُّ المادَّتَيْنِ غَلَبَتْ عَلَى ٱلأُخْرَى غَلَبَتْ عَلَيْهِ."

(رواه الإمام أحمد. حديث صحيح)

Narrated Abū Sa'īd al-Khudrī: "There are four types of hearts: the naked (*ajrad*) heart in which there is a light similar to a lantern which illuminates; the heart which is locked (*aghlaf*) in an envelope; the inverted (*mankūs*) heart; and the divided heart (*muṣfaḥ*). The naked heart is that of the believer, and the lantern therein is its light [from God]; the locked heart is that of the non-believer; the inverted heart is that of the hypocrite who knows but refuses [the truth]; the divided heart is that in which there is part faith and part hypocrisy. The part of faith therein is comparable to a good plantation irrigated by pure water; and the part of hypocrisy therein is comparable to a wound washed by both pus and blood. The stronger of these two tendencies will dominate the heart."

(Quoted by Aḥmad ibn Ḥanbal. Authenticated *ḥadīth*)

Commentary

Among the four types of heart mentioned in this *ḥadīth*, the divided heart has received most attention from the commentators. This heart, in fact, is that of the majority of believers, and the goal of all spirituality is precisely to enable the believer to pass from a state of inner division to a state in which faith radiates within him without meeting any obstacle: "The naked heart is that of the believer and the lantern therein is its light [from God]." Upon commenting on this *ḥadīth* al-Ghazzālī emphasizes the central role of *dhikr* as a means of spiritual purification and a path to the illumination of the heart.

al-Ghazzālī

Another version of this *ḥadīth* ends with the following words: "The stronger of these two tendencies will win the heart."

[One can compare this *ḥadīth* to] the verse: *Lo! those who are wary (of God), when a thought of evil from the devil troubleth them, they do but remember and behold them seers!*[42] God therefore informs us that purity of the heart and its ability to see clearly follows the invocation of God, and that only those who are wary of God are in a position to practice *dhikr*. God-wariness is the door to the invocation (*al-taqwā bāb al-dhikr*) which in its turn is the door of unveiling (*al-dhikr bāb al-kashf*). Unveiling itself is the door of the great success (*al-fawz al-akbar*) which is the meeting with God, Exalted is He.

(*Iḥyā'*, III, p. 12)

42. VII: 201.

Ḥadīth 44

عن ابن عمرو : "الزُّهْدُ فِي ٱلدُّنْيا يُرِيحُ ٱلقَلْبَ وَٱلبَدَنَ وَٱلرَّغْبَةُ فِيها تُكْثِرُ ٱلْهَمَّ وَٱلْحَزَنَ، وَٱلبَطالَةُ تُقَسِّي ٱلقَلْبَ."

(رواه السيوطي. حديث حسن)

Narrated Ibn 'Amr: "Detachment from the world appeases the heart and the body whereas worldly desire generates worry and distress, and idleness hardens the heart."

(Quoted by al-Suyūṭī. Validated *ḥadīth.*)

Commentary

The appetite of the ego for the possessions of this world in reality is insatiable and it is precisely this insatiability that wears out the heart and the body. The mystics often quote the verse:

﴿أَلْهاكُمُ ٱلتَّكاثُرُ حَتَّىٰ زُرْتُمُ ٱلْمَقابِرَ﴾

Rivalry in worldly increase distracteth ye until ye come to the graves.[43]

A statement has been related from Bishr ibn al-Ḥārith (d. 227/840) on the subject of the love of the world, announcing what other spiritual masters would later elaborate: "Whoever loves the world does not taste the sweetness of the worship of God. Jesus, the son of Mary, said: 'The origin of every fault is the love of this world.'"

Shaykh al-Darqāwī

Dedicate yourselves, O brothers—may God have mercy on you—to that which will annihilate your egos and vivify your hearts. No virtue can bloom before you have emptied your hearts of the love of the world. Conversely, all defects develop from love of the world when it remains in the heart . . .

Be, therefore, as I have asked you to be, for none shall reach the Presence of our Lord without passing through the death of the ego and the revitalization of the heart, and whatever be our knowledge. As the great friend of God Abū Madyan has said: "Whoever does not die to himself will not see the Real."

(*Rasā'il*, letter 8)

43. CII: 1-2.

Ḥadīth 45

عن ابن عباس : "عَلَيْكُمْ بِٱلْحُزْنِ فَإِنَّهُ مِفْتاحُ ٱلْقَلْبِ،
أَجِيعُوا أَنْفُسَكُمْ وَأَظْمِئُوها."

(رواه الطبراني. حديث حسن)

Narrated Ibn 'Abbās: "I recommend for you nostalgic sadness, for it is the key of the heart: leave your egos hungry and thirsty."

(Quoted by al-Ṭabarānī. Validated *ḥadīth*)

Commentary

The expression 'key to the heart' (*miftāḥ al-qalb*) is the most important element of this *ḥadīth*: the teachings it contains allow the believer to receive that key. How should one understand nostalgic sadness (*ḥuzn*)? Is it the lucidity that is born from the awareness of that which awaits man in the Hereafter, and concerning which the Prophet ﷺ has said: "If you knew what I know, you would laugh less and weep more"? As is often the case, the teachings of the Prophet ﷺ synthesize multiple elements: distancing oneself from the ego allows one to regain access to the heart, which is vivified by nostalgic sadness (*ḥuzn*). Nevertheless, the *ḥadīth* does not explain *how* this takes place: To what extent does nostalgic sadness offer access to the heart? And what is the link between detachment and nostalgia for God?

Shaykh al-Darqāwī

The disciples of the early generations sought only that which would annihilate their egos and vivify their hearts, whereas we, on the contrary, are preoccupied with killing our hearts and vivifying our egos! They would exert themselves in getting rid of their passions and in dethroning their ego; whereas we aspire to the satisfaction of our sensual desires and the exaltation of our ego. This is why we are with our backs to the door, and our face to a wall. I am only telling you this because I have seen the graces (*mawāhib*) that God accords to whomever dies to his ego and vivifies his heart.

We are content with very little; and yet, only the ignorant one is content before having reached the end of the Path. I have wondered whether there is something else depriving us from the Divine gifts besides our concupiscent desires and the exaltation of the ego, and—God be my witness—I found that the absence of spiritual nostalgia is also a veil. In fact, intuitions (*ma'ānī*) are generally only given to one whose heart is pierced by an intense nostalgia and a great desire to contemplate the Essence and the Lord.

It is in such a one that the intuitions of the Divine Essence flow until he is extinguished in the Essence, liberating himself from the illusion of a reality other than It. On the contrary, he who aspires to either take knowledge or action separately, does not receive intuition upon intuition; he will not delight then, since his aspiration aims at something other than the Divine Essence, and because God—exalted be He—blesses His servant to the measure of his aspiration.

(*Rasā'il*, letter 13, p. 43; *Lettres d'un maître*, pp. 51-52)

Ḥadīth 46

عن أبي موسى : "إِنَّما سُمِّيَ ٱلقَلْبُ مِنْ تَقَلُّبِه إِنَّما مَثَلُ ٱلقَلْبِ كَمَثَلِ رِيشَةٍ مُعَلَّقَةٍ فِي أَصْلِ شَجَرَةٍ يُقَلِّبُها ٱلرِّيحُ ظَهْراً لِبَطْنٍ."

(رواه الإمام أحمد. حديث صحيح)

Narrated Abū Mūsā: "The heart has been so called because of its turnings: it is similar to a feather hanging from a tree which the wind blows around back and forth."

(Quoted by Aḥmad ibn Ḥanbal. Authenticated *ḥadīth.*)

Ḥadīth 47

عن المقداد بن الأسود : "لَقَلْبُ ٱبْنِ آدَمَ أَشَدُّ ٱنْقِلاباً مِنَ ٱلقِدْرِ إِذا ٱسْتَجْمَعَتْ غَلَياناً."

(رواه الإمام أحمد. حديث صحيح)

Narrated al-Miqdād ibn al-Aswad: "Verily, the heart of the son of Adam gets overturned more easily than water boiling in a pot."

(Quoted by Aḥmad ibn Ḥanbal. Authenticated *ḥadīth.*)

Commentary

One of the constants of the spiritual life is that it does not unfold in a linear fashion and very often the believer has the impression of having distanced himself from God, and that his faith has weakened. Spiritual life is subject to the extreme sensibility of the heart to the most diverse influences, be they positive or negative, hence the image of the "feather hanging from a tree which the wind blows back and forth."

al-Ghazzālī

Know that the heart is torn apart by the different tendencies, such as those that we have seen, and that it is marked by spiritual influences and states which we have referred to . . .

At times the heart is under the influence of a demon which invites it to caprice (*hawā*), and at other times it is under the influence of an angel which rescues it. But when one demon succeeds in influencing the heart, another demon starts influencing it. Conversely, when the heart lets itself be drawn by an angel, another angel comes and pulls it away. The heart can therefore be divided between two angels, two demons, or between an angel and a demon; but it is never left to itself. This is what the verse *And We will turn their hearts and their sights*[44] alludes to. Since the Messenger of God ﷺ knew the marvels of God's creation related to the heart and its turnings, he would swear by saying: "Nay, by the One who turns hearts." He would also repeat the following supplication: "O Turner of hearts, make our hearts firm in Thy religion."[45]

(*Iḥyā'*, III, p. 44)

44. VI: 110.

45. *Yā Muqalliba l-qulūb, thabbit qulūbanā 'alā dīnik.*

Ḥadīth 48

عن عبد الله بن عمرو : "إِنَّ قُلُوبَ بَنِي آدَمَ كُلَّها بَيْنَ إِصْبَعَيْنِ مِنْ أَصابِعِ ٱلرَّحْمٰنِ كَقَلْبٍ واحِدٍ يُصَرِّفُهُ حَيْثُ يَشاءُ. ثُمَّ قالَ رَسُولُ ٱللهِ ﷺ : "اللَّهُمَّ مُصَرِّفَ ٱلقُلُوبِ صَرِّفْ قُلُوبَنا عَلى طاعَتِكَ."

(رواه مسلم. حديث صحيح)

Narrated ʿAbd Allah ibn ʿAmr: "Verily, the hearts of all men are held between two fingers of the All-Merciful like a single heart: He turns it in any (direction) He likes."

Then, the Messenger of God ﷺ said: "O He who is the Turner of hearts, turn our hearts to Thine obedience."

(Quoted by Muslim. Authenticated *ḥadīth*.)

Commentary

ʿAbd al-ʿAzīz al-Dabbāgh

The two fingers are symbolic: they denote two modes of turning hearts . . .

These dispositions are relative to the body and to the soul. The body comes from the earth and inclines towards concupiscent desires, whereas the soul is created from light and inclines towards knowledge and spiritual truths. They are therefore in perpetual opposition.

The actions of the angel or of the devil on man are but consequences of that which we shall expound upon, and which shed light on the origin of the problem.

Every man, pious or not, is the scene of self-propagating thoughts (*khawāṭir*) which lead him to salvation or to damnation. Depending on the nature of his thoughts, man will be approached by the angel or the devil who in turn inspires him . . .

(*Ibrīz*, I, p. 292)

Ḥadīth 49

عن ابن عمر : "مَنْ جَعَلَ ٱلْهُمُومَ هَمّاً واحِداً، كَفاهُ ٱللّٰهُ ما أَهَمَّهُ مِنْ أَمْرِ ٱلدُّنْيا وَٱلآخِرَةِ، وَمَنْ تَشاعَبَتْ بِهِ ٱلْهُمُومُ لَمْ يُبالِ ٱللّٰهُ فِي أَيِّ أَوْدِيَةِ ٱلدُّنْيا هَلَكَ."

(رواه الحاكم. حديث صحيح)

Narrated Ibn 'Umar: "Whoever unifies all his preoccupations in order to keep but one will be protected by God from all the worries of this world and the next. As for he who lets himself be dispersed by his preoccupations, God hardly cares about the way in which he shall perish!"

Commentary

One of the gravest pitfalls in the spiritual life is dispersion: nothing is possible [to achieve in the spiritual Path] without inner unification. This unification must be realized around the immutable axis of the invocation of God (*dhikr Allāh*).

al-Ghazzālī

Know for certain that Satan is from amongst those who have received a delay (*al-munẓirūn*)[46] [from God] and that he will not humble himself before you by postponing his suggestions [even if the struggle were to be prolonged] until the Day of Judgment, except if all your preoccupations disappear to the benefit of a single one: that your heart be entirely absorbed by the remembrance of God, the Unique. The Accursed one will no longer have a hold on you and you will be amongst the perfectly devoted slaves of God, who escape the domination of the Satan.[47]

Do not think that he (Satan) is absent from an empty heart. Quite the contrary, he circulates within the son of Adam like blood [in the body].[48] Its flow is comparable to that of air in a cup: if you wish the air not to enter the cup without filling it with water or some other [liquid], you are wishing the impossible, for where emptiness reigns, air inevitably penetrates. In

46. Reference to VII:14-15. (tr.)

47. Allusion to the verses, *He said: My Lord! Because Thou hast sent me astray, I verily shall adorn the path of error for them in the earth, and shall mislead them every one, save such of them as are Thy perfectly devoted slaves.* (XV:39-40)

48. Reference to the *ḥadīth*, "Verily, Satan circulates within the son of Adam like blood [in the body]. Diminish its flow through hunger." (Narrated by Ṣafiyya; quoted by al-Bukhārī and Muslim).

the same way, a heart occupied with meditation on an important aspect of religion escapes the turnings of Satan.

(*Iḥyā'*, IV, p. 73)

Ḥadīth 50

عن أم سلمة :"إِذا أَرادَ ٱللهُ بِعَبْدٍ خَيْراً جَعَلَ لَهُ واعِظاً مِنْ قَلْبِهِ."

(رواه الديلمي. حديث حسن)

Narrated Umm Salama: "When God wants the best for a servant, He bestows upon him an exhortation coming from his heart."

(Quoted by al-Daylamī. Validated *ḥadīth*.)

Commentary

The Arabic term *wā'iẓ*, translated here as "exhortation" alludes to an inner call, giving rise to a spiritual impetus towards God. As al-Ghazzālī frequently reminds us, this call comes to the heart through the intermediary of an angel in charge of guidance. On this subject the Qur'ān declares,

﴿فَمَنْ يُرِدِ ٱللهُ أَنْ يَهْدِيَهُ يَشْرَحْ صَدْرَهُ لِلإِسْلامِ﴾

And whomsoever it is God's will to guide, He expandeth his bosom unto submission to [God].[49]

al-Ghazzālī

The heart is similar to a mirror (*mir'āt*) which, surrounded as it is by numerous objects, must reflect them. Positive influences and negative influences therefore reach the heart. The beneficial ones augment its purity, brilliance, and light until Truth is reflected perfectly therein, and the reality of religion is unveiled to it. It is to this heart that the following *ḥadīth* of the Prophet ﷺ refer: "When God wants the best for a servant, He bestows upon him an exhortation coming from his heart"; and, "He who receives an exhortation from the heart is protected by God." Only such a heart is capable of settling lastingly in the invocation of God: *Verily in the remembrance of God do hearts find rest*![50]

(*Iḥyā'*, III, p. 11)

49. VI: 125
50. XIII: 28.

Ḥadīth 51

عن أبي هريرة : "إِنَّ ٱلْمُؤْمِنَ إِذا أَذْنَبَ كانَتْ نُكْتَةٌ سَوْداءُ فِي قَلْبِهِ فَإِنْ تابَ وَنَزَعَ وَٱسْتَغْفَرَ صُقِلَ قَلْبُهُ فَإِنْ زادَ زادَتْ، فَذٰلِكَ ٱلرَّانُ ٱلَّذي ذَكَرَهُ ٱللهُ فِي كِتابِهِ ﴿كَلَّا بَلْ رانَ عَلَىٰ قُلُوبِهِمْ ما كانُوا يَكْسِبُونَ﴾."

(رواه ابن حبان. حديث صحيح)

Narrated Abū Hurayra: "When a believer commits a sin, a black spot appears on his heart. If he repents and seeks forgiveness, his heart becomes purified. If he advances in sin, the black spots increase and this is the rust mentioned by God in His Book: *Nay, but that which they have earned is rust upon their hearts.*"[51]

(Quoted by Ibn Ḥibbān. Authenticated *ḥadīth.*)

Commentary

The idea according to which the heart is progressively covered with "rust" has been explained by numerous spiritual masters. This is, for example, how the celebrated al-Junayd distinguishes between the rust (*rayn*) and the thin veil (*ghayn*): "Rust stems from dispositions anchored within man (*al-waṭanāt*) and the thin veil of self-propagating thoughts (*al-khaṭarāt*). And yet, the former are permanent, and the latter transitory."[52]

al-Ghazzālī

Negative influences have an effect comparable to thick smoke veiling the mirror of the heart. If this smoke is maintained, it does not cease to thicken until the heart becomes black and dark: it is then completely veiled from God. This is the meaning of the seal (*ṭab'*) and the rust (*rayn*) mentioned by God: *Nay, but that which they have earned is rust upon their hearts; If We will, We can smite them for their sins and set a seal upon their hearts so that they hear not.*[53] God therefore links the permanent incapability of listening to the seal created by the sins . . .

When sins become many, they stamp a seal on the heart which then becomes deaf and can no longer perceive the Truth and the beauty of reli-

51. LXXXIII: 14.
52. *Tāj*, p. 122.
53. VII: 100.

gion. Likewise, this heart will not attach any importance to the Hereafter, dedicating itself completely to the here-below . . .

This is how the heart can become blackened by sin according to what has been related to us by the Qur'ān and the *Sunna*.

(*Iḥyā',* III, p. 11)

Ḥadīth 52

عن ابن مسعود : "إذا دَخَلَ ٱلنُّورُ ٱلقَلْبَ انْفَسَحَ وَانْشَرَحَ.
قالُوا : وَما عَلامَةُ ذٰلِكَ يا رَسُولَ الله ؟ قالَ : الإنابَةُ إلى
دارِ ٱلخُلُودِ وَٱلتَّجافِي فِي دارِ ٱلغُرُورِ وَٱلاِسْتِعْدادُ لِلْمَوْتِ
قَبْلَ نُزُولِه."

(رواه الحاكم. حديث صحيح)

Narrated Ibn Mas'ūd: "When light enters the heart, it dilates and expands." Someone asked: "What is the sign testifying to this?" The Prophet ﷺ replied: "The fact of turning towards the eternal Abode, being disinterested in the abode of the unreal, and preparing for death before it arrives."

(Quoted by al-Ḥākim. Authenticated *ḥadīth*)

Commentary

Ḥadīth 45 stresses the importance of spiritual nostalgia as "key to the heart", thus giving us signs of the opening of the heart to Divine light. These two *ḥadīth* shed light upon each other, and it is evident that one cannot turn to "the Abode of the Eternal" without an intense spiritual nostalgia.

Ḥadīth 53

عن أنس : "الشَّيْطانُ يَلْتَقِمُ قَلْبَ ابْنِ آدَمَ فَإذا ذَكَرَ ٱللّٰهَ خَسَنَ عِنْدَهُ وَإذا نَسيَ ٱللّٰهَ ٱلْتَقَمَ قَلْبَهُ."

(رواه الحكيم. حديث حسن)

Narrated Anas: "Satan tries to devour the heart of the son of Adam: If he invokes God, Satan shrinks away from him but if he forgets God, he devours his heart."

(Quoted by al-Ḥākim. Authenticated *ḥadīth.*)

al-Ghazzālī

Whoever forgets God Most High for an instant has in that precise moment Satan for companion. For this reason, God the Most High has said: *And he whose sight is dim to the remembrance of the Beneficent, We assign unto him a devil who becometh his companion.*[54]

The Prophet ﷺ has said: "Verily, God Most High hates a lazy youth." Indeed, when a youngster is inactive, his "interior" must become occupied with permissible things which will help him in his religion. For when he does nothing, he is outwardly idle but his heart does not remain unoccupied even for a single moment. Quite the contrary, Satan comes to make his nest there and to lay his eggs in order to reproduce therein. The eggs reproduce and this is how the progeny of Satan multiplies faster than any animal whatsoever, because its natural tendency is that of fire; if it finds dry wood, its reproduction becomes even faster, fire feeding fire.

(*Iḥyā'*, III, p. 73)

54. XLIII: 36.

Ḥadīth 54

عن أبي هريرة : "لَوْلا أَنَّ ٱلشَّياطِينَ يَحُومُونَ عَلَى قُلُوبِ بَنِي آدَمَ لَنَظَرُوا إِلَى مَلَكُوتِ ٱلسَّماواتِ."

(رواه الإمام أحمد. حديث صحيح)

Narrated Abū Hurayra: "Were it not for the devils encircling the hearts of the children of Adam, they would be able to perceive the Kingdom of Heaven."

(Quoted by Aḥmad ibn Ḥanbal. Authenticated *ḥadīth*.)

Commentary

The Arabic term *malakūt*, translated here as "Kingdom of Heaven," refers to the world of spiritual truths and angelic presences. Ibn al-ʿArabī defines *malakūt* as the world of the Unseen (*ʿālam al-ghayb*) as opposed to the *mulk* which is the sensible world (*ʿālam al-shahāda*).

Ibn al-ʿArabī

Among all these sciences,[55] there are those which become the cause of obstacles for us to perceive what the messengers of God perceived. This is what is referred to in the *ḥadīth* authenticated through unveiling (*kashf*), in which the Prophet ﷺ has said: "Were it not for the abundance of your words and the unease in your hearts, you would see what I see and you would hear what I hear." In saying this, he showed the path which leads to the station where he could see what he could see, and hear what he could hear. To the question of whether there are persons who have lost that thing within themselves preventing them from perceiving what the messengers of God perceived, we reply: Yes, it is possible to lose this obstacle. In fact, God ordered His Prophet ﷺ to *make clear to men what has been revealed to them*[56] a consequence of which is that no obstacle to spiritual elevation can appear which cannot be overcome, and there can be no degree of nearness to God that cannot be realized. Whoever exerts himself seriously ends up by reaching the goal (*man jadda wajada*). As for him whose efforts are insufficient, he has but himself to blame.

(*Fut.*, III, p. 131)

---

55. That is, the list of the sciences belonging to the initiatic abode of the renewal of the non-existents (*tajdīd al-maʿdūm*). For the list of sciences concluding the chapters of *Futūḥāt* dedicated to the initiatic abode, refer to our work *Le Mahdī et ses Conseillers*. pp. 10-19.

56. Reference to the verse, *We have revealed unto thee the Remembrance that you may make clear to men what hath been revealed to them, and that haply they may reflect* (XVI: 44).

Predispositions: الاستعدادات

Ḥadīth 55

عن أبي هريرة : "النَّاسُ مَعادِنُ كَمَعادِنِ ٱلفِضَّةِ وَٱلذَّهَبِ، خِيارُكُمْ فِي ٱلجاهِلِيَّةِ خِيارُكُمْ فِي ٱلإِسْلامِ إِذا فَقُهُوا."

(رواه البخاري. حديث صحيح)

Narrated Abū Hurayra: "People are comparable to silver and gold: the best amongst you during the time of ignorance are the best amongst you in Islam, as long as they understand religion."

(Quoted by al-Bukhārī. Authenticated *ḥadīth*)

Commentary

The image of silver and gold clearly implies that people have different predispositions impossible to overlook. In keeping with the image of these precious minerals, which can be purified by melting, man can follow a path of purification but cannot *change* the predispositions granted to him from the Real since pre-eternity. In this sense, the above *ḥadīth* is a textual support for the doctrine of predestination. Moreover, it provides a foundation for this doctrine which is perfectly in line with a metaphysical perspective emphasizing the nature of things and absence of arbitrariness in one's destiny. The following text is written from the same perspective.

Amīr 'Abd al-Qādir

The Most High has said: *Lo! We shall pay them their whole due unabatedly.*[57] Each creature's position depends upon its inner nature (*ḥaqīqa*) and its predispositions, which are innumerable. This is also the meaning of the verse, *Our Lord is He Who gave unto everything its nature, then guided it aright.*[58]

Thus every creature possesses a predisposition which is the part accorded to it by the Real—exalted be He. This predisposition cannot be identical in every respect from one creature to another. The reason for this difference is linked to the particular aspect of the Real that is turned towards each creature. As a matter of fact, every created being—all the way

57. XI: 109.

58. XX: 50.

down to the atom—possesses a particular name that no other created being partakes of. This name is in fact the very reality of this creature, since this is what distinguishes it from others: *God is All-embracing, All-knowing.*[59] There cannot be any repetition in existence. That which supplicates God within a creature, and is then fulfilled, is none other than predisposition. This is the meaning of the verse, *I answer the prayer of the supplicant when he crieth unto Me.*[60] . . .

Predisposition is always fulfilled, whether the demands formulated by the tongue conform to it or not. This is the meaning of that which has been quoted in the *ḥadīth*: "Everyone will be easily disposed to that for which they are created."[61]

---

59. II: 247.
60. II: 186.
61. Cf. *ḥadīth* 60.

Ḥadīth 56

عن أبي موسى الأشعري : "مَثَلُ ما بَعَثَني ٱللهُ بِهِ مِنَ ٱلْهُدَى وَٱلعِلْمِ كَمَثَلِ ٱلغَيْثِ ٱلكَثيرِ أَصابَ أَرْضاً، فَكانَ مِنْها نَقِيَّةٌ، قَبِلَتِ ٱلْماءَ، فَأَنْبَتَتِ ٱلكَلأَ وَٱلعُشْبَ ٱلكَثيرَ. وَكانَتْ مِنْها أَجادِبُ، أَمْسَكَتِ ٱلْماءَ، فَنَفَعَ ٱللهُ بِها ٱلنَّاسَ، فَشَرِبُوا وَسَقَوا وَزَرَعُوا. وَأَصابَتْ مِنْها طائِفَةً أُخْرَى، إِنَّما هِيَ قِيعانٌ لا تَمْسِكُ ماءً وَلا تُنْبِتُ كَلأً. فَذٰلِكَ مَثَلُ مَنْ فَقُهَ فِي دِينِ ٱللهِ وَنَفَعَهُ ما بَعَثَني ٱللهُ بِهِ فَعَلِمَ وَعَلَّمَ وَمَثَلُ مَنْ لَمْ يَرْفَعْ بِذٰلِكَ رَأْساً وَلَمْ يَقْبَلْ هُدى ٱللهِ ٱلَّذي أُرْسِلْتُ بِهِ."

(رواه البخاري. حديث صحيح)

Narrated Abū Mūsā al-Ash'arī: "The guidance and the knowledge which God has sent to me are comparable to abundant rain watering the earth. Fertile earth will absorb water and will bring forth pastures and herbs in abundance. Arid earth will not absorb water, but will hold it, and thus God will benefit people, for they will drink from it and will water their cattle and their plantations with it. Dry and flat earth will let the water flow off without retaining it and nothing will grow. This is the same (with regard to different categories of people): Those who are able to receive an understanding of the religion of God and profit from that with which I have been sent, learn the knowledge and teach it; or those who do not raise their heads and accept the guidance with which I have been sent."

(Quoted by al-Bukhārī. Authenticated *ḥadīth*.)

Commentary

This *ḥadīth* mentions three categories of persons with regard to their disposition *vis-à-vis* the message of Islam. These three categories are referred to through simple and clear images: the heart of man is a piece of earth and the message of Islam is water from the sky seeking to make this earth fertile.

The intermediary category—denoted by the image of the earth holding the water—is considered by the spiritual masters as designating scholars who have only a bookish knowledge which has not transformed them inwardly, and through which they seek worldly gains. This bookish knowledge can be compared to the "discursive science" (*'ilm 'alā lisān*).[62]

In the following text, al-Sha'rānī mentions the process of progressive interiorisation of bookish knowledge, a process which leads to veritable knowledge for the person who has started his divinity studies before having received spiritual discipline.

al-Sha'rānī

I have received the following teaching from 'Alī al-Khawwāṣ: "For us, the only true scholar is he who can trace back all the opinions of the founders of the legal schools (*madhāhib*) to the Book and the *Sunna*, and who knows how to go beyond the apparent contradictions amongst these opinions. Then he is no longer part of the common people and he deserves the title of scholar. This is the first degree that has to be attained. After this degree, the scholar will be elevated until he is able to draw from the Chapter al-Fātiḥa all the prescriptions of the Qur'ān, for the Fātiḥa is the mother of the Book. Indeed, the reward for reading this chapter during the prayers is equivalent to that of reading the entire Qur'ān. He will be further elevated to being able to draw from any letter of the Qur'ān at all all the legal opinions formulated by the scholars concerning the Law (*Sharī'a*). This is how the perfect scholar should be."

(*Khiḍriyya*, p. 39)

62. Cf. *ḥadīth* 71.

Ḥadīth 57

عن عبد الله بن عمر: "إِنَّما ٱلنَّاسُ كَٱلإِبِلِ ٱلْمِئةِ لا تَكادُ تَجِدُ فِيها راحِلَةً."

(رواه البخاري. حديث صحيح)

Narrated ʻAbd Allāh ibn ʻUmar: "People are similar to a herd of camels: out of a hundred, you will hardly find a single one capable of long journeys."

(Quoted by al-Bukhārī [and Muslim]. Authenticated *ḥadīth*).

Commentary

In order to express the diversity of spiritual dispositions, the Prophet ﷺ has recourse to an image capable of impressing the imagination of his contemporaries. The Arabs of the time knew well that in terms of endurance and capacity for great distances, all camels were not the same. Likewise, not all men are qualified for the long journeying (*sulūk*) on the Path.

al-Junayd

Some time ago, I wrote to some brothers from Isfahan. My letter was opened and the text was handled. Some had misunderstood certain things that were said therein, and I had much of trouble getting through the embarrassment. As a consequence, these people gave me a lot of trouble. One has to be blunt with people, not so much in order to show leniency towards them as to make plain to them something they do not understand, even if it happens that this is not done willingly or deliberately.

May God be your protection and your shield and may He preserve you and me! You must therefore—may God have mercy on you—choose your words, and you must know your contemporaries well. Speak to people about what they know[63] and spare them what they cannot grasp. It rarely happens, in fact, for a man not to be hostile to what he does not know, and "People are similar to a herd of camels: out of a hundred, you will hardly find a single one capable of long journeys." God has nevertheless made the scholars and the sages a mercy out of His mercy and He gratifies His servants; therefore act in such a way that you may be a mercy for others, even if He has made you a trial for yourself! Present yourself not in accordance with your inner state but theirs; speak to them from the heart but according to what suits them and this will work out better for them and for you.

(*Enseignement*, "Lettre à Abū Bakr Kisā'ī", pp. 69-70)

63. See *ḥadīth* 61.

Ḥadīth 58

عن أبي الدرداء : "بَيْنَما نَحْنُ عِنْدَ رَسُولِ ٱللهِ ﷺ نَتَذاكَرُ ما يَكُونُ إِذْ قالَ رَسُولُ ٱللهِ ﷺ : إذا سَمِعْتُمْ بِجَبَلٍ زالَ عَنْ مَكانِه فَصَدِّقُوا بِهِ وَإِذا سَمِعْتُمْ بِرَجُلٍ تَغَيَّرَ عَنْ خُلُقِه فَلا تُصَدِّقُوا بِهِ فَإِنَّهُ يَصِيرُ إِلى ما جُبِلَ عَلَيْهِ."

(رواه الإمام أحمد. حديث حسن)

Narrated Abū al-Dardā': "We were once in the presence of the Messenger of God ﷺ and we mentioned certain realities, at which he told us: 'If you hear that a mountain has been removed, believe it; but if you hear that the character (*khulq*) of a man has changed, do not believe it, because man only displays the nature that has been given to him (*mā jubila 'alayhi*)."[64]

(Quoted by Aḥmad ibn Ḥanbal. Authenticated *ḥadīth*).

Commentary

This *ḥadīth* categorically negates the possibility of change in a person's character. It has to be specified, however, that it is the substance of a person which can never change, but obviously the blameworthy tendencies of the character can and should die, as they are more or less accidental. The distinction between what is substantial and what is accidental in one's character is expressed eloquently by the following sentence in the text below: "Although a cold object can be heated, the cold itself cannot turn into heat."

Amīr 'Abd al-Qādir

God does not decree for the one who submits to His Order except what one's intimate nature requires, so that eventually the respective decisions of God are nothing but the "decisions" of that creature. This is why when the damned cry out with a view to chastisement: *Oh, would that we might return! Then would we not deny the revelations of our Lord but we would be of the believers!* God then counters them with a formal refutation: *Nay, but that hath become clear unto them which before they used to hide. And if they were sent back they would return unto that which they are forbidden. Lo! they are liars.*[65] This is how we learn that their pretensions of no

---

64. The Arabic verb *jabala* has the meaning of forming, creating. To the same root belongs the noun *jibilla* which denotes one's innate nature.

65. VI: 27-28.

longer denying the revelations of God and becoming believers are illusory. If they were to be given yet another opportunity, they would not be able to act differently from before, due to their particular predispositions or—which amounts to the same—their intimate reality. Realities cannot in fact undergo any transformation: Although a cold object can be heated, the cold itself cannot turn into heat . . .

Only ignorance, stubbornness, and disbelief have pushed them to transgress the Divine orders: had they been able to know their own predispositions and what follows them, they would have never deserved damnation! And that which would have outwardly appeared as a transgression, would not have been accomplished except after an unveiling. This is why God does not demand any taking to task amongst heirs, to whom He has accorded the knowledge of their predispositions. Taking into consideration the initiatic unveiling with which they were gratified, He takes them to count neither with regards to what He has done with them, nor what He has created in them. Whatever their actions may be, they cannot be likened to sins and they will not bring them any chastisement in the Hereafter, even if they appear like transgressions of the outward Law, the role of which is precisely to place everything at its own level . . .

Those who are veiled with regard to their predispositions cannot claim such justifications because they ignore the real meaning of what their intimate nature requires in terms of disbelief, transgression, and sin.

What we have just explained is one of the foundations of the "secret of predestination." However, the Lawmaker has forbidden us from expounding on this issue, for fear of disturbing weak souls. In fact, such a reflection would lead them almost inevitably to denial, or even rejection of all the revealed Laws.

(*Mawāqif*, no 145)

Ḥadīth 59

عن عائشة : "الأَرْوَاحُ جُنُودٌ مُجَنَّدَةٌ، فَما تَعارَفَ مِنْها ٱئْتَلَفَ وَما تَناكَرَ مِنْها ٱخْتَلَفَ."

(رواه البخاري. حديث صحيح)

Narrated 'Ā'isha: "Souls are similar to an army in ranks: Those who know each other have affinity, and those who do not are in opposition."

(Quoted by al-Bukhārī. Authenticated *ḥadīth*)

Commentary

By affirming the pre-existence of souls, this *ḥadīth* clarifies the reasons for spiritual affinity amongst certain people, as well as opposition amongst others. In this sense, it brings to light important aspects of the predispositions of each group. Certain commentators have also considered that this *ḥadīth* alludes to the spiritual station which souls occupy depending on their spiritual elevation.

Abū l-Ḥasan al-Daylamī

Love amongst the elite of believers is proof of the fact that they knew each other in the spiritual realm. Those who know each other have an affinity, whereas those who do not know each other are in opposition . . .

It is related that 'Ikrīma quoted al-Ḥārith ibn 'Umayr as saying: "I met with Sulaymān who asked me: 'How are you, O Ḥārith ibn 'Umayr?' [al-Ḥārith responded]: 'How do you know me?' [Sulaymān responded]: 'My soul has met with yours.'"

Al-Ḥārith added, "Souls are similar to an army in rows: Those who know each other have affinity, and those who do not are in opposition."

(*Kitāb 'aṭf al-alif*, p. 105)[66]

al-Sarrāj

What are the spiritual stations (*maqāmāt*)? One can say that they are the "inner loci" the believer holds onto when presenting himself before his Lord for his acts of worship, his inner exertions (*mujāhadāt*), his spiritual exercises (*riyāḍāt*), and his contemplative retreats. God Most High has said, *This is for him who feareth My station (maqāmī) and feareth My threats;*[67] *There is not one of us but hath his known station.*[68]

Abū Bakr al-Wāsiṭī was asked about the saying of the Prophet ﷺ,

66. I.F.A.O, 1962.

67. XIV: 14

68. XXXVII: 164. The Qur'ān attributes these words to the angels.

"Souls are like an army in ranks . . . " He replied, "*In ranks* means according to the station they occupy. The stations are repentance, scruple, detachment, poverty, patience, satisfaction, confidence, etc."

(*Luma'*, p. 65)

Ḥadīth 60

عن عمران بن حصين : "قِيلَ : يا رَسُولَ ٱللهِ أَعُلِمَ أَهْلُ ٱلْجَنَّةِ مِنْ أَهْلِ ٱلنَّارِ ؟ فَقالَ : نَعَم. قِيلَ : فِيما يَعْمَلُ ٱلعامِلُون ؟ قالَ : كُلٌّ مُيَسَّرٌ لِما خُلِقَ لَهُ."

(رواه مسلم. حديث صحيح)

Narrated 'Imrān ibn Ḥuṣayn: "It was said to the Messenger of God ﷺ: 'Has a distinction been drawn between the people of Paradise and the denizens of Hell?' He said: 'Yes.' He was asked again: 'Then what is the meaning of our deeds?' Thereupon he said: 'Everyone is easily disposed to that for which they are created.'"

(Quoted by Muslim. Authenticated *ḥadīth*.)

Commentary

The question of predestination and free will is one of the most complex ones in Muslim theology. From the point of view of reason, it is insolvable. In this *ḥadīth* the Prophet ﷺ presents predestination and free will as two faces of the same reality. However, only the eye of the heart can perceive these two faces at the same time, which is not the case with reason, because when reason considers predestination it ignores free will and conversely . . .

Amīr 'Abd al-Qādir

If God—exalted be He—were to unveil to one of His chosen servants that which He knew beforehand in His knowledge—that is, what the immutable archetype of that being (*'aynuhu al-thābita*) requires—then it would be right and acceptable for this servant to say: "I have done this by the will of God and through His order," an order which goes beyond the categories of good and evil. He has also said, *Have ye any (certain) knowledge? If so, bring it forth for us*,[69] which means: do you possess knowledge of what your essential predispositions imply? Have your immutable archetypes been unveiled to you? [. . .]

Being the Generous One *par excellence*, God does not reject the demand of the essential predispositions or, in other terms, the requirements of the Names and the particular Divine aspects constituting the principal realities possessed by created beings. Thus He does not judge them except through themselves and starting from themselves. Or to put it better, you are your own judges. And the judge is bound to judge every matter in accordance with its nature.

(*Mawāqif*, no 236. French translation M. Chodkiewicz, *Écrits spirituels*, pp. 142-143.)

69. VI: 148.

Knowledge and Gnosis: العلم والمعرفة

Ḥadīth 61

عن علي بن أبي طالب : "حَدِّثُوا ٱلنَّاسَ بِما يَعْرِفُونَ أَتُحِبُّونَ أَنْ يُكَذَّبَ ٱللهُ وَرَسُولُهُ ؟"

(رواه البخاري. حديث صحيح)

Narrated 'Alī ibn Abī Ṭālib: "Speak to people according to their understanding: would you like to belie God and His messenger?"

(Quoted by al-Bukhārī. Authenticated *ḥadīth*.)

Commentary

Concerning spiritual knowledge, certain literalists amongst the proponents of a narrow-minded exoterism negate the existence of a "hidden knowledge" in Islam, a knowledge which is inaccessible to simple mental understanding. The favored reference of these literalists is, after the Qur'ān, the *ḥadīth* collection of al-Bukhārī, and they quote the following "motto" on every occasion: "The most truthful book after the Book of God is the collection of authentic *ḥadīth* by al-Bukhārī." And yet, a careful and frank reading of this collection shows that it contains a certain number of *ḥadīth* pointing to the existence of a kind of knowledge which should not be divulged to all believers and which should be reserved instead to those who have the inner disposition required to understand it. But al-Bukhārī goes even further, as he is not satisfied with quoting these *ḥadīth* in a scattered fashion but devotes the forty-ninth section of his Chapter on Knowledge (*Kitāb al-'ilm*) entitled: *On Those who Relate Knowledge to a Category of Persons (qawm) to the Exclusion of the Others, from Fear that the Latter will not Understand it*. Furthermore, it is known that the word *qawm* is a term designating the Sufis themselves. This section contains three *ḥadīth*: the one narrated by 'Alī which we quoted here, and two others—quoted below—mentioning the value of the *shahāda* and professing God's Unity.

Ibn al-'Arabī

The Messenger of God ﷺ has said: "Abū Bakr is not your superior by reason of much fasting and prayer, but because of something which hath been fixed in his breast." He did not explain what this something was and kept silence on this matter. Not all knowledge must be necessarily divulged by one who possesses it, and the Prophet ﷺ has said: "Speak to people according to the capacity of their intelligence."

Hence, when someone finds a book dealing with a science he does not know and who has not followed the inner path, he should not meddle in it, but he must return the book to those who have authority in that domain, without being obligated to believe or disbelieve in it, or even talk about it.

> *Nay, but they denied that, the knowledge whereof they could not compass . . .*[70]

> *Why then argue ye concerning that whereof ye have no knowledge? . . .*[71]

These verses teach us that people are blameworthy when they speak about a reality, the path to which they have not traversed and so have not realized it.

(*Extinction*, pp. 31-32)

70. X: 39.
71. III: 66.

Ḥadīth 62

عن أنس بن مالك : "أَنَّ ٱلنَّبِيَّ صَلَّى ٱللهُ عَلَيْهِ وَسَلَّمَ، وَمُعاذٌ رَدِيفُهُ عَلَى الرَّحْلِ، قالَ : يا مُعاذَ بْنَ جَبَلٍ. قال : لَبَّيْكَ يا رَسُولَ ٱللهِ وَسَعْدَيْك، قال : يا مُعاذ. قال : لَبَّيْك يا رَسُولَ ٱللهِ وَسَعْدَيْك، ثَلاثاً، قال : ما مِنْ أَحَدٍ يَشْهَدُ أَنْ لا إِلٰـه إِلاَّ ٱللهُ وَأَنَّ مُحَمَّداً رَسُولُ ٱللهِ، صِدْقاً مِنْ قَلْبِه إِلاَّ حَرَّمَهُ ٱللهُ عَلَى ٱلنَّار. قالَ : يا رَسُولَ ٱللهِ، أَفَلا أُخْبِرُ بِهِ ٱلنَّاسَ فَيَسْتَبْشِرُوا ؟ قالَ : إِذاً يَتَّكِلُوا. وَأَخْبَرَ بِها مُعاذ عِنْدَ مَوْتِه تَأَثُّماً."

(رواه البخاري. حديث صحيح)

Narrated Anas ibn Malik: "Once Mu'ādh was riding along with the Messenger of God ﷺ, as a companion rider. The Messenger of God ﷺ said, 'O Mu'ādh ibn Jabal.' Mu'ādh replied, 'At your service, O Messenger of God!' Again the Prophet ﷺ said, 'O Mu'ādh!' Mu'ādh said thrice, 'At your service, O Messenger of God!' The Prophet ﷺ said, 'Whoever testifies with a sincere heart that there is no god but God and that Muhammad is his Messenger, God will save him from the Hell-fire.' Mu'ādh said, 'O Messenger of God! Should I not inform the people about this so that they may have glad tidings?' He replied, 'When the people hear about this, they will depend on it solely.' Then Mu'ādh narrated this *ḥadīth* just before his death, being afraid of committing sin (by not relating the knowledge)."

(Quoted by al-Bukhārī. Authenticated *ḥadīth*.)

Commentary

The element which could lead people who hear this *ḥadīth* in error is the forgetting of the expression "with a sincere heart" (*ṣidqan min qalbihi*). Indeed, although it is easy to pronounce a formula "by the tongue," it is much more difficult to realize it with the heart. In its inner realization, the phrase of testimony to God's Unity may therefore be considered as the journey on the spiritual path. Due to the fact that it is inevitable that people lose sight of the inner meaning of a message in favor of its outward meaning, the mystics have always avoided conveying their teachings to those not qualified to understand their meanings and who are not called to realize them in practice.

Ibn al-'Arabī

When Ḥasan al-Baṣrī (who would regularly deliver a public lecture) wanted to speak about mysteries which should not be met on the path of those who are not worthy of them, he would call upon Farqad al-Sabakhī and Mālik ibn Dinār as well as others amongst the folk of spiritual taste (*ahl al-dhawq*) to close the doors to others, speaking only about these mysteries in intimate session. Had it not been necessary to observe secrecy, Hasan would not have proceeded in that manner . . .

In speaking about the verse *God it is who hath created seven heavens, and of the earth the like thereof,*[72] Ibn 'Abbās declared: "If I were to comment on this verse before you as I heard it commented upon by the Prophet ﷺ himself you would stone me." As for 'Alī ibn Abī Ṭālib, he used to beat his breast and say: "Surely, here is abundant knowledge! If only I could find people capable of bearing it!"

(*Extinction*, pp. 30-31)

72. LXV: 12

Ḥadīth 63

عن أبي هريرة : "يا رَسُولَ ٱللهِ، إِنِّي أَسْمَعُ مِنْكَ حَدِيثاً كَثِيراً أَنْساه. قالَ : ٱبْسُطْ رِداءَك. فَبَسَطْتُهُ فَغَرَفَ بِيَدَيْهِ، ثُمَّ قالَ : ضُمَّهُ. فَضَمَمْتُهُ، فَما نَسِيتُ شَيْئاً بَعْدَه."

(رواه البخاري. حديث صحيح)

Narrated Abū Hurayra: "'O Messenger of God, I hear many narrations from you but I forget them.' The Messenger of God ﷺ said, 'Spread your garment.' I did accordingly and then he moved his hands as if filling it with something, and then said, 'Wrap it around your body.' I did so and thereafter I never forgot anything."

(Quoted by al-Bukhārī. Authenticated *ḥadīth*.)

Ḥadīth 64

عن ابن عباس : "ضَمَّنِي رَسُولُ ٱللهِ ﷺ وَقالَ : اللَّهُمَّ عَلِّمْهُ ٱلكِتاب."

(رواه البخاري. حديث صحيح)

Narrated Ibn 'Abbās: "The Prophet ﷺ embraced me and said, 'O God! Teach him (the knowledge of) the Book.'"

(Quoted by al-Bukhārī. Authenticated *ḥadīth*.)

Ḥadīth 65

عن محمود بن الربيع قال : "عَقَلْتُ مِنَ ٱلنَّبِيِّ ﷺ مَجَّةً مَجَّهَا فِي وَجْهِي، وَأَنا ٱبْنُ خَمْسِ سِنِينَ مِنْ دَلْو."

(رواه البخاري. حديث صحيح)

Narrated Maḥmūd ibn al-Rabī‘: "When I was a boy of five, I remember the Prophet ﷺ took water from a bucket with his mouth and threw it on my face."

(Quoted by al-Bukhārī. Authenticated *ḥadīth*.)

Commentary

"The assimilation of spiritual knowledge cannot be reduced to a mental process: it requires an inward opening which is related to grace. The actions of the Prophet ﷺ mentioned in these *ḥadīth*, like the use of the robe of his disciple and companion Abū Hurayra, his saliva for Maḥmūd ibn al-Rabī‘ when he was still a child, or embracing Ibn ‘Abbās, are acts of grace.

Ibn al-‘Arabī

Know—may God support you with the spirit of sanctity—that we have made known to you that the Christic[73] (*‘īsāwī*) pole (*quṭb*) is he who unifies in himself two heritages: the heritage which allows for spiritual receptivity (*infi‘āl*) and the Muḥammadan heritage received through "taste" (*dhawq*) from Jesus. Since we have mentioned the stations and the states of these poles, we have to say a few words about their secrets. When these poles wish to transmit one of their spiritual states to someone who they know through unveiling or Divine indication to posses the qualifications to receive it, they perform this transmission by the hand or by wrapping the person round themselves. They can also do it by giving this person a cloth belonging to them. They ask him to wear this cloth, pouring therein what they wish to transmit to him. Then they say to him: "Apply this cloth against your chest" or "Wear this cloth" depending on the state they wish to transmit to them . . .

I have seen this in some of my masters . . . When Makkī al-Wāsiṭī—student of Ardashīr who is buried in Mecca—was captivated by a spiritual state (*ḥāl*), he would ask the person with him to hold him in his arms . . . Then this person would receive this state.

Jābir ibn ‘Abdullāh complained to the Prophet ﷺ about being unable to

73. On the notion of prophetic heritage, see *ḥadīth* 147 and 174.

sit on a horse. The Prophet ﷺ hit him with his hand on the chest and Jābir never fell from the horse again . . . Similarly, Abū Hurayra complained to the Prophet ﷺ of forgetting what he heard from him. The Prophet ﷺ told him: "O Abū Hurayra, spread your garment." Abū Hurayra did so, and the Prophet ﷺ poured something invisible from his hands onto the garment of Abū Hurayra and then requested of him: "Wrap it around yourself!" Since that moment, Abū Hurayra never forgot anything he heard from the Prophet ﷺ.

(*Fut.*, I, p. 227)

Ḥadīth 66

عن أبي هريرة : "حَفِظْتُ مِنْ رَسُولِ ٱللهِ ﷺ وِعاءَيْنِ فَأَمَّا أَحَدُهُما فَبَثَثْتُهُ وَأَمَّا ٱلآخَرُ فلَوْ بَثَثْتُهُ قُطِعَ هٰذا ٱلبُلْعُومُ."

(رواه البخاري. حديث صحيح)

Narrated Abū Hurayra: "I have memorized two kinds of knowledge from the Messenger of God ﷺ. I have divulged one of them to you and if I divulged the second, my throat would be cut."

(Quoted by al-Bukhārī. Authenticated *ḥadīth*.)

Commentary

For the spiritual masters, the two forms of knowledge mentioned by Abū Hurayra in this *ḥadīth* are of a very different nature. That which was not divulged could not be transmitted directly to all people because it exceeds the limited capacities of reason (*fawqa ṭawri l-'aql*), as emphasized by Ibn al-'Arabī. The heart may nonetheless receive this form of knowledge if it is vivified by a spiritual path.

Ibn al-'Arabī

When a believer is dedicated entirely to the spiritual retreat (*khalwa*) and the invocation (*dhikr*), and he breaks away from thoughts, and realizes complete poverty by standing at the door of his Lord, then he receives from the Most High a part of the "knowledge from God" (*al-'ilm biHi*), Divine mysteries (*asrār ilāhiyya*), and lordly knowledge (*ma'ārif rabbāniyya*). This is what God bestowed upon Khiḍr: . . . *one of Our slaves, unto whom We had given mercy from Us, and had taught him knowledge from Our presence*.[74] In addition, God has said: *Be wary of God and God will teach you* . . . ;[75] *If ye are wary of God, He will give you discernment (furqān)* . . . ;[76] *He will give you twofold of His mercy and will appoint for you a light wherein ye shall walk* . . . [77] Al-Junayd was asked, "How did you achieve your spiritual degree?" He replied, "By sitting on these stairs for thirty years." Abū Yazīd al-Basṭāmī declared: "You take your knowledge dead from the dead; we take our knowledge from the Living who does not die."

Therefore, he who is determined in his spiritual retreat with God will receive sciences which no theologian (*mutakallim*) can attain to. In reality,

74. XVIII: 65.
75. II: 282.
76. VIII: 29.
77. LVII: 28.

whoever limits himself to theoretical knowledge (*ṣāḥib naẓar*) and demonstration (*burhān*) will not be able to reach the state we are referring to, for it is beyond reason. There are three types of knowledge:

- rational knowledge (*'ilm al-'aql*): that which imposes itself naturally on us[78] or which follows from the analysis of an argument (*dalīl*) . . .
- the knowledge of the spiritual states (*'ilm al-aḥwāl*): it can only be acquired through "tasting" (*dhawq*) . . .
- the science of the secrets (*'ilm al-asrār*): this is a science which transcends reason (*fawqa ṭawri al-'aql*) and which is an inspiration from the spirit of sanctity (*rūḥ al-qudus*) in the inner conscience. This inspiration is proper to a prophet or a saint . . .

Therefore, when a possessor of the science of the secrets comes with a knowledge that is acceptable from the point of view of reason and on which the sacred Law has not spoken, we must not reject it outright and we have the choice to make it ours or not . . .

Indeed, if these sciences were not negated by certain people, the following saying of Abū Hurayra would make no sense: "I have memorized two kinds of knowledge from the Messenger of God ﷺ. I have divulged one of them to you and if I divulged the second, my throat would be cut."

(*Fut.*, [O.Y.], I, pp. 138-142)

Al-Junayd said: "No one realizes the Truth without a thousand truthful ones (*ṣiddīqīn*) accusing him as a heretic." It is so because those who realize the truth know from God that which no one else can know. The knowledge which they hold is that to which 'Alī ibn Abī Ṭālib alluded when he hit his breast sighing: "Surely, here is abundant knowledge! If only I could find persons capable of bearing it!" In fact, 'Alī was one of the solitaries (*afrād*) and this type of knowledge was not transmitted to anyone at the time except to Abū Hurayra, from whom al-Bukhārī quoted the following saying: "I have memorized two kinds of knowledge from the Messenger of God. I have divulged one of them to you and if I divulged the second, then my throat would be cut."

Abū Hurayra therefore reports that he had received this knowledge from the Messenger of God ﷺ: he was its trustee without having tasted it. He only possessed it insofar as he had heard it from the Messenger of God ﷺ. And yet, we have spoken about the person who has received the profound comprehension of the Word of God, for this is the knowledge of the solitaries, amongst whom was 'Abd Allāh ibn 'Abbās. He was nicknamed "the Ocean" due to his grasping of this knowledge. In speaking about the verse *God it is who hath created seven heavens, and of the earth the like*

78. Such as the principles of logic.

thereof,[79] he declared: "If I were to comment on this verse before you as I heard it commented upon by the Prophet ﷺ himself you would stone me."
(*Fut.*, [O.Y.], III, pp. 248-249)

79. LXV: 12

Ḥadīth 67

عن أنس بن مالك : "خَطَبَنا رَسُولُ ٱللهِ ﷺ خُطْبَةً ما سَمِعْتُ مِثْلَها قَطُّ، فَقالَ : "لَوْ تَعْلَمُونَ ما أَعْلَمُ لَضَحِكْتُمْ قَليلاً وَلَبَكَيْتُمْ كَثيرا." فَغَطَّى أَصْحابُ رَسُولِ ٱللهِ ﷺ وُجُوهَهُمْ وَلَهُمْ خَنين."

(رواه البخاري. حديث صحيح)

Narrated Anas ibn Mālik: "The Messenger of God ﷺ delivered a sermon the like of which I had never heard before. He said, 'If you but knew what I know, you would laugh little and weep much.' Upon hearing that, the companions of the Prophet ﷺ covered their faces and the sound of their weeping was heard."

(Quoted by al-Bukhārī. Authenticated *ḥadīth*.)

Commentary

The tears of the Companions which followed after this declaration of the Prophet ﷺ were interpreted on two levels: that of fear of what awaits man in the Hereafter (*aḥwāl al-ākhira*), and that of incapacity of the Companions to completely understand the Prophet. In his *Iḥyā'*, al-Ghazzālī takes up the second interpretation:

> Know that the division of sciences into hidden sciences (*'ulūm khafiyya*) and manifested sciences (*'ulūm jaliyya*) must be accepted by all the folk of spiritual perception (*baṣīra*): this division is negated only by those who desperately cling to simplistic and childish ideas recurring to them. They have no aspiration to spiritual elevation (*sha'w al-'alā*), and to the stations of the scholars and the saints.
>
> The Prophet ﷺ has said: "If you but knew what I know then you would laugh little and weep much." Why then did he not unveil to his Companions what he had in mind at that moment except that they could not grasp it? In the end there is no doubt that whatever he had told them, they would not have believed him.
>
> (*Iḥyā'*, I, p. 99)

Ḥadīth 68

عن أبي هريرة : "العِلْمُ خَيْرٌ مِنَ ٱلعِبادَةِ، وَمِلاكُ ٱلدِّينِ ٱلوَرَعُ."

(رواه ابن عبد البر. حديث حسن)

Narrated Abū Hurayra: "Knowledge is better than worship, and the foundation of religion is piety."

(Quoted by Ibn 'Abd al-Barr. Validated *ḥadīth.*)

Ḥadīth 69

عن أبي أمامة : "فَضْلُ ٱلعالِمِ عَلَى ٱلعابِدِ كَفَضْلي عَلى أَدْناكُمْ، إِنَّ ٱللهَ عَزَّ وَجَلَّ وَمَلائِكَتُهُ وَأَهْلُ ٱلسَّماواتِ وَٱلأَرَضينَ حَتَّى ٱلنَّمْلَةُ في جُحْرِها وَحَتَّى ٱلْحُوتُ لَيُصَلُّونَ عَلَى مُعَلِّمِ ٱلنَّاسِ ٱلْخَيْرَ."

(رواه الترمذي. حديث صحيح)

Narrated Abū Umāma: "The superiority of a scholar over the worshiper is similar to my superiority over the simplest of you. Lo! God—the Almighty and the Majestic—as well as His angels, the habitants of the heavens and the earths, down to the ant in its hole and fish in the sea, call down blessings upon whoever teaches good to people."

(Quoted by al-Tirmidhī. Authenticated *ḥadīth*)

Commentary

Nobility of knowledge is only understood if what is meant by this term is the knowledge granted to someone whose heart is illuminated by faith.

al-Ghazzālī

God bears witness that there is no god but He, and (so do) the angels and those possessed of knowledge, maintaining His creation with justice; there is no god but He, the Mighty, the Wise.[80]

80. III: 18.

Observe how God Most High has mentioned Himself, then the angels, and then those possessed of knowledge (*'ilm*). With this, He bestows a blessing and a favor, purity and nobility. [. . .]

Faṭh al-Mawṣilī once asked, "Will not the sick person die if they deprive him of food and drink?"

Those around him replied, "Surely, he will!"

He then said, "It is the same for the heart. When it is deprived of wisdom and knowledge for three [consecutive] days, it dies."

What he said is the truth: just as the nourishment of the body is food, the nourishment of the heart is knowledge and wisdom, as it lives from them. Whoever lacks knowledge possesses a sick heart on the point of dying. However, he does not realize it because when the heart is in love with the here-below and preoccupied with it, the heart loses its sensitivity, just as someone experiencing strong fear no longer feels the pain, even if he is wounded. But when death frees him from the worries of this life, he will become conscious of his ruin: his regret will be immense but that will not serve him at all. He is similar to the one who comes to his senses after intoxication; only then he realizes the evil that awaits him.

We seek refuge in God from the day when the veil is lifted: People are asleep and when they die they wake up!

(*Iḥyā'*, I, pp. 5-9)

al-Junayd

O young man! Attach yourself to knowledge, regardless of any spiritual state that occurs in you, because it will remain your companion when your spiritual states fade. God has said, *And those who are firmly rooted in knowledge say: We believe in it, it is all from our Lord; and none pay heed except those having understanding.*[81]

(*Enseignement*, p. 187)

81. III: 7.

Ḥadīth 70

عن معاوية : "مَنْ يُرِدِ ٱللّٰهُ بِهِ خَيْراً يُفَقِّهْهُ فِي ٱلدِّينِ."

(رواه البخاري. حديث صحيح)

Narrated Mu'āwiya: "When God wishes good for a servant, He grants him a [deep] understanding of religion."

(Quoted by al-Bukhārī. Authenticated *ḥadīth*.)

Commentary

[Deep] understanding of religion (*al-fiqh fī al-dīn*) is a Divine grace and not the fruit of bookish studying. The Arabic term *fiqh* did not yet signify in the Qur'ān and *Ḥadīth* the set of legal rulings and prescriptions constituting the *Sharī'a*—as would be the case a few centuries later—but an inner comprehension of the Qur'ānic and Prophetic message.

al-Munāwī

The term *khayr*, which is used in this *ḥadīth*, denotes the totality of Divine blessings because it is not specified. In fact, the grammatical indetermination (*nakira*) expresses generality.

The expression "He grants him understanding (*fiqh*) of the religion" means that God gives to His servant the understanding of the secrets concerning the obligations and prohibitions laid out by the Legislator. This grace is a godly light (*nūr rabbānī*) that God puts in the heart of His servant as indicated by this saying of Ḥasan [al-Baṣrī]: "The *faqīh*[82] is he who understands what God has obligated and prohibited. However, only he who puts into practice what he knows [in theory] can become a *faqīh*."

In the same way, it is related from the Proof of Islam (*Ḥujjat al-Islām*, i.e., al-Ghazzālī) that:

> True *fiqh* in religion is knowledge which springs up in the heart, and which is manifested by the tongue, and which is then conducive to virtuous action and gives rise to the fear of God. As for those who pursue long studies in religion, and become proud, they are excluded from the high station we referred to.

[al-Ghazzālī] has also written:

> *Fiqh* is nothing but the knowledge of God and His Attributes. As for the *fiqh* understood as knowledge of the legal rulings (*aḥkām shar'iyya*), Satan governs most of those who devote themselves to it! They are

82. That is, one who possesses the understanding of religion. Today, this term denotes the jurist.

drowned in distraction and seek only the advantages of the here-below. They see the good as evil and the evil as good. That is why knowledge of religion has become so rare, and the standard of guidance so invisible!

Therefore, it has to be understood that the term *fiqh* denotes the knowledge leading to the Hereafter which is an individual obligation (*farḍ ʻayn*) . . . If a jurist is asked about the purity of intention (*ikhlāṣ*), reliance on God (*tawwakul*) or how to prevent ostentation (*riyā'*), he will not be able to answer! It is, however, an obligation to know this and neglecting it leads to perdition. On the contrary, if he is asked about the oath of anathema (*li'ān*) or that of continence (*ẓihār*),[83] he may provide their precise definitions though they are unnecessary. In His Book, God shows the path to the Hereafter through the following terms: understanding (*fiqh*), wisdom (*ḥikma*), clarity (*ḍiyā'*), light (*nūr*) and right guidance (*rushd*).

(*Fayḍ al-Qadīr*, *ḥadīth* no. 9103)

83. That is, the two particular modes of divorce in Islam.

Ḥadīth 71

عن جابر : "العِلْمُ عِلْمان : عِلْمٌ فِي ٱلقَلْبِ فَذٰلِكَ ٱلعِلْمُ ٱلنَّافِعُ وَعِلْمٌ فِي ٱللِّسانِ فَذٰلِكَ حُجَّةُ ٱللهِ عَلى ٱبْنِ آدَمَ."

(رواه الخطيب. حديث حسن)

Narrated Jābir: "Knowledge is of two kinds: one is situated in the heart, which is beneficial knowledge, and the other is nothing but discourse and therein is a proof from God for the son of Adam."

(Quoted by al-Khaṭīb. Validated *ḥadīth.*)

Ḥadīth 72

عن زيد بن ثابت : "نَضَّرَ ٱللهُ ٱمْرَأً سَمِعَ مِنَّا حَدِيثاً فَحَفِظَهُ حَتَّى يُبَلِّغَهُ غَيْرَهُ، فَرُبَّ حامِلِ فِقْهٍ إِلَى مَنْ هُوَ أَفْقَهُ مِنْهُ، وَرُبَّ حامِلِ فِقْهٍ لَيْسَ بِفَقِيهِ !"

(رواه الترمذي. حديث صحيح)

Narrated Zayd ibn Thābit: "May God brighten the face of His servant who, having heard some of my words, memorizes them in order to pass it on. Indeed, it may happen that someone transmits knowledge (*fiqh*) to another, who is gifted with a greater intelligence. And it may happen that a 'bearer of knowledge' is not gifted with intelligence!"

(Quoted by al-Tirmidhī. Authenticated *ḥadīth*)

Commentary

The distinction between the two kinds of knowledge pertaining to religion was mentioned in the commentary on the previous *ḥadīth*. Very much like al-Ghazzālī, Ibn al-'Arabī warns against the dangers of bookish knowledge that is not illuminated by the light of the heart. However, he makes it clear that he is not attacking Islamic exoterism—for him exoterism is a dimension of the Path—but the "exoterist mentality" which is a real prison.

Ibn al-'Arabī

May God protect you, brother, from evil thoughts in imagining that I blame the jurists as such, or for their work in jurisprudence, as such an attitude is not permitted for a Muslim and the nobility of *fiqh* cannot be doubted. However, I blame the type of jurist who is greedy for the goods of this world, and who studies *fiqh* for vanity, so that he may be noticed and mentioned, and in order to bask in sterile quibbles and controversies. It is this kind of person who attacks the God-fearing folk of the Hereafter, who receive knowledge from Him (*min ladunHu*). These jurists seek to refute a knowledge they do not know; and with whose principles they are unfamiliar . . .

In the same way, I have reproached certain "Sufis"; not the sincere ones, but those who feign in the eyes of people a sanctity which contradicts their inner nature . . .

The jurists I am speaking about are dominated by their egotistic and passionate desires; they are under the sway of Satan. Insofar as they seek to harm the Friends of God (*awliyā' Allāh*), their account will make them perish, as we know from the Prophet ﷺ.[84]

I have never ceased defending the rights of the *fuqarā'*[85] before such jurists and I have always sought to protect the former from the latter. In this I was inspired, for whoever starts to blame the Friends of God in general or in particular, and whoever—without having shared their company—attacks those who visit them, such a person only shows his ignorance and will never gain salvation.

(*Soufis*, pp. 95-98)

84. Allusion to the famous *ḥadīth qudsi*: "Whoever shows enmity to one My friends, I declare war to him . . . " Cf. *ḥadīth* 197.

85. The term *faqīr* (pl. *fuqarā'*) meaning "poor in God" denotes the disciples and the masters of the Path.

Ḥadīth 73

عن ابن عباس : "عَلَيْكَ بِٱلعِلْمِ فَإِنَّ ٱلعِلْمَ خَلِيلُ ٱلْمُؤْمِنِ وَٱلْحِلْمَ وَزِيرُهُ وَٱلعَقْلَ دَلِيلُهُ وَٱلعَمَلَ قَيِّمُهُ وَٱلرِّفْقَ أَبُوهُ وَٱللِّينَ أَخُوهُ وَٱلصَّبْرَ أَمِيرُ جُنُودِهِ."

(رواه الحكيم. حديث حسن)

Narrated Ibn 'Abbās: "Seek knowledge, for it is the intimate friend of the believer. Moreover, forbearance is the minister of knowledge, intellect its guide, action its pivot, benevolent character its father, gentleness its brother, and patience is the general of its armies."

(Quoted by al-Ḥakīm. Validated *ḥadīth*)

Commentary

The close link between spiritual knowledge and virtue—emphasized eloquently by this *ḥadīth*—is not easy to grasp for one who confuses intellect with reason. As an organ of spiritual knowledge, the intellect surpasses the individual as such, and by this very fact leads him to transcend his limits.

Frithjof Schuon ('Īsā Nūr al-Dīn)

When metaphysical knowledge is effective it produces love and destroys presumption. It produces love; that is to say, the spontaneous directing of the will towards God and the perception of "myself"—and of God—in the neighbour.

It destroys presumption: for knowledge does not allow man to overestimate himself or to underestimate others. By reducing to ashes all that is not God, it orders all things.

(*Perspectives*, p. 186)

There is something in man which is contrary to God and something which is conformable to Him: on the one hand, the impassioned will, and on the other, the pure intellect. For those ways which are founded on the first aspect, the turning back of the will—ascesis—is all in all and doctrinal truth is a background. For the ways which are founded on the second element, it is the intellect—and so intellection—which is all in all and ascesis is an auxiliary.

But these two perspectives give rise to indefinitely varied combinations in line with the inexhaustible diversity of spiritual and human possibilities.

(*Perspectives*, p. 190)

Ḥadīth 74

عن عائشة: "إِنَّ ٱلرَّجُلَ لَيُدْرِكُ بِحُسْنِ خُلُقِهِ دَرَجَةَ ٱلصَّائِمِ ٱلقائِمِ وَلا يَتِمُّ لِرَجُلٍ حُسْنُ خُلُقِهِ حَتَّى يَتِمَّ عَقْلُهُ فَعِنْدَ ذٰلِكَ تَمَّ إِيْمانُهُ وَأَطاعَ رَبَّهُ وَعَصى عَدُوَّهُ إِبْلِيسَ."

(رواه الترمذي. حديث صحيح)

Narrated 'Ā'isha: "Verily, through the acquisition of the virtues (*ḥusn al-khuluq*) man can attain the degree of the person who fasts during the day keeps night vigils (*al-qā'im al-ṣā'im*). However, the virtues cannot be complete unless the intellect is perfected. Then the faith of such a person will be perfect; he will obey his Lord and disobey his enemy Iblīs."

(Quoted by al-Tirmidhī. Authenticated *ḥadīth*.)

Commentary

This *ḥadīth* mentions in hierarchical order the three types of spirituality: the path of action—summarized here by prayer and fasting; the path of love or the acquisition of the virtues; and the path of knowledge. It clearly places at the summit of this hierarchy the third path, which can be described as restoring the "plenitude of intelligence" within man. According to the end of this *ḥadīth*, fleeing from different forms of distraction in order to conform entirely to the Truth is a prerogative of intelligence. Thus only the path of knowledge (*ma'rifa*) allows an escape from the pitfalls of sentimentalism, pious exaggeration, and excess zeal.

Frithjof Schuon ('Īsā Nūr al-Dīn)

The key to many enigmas in the realm of spiritual thought is the fact that God requires of men that they be pious and virtuous, and not that they be intelligent; this provides the justification for a pious unintelligence, but is unconnected with gnosis and esoterism. Obviously God forbids men to make bad use of their intelligence—as persistent error is in the will rather than in the mind—but He cannot blame them for not possessing an intelligence which was not given to them. One is forced to admit that unintelligence can set up house with piety, that it can even, accidentally and sporadically, enter the realm of what should be wisdom, although in certain cases one hesitates to do so for fear of being disrespectful or ungracious; moreover, one all too often forgets the blinding evidence that it is better to follow truth stupidly than to follow error intelligently, all the more so as truth in any case neutralizes unintelligence at least to a certain extent, whereas on the contrary, error can only pervert and corrupt the mind. [. . .]

The miracle of humility is precisely that it alone is able to transmute unintelligence into intelligence, as far as this is possible; the humble man is intelligent by his very humility.

God requires from each man what he can give; but from the intelligent man he requires in addition intelligence in the service of truth, for which it is made and through which it lives. In some people, moreover, intelligence resides less in their theology than in their sanctity; nonetheless the spiritual norm lies in an equilibrium between thought and virtue, between mind and beauty.

Intelligence is only beautiful when it does not destroy faith, and faith is only beautiful when it is not opposed to intelligence.

(*Sufism*, pp. 81-82)

Ḥadīth 75

عن أبي هريرة : "ما أَخافُ عَلى أُمَّتِي إِلاَّ ضَعْفَ ٱليَقِينِ."

(رواه الطبراني. حديث حسن)

Narrated Abū Hurayra: "I fear but one thing for my community: weakness of certainty."

(Quoted by al-Ṭabarānī. Validated *ḥadīth*)

Commentary

Certainty is a central element of faith. However, this certitude gets dulled, as it were, when the ephemeral character of things is forgotten. Conversely, it is reinforced to the extent that discerning the Absolute from the relative is deepened and rooted in being.

Frithjof Schuon ('Īsā Nūr al-Dīn)

If Islam, the last to appear in the series of great Revelations, is not founded on miracles—though of necessity admitting them, for otherwise it could not be a religion—this is also because the Antichrist "will lead many astray by his wonders." Now spiritual certainty, which is at the very opposite pole from the "inversion" produced by miracles—and which Islam offers in the form of a penetrating unitary faith, an acute sense of the Absolute—is an element to which the devil has no access; he can imitate a miracle but not what is intellectually evident; he can imitate a phenomenon but not the Holy Spirit, except in the case of those who want to be deceived and in any case have no sense either of the truth or of the sacred.

(*Understanding Islam*, pp. 20-21)

What is the certainty possessed by man? On the plane of ideas it may be perfect, but on the plane of life it but rarely pierces through illusion.

Everything is ephemeral and every man must die. No man is ignorant of this and no one knows it.

(*Perspectives*, p. 188)

Ḥadīth 76

عن الحسن بن علي : "حَفِظْتُ مِنْ رَسُولِ ٱللهِ ﷺ : دَعْ ما يُرِيبُكَ إِلَى ما لا يُرِيبُكَ."

(رواه الترمذي. حديث صحيح)

Narrated Ḥasan ibn 'Alī: "I have memorized from the Messenger of God ﷺ: 'Leave what provokes doubt in you for what does not stir up any doubt in you.'"

(Quoted by al-Tirmidhī. Authenticated *ḥadīth*)

Commentary

Together with Ḥusayn, Ḥasan ibn 'Alī is one of the two grandsons of the Prophet, whose love for them is well-known. The education he transmitted to his grandsons—besides that which they received from their father 'Alī—could not but be profoundly spiritual. Besides, Ḥasan starts this *ḥadīth* with the expression "I have memorized from the Messenger of God ﷺ," which testifies to the importance he attached to this lesson.

The Arabic verb *arāba* translated by the expression "provokes doubt," derives from the root r-y-b expressing doubt, uncertainty, confusion. The term *rayb* is quoted several times in the Qur'ān, essentially with regard to the Book and the Day of Reckoning. Thus the Qur'ān declares about itself: *This is the Book whereof there is no doubt . . .* [86]

This *ḥadīth* invites the believer to live his life and his faith based on what avoids doubt, itself a generator of trouble. Man cannot avoid being confronted with the uncertain, but even in this case he will have to cling to what he knows with certainty. This is how the Qur'ān warns against the temptation to judge what is inaccessible to us:

﴿وَلا تَقفُ ما لَيسَ لَكَ بِهِ عِلْمٌ إِنَّ ٱلسَّمْعَ وَٱلْبَصَرَ وَٱلْفُؤادَ كُلُّ أُولَئِكَ كانَ عَنْهُ مَسئُولاً﴾

Follow not that whereof thou hast no knowledge. Lo! the hearing and the sight and the heart—each of these will be asked.[87]

On a higher level, the attitude described in this *ḥadīth* invites man to base

86. II: 2.

87. XVII: 36.

his spirituality on certainty and not on conjecture, on evidence conferred by the Truth and not on the conviction that gives rise to events such as dreams, visions, or inspirations.

Ibn ʿAjība

In everything [he does], the Perfect Man will only rely on evidence (*bayyina*) coming from his Lord. Outwardly he is led by the sacred Law and inwardly by the holy Truth. If he receives inspirations (*wāridāt*) or self-propagating thoughts (*khawāṭir*), he will confront them with the Book and the Sunna. If they conform to these two sources, he will be able to make them known and act accordingly; otherwise, he will hide and reject them . . .

The majority of spiritual authorities recognize that a Muslim cannot bring forth anything before knowing the Divine decree on that subject. This is what the verse *Follow not that whereof thou hast no knowledge* refers to.

When a Muslim does not find any answer in the Book or the Sunna, he will consult his heart—if the latter is exempt from the thrall of the senses. Otherwise, he will consult the folk of Purity (*ahl al-ṣafāʾ*) who are none other than the folk of Remembrance (*ahl al-dhikr*) about whom the Most High has said: *Ask the folk of Remembrance if ye know not.*[88] The believer will not ask the "folk of conjecture" (*ahl al-ẓunūn*) who are the people of outward knowledge, for God has said concerning this matter, *and surely conjecture does not avail against the Truth.*[89]

(*Baḥr*, III, p. 200)

88. XVI: 43.

89. LIII: 28.

Wisdom: الحكمة

Ḥadīth 77

عن ابن مسعود : "رَأْسُ ٱلْحِكْمَةِ مَخافَةُ ٱللهِ تَعالَى."

(رواه الحكيم. حديث صحيح)

Narrated Ibn Mas'ūd: "The beginning of wisdom is the fear of God Most High."

(Quoted by al-Ḥakīm. Authenticated *ḥadīth*)

Commentary

Fear of God must not be taken here in a sentimental and subjective sense, for then how could it be a path of access to wisdom? In spiritual wayfaring, fear of God is an "attitude of the intelligence and the will" as emphasized by F. Schuon ('Īsā Nūr al-Dīn).

Like every spiritual station, fear possesses numerous degrees which can be summarized in three groups corresponding to three categories of people. This is the method largely used by the spiritual masters of Islam. Khwāja 'Abd Allāh al-Anṣārī, while expounding on what fear (*khawf*) of God corresponds to in these three categories of men, shows how it opens into wisdom when it is taken to its highest degrees.

Frithjof Schuon ('Īsā Nūr al-Dīn)

The fear of God is not in any way a matter of feeling, any more than is the love of God. Like love, which is the tendency of our whole being towards transcendent Reality, fear is an attitude of the intelligence and the will. It consists in taking account at every moment of a Reality which infinitely surpasses us, against which we can do nothing, in opposition to which we could not live and from the teeth of which we cannot escape.

(*Perspectives*, pp. 279)

al-Anṣārī

God has said: *They fear their Lord above them.*[90] Fear means to rouse oneself from the quietude of security by considering the Divine Word. Fear comprises three degrees:

The first degree is fear of chastisement. This degree ensures the ex-

90. XVI: 50.

istence of faith and constitutes the common fear of people. It arises from belief in the Divine threat, of remembering its detrimental effects and understanding the issues.

The second degree is fear of Divine craftiness[91] when the emanations of spiritual uplifting occur, which provide great pleasure. At the level of the elite, fear of God does not generate any state of tension except that it is caused by the Divine majesty which then becomes reverential fear (*haybat al-ijlāl*).

The last degree is the supreme degree which can be mentioned in the context of fear: it concerns the person to whom God unveils Himself when the former addresses himself to Him; it protects the person who contemplates Him during intimate confiding; and it breaks the person who perceives Him under the impact of the Divine grandeur . . .

(*Manāzil*, no. 12, p. 20 of the Arabic text)

91. Through which one can lose one's guidance and be thrown even lower (*istidrāj*). Divine craftiness can hit those who take pride in themselves openly or secretly.

Ḥadīth 78

عن أبي هريرة : "اَلْحِكْمَةُ عَشْرَةُ أَجْزاءٍ : تِسْعَةٌ مِنْها فِي اَلعُزْلَةِ وَواحِدٌ فِي اَلصَّمْتِ."

(رواه السيوطي. حديث حسن)

Narrated Abū Hurayra: "Wisdom is divided into ten parts, nine of which are associated with solitude, and one with silence."

(Quoted by al-Suyūṭī. Validated *ḥadīth.*)

Commentary

The two sources of wisdom mentioned in this *ḥadīth* are in reality very near to one another, solitude and knowledge being intimately linked. The matter involves avoiding dispersion, which is inherent to everyday life, and putting the emphasis on spirituality. Spiritual masters continually warn their disciples against the poison of bad company, i.e., that which does not elevate one and which invites to dispersion in any form.

Ibn 'Aṭā' Allāh

Nothing benefits the heart more than a spiritual retreat wherein it enters the domain of meditation.

(*Ḥikam*, no. 12)

Shaykh al-Darqāwī

O disciple, in order to be protected spiritually (*salāma*) one must escape from people, except from those whose spiritual state is beneficial to others and whose words remind one of God.[92] In fact, people do not know the Tradition of their Prophet ﷺ, and they do not know their ignorance! God protect us! How great is their ignorance! It is such that when they see someone humbling his soul, they do not attribute him any value, considering him as contemptible, humiliating him and making nothing of it. Moreover, with regards to his parting from this world and its people, they underestimate him, and do not recognize in him any value, finding him bad, cumbersome, repulsive, and they start having an aversion to him. Then they consider him to have gone outside of the pale of tradition and to be a person of innovation (*bid'a*). They do not realize that the Muḥammadan tradition is precisely the

92. Advice which is reminiscent of a *ḥikma* from Ibn 'Aṭā' Allāh:

لا تَصْحَبْ مَنْ لا يُنْهِضُكَ حالُهُ وَلا يَدُلُّكَ عَلَى ٱللهِ مَقالُه.

"Do not keep company with one whose inner state does not inspire you and whose discourse does not lead you to God." (*Ḥikam*, no. 40)

Path he follows and that the innovation is precisely theirs.

The origin of these people's ignorance is the domination of their senses and of the material world (*al-ḥiss*), which have seized their hearts and their limbs making them dumb (and) blind, so they do not understand.[93]

This is incredible indeed! How could the realities (*ḥaqā'iq*) of things have been reverted to the point that the tradition be considered an innovation, and innovation be considered the tradition, and that the blind start dictating the way to one who sees?

Lo! we are God's and lo! unto Him we are returning.[94] There is no strength nor might save in God Most High, the Almighty.

(*Rasā'il*, letter 28, pp. 55-56)

The following passage is a testimony from the celebrated Ibrāhīm ibn Adham (d. 161/777), a mystic belonging to the period of the predecessors (*Salaf*) who is often cited by later masters as a model in the domain of asceticism. In this testimony, Ibn Adham relates how he received gnosis (*ma'rifa*) on solitude and silence through the teaching of a Christian monk. By means of a simple and concrete teaching, Father Simon emphasizes that gnosis is based on the discernment between the Absolute and the relative, the Real and the illusory.

Ibrāhīm ibn Adham

I received gnosis through the teaching of a monk called Father Simon. Having visited him in his cell, I asked him:

Father Simon, how long have you been in this cell?

Seventy years.

What do you feed yourself?

O Ḥanīf, what makes you ask this question?

The desire to know.

Each night a chickpea.

What vivifies your heart that you manage to content yourself with this?

Do you see that monastery? The monks who live there visit me once a year. They decorate my cell and circumambulate around it as a sign of reverence. When my soul shows signs of weakening in the worship of God, I recall those moments, and that is how I bear the pains of an entire year in view of one hour. [If I can do that], then bear O Ḥanīf the pains of an hour for the glory of eternity!

When he told me that, gnosis set in my heart.

(*Ḥilyat al-awliyā'*, VIII, p. 29)

93. II: 171.

94. II: 156.

Ḥadīth 79

عن ابن مسعود : "لا حَسَدَ إلاَّ في ٱثْنَيْن : رَجُلٍ آتاهُ ٱللّٰهُ مالاً فَسَلَّطَهُ عَلَى هَلَكَتِهِ في ٱلْحَقِّ، وَرَجُلٍ آتاهُ ٱللّٰهُ ٱلْحِكْمَةَ فَهُوَ يَقْضِي بِها وَيُعَلِّمُها."

(رواه البخاري. حديث صحيح)

Narrated Ibn Mas'ūd: "There is no envy except of two [types of people]: a person to whom God has given wealth and he spends it in the right way, and a person to whom God has given wisdom and he judges accordingly and teaches it to the others."

(Quoted by al-Bukhārī. Authenticated *ḥadīth*)

Commentary

If being envious—in the sense of a healthy emulation—towards a person who possesses wisdom is permissible, that is because wisdom is a great blessing, not only for the one possessing it but for all those who are directly influenced by its teachings, and eventually, for the community of believers at large because its great sages revive religion even if not everyone realizes it. Concerning the great privilege that the gift of wisdom represents, the Qur'ān affirms:

﴿يُؤْتِي ٱلْحِكْمَةَ مَنْ يَشاءُ وَمَنْ يُؤْتَ ٱلْحِكْمَةَ فَقَدْ أُوْتِيَ خَيْراً كَثِيراً وَما يَذَّكَّرُ إلاَّ أُولُو ٱلأَلْبابِ﴾

He giveth wisdom unto whom He will, and he unto whom wisdom is given, he truly hath received abundant good. But none will grasp the message except men of understanding.[95]

95. II: 269.

Ḥadīth 80

عن أبي هريرة : "اَلْكَلِمَةُ ٱلْحِكْمَةُ ضَالَّةُ ٱلْمُـؤْمِنِ حَيْثُمَـا وَجَدَها فَهُوَ أَحَقُّ بِهَا."

(رواه ابن ماجه. حديث حسن)

Narrated Abū Hurayra: "The believer is in search of words of wisdom; wherever he finds them, he is most entitled to make them his own."

(Quoted by Ibn Mājah. Validated *ḥadīth.*)

Commentary

In affirming that wisdom constitutes the object of the believer's quest, this *ḥadīth* clearly displays the universality of spiritual seeking in Islam. This universality is underlined by the expression: "wherever he finds it", in a close relationship with the saying attributed to the Prophet: "Seek knowledge even [if it be as far as] China!"

The fact is, this universalist attitude is very rarely put to practice, and the reasons for this are numerous. First of all, there is the reduction of the truth to the forms it has taken in the message of Islam. Thus all truth which is expressed in a non-directly Islamic manner will be considered by certain Muslims as a useless human invention, or even a dangerous straying. Islam explicitly recognizes the Divine origin of the Abrahamic religions, while quite often pointing out that everything which does not resemble the teachings of Islam is not part of the original messages but just a product of human deviation. This attitude affirms that the message of original Christianity, for example, was no different from that of Islam. The only differences commonly admitted are those pertaining to the revealed Laws (*sharāi'*), which can change from one religion to another. As for the creed (*'aqā'id*), it is supposedly the same in all revealed religions. However, a distinction must be made between the "underlying truth" and the form that this truth takes at a certain time and in a certain environment. The underlying truth must be unique, hence the Sufi adage *al-tawḥīd wāḥid*[96]—but the mode of expressing it and the means of realizing it are necessarily multiple and adapted to the people for whom they are destined. Thus the preaching of Jesus, far from completely resembling that of the Prophet ﷺ of Islam, insists on the immanence of God—or His Presence in creation—and the detachment from the seductions and the illusions of the world. Addressing himself to a people where the Unity and transcendence of God were accepted, he could not have stressed this aspect of Divine nature. Without negating

96. *The doctrine of Unity is unique.*

transcendence, he emphasized its complementary aspect: "The Kingdom of God is within you."[97] This did not prevent him from occasionally affirming God's transcendence with force: "Why do you call me good. No one is good except God alone!"[98]

Seeking to know the reality of the Divine nature does not mean insisting only on immanence (*tashbīh*) or only on transcendence (*tanzīh*), but trying to realize inwardly the complementarity of these two aspects. The dogmatic attachment to only one of these two faces of the Divine reality leads inevitably to literalism and to spiritual death. On this subject, a *ḥikam* of Shaykh al-ʻAlawī affirms: "The people most removed from their Lord are those who insist more on transcendence."[99]

On the other hand, the message of Islam addressed to a largely polytheist community had to pass over in silence the question of God's immanence and to affirm in a clear and simple manner His transcendence. Immanence, however, is not absent from the teachings of the Qur'ān: *He is with you wherever you are*[100] and *We are nearer to man than his jugular vein.*[101] Likewise, the Prophet ﷺ related a holy tradition (*ḥadīth qudsī*) in which God affirms His being the Hearing with which the friend of God hears, the Sight with which he sees, the Hand with which he grasps . . . [102] Ibn al-ʻArabī affirms the complementarity of the aspects of immanence and of transcendence, underlining the danger in every unilateral affirmation: "For the Folk of Divine realities (*ahl al-ḥaqā'iq*), affirming that God is incomparable to things means limiting the concept of the Divine reality and to render it conditional; whoever negates all similarity with regards to God, without leaving this exclusive point of view, manifests both ignorance and lack of respect (*adab*). The exoterism which one-sidedly insists on the Divine transcendence (*al-tanzīh*) slanders God and His messengers—peace be upon them all. Without noticing it, imagining that he hits the target, he misses widely; for he is one of those who accept only a part of the Divine revelation while rejecting the other."[103]

The above observations allow us to see that it is not easy to recognize the truth when it manifests itself in forms different from those to which we are accustomed. The putting into practice of this *ḥadīth* requires a certain spiritual maturity and a sufficiently profound knowledge of Islam and of its perspective.

---

97. Luke, 17:21.
98. Mark, 10:18.
99. *Ḥikmatuhu*, no. 25.
100. LVII: 4
101. L: 16.
102. Cf. *ḥadīth* 197.
103. Tr. by T. Burckhardt in *La Sagesse des Prophètes*, p. 61 (Albin Michel: 1989).

Ibn al-'Arabī

The revealed religions are diverse only through the diversity of the Divine aspects (*nisab ilāhiyya*) they envisage. In fact, if the Divine aspect according to which a certain thing is permissible in the revealed law (*shar'*) were the same as that according to which the same thing should be prohibited, there would be no divergences between the legal ruling (*ḥukm*) of a Law and that of another. However, it has been well established that such divergences exist. Furthermore, if such were not the case, this Divine saying would make no sense: *For each (of you) We have appointed a Divine Law and a traced-out way.*[104] Nevertheless, it is true that each community possesses a Law and a traced-out way of their own which were brought to them by their prophet or their messenger who, on one hand confirmed the preceding religions and on the other manifests new elements.

Therefore, we know with complete certainty that the Divine aspect through which God accorded His law to Muhammad ﷺ is different from the aspects through which He revealed His law to the other prophets. Had this not been the case, and if the Divine aspect which is at the origin of the revealed law were unique in all its facets (*min kulli wajh*), then the revealed religions would be one in all their facets.

If it is asked, why do the envisaged Divine aspects differ from one religion to another? We will respond: Due to the different inner dispositions (*aḥwāl*). Thus a sick person will supplicate: "O Thou who curest the illness and gives the remedy"; a hungry person will cry out: "O Thou who providest sustenance"; a person who is about to be drowned will call out: "O Thou who givest succour." . . . Therefore, the Divine aspects[105] vary according to the different inner dispositions.

(*Fut.*, I. p. 265)

---

104. V: 48.

105. Represented by the different Divine Names in the above example by Ibn al-'Arabī.

Ḥadīth 81

عن ابن عباس : "ما مِنْ آدَميٍّ إلاّ فِي رَأْسِهِ حِكْمَةٌ بِيَدِ مَلَكٍ. فَإِذا تَواضَعَ قِيلَ لِلْمَلَكِ : ارْفَعْ حِكْمَتَهُ، وَإِذا تَكَبَّرَ قِيلَ لِلْمَلَكِ : ضَعْ حِكْمَتَه."

(رواه الطبراني. حديث حسن)

Narrated Ibn 'Abbās: "There is no person who does not possess in his head wisdom governed by an angel. When man shows humility, the angel receives the order to increase his wisdom, and when man shows pride, the angel receives the order to decrease his wisdom."

(Quoted by al-Ṭabarānī. Validated *ḥadīth*.)

Commentary

According to this *ḥadīth*, any person can receive a certain amount of wisdom through inspiration. The amount of wisdom which he receives is determined by his humility. All in all, man's intelligence cannot be total unless it rids itself of pride: "The miracle of humility is precisely that it alone is able to transmute unintelligence into intelligence, as far as this is possible; the humble man is intelligent by his very humility."[106]

al-Ghazzālī

God Most High through His grace and the vastness of His generosity has honored the children of Adam and has elevated them above animals. He has assigned to each person two angels: the first one guides him and the second strengthens him.

Knowledge granted by these two angels distinguishes humans from animals. Therefore, human beings possess two specific qualities. The first is the knowledge of God Most High and of the Messenger, and the second is the means of reaching happy outcomes. All this comes about through the angel in charge of knowledge. As for animals, they possess neither knowledge nor guidance that would lead them to happy outcomes; they only know how to satisfy their immediate needs. This is why they seek nothing except the pleasurable. The beneficial remedy, which may be unpleasant at the time, is never sought.

Through the light of guidance man knows that following his desires brings unfortunate consequences for him.

This guidance, however, is not sufficient because man does not have

106. Cf. commentary of *ḥadīth* 74.

the power to separate himself from that which is harmful. Many a misfortune such as illness hits man without him being able to repel it. Therefore he needs power (*qudra*) and strength (*quwwa*) which will help him in defeating his desires: he will struggle against them, thanks to this force, in order to defeat this hostility.

For this purpose, God Most High has assigned him an angel who strengthens and assists him with the invisible "armies" (*junūd*). They are charged to fight the forces of concupiscent desires which can sometimes diminish and sometimes grow stronger. This depends on the assistance (*ta'yīd*) that God grants to His servant. In the same manner, guidance is different in different persons and remains indeterminable.

The two angels we mentioned are assigned to every human being.

If you know that the degree of the angel charged with guidance is higher than that which is charged with spiritual support, you will not miss the fact that the right side, the noblest of the two sides, is occupied by the first. It befits the servant to submit himself to him.

The servant is aware of two situations: heedlessness (*ghafla*) and attentiveness (*fikr*), abandonment and struggle.

In heedlessness, he turns away from the angel of the right side. In so doing, he is unjust towards himself. One evil deed will then be written for him. Inversely, through attentiveness he turns towards the angel to receive guidance. Thus he shows himself to be beneficent. A good deed will be written for him.

In the same way, in abandonment, he turns away from the angel of the left side and loses the source of his strength. In doing so, he is unjust to himself. An evil deed will be written for him. Inversely, through effort, he is strengthened by the "armies" of the angel and a good deed will be written for him.

(*Iḥyā'*, IV, p. 62)

Interpretation of Dreams: الرؤيا وتعبير الأحلام

Ḥadīth 82

عن حذيفة بن أسيد : "ذَهَبَتِ ٱلنُّبُوَّةُ فَلا نُبُوَّةَ بَعْدي إلاّ ٱلْمُبَشِّرات : الرُّؤْيا ٱلصَّالِحةُ يَراها ٱلرَّجُلُ أَوْ تُرى لَهُ."

(رواه الطبراني. حديث صحيح)

Narrated Ḥudhayfa ibn Asyad: "Prophecy has come to an end and there will be no prophets after me. Only heralds remain: the pious vision which man sees or which is shown to him."

(Quoted by al-Ṭabarānī. Authenticated *ḥadīth*.)

Ḥadīth 83

عن أنس بن مالك : "رُؤْيا ٱلْمُؤْمِنِ جُزْءٌ مِنْ سِتَّةٍ وَأَرْبَعِينَ جُزْءاً مِنَ ٱلنُّبُوَّة."

(رواه البخاري. حديث صحيح)

Narrated Anas: "A believer's [oneiric] vision constitutes one forty-sixth of prophethood."

(Quoted by al-Bukhārī. Authenticated *ḥadīth*)

Commentary

Insofar as the above *ḥadīth* mention that [oneiric] vision constitutes a part of prophethood, it is natural to envisage the role of dreams in the spiritual life of the believer. However, it is not easy to demonstrate the relationships existing between [oneiric] vision and prophethood. Surely, it is known from a *ḥadīth* conveyed by 'Ā'isha that before receiving the revelation, the Prophet ﷺ had a period of time during which he had pious [oneiric] visions (*ru'yā ṣāliḥa*).[107] But in order to grasp the correlation between [oneiric] vision and prophethood, one has to look into their common language, which

107. Cf. al-Bukhārī, *Ṣaḥīḥ*, *Bad' al-waḥy ilā Rasūli-Llāh.*

is symbolism. Prophethood, much like dreams—although of a different and much more elevated nature—is expressed through symbols, hence the need for interpretation. Symbols (*mithāl*) are not simple, arbitrary allegories, they transmit something of the reality of that which they symbolize. In order to underline the importance of the link between symbols and the spiritual reality they point out, al-Ghazzālī uses the terms "homology" (*muwāzana*), "similitude" (*mumāthala*), and "correlation" (*muṭābaqa*).

al-Ghazzālī

Know that the world is twofold: spiritual (*rūḥānī*) and corporeal (*jismānī*), or if you prefer, intelligible (*'aqlī*) and sensory (*ḥissī*), or superior (*'ulwī*) and inferior (*suflī*). All these expressions are almost equivalent: only the points of view differ. [. . .]

The sensible world is a point of support for elevating (*marqāt*) oneself towards the intelligible world. Were there no link (*ittiṣāl*) and correspondence (*munāsaba*) between them, the way to reach there would have been closed. And if this had not been possible, no one would have been elevated towards the Presence of the Lord nor would anyone have been drawn nigh unto Him. [. . .]

Divine Mercy has established a parallel relation (homology) (*muwāzana*) between the visible world and the celestial kingdom. As a consequence, there is nothing in the former which is not a symbol (*mithāl*) of something in the latter. It is possible for a single earthly thing to be a symbol of several things of the celestial world, and conversely a single thing of the celestial world can be represented by several symbols of the visible world. A thing is a symbol of another if the former represents the latter by virtue of a similitude (*mumāthala*) and if it corresponds to it by virtue of a certain correlation (*muṭābaqa*).

(*Mishkāt*, pp. 70-71)

Ḥadīth 84

عن أبي هريرة : "اللَّبَنُ فِي ٱلْمَنامِ فِطْرَةٌ."

(رواه البزار. حديث صحيح)

Narrated Abū Hurayra: "In dreams, milk corresponds to the primordial nature."

(Quoted by al-Bazzār. Authenticated *ḥadīth*)

Ḥadīth 85

عن عبد الله بن عمرو بن العاص : "رَأَيْتُ فِيما يَرى ٱلنَّائِمُ لَكَأَنَّ فِي إِحْدَى أَصْبَعَيَّ سَمْناً وَفِي ٱلأُخْرَى عَسَلاً فَأَنا أَلْعَقُهُما فَلَمَّا أَصْبَحْتُ ذَكَرْتُ ذٰلِكَ لِرَسُولِ ٱللهِ ﷺ فَقالَ : تَقْرَأُ ٱلكِتابَيْنِ ٱلتَّوْراةَ وَٱلفُرْقانَ. فَكانَ يَقْرَؤُهُما."

(رواه الإمام أحمد. حديث حسن)

Narrated 'Abd Allāh ibn 'Amr ibn al-'Āṣ: "I saw myself in a dream licking my two fingers: on one of them there was butter and on the other honey. Upon waking, I related this to the Messenger of God ﷺ who told me, 'You will be able to read the two books: the Torah and the Qur'ān.' And this is what happened eventually."

(Quoted by Aḥmad ibn Ḥanbal. Validated *ḥadīth*.)

Commentary

The understanding of the message sent by God to a servant by means of a dream requires, as we have seen, an interpretation. The latter consists in linking the tangible symbol to the spiritual reality which it symbolizes. Thus the first *ḥadīth* teaches us that milk in a vision is the symbol of the primordial nature (*fiṭra*). The Qur'ān also gives some examples of this interpretative process, notably with regards to the prophet Yūsuf who had received the gift of interpreting dreams or parables (*ta'wīl al-aḥādīth*):[108] in his dream, the stars symbolize his parents and his brothers.[109] This "transposition" from the tangible to the intelligible is called *i'tibār* by al-Ghazzālī,

108. Cf. XII: 6.
109. XII: 100.

who considers it to be essentially the same process as that through which the symbols of the revealed Book should be interpreted. This kinship in the interpretative process is therefore underlined by the *ḥadīth* which affirms that "a believer's vision is a message granted to the servant by his Lord during sleep." The Arabic term *kalām* translated here as "message" is the same as that which denotes the Divine Word.

Al-Ghazzālī nevertheless specifies that the interpretation of the Book does not imply at all the rejection of the literal meaning of its verses.

al-Ghazzālī

From the above elements and the symbolic interpretation do not deduce that I would allow myself to reject the literal meaning and that I would be convinced of their falsity. This would lead me to maintain that Moses did not have any "sandals" and that he did not hear God say to him: "Take off your sandals!"[110] God forbid! The negation of the literal sense is the opinion of the *bāṭiniyya* who are truly one-eyed and see only one of the two worlds; they ignore the homology existing between the two and do not understand it. Reversely, the negation of the secrets [contained in the Revelation] is the position of the crude literalists (*ḥashwiyya*). Thus whoever isolates the apparent meaning is a literalist and whoever isolates the hidden meaning is a *bāṭinī*, whereas whoever unites the two is perfect [in his interpretation]. This is why the Prophet ﷺ has said: "The Qur'ān has an interior (*baṭn*) and an exterior (*ẓahr*), a limit (*ḥadd*) and a point of ascension (*maṭla'* or *maṭli'*)."[111]

I would therefore say that Moses understood that the order to take off his sandals meant the rejection of both worlds; he then obeyed the outward meaning by taking them off, and the inward meaning by rejecting both worlds. This is what it means to practice the "transposition" (*i'tibār*), that is, passing from one thing to another: from the literal meaning to the profound meaning.

(*Mishkāt*, p. 77)

---

110. A reference to the Divine injunction received by Moses when he came near the burning bush: *Lo! I am thy Lord, So take off thy shoes, for lo! thou art in the holy valley of Tuwa.* (XX: 12)

111. See *ḥadīth* 135.

Ḥadīth 86

عن أبي هريرة : "إذا رَأَى أَحَدُكُمْ ٱلرُّؤيا ٱلْحَسَنَة فَلْيُفَسِّرْها وَلْيُخْبِرْ بِها وَإِذا رَأَى ٱلرُّؤْيا ٱلْقَبِيحة فَلا يُفَسِّرْها وَلا يُخْبِرْ بِها."

(رواه الترمذي. حديث حسن)

Narrated Abū Hurayra: "When one of you has had a good dream, he should interpret and share it with the others. But whoever has a bad dream should neither interpret it nor share it."

(Quoted by al-Tirmidhī. Validated *ḥadīth*)

Commentary

A bad dream (*ru'yā qabīḥa*) is one which announces a misfortune and brings distress (*ru'yā muḥzina*); speaking about it and attempting to interpret it implies according too great an importance to it, and to contribute involuntarily to its realization.

'Abd al-'Azīz al-Dabbāgh

I asked ['Abd al-'Azīz al-Dabbāgh] about distressing dreams (*ru'yā muḥzina*); under what conditions are they harmful and under which ones are they not? I told him the story of a woman who dreamt that her house was destroyed and her newborn baby was one-eyed; when she had this dream her husband was away on a trading trip. She related this dream to the Prophet ﷺ who told her: "Your husband will arrive safe and sound, God willing, and your child will be healthy." At first, the woman looked for the Prophet ﷺ but did not find him; then she related her dream to 'Ā'isha who told her: "If your dream is authentic, your husband will die and you will bring to life a wicked child!" When the Prophet ﷺ returned, 'Ā'isha informed him about the dream as well as her interpretation. Then he reproached her: "O 'Ā'isha! When you interpret the dream of a believer, do it in a positive sense, for a dream is realized according to the interpretation it has received!" Ibn Ḥajar confirms that this *ḥadīth* is quoted by Dārimī and its chain is valid.

Shaykh al-Dabbāgh said: "The distressful dream is a warning (*tanbīh*) from God for His servant as well as a test (*ikhtibār*): will he remain turned towards his Creator or will he distance himself from Him? The servant who is firmly attached to the Most High does not pay any attention to the distressing dream because he knows that everything comes from Him who is in charge of everything and that the dream in question has no effect on him. Therefore he will not give any importance to it. The distressing dream will not harm such a person."

(*Ibrīz*, I, pp. 246-247)

Divine Inspiration: الإلهام الرباني

Ḥadīth 87

عن البراء بن عازب : "قَالَ ٱلنَّبِيُّ ﷺ لِحَسَّان : ٱهْجُهُمْ أَوْ هاجِهِمْ وَجِبْرِيلُ مَعَك."

(رواه البخاري. حديث صحيح)

Narrated al-Barrā' ibn 'Āzib: "The Prophet ﷺ said to [the poet] Ḥassān: 'Compose a poem to scoff them, and may Gabriel assist you!'"

(Quoted by al-Bukhārī. Authenticated *ḥadīth*)

Ḥadīth 88

عن عائشة : "كانَ ٱلنَّبِيُّ ﷺ يَضَعُ لِحَسَّان مِنْبَراً فِي ٱلْمَسْجِد يَقُومُ عَلَيْه قائماً يُفاخِرُ عَنْ رَسُولِ ٱللهِ ﷺ، يَقُولُ ٱلرَّسُولُ : "إِنَّ ٱللهَ يُؤَيِّدُ حَسَّان بِرُوحِ ٱلْقُدُسِ ما نافَخَ أَوْ فاخَرَ عَنْ رَسُولِ ٱللهِ."

(رواه الترمذي. حديث صحيح)

Narrated 'Ā'isha: "The Prophet ﷺ used to put in his mosque a pulpit (*minbar*) at Ḥassān's disposal. The latter would stand on it and then would praise God and the Messenger of God ﷺ. The Prophet ﷺ would say about him: 'Verily, God assists Ḥassān through the Holy Spirit when he praises the Messenger of God.'"

(Quoted by al-Tirmidhī. Authenticated *ḥadīth*)

Commentary

These two *ḥadīth* are important in more than one way. They insist on the possibility that a poem can come from heavenly inspiration, and that this heavenly inspiration—besides emanating from the Holy Spirit (*al-Rūḥ al-*

qudus)—is not reserved exclusively for the Prophets. For many commentators, the Holy Spirit is none other than the angel Gabriel. This identification is confirmed by looking at the two *ḥadīth*. A verse mentioning the revelation of the Qur'ān also supports the meaning of this identification: *Say: The holy Spirit hath delivered it from thy Lord with the Truth . . .* [112]

One of the most celebrated poems of the Muslim world remains *al-Burda* written by Shaykh Sharaf al-Dīn al-Būṣīrī (d. 694/1294). This beautiful praise of the Prophet ﷺ owes its fame to both its intrinsic value and the circumstances surrounding its composition. It is related that, affected by hemiplegia, Būṣīrī dreamt of the Prophet, who put his hand on the paralyzed spot and covered it with his mantle (*burda*). When he woke up he realized he had miraculously been healed. Even though Būṣīrī was discrete about what had happened, the news spread rapidly and his poem received the title *Burdat al-madīḥ*. This long poem of 160 verses is still commonly read and sung to this day during religious celebrations.

Ibn al-'Arabī

There was amongst us in Damascus a gracious (*min ahl al-faḍl*), cultivated and, pious man, whose name was Yaḥyā ibn al-Akhfash. He was originally from Marrakech where his father taught Arabic. Once when I was in Damascus, he wrote to me the following letter: "My friend in God, yesterday I saw the Prophet ﷺ in my dream. The scene took place in the Great Mosque of Damascus. He was standing before the place of sermons (*maqṣūrat al-khaṭāba*), which is situated beside the box containing the copy of the Qur'ān attributed to 'Uthmān. People pushed forward in order to pay allegiance to him. I waited until the crowd became smaller and then I went before him and took his hand [to pay my allegiance]. He told me: 'Do you know Muḥammad?' I asked him which one he meant, and he told me: 'Ibn al-'Arabī.' I replied, 'Yes, I know him.' Then he said to me: 'We have a task to entrust to him. Tell him that the Messenger of God asked him to carry out the command which he received. As for you, be his companion, you will benefit from it. Tell him: the Messenger of God asks you to praise the Helpers (*Anṣār*) and especially Sa'd ibn 'Ubāda. Then the Prophet ﷺ called Ḥassān ibn Thābit and told him: 'O Ḥassān, teach him a verse which he will transmit to Muḥammad Ibn al-'Arabī and based on which the latter will compose his poem in keeping with its rhyme and meter.' Ḥassān turned to me and said: 'O Yaḥyā, this is for you:

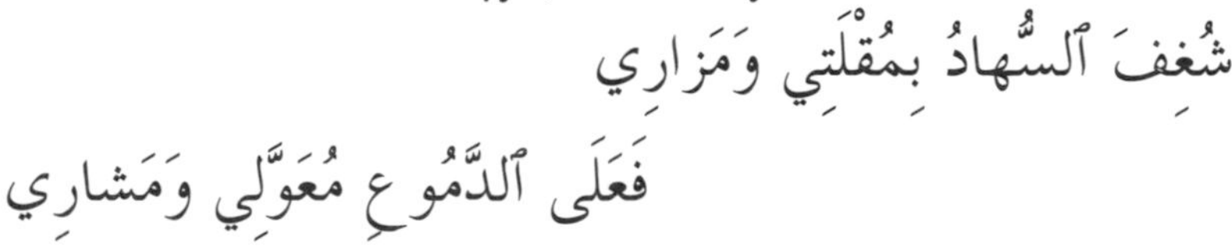

شُغِفَ ٱلسُّهادُ بِمُقْلَتِي وَمَزارِي
فَعَلَى ٱلدُّمُوعِ مُعَوَّلِي وَمَشارِي

112. XVI: 102.

> *My sleepless nights are spent in my weeping and my pious visits*
> *My tears are my hope and my sole refuge.'*

He repeated this verse to me until I memorized it. Then the Messenger of God ﷺ told me: 'When he has composed this praise of the Helpers, transcribe it in your most beautiful handwriting and bring it on Thursday evening to the tomb you call *qabr as-sitt*; there you will find a man named Ḥāmid, give him this poem.'"

(*Fut.*, I, pp. 196-8 [O.Y.])

Ḥadīth 89

عن أبي : "إِنَّ مِنَ ٱلشِّعْرِ حِكْمَة."

(رواه البخاري. حديث صحيح)

Narrated Ubayy: "Verily, there is wisdom in poetry."
(Quoted by al-Bukhārī. Authenticated *ḥadīth*)

Commentary

Poetry allows the masters of the Path to express truths which are sometimes too subtle to fit into the "mold of common language." Wisdom—and therefore knowledge also—surpasses ordinary understanding and certain of its modes cannot be mentioned except through allusions. It must be added that the rhyme and the sonorities of a poem as well as the beauty and harmony attached to it contribute to the transmission of a wisdom which would otherwise remain incommunicable.

Ibn al-'Arabī

Know that this poem—like all the poems that begin each chapter of this book—does not aim to express synthetically that which will be expounded in prose in the chapter, the poem is in itself part of the treatise. [What is taught by the poem] is therefore not repeated in the prose that follows. Thus, one must equally turn one's attention to the poetry as well as the prose contained in this work. The poems of this book in fact contain original and independent matters (*masā'il*) which are not found in the prose. There is, however, a link (*rābiṭ*) between these different matters. A treatise on man, for example, is inseparable from a treatise on the animal kingdom, since man shares with the animals the senses; and finally, it is inseparable from a treatise on the mineral world, since man too possesses certain parts of the body which are insensible like the nails and the hair . . . Every existing thing maintains a relationship (*irtibāṭ*) with another. This is so even between the Lord and the servant, for the creature cannot be envisaged but in relation to the Creator, and inversely.

(*Fut.*, II, p. 665)

Ḥadīth 90

عن أبي هريرة : "أَصْدَقُ كَلِمةٍ قالَها ٱلشَّاعِرُ كَلِمَةُ لَبِيد :
أَلا كُلُّ شَيْءٍ ما خَلا ٱللهَ باطِلُ."

(رواه البخاري. حديث صحيح)

Narrated Abū Hurayra: 'The most truthful word pronounced by a poet was that of Labīd: "Except God, is not everything unreal (*bāṭil*)?"

(Quoted by al-Bukhārī. Authenticated *ḥadīth*.)

Commentary

The illusory character of the world is a recurring theme in the teachings of the spiritual masters. This can be easily understood since spirituality consists precisely in getting rid of the illusion which tends to attribute to Creation—which in that capacity is ephemeral and transitory—a stability and a reality befitting only that which is eternal. In this sense, not only the external world but also the ego is illusory.

Hence, it is not out of place to ponder on the status of this cosmic and egocentric "double illusion." At first, one can oppose the word of Labīb by the verse from the Qur'ān: *Lord! Thou did not create this in vain (bāṭilan)*[113] which seems to express a truth altogether contrary to that which is contained in the words of the poet. In fact, we find the same term *bāṭil* in both citations, and in both instances it is applied to Creation. However, the two usages of this term are not antithetical as long as we understand that the illusory existence of the world and of the ego is not pure nothingness, which would, properly speaking, amount to nonsense. If Creation considered in itself appears as devoid of reality, it is also, with respect to existence, a plane of reflection of the Divine qualities, a mirror of theophanies.

It is this aspect of things that constituted the major theme of the dialogue between Ibn al-'Arabī and the Prophet Hārūn during their spiritual encounter during his "ascension" (*mi'rāj*):

> I told him: "O Hārūn, certain men of knowledge claim that as far as they are concerned existence is annihilated and that they only see God. According to them, the world no longer has any reality and nothing justifies their paying attention to someone else beside God. And yet, it is certain that their spiritual degree cannot equal yours and your likes: *make not my enemies rejoice over me*.[114] For this reason, you take heed

113. III: 191.
114. VII: 150.

> of your enemies. Your spiritual type (*ḥāl*) is therefore quite different from that of these men of knowledge." Hārūn replied: "These men of knowledge are truthful, for they have said nothing but what their own existence conferred upon them. So, does everything in the world that ceases to exist in their eyes effectively cease to be?" I did not reply. Then he said: "The limitation of their knowledge with regards to the veritable nature of things is proportional to what escapes them. What they are missing with respect to the science of Divine Reality (*al-Ḥaqq*) is in proportion to that which is veiled from the reality of the world. In its totality, the world is nothing but the theophany of the Divine Reality for whomever knows It."[115]

In another text, Ibn al-'Arabī explains that God possesses a "particular Face" in everything that exists, and that this is precisely what allows a creature to be:

> Nothing can be deprived of a "face" of God—Exalted is He. He is the reality of that face. If this were not so, He would not be [the only] divinity and the world would be sufficient unto itself, which is however impossible.
>
> (*Fut.*, II, p. 299)

115. This text contains allusions which are impossible to render into French (or English-editor's note). Thus by "knowledge" we translate the term *'ilm* and by "world" the term *'ālam*. These two terms come from the same root, which suggests the idea that the world is a support for the knowledge of God.

The Invocation of God: ذكر الله تعالى

Ḥadīth 91

عن أبي الدرداء : "أَعْظَمُ ٱلنَّاسِ دَرَجةً ٱلذَّاكِرُونَ ٱللهَ."

(رواه البيهقي. حديث حسن)

Narrated Abū al-Dardā': "Those who are given the highest spiritual degree are those who practice the invocation of God."

(Quoted by al-Bayhaqī. Validated *ḥadīth*.)

Commentary

The term *dhikr*, which we have translated as "invocation," can also be translated as "remembrance," "reminder," or "mention." In order to respect this polysemy, the following phrase can be used as a definition: [*Dhikr* is the] remembrance of God through the repetition of a sacred formula.

After reading this *ḥadīth*, one may ask: "How does invocation confer the highest degree of spirituality?" This question can also be formulated in the following way: "Why does the repetition of the Divine Name or the Shahāda—and not another rite—confer the highest degree of spirituality?"

This *ḥadīth* in itself clarifies the meanings of the Qur'ānic verse affirming the primacy of the invocation:

﴿إِنَّ ٱلصَّلَاةَ تَنْهَى عَنِ ٱلْفَحْشَاءِ وَٱلْمُنْكَرِ وَلَذِكْرُ ٱللهِ أَكْبَرُ﴾

Surely prayer keeps away from indecency and evil, and certainly the remembrance of God is the greatest.[116]

Nevertheless, in order to reply to the twofold question, one has to look into the nature and the role of invocation in the spiritual path. For this, it is necessary to clarify the role of invocation in surpassing the limits of the mind, a process through which access to the heart becomes possible.

Martin Lings (Abū Bakr Sirāj al-Dīn)

All doctrine is related to the mind; but mystical doctrine, which corresponds to the Lore of Certainty, is a summons to the mind to transcend itself. The

116. XXIX: 45.

Divine Name Allāh is the synthesis of all truth and therefore the root of all doctrine, and as such it offers certainty to the Heart and to those elements of the soul which are nearest to the Heart. But being a synthesis, it cannot in itself meet the needs of the mind; and so, in order that the whole intelligence including the mind may participate in the spiritual path, the Name as it were holds out a hand to the mental faculties, an extension of itself which offers them lore as well as certainty and which, in addition to being a synthesis, has an analytical aspect on which it can work. The extension of the Name is the divinely revealed testification (*shahāda*) that there is no god but God (*lā ilāha illā 'Llāh*).[117]

No god but God: for the mind it is a formulation of truth; for the will it is an injunction with regard to truth; but for the Heart and its intuitive prolongations of certainty it is a single synthesis, a Name of Truth, belonging as such to the highest category of Divine Names. This synthetic aspect makes itself felt even when the Shahāda is taken in its analytical sense, for the synthesis is always there in the background, ever ready as it were to reabsorb the formulation back into itself. Thus while necessarily inviting analysis, as it must, the Shahāda seems in a sense to defy analysis. It is both open and closed, obvious and enigmatic; and even in its obviousness it is something of a stranger to the mind which it dazzles with its exceeding simplicity and clarity, just as it also dazzles because it reverberates with hidden implications.

(*What is Sufism?*, pp. 63-64)

117. One of the reasons why the Name as an invocation is 'greatest' is that by refusing to address itself to the mind, it compels the centre of consciousness to recede inwards in the direction of the Heart. (M.L.)

Hadīth 92

عن شداد بن أوس : "كُنَّا عِنْدَ ٱلنَّبِيِّ ﷺ فَقال : "هَلْ فِيكُمْ غَرِيب ؟" يَعْنِي أَهْلَ ٱلكتاب. فَقُلْنا : "لا، يا رَسُولَ ٱللهِ." فَأَمَرَ بِغَلْقِ ٱلباب وَقال : "ارْفَعُوا أَيْدِيَكُمْ وَقُولُوا : لا إِله إِلاَّ ٱللهُ." فَرَفَعْنا أَيْدِينا ساعَةً ثُمَّ وَضَعَ رَسُولُ ٱللهِ ﷺ يَدَهُ ثُمَّ قال : "ٱلْحَمْدُ لله، اللَّهُمَّ بَعَثْتَنِي بِهٰذِه ٱلكَلِمَة وَأَمَرْتَنِي بِها وَوَعَدْتَنِي عَلَيْها ٱلْجَنَّةَ وَإِنَّكَ لا تُخْلِفُ ٱلْمِيعاد." ثُمَّ قالَ : "أَبْشِرُوا ! فَإِنَّ ٱللهَ قَدْ غَفَرَ لَكُمْ."

(رواه الحاكم. حديث صحيح)

Narrated Shaddād ibn Aws: "We were in the company of the Prophet ﷺ when he asked: 'Is there any stranger amongst you?' by which he meant the People of the Book. We replied: 'No, O Messenger of God.' He then ordered the door to be closed and said: 'Raise your hands and say: *Lā ilāha illa-Llāh*.' We raised our hands for a moment, then the Messenger of God ﷺ lowered his hands and said: 'Praise belongs to God! O God, Thou hast sent me with this word, Thou hast ordered me to repeat it and promised me Paradise for it. Verily, Thou never breakest Thy promise.' Then he told us: 'Rejoice, for in truth God has forgiven you.'"

(Quoted by al-Ḥākim. Authenticated *ḥadīth*.)

Commentary

The Sufi path is based on the transmission of invocatory formulae. In order to be recited according to all the required spiritual conditions, these formulae have to be received through a chain of transmission (*silsila*) going back to the Prophet. This *ḥadīth* is often considered a textual proof for the reality of such a transmission.

Shaykh al-'Alawī

This *ḥadīth* constitutes the first link in the chain of transmission of the teaching of the Sufis. The Prophet ﷺ ordered that the door be locked before he instructed the Companions in a group and asked them: "Are there any strangers amongst you?" in order to indicate that the path of the Sufis is founded on secrecy. Those who are strangers [to the path] and who do not believe in it cannot be present at such an instruction; their absence is necessary because their lack of qualification might lead them to denigrate what they witness therein.

(*Qawl*, p. 37)

Ḥadīth 93

عن علي :سأل النبي ﷺ بقوله "يا رَسُولَ الله : "دُلَّني عَلى
أَقْرَبِ ٱلطُّرُقِ إِلى ٱللهِ وَأَسْهَلِها عَلى عِبادِهِ وَأَفْضَلِها عِنْدَهُ
تَعالى." فَقالَ ﷺ : "يا عَلِيّ عَلَيْكَ بِمُداوَمَةِ ذِكْرِ ٱللهِ سِرّاً
وَجَهْراً..." فَقالَ عَلِيّ : "كَيْفَ أَذْكُرُ ؟" قالَ ٱلنَّبِيُّ ﷺ :
"غَمِّضْ عَيْنَيْكَ وَٱسْمَعْ مِنِّي لا إِلَهَ إِلاَّ ٱللهُ ثَلاثَ مَرّاتٍ ثُمَّ
قُلْها ثَلاثاً وَأَنا أَسْمَعُ."

(رواه الطبراني. حديث حسن)

'Alī narrated that he asked the Prophet ﷺ: "O Messenger of God, indicate to me the shortest way leading to God, the easiest one for His worshippers and the most elevated one in the eyes of the Exalted." The Prophet ﷺ replied: "O 'Alī, you have to practice the invocation incessantly, sometimes in silence and sometimes aloud." 'Alī asked: "How should I invoke?" The Prophet ﷺ told him: "Close your eyes and listen to me say three times: *lā ilāha illa-'Llāh*, then say this formula three times so that I can hear you."

(Quoted by al-Ṭabarānī. Validated *ḥadīth*).

Commentary

The most important expressions of this *ḥadīth* are the following: "the shortest way leading to God" (*aqrab al-ṭuruq ilā-Llāh*), "the easiest" (*ashaluhā*), and "the most elevated" (*afḍaluhā*). They demonstrate yet again the primacy of the path of invocation. But this *ḥadīth* also shows that invocation—in the sense of an initiatic practice—must be received through an oral and living transmission. In this sense, this *ḥadīth*, just as the one preceding it, is a textual proof for the transmission (*talqīn*) of the invocation amongst the Sufis.

Although the invocation of God by means of the formula *lā ilāha illa-Llāh* constitutes a common invocation recommended for every believer,[118] 'Alī received it from the Prophet ﷺ through a particular transmission. It therefore became, in his case, an initiatic practice. This clearly follows from the request of 'Alī. In addition, it is known that 'Alī transmitted the initiation to several Companions and thus became

118. Cf. *ḥadīth* 95.

the origin of numerous orders.[119]

The importance of the living transmission of the invocation is also pointed out by a *ḥadīth* according to which certain servants of God are veritable keys to the invocation:

عن ابن مسعود : "إِنَّ مِنَ ٱلنَاسِّ مَفاتِيحَ لِذِكْرِ ٱللهِ إِذا رُؤُوا ذُكِرَ ٱللهُ."

(رواه الطبراني. حديث حسن)

Narrated Ibn Mas'ūd: "Verily, certain persons are keys for the invocation of God: they arouse the invocation of God when they are seen."[120]
(Quoted by al-Ṭabarānī. Validated *ḥadīth*)

Having realized a very high degree of the invocation of God, 'Alī became a "key" for the others, engaging them in the path of God's proximity. The function which 'Alī assumed earned him the following important testimony of the Prophet:

عن عبد الله بن مسعود : "النَّظَرُ إِلَى وَجْهِ عَلِيٍّ عِبادَةٌ."

(رواه الحاكم. حديث صحيح)

Narrated Ibn Mas'ūd: "Looking at the face of 'Alī is an act of worship."
(Quoted by al-Ḥākim. Authenticated *ḥadīth*.)[121]

---

119. The same is true for Abū Bakr.

120. Cf. also *ḥadīth* 187 and 188.

121. Ibn al-Jawzī (d. 597/1200) and al-Dhahabī (d. 748/1348), disturbed by the meaning of this *ḥadīth*, declared it forged (*mawḍū'*). Al-Suyūṭī emphasizes its authenticity by reminding us that it was related by eleven Companions, which gives it the status of a *mutawātir ḥadīth*. In addition, the celebrated contemporary *muḥaddith* 'Abd al-'Azīz ibn al-Ṣiddīq al-Ghumarī (d. 1997) has devoted a treatise to the authentication of this *ḥadīth*: *al-Ifāda fī ṭuruq ḥadīth "al-naẓar ilā 'Alī 'ibāda"*.

Ḥadīth 94

عن أنس بن مالك : "عَلامةُ حُبِّ ٱللهِ تعالى حُبُّ ذِكْرِ ٱللهِ
وعَلامةُ بُغْضِ ٱللهِ بُغْضُ ذِكْرِ ٱللهِ."

(رواه البيهقي. حديث حسن)

Narrated Anas ibn Mālik: "The criterion of the love of God is the love of His invocation (*dhikr*), and the criterion of the hatred of God is the hatred of His invocation."

(Quoted by al-Bayhaqī. Validated *ḥadīth*.)

Commentary

Loving God and loving to invoke Him are indissolubly linked because the invocation makes present the Invoked. Concerning this subject, al-Junayd has been quoted as saying: "The sign of perfect love of God is the continuous invocation in the heart accompanied by joy, delight, ardent desire (*shawq*), and contentment in the [spiritual] intimacy (*uns*)."

al-Ghazzālī

Know that every man claims to love. And yet, if pretending is easy, realizing is much more difficult. Therefore, man must not be deluded by the deceptions of Satan and the trickeries of the ego pretending to the love of God Most High. One must confront the pretensions of the ego with criteria (*'alāmāt*) and proofs.

Love is like a goodly tree, its root set firm, its branches reaching into heaven;[122] its fruits appear in the heart, the tongue and the limbs. These manifestations testify to love just as smoke testifies to the existence of fire, and fruit to a tree's nature. These manifestations are numerous. Amongst the signs of love is the desire of meeting with the Beloved by means of unveiling and contemplation in the abode of peace (*dār al-salām*). In fact, one cannot conceive of a heart which experiences love while not seeking to contemplate and to meet with its beloved. [. . .] In the same way, whoever loves God will love madly the invocation of God: his tongue will invoke Him constantly and his heart will not be able to spend a single moment without it. In fact, whoever loves a thing necessarily mentions amply that thing as well as everything related to it. This is the reason why the criterion of the love of God is the love of His invocation, the love of the Qur'ān which is His Word, the love of the Messenger of God ﷺ and all that concerns him. When love is strong, it extends to everything related to the Beloved. This is

122. Allusion to XIV: 24.

not a dispersion in love (*shirka fī l-ḥubb*), for he who loves the Messenger of the Beloved because he is "His" messenger, and loves His Word because it is "His," loves nothing other than Him! On the contrary, this testifies to the perfection of his love. Moreover, a man whose heart is dominated by the love of God will love all creatures because they are God's: how can he not love the Qur'ān, the Mesenger and the serving Friends of God?

(*Iḥyā'*, IV, pp. 320-323)

al-Junayd

The question of love was raised in a session of spiritual masters in Mecca during the season of Pilgrimage. They asked al-Junayd, who at the time was the youngest amongst them: "And what is your opinion, O Iraqi?" Al-Junayd lowered his head, tears going down his face, and then he said: "Love requires the servant to have abandoned his individuality, to constantly invoke his Lord, to perform all his duties before Him, to have his heart turned to Him until he is consumed by the lights of His Being, to drink the pure water of His affection so that God lifts the veils covering His mysteries. When such a man speaks, it is for God; if he expresses himself, it is on the subject of God; if he performs an act, it is by the order of God; if he rests, it is with God. He is from God, for God, with God."

The spiritual masters then started weeping and confessed: "What more can one say? May God reward you, the Crown of the Sages!"

(*Enseignement*, pp. 194-5)

Ḥadīth 95

عن أبي هريرة : "جَدِّدُوا إِيْمانَكُمْ : أَكْثِرُوا مِنْ قَوْلِ لا إِلَـٰهَ إِلاَّ ٱللهُ."

(رواه الحاكم. حديث صحيح)

Narrated Abū Hurayra: "Renew your faith by multiplying the repetition of the formula 'There is no god but God.'"

(Quoted by al-Ḥākim. Authenticated *ḥadīth*)

Commentary

Faith, considered as a profound adherence of the heart, has to be renewed because, on the one hand, this adherence can decrease in intensity depending on numerous factors, and on the other, because faith consists of many degrees which can only be realized progressively and in accordance with one's spiritual commitment. The realization of these different degrees can be experienced as spiritual rebirths. This *ḥadīth* therefore presents the invocation of God through the formula *lā ilāha illa-'Llāh* as the privileged means of living these rebirths.

al-Munāwī

"Renew your faith!" The Companions then asked: "O Messenger of God, how shall we renew our faith?" He told them: "Multiply the repetition of the formula There is no god but God." Practicing this invocation regularly and with perseverance (*mudāwama*) renews faith in the heart, filling it with light and letting certitude (*yaqīn*) grow therein. This invocation opens the heart to access secrets known by people of spiritual perceptions (*ahl al-baṣā'ir*) and which are only denied by people without faith or a law.

(*Fayḍ al-Qadīr*, *ḥadīth* 3581)

Ḥadīth 96

عن الحارث الأشعري : "وَآمُرُكُمْ أَنْ تَذْكُرُوا ٱللَّهَ تَعَالَى

فَإِنَّ ذٰلِكَ مَثَلُ رَجُلٍ خَرَجَ ٱلْعَدُوُّ فِي أَثَرِهِ سِرَاعاً حَتَّى إِذَا

أَتَىَ إِلَى حِصْنٍ حَصِينٍ فَأَحْرَزَ نَفْسَهُ مِنْهُمْ كَذٰلِكَ ٱلْعَبْدُ لَا

يُحْرِزُ نَفْسَهُ مِنَ ٱلشَّيْطَانِ إِلَّا بِذِكْرِ ٱللَّهِ."

(رواه الترمذي. حديث صحيح)

Narrated al-Ḥārith al-Ashʿarī: "And I enjoin you to practice the invocation of God the Most High, for just as a soldier is not safe from the enemy pursuing him until he enters a fortress, so is the servant unprotected from Satan except through the invocation of God."

(Quoted by al-Tirmidhī. Authenticated *ḥadīth*)

Commentary

The invocation is compared here to a fortress: it repels the spiritual enemy and reintegrates the being into the inviolable Purity. The Qurʾān enjoins basically the same attitude in these terms: *Flee then unto God . . .* [123]

This *ḥadīth* therefore suggests the invocation as refuge: it is only by invoking that the will shall be able to escape the tyranny of desires, distractions and sterile thoughts. Through this attitude, the believer realizes detachment, which is a fundamental virtue for the spiritual life.

Frithjof Schuon (ʿĪsā Nūr al-Dīn)

Human nature comprises three planes: the plane of the will, the plane of love, and the plane of knowledge; each is polarized into two complementary modes, which appear, respectively, as renunciation and act, peace and fervor, discernment and union.

The will is divided in a certain sense into an affirmative mode and a negative mode, for it can only accomplish or abstain: it must either do "good" or avoid "evil." In the spiritual life, the negative attitude comes in principle before the positive or affirmative act, because the will is *a priori* entrenched in its state—natural since the fall—of passional and blind affirmation; every spritual path must start with a "conversion," an apparently negative turning round of the will, an indirect movement towards God in the form of an inner separation from the false plenitude of the world. This withdrawal corresponds to the station of renunciation or detachment, of

---

123. LI: 50.

sobriety, of fear of God: what has to be overcome is desire, passional attachment, idolatry of ephemeral things; the error of passion is proven by its connection with impurity, corruption, suffering and death. The Divine prototype of the virtue of detachment is Purity, Impassibility, Immortality; this quality, whether we envisage it *in divinis* or in ourselves, or around us, is like crystal, or snow, or the cold serenity of high mountains; in the soul the virtue of detachment is a spiritual anticipation of death and thereby a victory over it. It is fixation in instantaneity, in spiritual motionlessness, in the fear of God.

(*Stations*, pp. 191-2)

Ḥadīth 97

عن معاذ بن جبل : "سُئِلَ ﷺ أيُّ ٱلْمُجاهدينَ أَعْظَمُ أَجْراً ؟ قال أَكْثَرُهُمْ لله تبارَكَ وتَعالى ذِكْراً. فَسُئِلَ عَنْ ٱلصَّلاةِ وَٱلزَّكاةِ وَٱلحَجِّ وَٱلصَّدَقة. كُلُّ ذٰلكَ يَقولُ : أَكْثَرُهُمْ لله تَبارَكَ وتَعالى ذِكْراً. فَقالَ أَبُو بَكْرٍ لِعُمَرَ : يا أَبا حَفْصٍ ذَهَبَ ٱلذّاكِرُونَ بِكُلِّ خَيْرٍ. فَقالَ رَسولُ ٱللهِ ﷺ : أَجَل."

(رواه الإمام أحمد. حديث صحيح)

Narrated Mu'ādh ibn Jabal: "The Prophet ﷺ was asked which type of warriors would achieve the greatest reward. He replied: 'Those who invoke God the Exalted the most.' Then they asked him about prayer, the tithe, pilgrimage, almsgiving, and each time he replied: 'Those who invoke God the Exalted the most.' Then Abū Bakr said to 'Umar: 'O father of Ḥafṣa, the invokers have taken all the good.' The Messenger of God ﷺ then added: 'Precisely.'"

Ḥadīth 98

عن ابن مسعود : "ذاكِرُ ٱللهِ فِي ٱلغافِلينَ بِمَنْزِلَةِ ٱلصّابِرِ فِي ٱلفارِّينَ."

(رواه مسلم. حديث صحيح)

Narrated Ibn Mas'ūd: "Whoever practices the invocation of God amongst the heedless is akin to the person who faces up the battle amongst those who are running away."

(Quoted by Muslim. Authenticated *ḥadīth*)

Commentary

If the preceding *ḥadīth* presented invocation to us as the ultimate refuge, the first of these two *ḥadīth* presents it as the "supreme merit": It constitutes the best action or action *par excellence*. Being the struggle against the fallen soul, the invocation represents the perfection of activity and of combativeness. This is the reason why the second *ḥadīth*, to describe the *dhākir*, mentions "the person who faces the battle amongst those who are running away."

Frithjof Schuon ('Īsā Nūr al-Dīn)

The will, as we have said, must both deny and affirm: if it must deny by reason of the falsity of its habitual objects, which are impermanent, it must on the other hand affirm by reason of its positive character, which is freedom of choice. Since the spiritual act must assert itself with force against the lures of the world or of the soul which seek to engross and corrupt the will, it involves the combative virtues: decision, vigilance, perseverance . . .

What has to be actively conquered is natural and habitual passivity towards the world and towards the images and impulsions of the soul; spiritual laziness, inattention, dreaming, all have to be overcome; what gives victory is the Divine Presence which is "incarnate" as it were in the sacred act—prayer in all its forms—and thus regenerates the individual substance.

(*Stations*, pp. 192-3)

Ḥadīth 99

عن أبي سعيد الخدري : "لا يَقْعُدُ قَوْمٌ يَذْكُرُونَ ٱللهَ عَزَّ وَجَلَّ إِلاَّ حَفَّتْهُمُ ٱلْمَلائكةُ وَغَشِيَتْهُمُ ٱلرَّحْمةُ وَنَزَلَتْ عَلَيْهِمُ ٱلسَّكِينةُ وَذَكَرَهُمُ ٱللهُ فِيمَنْ عِنْدَهُ."

(رواه مسلم. حديث صحيح)

Narrated Abū Sa'īd al-Khudrī: "No group of people sits and remembers God Most High but they are surrounded by angels and enshrouded in Mercy, and there descends upon them tranquillity (*Sakīna*) as they remember God, and God mentions them to those who are near Him."

(Quoted by Muslim. Authenticated *ḥadīth*.)

Commentary

In the previous two *ḥadīth* we saw that invocation makes it possible to liberate and regenerate the will. The present *ḥadīth* mentions certain aspects of the invocation which are related to love. Like the will, love too possesses a passive mode and an active mode. The former derives from the awareness that everything we love is found infinitely in God: it therefore represents a perfection of contentment. This "passivity" ought not to be taken in the negative sense of giving up: through it, the believer is "actively passive" since it is a question of rejecting all dispersion, all dissipation, and all agitation in order to be united in love. Regarding this matter, the Qur'ān remarks:

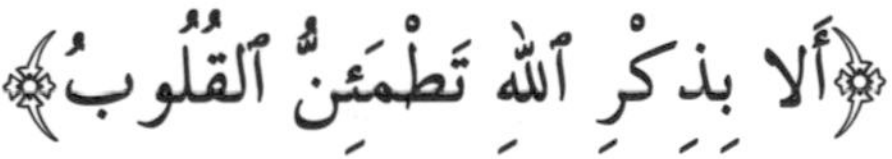

Verily in the remembrance of Allah do hearts find rest![124]

The *ḥadīth* mentions the *Sakīna*, the Tranquility that the Presence of God confers. It penetrates the heart of the believers, introducing serenity and contentment therein.

The second mode of the love of God is dynamic: it is fervor, confident faith. This will be discussed in the next *ḥadīth* and its commentaries.

Frithjof Schuon ('Īsā Nūr al-Dīn)

On the plane of love, of the affective life of the soul, we can distinguish an active mode and a passive mode, as in everything that lives. Passive virtue

124. XIII: 28.

is made of contemplative contentment, hence also of patience; it is the calm of that which rests in itself, in its own virtue; it is generous relaxation, harmony; it is repose in pure Being, equilibrium of all possibilities. This attitude loosens the knots of the soul, it removes agitation, dissipation, and the contraction which is the static counterpart of agitation; there is in it neither curiosity nor disquiet. The quality of calm derives from the Divine Peace, which is made of Beatitude, of infinite Beauty; beauty everywhere and always has at its root an aspect of calm, of existential repose, of equilibrium of possibilities; this is to say that it has an aspect of limitlessness and of happiness. The essence of the soul is beatitude; what makes us strangers to ourselves is dissipation, which casts us into destitution and ugliness, into a state of sterile dilapidation similar to shaking palsy, a disordered movement which has become a state, whereas normally it is the static which is at the basis of the dynamic and not the converse. [. . .]

It is the calm, simple and generous perfection of the pool which mirrors the depth of the sky with all its serenity; it is the beauty of the water lily, of the lotus opening to the light of the sun. It is repose in the center, resignation to Providence, quietude in God. We can distinguish in this station a gentle aspect and a stern aspect, namely the happy quietude founded on the certainty that all we love is to be found infinitely in God, and the ascetic contentment founded on the idea that God suffices us.

(*Stations*, pp. 193-4)

Ḥadīth 100

عن معاذ بن جبل : "ما عَمِلَ آدَمِيٌّ عَمَلاً قَطُّ أَنْجى لَهُ مِنْ عَذابِ ٱللهِ مِنْ ذِكْرِ ٱللهِ عَزَّ وَجَلَّ."

(رواه الإمام أحمد. حديث صحيح)

Narrated Mu'ādh ibn Jabal: "Nothing protects the son of Adam from the chastisement as much as the invocation of God."

(Quoted by Aḥmad ibn Ḥanbal. Authenticated *ḥadīth*.)

Ḥadīth 101

عن أنس بن مالك : "مَنْ ذَكَرَ ٱللهَ فَفاضَتْ عَيْناهُ مِنْ خَشْيَةِ ٱللهِ حَتّى يُصيبَ ٱلأَرْضَ مِنْ دُموعِهِ لَمْ يُعَذِّبْهُ ٱللهُ يَوْمَ ٱلقِيامةِ."

(رواه الحاكم. حديث صحيح)

Narrated Anas ibn Mālik: "Whoever invokes God and weeps out of fear of God so that his tears touch the ground, shall not be chastised on the Day of Resurrection."

(Quoted by al-Ḥākim. Authenticated *ḥadīth*.)

Commentary

The sincere and persevering invocation of God leads to certain salvation because it is a way of opening oneself to Mercy. These two *ḥadīth* affirm that nothing can protect from chastisement as the invocation, which therefore aims at increasing fervor and faith, representing the dynamic aspect of love. The "gift of tears" mentioned by the second *ḥadīth* pertains to the warmth of love which alone is capable of performing the "spiritual melting of the ego."

Frithjof Schuon ('Īsā Nūr al-Dīn)

But beside this repose in our initial equilibrium or in our existential perfection, there is a positive tendency that is converse, a "going out of oneself" in active mode; this is fervor, confident and charitable faith; it is the melting of the heart in the Divine warmth, its opening to Mercy, to essential Life, to infinite Love. Man, in his fallen state, is closed to the Mercy which seeks to save him; this is hardness of heart, indifference towards God and the neighbor, egoism, greed, mortal triviality; such triviality is as it were the inverse counterpart of hardness, it is the fragmenting of the soul amongst sterile facts, amongst their insignificant and empty multiplicity, their desiccating, drab monotony; it is the chop and change of "ordinary life" where ugliness and boredom pose as "reality." In this state, the soul is both hard like stone and pulverized like sand, it lives amongst the dead husks of things and not in the Essence which is Life and Love; it is at once hardness and dissolution. Wholly different from this dissolution is the spiritual liquefaction of the ego; this is fervor, intense unification of the movements of the soul in an upsurge of faith in the Divine Mercy [. . .]

Besides its active aspect founded on the conviction that God surely responds to our fervor, this station includes a passive aspect, founded on the melting of the heart in the Divine Warmth; there is in this second attitude as it were a noble sadness, something related to the gift of tears and the path of mystical love; it is like nostalgia for the Beauty of the Loved One. Joy and melancholy meet in fervor, as beatitude and sobriety—or hope and resignation—meet in peace.

(*Stations*, pp. 194-5)

Ḥadīth 102

عن أبي سعيد الخدري : "أَكْثِرُوا ذِكْرَ ٱللهِ تَعالَى حَتَّى يُقالَ إِنَّهُ مَجْنُون."

(رواه ابن حبان. حديث صحيح)

Narrated Abū Sa'īd al-Khudrī: "Multiply the invocation of God—exalted be He—until they say: there is a fool!"

(Quoted by Ibn Ḥibbān. Authenticated *ḥadīth*)

Commentary

For the heart of the aspirant who dedicates himself to the invocation with fervor and perseverance, [the invocation] becomes a source of light. And yet, the heart can sometimes be overwhelmed by the brightness of the Divine light and be instantly carried away by the power of God's love, which explains why this state can appear as foolishness in the eyes of a profane person.

Ibn 'Aṭā' Allāh

Know that through His Name—which we have spoken of in an earlier chapter—God illuminates the person who hears it with His Knowledge, through which God conveys inspiration and comprehension to him. The spiritual motive for which God invites to the abundant invocation of His Name, which He prefers to any other invocation—a fact demonstrating the love and high esteem that God has for His servant—is for no other reason except the meditation (*tafakkur*) on the intelligible meanings of the secrets of the Name. This is how the suns of the lights rise in the hearts and the bodies, and the invokers are rooted firmly in Knowledge, and how their love is intensified and they become God's elect. Hence, the sign of the love of God is abundant invocation . . .

As the poet said:

Repeat the invocation of His Names to me,
Polish the hearts through His light and His brightness.
Spread the blows before the souls,
They will be eager to taste this nectar.
Through this Name the world received light
The earth, the air, and the heavens.
Perplexed are the intellects of the aspirants,
Before the grandeur of His Attributes.
The hearts of the creatures are set ablaze before His brightness.
And when His majesty is unveiled to the hearts,
They receive the secret of His elevation and His clarity.

(*Qaṣd*, pp. 80-81)

Ḥadīth 103

عن أبي هريرة : "سَبَقَ ٱلْمُفْرَدُونَ. قالُوا وَما ٱلْمُفْرَدُونَ يا رَسُولَ ٱللهِ ؟ قالَ : الذَّاكِرونَ ٱللهَ كَثِيراً وٱلذَّاكِراتِ."

(رواه مسلم. حديث صحيح)

Narrated Abū Hurayra: "The Solitary ones are ahead of everybody. Someone asked: 'Who are the Solitaries, O Messenger of God?' He said: 'The (believing) men and women who practice abundantly the invocation of God."

(Quoted by Muslim. Authenticated *ḥadīth*)

Ḥadīth 104

عن أبي هريرة : "سَبَقَ ٱلْمُفْرَدُونَ. قالوا : وَما ٱلْمُفْرَدُونَ يا رَسُولَ ٱللهِ ؟ قال : الْمُسْتَهْتَرُونَ فِي ذِكْرِ ٱللهِ. يَضَعُ ٱلذِّكْرُ عَنْهُمْ أَثْقالَهُمْ فَيَأْتُونَ يَوْمَ ٱلقِيامةِ خِفافاً."

(رواه الترمذي. حديث صحيح)

Narrated Abū Hurayra: "The Solitary ones are ahead of everybody. Someone asked: 'Who are the Solitary ones, O Messenger of God?' He said: 'Those who love the invocation of God tremendously (*al-mustahtarūn*). It relieves them of the pains they suffer, and thus they meet God with their hearts at ease on the Day of Resurrection."

(Quoted by al-Tirmidhī. Authenticated *ḥadīth*.)

Commentary

The Solitary ones (*al-mufradūn*) are those who have broken away from all worldly attachments. Being dominated by nothing outward they have realized true freedom, and hence they are capable of worshipping God "in spirit and in truth." Solitude is simply the realization of detachment and of sincerity through the invocation of God. If "the Solitary ones are ahead of everybody," this is because the invocation is the "royal path" in the long journey of spiritual wayfaring. This slow and progressive realization is described with great force and beauty in this *ḥikma* of Ibn 'Aṭā' Allāh:

Do not abandon the invocation (*al-dhikr*) because you do not feel the

Presence of God therein. For your forgetfulness of the invocation of Him is worse than your forgetfulness in the invocation of Him. Perhaps He will take you from an invocation with forgetfulness (*ghafla*) to one with vigilance (*yaqaẓa*), and from one with vigilance to one with the Presence of God (*ḥuḍūr*), and from one with the Presence of God to one wherein everything but the Invoked (*al-Madhkūr*) is absent.

(*Ḥikam*, no. 44)

Ḥadīth 105

عن عبد الله بن بسر : "أَنَّ رَجُلاً قَالَ : يَا رَسُولَ ٱللّٰهِ إِنَّ شَرَائِعَ ٱلإِسْلَامِ قَدْ كَثُرَتْ عَلَيَّ فَأَخْبِرْنِي بِشَيْءٍ أَتَشَبَّثُ بِهِ. قَالَ : لَا يَزَالُ لِسَانُكَ رَطْبًا مِنْ ذِكْرِ ٱللّٰهِ."

(رواه الترمذي. حديث صحيح)

Narrated 'Abd Allāh ibn Busr: "A man asked, 'O Messenger of God, the prescriptions of the *Sharī'a* are too numerous for me: teach me something to which I can cling firmly!' The Prophet ﷺ told him: 'Let your tongue be always busy with the invocation of God.'"

(Quoted by al-Tirmidhī. Authenticated *ḥadīth*.)

Commentary

This *ḥadīth* clearly announces the primacy of the remembrance or invocation of God (*dhikr Allāh*). Without abolishing the prescriptions of the *Sharī'a*, this *ḥadīth* puts them into perspective by recalling the essential in the path to God. Because it actualizes the Presence of the Invoked, invocation is the royal path towards knowledge: both of the inner reality of man and of God.

Ibn 'Aṭā' Allāh

If He opens a door for you, thereby making Himself known, pay no heed if your deeds do not measure up to this. For, in truth, He has not opened it for you but out of a desire to make Himself known to you. Do you not know that He is the one who has presented the knowledge of Himself (*ta'arruf*) to you, whereas you are the one who presented Him with deeds? What a difference between what He brings to you and what you present to Him!

(*Ḥikam*, no. 8)

Frithjof Schuon ('Īsā Nūr al-Dīn)

In Islam, the implicit doctrine of the Name of God is Unity; Unity must be understood to mean that God is the Absolute and that there is but one Absolute; that it is this global aspect of evidentness or of absoluteness which "unifies," that is to say transmutes and delivers. He who says Allāh says "there is no Truth or Absolute but the one Truth, the one Absolute" (to paraphrase the Shahāda: *Lā ilāha illā 'Llāh*), or in Vedantic terms: "The world is false, Brahma is real"; or again: "Nothing is evident, if not the Absolute." And this amounts to saying that Islam takes its starting point not in our fallen, passional nature, but in the theomorphic, inalterable character of our humanity, that is, in what distinguishes us from animals, namely objective and in principle limitless intelligence. Now the normal content of the intelligence—that for which it is made—is the Absolute-Infinite; in a word, man is intelligence at once integral and transcendent, horizontal and vertical, and the essential content of this intelligence is at the same time our Deliverance; man is delivered by consciousness of the Absolute, his salvation is the remembrance of God.

(*Stations*, pp. 180-181)

Ḥadīth 106

عن ابن عباس : "ما مِنْ صَدَقةٍ أَفْضَلُ مِنْ ذِكْرِ ٱللهِ تَعالَى."

(رواه الطبراني. حديث حسن)

Narrated Ibn 'Abbās: "There is no better alms than the invocation of God the Exalted."

(Quoted by al-Ṭabarānī. Validated *ḥadīth*)

Commentary

Alms (*ṣadaqa*) are considered a form of generosity primarily for the needy; in general it pertains to providing for basic needs. This *ḥadīth* emphasizes that the invocation (*dhikr*), despite being immaterial, constitutes alms *par excellence*. How can such an affirmation be understood since the invocation distances the invoker from others and centers the soul exclusively upon God?

Frithjof Schuon ('Īsā Nūr al-Dīn)

No "egoism" is possible in the attitude of the pure contemplative, for his "I" is the world, the "neighbor." What is realized in the microcosm radiates in the macrocosm, by reason of the analogy between all the cosmic orders. Spiritual realization is a kind of "magic," which necessarily communicates itself to its surroundings. The equilibrium of the world has need of contemplatives.[125]

To lose oneself for God is always to give oneself to men.

(*Perspectives*, p. 280)

125. It is a question of a relative equilibrium consonant with particular cyclic conditions. St. John of the Cross said that "a spark of pure love is more precious to God, more useful for the soul and more rich in blessings for the Church than all other works taken together, even if to all appearances one does nothing."

Ḥadīth 107

عن أبي سعيد الخدري : "يَقُولُ ٱللهُ عَزَّ وَجَلَّ يَوْمَ ٱلْقِيامة : سَيُعْلَمُ أَهْلُ ٱلْجَمْعِ مِنْ أَهْلِ ٱلْكَرَمِ. فَقيلَ : وَمَنْ أَهْلُ ٱلْكَرَمِ ؟ فقالَ : أَهْلُ مَجالِسِ ٱلذِّكْرِ."

(رواه الإمام أحمد. حديث حسن)

Narrated Abū Sa'īd al-Khudrī: "God will say on the Day of Resurrection: 'A distinction will be made between the common folk and the folk of nobility.' They shall ask: 'Who are the folk of nobility?' He will answer: 'Those who participated in sessions of invocation.'"

(Quoted by Aḥmad ibn Ḥanbal. Validated *ḥadīth*)

Ḥadīth 108

عن أبي الدرداء : "الَّذينَ لا تَزالُ أَلْسِنَتُهُمْ رَطْبَةً مِنْ ذِكْرِ ٱللهِ يَدْخُلُ أَحَدُهُمْ ٱلْجَنَّةَ وَهُوَ يَضْحَك."

(رواه السيوطي. حديث حسن)

Narrated Abū al-Dardā': "Those persons whose tongues remain wet due to their constant invocation of God will enter Paradise laughing."

(Quoted by al-Suyūṭī. Validated *ḥadīth*)

Commentary

We have already seen the distinction between the common people, the elite, and the elite of the elite. The first *ḥadīth* mentions the distinction between exoterism and esoterism by means of two other expressions: "the common generality" (*ahl al-jam'*) and "the folk of nobility" or generosity (*ahl al-karam*). Again, the path of invocation is what characterizes esoterism.

The second *ḥadīth,* on the other hand, emphasizes that the invocation shall facilitate what will be experienced as "the terrible anxiety before the Judgment" by creatures. The laughing of the folk of invocation can be interpreted as a "holy carefreeness" and a total confidence in the Divine Mercy.

Ḥadīth 109

عن أبي هريرة : "قال الله تعالى : أَنا عِنْدَ ظَنِّ عَبْدي بي وَأَنا مَعَهُ إِذا ذَكَرَني فَإِنْ ذَكَرَني في نَفْسِهِ ذَكَرْتُهُ في نَفْسي وَإِنْ ذَكَرَني في مَلَأ ذَكَرْتُهُ في مَلَأ خَيْرٍ مِنْهُمْ، وَإِنْ تَقَرَّبَ إِلَيَّ بِشِبْرٍ تَقَرَّبْتُ إِلَيْهِ ذِراعاً، وَإِنْ تَقَرَّبَ إِلَيَّ ذِراعاً تَقَرَّبْتُ إِلَيْهِ باعاً، وَإِنْ أَتاني يَمْشي أَتَيْتُهُ هَرْوَلَة."

(رواه البخاري. حديث صحيح)

Narrated Abū Hurayra: "God Most High has said: 'I am with My slave's opinion of Me, and I am with him if He remembers Me. If he remembers Me in himself, I too, remember him in Myself; and if he remembers Me in a group of people, I remember him in a group that is better than they; and if he comes one span nearer to Me, I go one cubit nearer to him; and if he comes one cubit nearer to Me, I go a distance of two outstretched arms nearer to him; and if he comes to Me walking, I go to him running.'"

(Quoted by al-Bukhārī. Authenticated *ḥadīth*)

Commentary

This *ḥadīth* sets out, through a series of eloquent images, a crucial principle of the spiritual life: that of mystical reciprocity. This reciprocity is a fundamental key to understanding the link between the approach of man and the action of God in response. The initiative must come from man—at least apparently—and the response of God always surpasses what man's efforts may deserve.

Frithjof Schuon ('Īsā Nūr al-Dīn)

In fact, what separates man from Divine Reality is but a thin partition: God is infinitely close to man, but man is infinitely far from God. This partition, for man, is a mountain; man stands in front of a mountain that he must remove with his own hands. He digs away the earth, but in vain; the mountain remains. Man, however, goes on digging, in the Name of God. And the mountain vanishes. It was never there.

(*Echoes*, p. 10)

Ḥadīth 110

عن معاوية : " وَإِنَّ رَسُولَ ٱللَّه ﷺ خَرَجَ عَلَى حَلْقَةٍ مِنْ
أَصْحَابِه فَقَالَ : مَا أَجْلَسَكُمْ ؟ قَالُوا : جَلَسْنَا نَذْكُرُ ٱللَّهَ
وَنَحْمَدُهُ عَلَى مَا هَدَانَا لِلإِسْلاَمِ وَمَنَّ بِهِ عَلَيْنَا. قَالَ : آللَّهِ
مَا أَجْلَسَكُمْ إِلاَّ ذَاكَ ؟ قَالُوا : وَٱللَّهِ مَا أَجْلَسَنَا إِلاَّ ذَاكَ.
قَالَ : أَمَا إِنِّي لَمْ أَسْتَحْلِفْكُمْ تُهْمَةً لَكُمْ وَلَكِنَّهُ أَتَانِي
جِبْرِيلُ فَأَخْبَرَنِي أَنَّ ٱللَّهَ عَزَّ وَجَلَّ يُبَاهِي بِكُمُ ٱلْمَلاَئِكَةَ. "

(رواه مسلم. حديث صحيح)

Narrated Abū Saʿīd al-Khudrī:"The Messenger of God ﷺ went out to the circle of his Companions and said: 'What makes you sit (here)?' They said: 'We are sitting here in order to remember God and to praise Him for He hath guided us to the path of Islam and He hath conferred favors upon us.' Thereupon he adjured by God and asked if that was the only purpose of their sitting there. They said: 'By God, we are not sitting here but for this very purpose,' whereupon he said: 'I am not asking you to take an oath because of any allegation against you but for the fact that Gabriel came to me and he informed me that God, the Exalted and Glorious, was talking to the angels about your magnificence.'"

(Quoted by Muslim. Authenticated *ḥadīth*.)

Commentary

This *ḥadīth* is often quoted to support the fact that invocation sessions existed in the time of the Prophet, and though not established by him, they were nonetheless confirmed and encouraged.

Shaykh al-ʿAlawī

So is this not sufficient for you with regard to the permissibility of the session of invocation during the time of Prophet ﷺ? As for ʿUmar ibn al-Khaṭṭāb, it is said that he too encouraged his companions to invoke until they would grow tired, then directed them to some other activity.

(*Lettre*, p. 43)

Ḥadīth 111

عن أنس بن مالك : "إِذا مَرَرْتُمْ بِرِياضِ ٱلْجَنَّةِ فَٱرْتَعُوا.
قالُوا : وَما رِياضُ ٱلْجَنَّة ؟ قالَ : حِلَقُ ٱلذِّكْرِ."

(رواه الترمذي. حديث صحيح)

Narrated Anas ibn Mālik: "'If you walk through the gardens of Paradise, satiate yourselves!' They asked him: 'What are the gardens of Paradise?' He said: 'The circles of invocation.'"

(Quoted by al-Tirmidhī. Authenticated *ḥadīth*)

Commentary

The principal image of this *ḥadīth* is that of spiritual nourishment. It is known that amongst the delights of the gardens of Paradise, mentioned by the Qur'ān, are the appetizing delicacies. Since the circles of invocation are compared to the gardens in Paradise, they must also nourish the invoker, satiating him and thus satisfying "the thirst and hunger" which characterize every veritable aspiration. Hence the use of the word *rata'a*, meaning feasting and eating well.

al-Munāwī

"Satiate yourselves": Eat as much as you want and seek the graces . . .

"The circles of invocation": According to Ṭayyibī, they denote circles wherein God's glory and praises are proclaimed. Dedication to the invocation has been compared to a feast because the most precious thing God can give to His servant in this world is the invocation, just as the most precious gift of God in the Hereafter is the vision of His Face—exalted be He. Yet, the invocation of God in the here-below is comparable to the vision of the Face of God in the Hereafter. Thus, he who invokes God by the tongue with a present heart contemplates Him in the intimacy (*sirr*) of his heart and sees Him by his inner conscience (*fu'ād*): it is as if he received the delights of Paradise. Al-Nawawī has said: "Just as the invocation is recommended, so is the company of the folk of the invocation, and there are many textual proofs (*adilla*) of this matter."

(*Fayḍ al-Qadīr*, *ḥadīth* 859)

Ḥadīth 112

عن عبد الله بن عمرو : "قُلْتُ : يا رَسولَ الله ما غَنيمةُ مَجالِسِ ٱلذِّكْرِ؟ قالَ : غَنيمةُ مَجالِسِ ٱلذِّكْرِ ٱلْجَنَّةُ."

(رواه الإمام أحمد. حديث صحيح)

Narrated 'Abd Allāh ibn 'Amr: "I asked the Prophet, 'O Messenger of God, what is the recompense for the sessions of invocation?' He said: 'The recompense for the sessions of invocation is Paradise.'"

(Quoted by Aḥmad ibn Ḥanbal. Authenticated *ḥadīth.*)

Commentary

The sessions of invocation (*majālis al-dhikr*) are described as gardens of Paradise even in the here-below, as underlined in the previous *ḥadīth*. The present *ḥadīth* affirms that the celestial recompense of the sessions of invocation can be none other than Paradise itself. The term expressing the idea of reward in this *ḥadīth* is *ghanīma* which belongs to the semantic field of battling, and whose first meaning is the booty, the prey of war. This evidently evokes the greater *jihād*, the struggle against the negative tendencies of the ego.

Shaykh al-Darqāwī

It is said that through the invocation of God (*dhikr Allāh*) the believer attains such peace of soul that the great terror in the day of resurrection cannot distress him; how much less can he then be disturbed by the trials and setbacks he faces in this world? Hold fast then to the invocation of your Lord, my brother, as we have told you to, and you will see miracles (that God bestows on us through His grace). And yet, in our eyes the invocation does not consist in man always saying: Allāh, Allāh, in praying and fasting; and when misfortune strikes him, he looks for remedies everywhere and is afraid he will not find them. For those who have realized the Truth (may God be content with them), invocation requires that the invoker conform to rigorously prescribed laws, the most important of which is always abandoning what does not concern him. Then if his Lord becomes known to him, or shall we say, if He reveals Himself to him through one of His Names of Majesty or of Beauty,[126] he will recognize Him and he will not ignore Him. This, indeed, is the veritable invocation for those who invoke God, and not the state of the person who is continuously occupied with the cult of God and who, when his Lord reveals Himself to him in some form

126. Or of Rigor (*jalāl*) and Beauty (*jamāl*).

which is contrary to his desire, does not recognize Him at all. Therefore understand what God teaches us, Amen. And remain firm in patience with God, for He—exalted be He—will cover your weakness with His might, your abasement with His glory, your poverty with His richness, your impotence with His strength, your ignorance with His knowledge, your anger with His clemency, and so on, so that you will taste the eternal life in this world before dying. The reality of this life has not been hidden from you, since God says about those who are in it: *And We will remove whatever rancour may be in their breasts. As brethren, face to face, (they will rest) on couches raised. Toil cometh not unto them there, nor will they be expelled from thence.*[127]

(*Rasā'il*, letter no. 37; *Lettres d'un maître*, pp. 93-94)

127. XV: 47-48.

Remembrance of Death: ذكر الموت

Ḥadīth 113

عن ابن عمر : "أَكْثِرُوا مِنْ ذِكْرِ هاذمِ ٱللَّذَّاتِ : الْمَوْتُ."

(رواه الترمذي. حديث صحيح)

Narrated Ibn 'Umar: "Multiply the occasions to remember that which puts an end to the ephemeral pleasures: death."

(Quoted by al-Tirmidhī. Authenticated *ḥadīth*)

Commentary

The awareness that each day that passes brings us inexorably closer to death allows an inner detachment from worldly pleasures. Indeed, realizing the ephemeral character and the impermanence of all things enables us to not be defeated by trials and to keep a sense of proportion in each and every situation.

al-Ghazzālī

Know that a man who is absorbed (*munhamik*) by the distractions of the here-below, and who lets himself be deluded, and takes pleasure in the appetites (*shahawāt*), can only have a heart which is exempt from any remembrance of death: when he is reminded of it, he becomes tense and moves away. God has said about this kind of people: *Say (unto them, O Muḥammad): Lo! the death from which ye shrink will surely meet you, and afterward ye will be returned unto the Knower of the Invisible and the Visible, and He will tell you what ye used to do.*[128]

Also know that there are three categories of men: the man absorbed by his distractions, the novice who repents (*tā'ib mubtadi'*), and the accomplished gnostic (*'ārif muntahin*):

The man absorbed by distractions does not remember death at all, and when he does, it is while regretting bitterly the here-below. The reminder of death only distances such a man from God.

The repenting person remembers death frequently so that it may give rise to fear in his heart and that he may fully realize repentance. If death frightens him, this is because he fears that he may die before his repentance is realized and before he can prepare himself for the Hereafter. His apprehension of death is therefore legitimate and is not found in those about

128. LXII: 8.

whom the Prophet ﷺ has said: "Whoever detests meeting God, God detests meeting him."[129] In reality, such a man detests neither death nor the encounter with God but rather he fears he may be unworthy due to his shortcomings. He is therefore comparable to the person who, having encountered the beloved, falls behind because he prepares and wants to appear in his most beautiful shape. The sign of this state is that the repenting person must occupy himself exclusively with the encounter with God, otherwise he joins with the category of those absorbed by this world.

As for the gnostic, he always remembers death, for he is ready to meet his Beloved: the lover does not forget for a single moment the promised encounter with the beloved. The gnostic generally finds death to be slow in coming: he would like it to occur in order to leave this world of impiety and to be near the Lord of the worlds. The following words have been narrated from Ḥudhayfa, which were uttered by him when death was near: "The beloved is coming while I am destitute, but I regret nothing of this world: My God, if Thou knowest that poverty is better for me than wealth, that sickness is better for me than health, and that death is better for me than life, make my death easier so that I can encounter Thee!"

Just as the repenting person is not capable of apprehending death, so is the gnostic capable of wishing for it. But beyond these two attitudes is that which consists in leaving the matter in the hands of God by choosing neither life nor death. This means making God's choices one's own. Such a degree cannot be realized except through total love of God and through the realization of the station of submission (*taslīm*) and that of contentment (*riḍā*): these are the supreme degrees.

(*Iḥyā'*, IV, p. 434)

---

129. Related by Abū Hurayra, quoted by al-Bukhārī.

Ḥadīth 114

عن جابر : "يُبْعَثُ كُلُّ عَبْدٍ عَلَى ما ماتَ عَلَيْه."

(رواه مسلم. حديث صحيح)

Narrated Jābir: "Every person will be resurrected in the state in which death caught him."

(Quoted by Muslim. Authenticated *ḥadīth.*)

Commentary

This *ḥadīth* clearly expresses the reasons for which the last instants of one's life are so important for the believer. Ultimately, all the spiritual efforts made in this life can be considered as a preparation for death: the spiritual state in which death seizes the believer will determine his life in the Hereafter. In the commentary of the previous *ḥadīth* we cited the distinctions al-Ghazzālī makes in the awareness of the illusory character of the here-below: that which distinguishes the repenting novice (*tā'ib mubtadi'*) from the accomplished gnostic (*'ārif muntahin*)—the only one who has truly prepared for death—is the degree of the spiritual awakening or exit from both the cosmic and egocentric illusion. For the spiritual masters, overcoming this illusion is the true preparation for death.

al-Ghazzālī

Just as in God's creation the eyelids constitute a veil which must be lifted in order for vision to be possible, bodies, appetites and earthly tendencies also veil the soul. Indeed, the soul cannot contemplate and attain realities that surpass the faculty of imagination (*khayāl*).[130] This life is a veil for the soul just as eyelids are veils for the eyes . . .

While the veil of this life is lifted at death, the soul is still sullied by the impurity of the here-below: it is not liberated at once even in the other world. [At the moment of death, souls are in one of the following two situations]:

> Souls dominated by vice (*khubth*) and rust: they are similar to a mirror eroded by impurities which then becomes useless and impossible to polish. These are the people who are veiled from their Lord forever—may God protect us from it!
>
> Souls which, having not been totally covered by rust, can still be purified and polished: they will have to be submitted to the Fire in order for the impurities to be removed from them. The duration of this passing through the Fire depends on the degree of purification which this

130. A few lines before, al-Ghazzālī explains that this faculty can only perceive that which is of a formal order: the bodies having colors and forms.

> soul needs: for the believer this varies from an instant to seven thousand years, according to the *ḥadīth.* And yet no soul leaves this world without taking with itself some impurity, even if minute. This is why the Most High has said: *There is not one of you but shall approach it. That is a fixed ordinance of thy Lord. Then We shall rescue those who kept from evil, and leave the evil-doers crouching there.*[131]

After God has purified the soul, it will be exempt of all stain (*kudūrāt*) . . . At that moment the Real—exalted be He—should shine forth (*yatajallā*) for it. This theophany will be for the soul an additional unveiling with respect to the imaginal knowledge of God it had before . . .

The beatific vision is therefore a reality but it should not be understood in the sense of a perfection of the imaginal faculty and of its representations conditioned by form and space, because the Lord of the lords is too elevated for that . . .

I must further add that gnosis (*ma'rifa*) that has been reached on earth will be perfected and it will attain the perfect unveiling: it will become pure contemplation. And yet, there is no distinction between the gnosis realized on earth and contemplation in the Hereafter, except the higher degree of clarity and unveiling of the latter.

(*Iḥyā'*, IV, pp. 303-304)

Frithjof Schuon ('Īsā Nūr al-Dīn)

Life is the passage of an individual dream, a consciousness, an ego, through a cosmic and collective dream. Death withdraws the particular dream from the general dream and tears out the roots which the former has sent down into the latter. The universe is a dream woven of dreams; the Self alone is awake.

The objective homogeneity of the world proves, not its absolute reality, but the collective nature of the illusion, or of a particular illusion, a particular world.

For the ego the world is not a subjective state, it is an objective and polyvalent reality; but for the Divine Self the world—or a particular world—is a subjective unity like a particular soul. When the intellect, which is as it were hidden within us and in which we can participate under certain conditions of realization and of grace, has seen the Self and has penetrated us with this vision, then the world will appear to us as an uncertain and fugitive substance—and thus as a dream—and it is our spiritual consciousness that will be revealed as polyvalent and stable; call it realization, grace, knowledge, or what you will.

(*Perspectives*, p. 228)

131. XIX: 71-72.

Ḥadīth 115

عن أنس بن مالك : "...ما أَنْتُم بِأَسْمَعَ بِما أَقُولُ مِنْهُمْ غَيْرَ أَنَّهُمْ لا يَسْتَطِيعُونَ أَنْ يَرُدُّوا عَلَيَّ شَيْئاً."

(رواه البخاري. حديث صحيح)

Narrated Anas ibn Mālik: " . . . you do not hear what I say any better than [the dead] do, but they cannot reply."

(Quoted by al-Bukhārī. Authenticated *ḥadīth*.)

Commentary

As this *ḥadīth* shows, the Prophet ﷺ knew the posthumous states of the deceased and would sometimes speak about them to the Companions. According to al-Ghazzālī, this knowledge is the privilege of the prophets, but some saints can also be granted the same privilege.

al-Ghazzālī

Know that the lights of spiritual perception (*baṣīra*) when they are nourished by the Book of God, the Sunna of the Prophet ﷺ and the methodic meditation (*minhāj al-i'tibār*) make known for us the posthumous states of the dead in their generality. It is thus realized that amongst deceased persons there are those who are damned (*ashqiyā'*) and those who are happy (*su'adā'*). However, in principle, the particular state of an individual is not known . . . this knowledge is not accessible except through precise unveiling on the state of the being under consideration. In fact, when someone dies, he passes from the terrestrial and visible realm to the celestial and hidden world; he cannot be seen by the physical eye; he can nevertheless be seen by another eye placed in the heart of every man. Unfortunately, most men cover their hearts with the thick veils of concupiscent desires and distractions of this world: that is why the deceased are not seen by this eye. Nothing from the celestial world can be seen as long as the veils of the eye of the heart are not lifted. Since these veils were lifted for the prophets, nothing prevents them from perceiving that which is in the heavens, from contemplating their marvels, from seeing the dead and informing the living concerning them. This is how the Messenger of God ﷺ saw the grave squeeze Sa'd ibn Mu'ādh or his daughter Zaynab; he also saw that Jābir was put before God with no veil separating them.

Such contemplation is only granted to the prophets and to the saints whose degree is nearest to the prophets. As for us, the only accessible contemplation is weaker and of another kind, which is not a prophetic contemplation. I am alluding to contemplation during sleep, which is part of the light of prophethood (*anwār al-nubuwwa*). This is why the Messenger of God ﷺ said: "Pious [oneiric] vision is one forty-sixth of prophethood." This vision, too, is only obtained through the removal of the veils of the heart, and only the dreams of pious and sincere men can be given credit."

(*Iḥyā'*, IV, p. 488)

Ḥadīth 116

عن ابن مسعود : "كُنْتُ نَهَيْتُكُمْ عَنْ زِيارَةِ ٱلقُبُورِ فَزُورُوها فَإِنَّها تُزْهِدُ فِي ٱلدُّنْيا وَتُذَكِّرُ ٱلآخِرة."

(رواه ابن ماجه. حديث حسن)

Narrated Ibn Mas'ūd: "I had forbidden you to visit graves. From now on, do so, for it enables you to detach yourselves from the world and is a reminder of the Hereafter."

(Quoted by Ibn Mājah. Validated *ḥadīth.*)

Commentary

The reminder of death is recommended in this *ḥadīth* in order to support two fundamental components of the spiritual path: detachment (*zuhd*) from the things of this world and the inner attraction of celestial realities (*al-ākhira*). In this sense, visiting the tombs of saints contributes to liberating the soul from the gravity of earthly ambience.

al-Ghazzālī

Know that death is terrifying and it exposes the soul to terrible dangers; people forget this because they scarcely meditate about it. And when someone remembers death, it is done through a heart which is distracted and imprisoned with worldly desires! Under these conditions, the reminder of death cannot affect the heart.

The reminder of death is practiced by emptying one's heart from everything and by keeping nothing else in the mind; thus whoever prepares himself for a journey in dangerous lands or for crossing a tempestuous sea will apprehend the day of departure. When the reminder of death has impregnated the heart, this reminder will start to influence it, the heart will then lose all superficiality and worldly delight.

(*Iḥyā'*, IV, p. 436)

Frithjof Schuon ('Īsā Nūr al-Dīn)

The first thought capable of delivering man from earthly attachments is that of death, and more generally—and correlatively—that of the ephemeral character of all things. This meditation, which also implies the idea of suffering, and which is intimately linked to the attitude of renunciation, sheds light on a fundamental aspect of our existence; it can therefore serve as the basis and the symbol for a spiritual realization, despite its apparently negative character which is necessarily compensated by a positive aspect: indeed, to withdraw from the world is to open oneself to the Divine Ray, it is to be disposed to know the Eternity of God; to flee from the impurity of the created is to take refuge in the Purity of the Uncreated; to leave suffering is to enter into Beatitude.

(*Eye of the Heart*, p. 149)

Ḥadīth 117

عن معاذ بن جبل : "لَيْسَ يَتَحَسَّرُ أَهْلُ ٱلْجَنَّةِ عَلى شَيْءٍ إِلاّ عَلى ساعةٍ مَرَّتْ بِهِمْ لَمْ يَذْكُروا ٱللهَ سُبْحانَهُ فِيها."

(رواه الطبراني. حديث حسن)

Narrated Mu'ādh ibn Jabal: "The inhabitants of Paradise do not regret anything except the moments during which they did not invoke God."

(Quoted by al-Ṭabarānī. Validated *ḥadīth*)

Commentary

The verb *taḥassara* expresses the idea of a bitter and painful regret. In this *ḥadīth*, the regret is not having realized enough the importance of the invocation (*dhikr*) enough during this life. For al-Ghazzālī, the obstacles preventing the heart from evaluating things according to their true value and from knowing their profound nature are linked to distractions and dispersion in all forms (*shawāghil*).

al-Ghazzālī

After death, certain realities are unveiled to man which were veiled to him in this life, just as that which was veiled to a man during sleep is unveiled to him upon waking up: "People are asleep: when they die, they wake up." The first thing to be unveiled to man in the Hereafter is that which was harmful or beneficial in the actions he performed. In this life, even though this will be delivered in a "book" which is placed in the secret of man's heart, the latter has no access to it due to the distractions of this world (*shawāghil al-dunyā*). Upon death, these distractions no longer exist and all his actions appear to him as they are . . . and this is the meaning of the verse: *Read thy book. Thy soul sufficeth as reckoner against thee this day.*[132]

(*Iḥyā'*, IV, p. 478)

Frithjof Schuon ('Īsā Nūr al-Dīn)

What is the world, if not a flow of forms, and what is life if not a cup which seemingly is emptied between one night and another? And what is prayer, if not the sole stable point—a point of peace and light—in this dream universe, and the straight gate leading to all that the world and life have sought in vain? In the life of a man, these four certitudes are all: the present moment, death, the encounter with God, eternity. Death is an exit, a world which closes down; the meeting with God is like an opening towards a fulgurating and immutable infinitude; eternity is a fullness of being in pure light; and

132. XVII: 14.

the present moment is, in our duration, an almost ungraspable "place" where we are already eternal—a drop of eternity amid the ceaseless shiftings of forms and melodies. Prayer gives to the terrestrial instant its full weight of the eternal and its Divine value; it is the sacred boat bearing us through life and death, towards the further shore, towards the silence of light; but at bottom it is not prayer which traverses time as it repeats itself, it is time which, so to speak, stops before the already celestial unicity of prayer.

(*Echoes*, p. 116)

al-Ghazzālī

Above all, do not think that the spiritual knowledge (*ma'rifa*) of the Prophet ﷺ is reducible to the imitation (*taqlīd*) of Gabriel. In fact, your knowledge is nothing but an imitation which has not achieved the spiritual nature of the knowledge of the Prophet . . .

Imitation is not spiritual knowledge, it is a conforming practice and creed (*i'tiqād ṣaḥīḥ*). And yet, the prophets are gnostics. Their gnosis consists in the fact that the reality of things was unveiled to them as it is: they were able to contemplate it through the inner eye (*baṣīra bāṭina*), just as you perceive external objects through the physical eye. The prophets therefore teach what they have contemplated and not what they have heard or received from others. Thus the reality of the Spirit was unveiled to them: through this they realized that the Spirit belongs to the Command of God the Most High . . .

He who knows the secret of the Spirit knows his soul and whoever knows his soul knows his Lord. Therefore he who knows his soul and his Lord realizes, in his profound being and his original nature (*fiṭra*), a Divine reality (*amr rabbānī*). Then he knows that he is a stranger in the corporeal world and that his descent in this world is not in agreement with his essential nature, but was caused by a circumstance foreign to his essence. This foreign circumstance survived in Adam, and it is denoted by the term sin (*ma'ṣiyya*). It was the cause for the descent from Paradise. And yet, only the latter is truly in harmony with Adam, Paradise is in reality the abode of nearness to God, and Adam was a Divine reality. The desire to be near his Lord is therefore natural and essential in man. But a foreign world distances him from his own essence; he forgets himself and forgets his Lord. Each time man acts in this way, he wrongs his own soul, and this is why he was told, *And be not ye as those who forgot God, therefore He caused them to forget their souls. Such are the evil-doers*[133] that is to say, those who have strayed from their nature and have forsaken their true homeland . . .

All of this is an allusion to the mysteries whose premises suffice to shake the gnostics, but whose terms freeze the hearts of limited men (*qāṣirūn*).

(*Iḥyā'*, III, p. 371)

---

133. LIX: 19.

God and His Attributes: الله وصفاته

Ḥadīth 118

عن عمران بن حصين : "كَانَ ٱللهُ وَلَمْ يَكُنْ شَيْءٌ غَيْرُهُ وَكَانَ عَرْشُهُ عَلَى ٱلْماءِ وَكَتَبَ فِي ٱلذِّكْرِ كُلَّ شَيْءٍ وَخَلَقَ ٱلسَّماواتِ وَٱلأَرْضَ."

(رواه البخاري. حديث صحيح)

Narrated 'Imrān ibn Ḥuṣayn: "[Before the creation] God was, and there was nothing with Him: He created His Throne and placed it on water; He wrote all the things in the Reminder, and He created the heavens and the earth."

(Quoted by al-Bukhārī. Authenticated *ḥadīth*.)

Commentary

In order to clarify the metaphysical meaning of this *ḥadīth*, the spiritual masters often add, "And it is now as it was then" after the first words. This is what Ibn 'Aṭā' Allāh has done in a *ḥikma*:[134] "God was and there was nothing with Him, and He is now as He was." For Ibn al-'Arabī this addition is superfluous and it risks concealing the non-temporal meaning of the Arabic word *kāna*:

Ibn al-'Arabī

What is the meaning of this saying of the Prophet ﷺ: "God is, and nothing is with Him . . . "?

Answer: He is not accompanied by thingness, nor do we ascribe it to Him. Such is He, and there is no thing with Him. The negation of thingness from Him is one of His essential attributes, just as is the negation of "withness" (*ma'iyya*) from things. He is with the things, but the things are not with Him, since "withness" follows from knowledge: He knows us, so He is with us. We do not know Him, so we are not with Him.

Know that the word *kāna* denotes a temporal limitation [since it is a past tense form—and is usually translated as "was"]. But in this saying that limitation is not meant. What is meant by the word is the "being" (*kawn*) which is existence (*wujūd*). The word is therefore used in its ontological

---

134. Cf. *Ḥikam*, no. 34.

meaning and not its temporal meaning. This is the reason why the following saying reported by the literalists (*'ulamā' al-rusūm*) amongst the theologians (*mutakallimūn*) is not from the Prophet: "He is now as He was then." This addition in the *ḥadīth* testifies to the ignorance of science pertaining to the term *kāna* . . . In the same [i.e., ontological] sense we have in the Qur'ān, "God is (*kāna*) All-pardoning, All-forgiving" (4:99), and other instances where the word *kāna* is employed.

(*Fut.*, XII, pp. 168-170 [O.Y.])

Ḥadīth 119

عن أبي هريرة : "إِنَّ ٱللهَ تَعالَى لَمَّا خَلَقَ ٱلْخَلْقَ كَتَبَ بِيَدِهِ عَلَى نَفْسِهِ : إِنَّ رَحْمَتِي تَغْلِبُ غَضَبِي."

(رواه الترمذي. حديث صحيح)

Narrated Abū Hurayra: "When God the Most High created the world, He wrote: 'Verily, My mercy precedes My wrath.'"

(Quoted by al-Tirmidhī. Authenticated *ḥadīth*)

Commentary

The primacy of Divine mercy is an aspect of its universality: if it precedes wrath, this is because it encompasses all things, as affirmed by the Qur'ān: *And My mercy encompasses all things*.[135] This is why it is worth underlining that Divine wrath must not be understood as an absence of mercy—which may be the case for human wrath—since nothing is excluded from it. Divine wrath is but a particular form that mercy takes in the hands of whomever strays from the Divine norm.

Ibn al-'Arabī

When an individual becomes wrathful for a reason related to his soul, his wrath does not involve any kind of mercy. But if he becomes wrathful for God, then his wrath is that of God. However, God's wrath is never exempt from Divine mercy. His wrath in this world is represented by what He has instituted as corporal punishments and sanctions; His wrath in the Hereafter is represented by the chastisements of those who shall enter Hell. God's wrath is therefore purification since it is blended with mercy in this life and the life to come. It is so because, having precedence over wrath in this world, mercy embraces the entire universe and extends to everything. When wrath occurs in this world, it finds mercy already there preceding it. And yet, since it must occur in this world, wrath has no other choice but to blend with mercy, like milk and water: the former is never exempt from water! Similarly, [Divine] wrath is never exempt from mercy. The latter has authority over wrath because it is the "mistress of both abodes." Thus God's wrath with respect to those who have deserved it will eventually be extinguished, but His mercy is infinite.

(*Fut.*, III, p. 333)

135. VII: 156.

Ḥadīth 120

عن أبي موسى الأشعري : "إنَّ ٱللهَ لا يَنامُ وَلا يَنْبَغي لَهُ أَنْ يَنام... حِجابُهُ ٱلنُّورُ : لَوْ كَشَفَهُ لأَحْرَقَتْ سُبُحاتُ وَجْهِهِ ما ٱنْتَهى إِلَيْهِ بَصَرُهُ مِنْ خَلْقِهِ."

(رواه مسلم. حديث صحيح)

Narrated Abū Mūsā al-Ash'arī: "Verily the Exalted and Mighty God does not sleep, and it does not befit Him to sleep. His veil is light. Were He to withdraw it (the veil), the splendour of His countenance would consume His creation as far as His sight reaches."

(Quoted by Muslim. Authenticated *ḥadīth*.)

Commentary

There are other versions of this *ḥadīth* that mention "sixty-six," "seven hundred," or "seventy thousand" veils of light and darkness. It is this last version that al-Ghazzālī chooses to comment upon:

> I explain it thus. God manifests Himself and to Himself. Therefore there could only be a veil in relation to a being who is "veiled." Now, amongst men, these are of three kinds, in accordance with their veils: pure darkness, mixed darkness and light, or pure light.
>
> The subdivisions of these three are numerous . . . My clearest opinion, however, is that these numbers [in the *ḥadīth*] are not mentioned in the way of definite enumeration at all, for numbers are not infrequently mentioned without any intention of limitation, but rather to denote some indefinitely great quantity—and God knows best!
>
> 1. Those veiled by Pure Darkness
>
> These are the atheists: *who believe not in God, nor the Last Day.*[136] These are: *they who love this present life more than that which is to come,*[137] for they do not believe in that which is to come at all. [. . .]
>
> 2. Those veiled by mixed Light and Darkness
>
> The second division consists of those who are veiled by mixed light and darkness. It includes three main kinds: first, those whose darkness has its origin in the senses (*ḥiss*); second, in the imagination (*khayāl*); third, in false syllogisms of the intelligence (*maqāyis 'aqliyya fāsida*). [. . .]

136. IV:38, IX:45.

137. XIV:3, XVI: 107.

3. Those veiled by Pure Light
They also fall into several classes, and I will only refer to three of them:

The *first* of these have searched and understood the true meaning of the Divine attributes, and have grasped that when these Divine attributes are named Speech, Will, Power, Knowledge, and the rest, it is not according to our human mode of naming. And this has led them to avoid denoting Him by these attributes altogether, and to denote Him simply by reference to His creation, as Moses did in his answer to Pharaoh, when the latter asked, "And what, pray, is the Lord of the Universe?" and he replied, "The Lord, Whose Holiness transcends even the ideas of these attributes. He is the Mover and Orderer of the Heavens."

The *second* mount higher than these, inasmuch as they perceived that the Heavens are a plurality, and that the mover of every particular Heaven is another being, called an Angel [. . .]

The *third* mount higher than these also, and say that this direct communication of motion to the celestial bodies must be an act of service to the Lord of the Universe, an act of worship and obedience to His command, and rendered by one of His creatures, an Angel, who stands to the pure Light Divine in the relation of the moon to the other visible lights; and they assert that the Lord is the Obeyed-One (*al-Muṭā'*). [. . .]

But those who attain [union] (*wāṣilūn*) make up a *fourth* grade. [. . .] They have passed beyond Him who moves the heavens and who issued the command (*amara*) for their moving, and attained unto an Existent who transcends all that is comprehensible by human sight or human insight. The glories of His principal and supreme Face (*wajhuHu l-awwal al-a'lā*) have consumed all that they had seen within themselves and outside themselves. They found Him transcendent of and separate from every characterization we attributed to Him.

(*Mishkāt*, pp. 89-97)

Ḥadīth 121

عن أبي هريرة : "إِنَّ اللهَ عَزَّ وَجَلَّ قالَ : أَنا عِنْدَ ظَنِّ عَبْدي بِي إِنْ ظَنَّ خَيْراً فَلَهُ وَإِنْ ظَنَّ شَرّاً فَلَهُ."

(رواه الإمام أحمد. حديث صحيح)

Narrated Abū Hurayra: "God, the Mighty and Majestic, has said: 'I am with My servant's opinion of Me: If he thinks that I will act in his favor, that will benefit him, and if he thinks that I act to his detriment, that will be detrimental to him.'"

(Quoted by Aḥmad ibn Ḥanbal. Authenticated *ḥadīth*)

Ḥadīth 122

عن أبي هريرة : : "يقولُ ٱللهُ تَعالَى : "أَنا عِنْدَ ظَنِّ عَبْدِي بِي وَأَنا مَعَهُ إِذا دَعانِي."

(رواه مسلم. حديث صحيح)

Narrated Abū Hurayra: "God Most High has said: 'I am with My servant's opinion of Me and I am with him when he supplicates me.'"

(Quoted by Muslim. Authenticated *ḥadīth*)

Commentary

A believer's thinking well of (*ḥusn al-ẓann*) God, as it were, causes his Lord to conform to it. This good opinion is then at the origin of graces and blessings in a believer's life. Regarding this, Ḥasan al-Baṣrī has said: "It is because of his thinking well of God that a servant can achieve what is good; it is because of his thinking ill of God that the hypocrite commits evil deeds." According to Ibn 'Aṭā' Allāh, there are essentially two bases for thinking well of God: considering His attributes and the blessings He bestows, the first of which is more elevated and harder to realize. With regard to this, he has written: "If you have not improved your thinking of Him on account of His attributes, improve it because of His treatment of you. For has He accustomed you to anything but what is good? And has He conferred upon you anything but His favors?"[138]

138. *Ḥikam*, no. 37.

Ibn al-ʿArabī

The Real is with the servant according to his state: "I am with my servant's opinion of Me. Let him therefore have a good opinion of Me." Whatever the servant's state may be, the Real will be with Him and will treat Him in conformity to that state. The Exalted Lord has said: *Remember Me, and I will remember you.*[139] Thus if the servant remembers (invokes) God in himself, God will remember him in Himself, and if the servant remembers his Lord in a gathering, God will remember him in a better gathering.

Just as God can be with the servant, so can the servant be with God. Concerning this, God has said: *He loves them and they love Him.*[140] The Folk of the Path of God know what this degree implies: If God had not loved them beforehand, they could have not loved Him.

(*Fut.*, p. 152 [O.Y])

139. II: 152.
140. V: 54.

Ḥadīth 123

عن أبي هريرة : "يَنْزِلُ رَبُّنا تَبارَكَ وَتَعالَى كُلَّ لَيْلَةٍ إلى
سَماءِ ٱلدُّنْيا، حِينَ يَبْقَى ثُلُثُ ٱللَّيْلِ ٱلآخِرِ، فَيَقُولُ : "مَنْ
يَدْعُونِي فَأَسْتَجِيبَ لَهُ، مَنْ يَسْأَلُنِي فَأُعْطِيَهُ، مَنْ يَسْتَغْفِرُنِي
فَأَغْفِرَ لَه ؟"

(رواه البخاري. حديث صحيح)

Narrated Abū Hurayra: "Our Lord—exalted be He—comes down every last third of the night to the nearest Heaven to us, saying: 'Is there anyone invoking Me, so that I may respond to his invocation? Is there anyone petitioning Me, so that I may grant him his request? Is there anyone seeking My forgiveness, so that I may forgive him?'"

(Quoted by al-Bukhārī. Authenticated *ḥadīth*.)

Commentary

In addition, the first meaning regarding the end of the night, this *ḥadīth* also alludes to the end of times (*ākhir al-zamān*), as the spiritual masters like to call it. It is known that the end of times is described as a dark period, not only for Islam but for the majority of religions. However, there exist compensations for this inescapable decline: spiritual knowledge is less difficult to attain than in the past, and the "price to be paid" in order to obtain it is smaller. The end of times is therefore the period in which Mercy becomes nearer.[141]

Ibn al-'Arabī

The whole universe fell asleep when the Messenger of God ﷺ left this world . . . We are today, by the grace of God, in the last third of this night which is the sleep of the universe. And yet, the Real manifests Itself during the last third of the night and it is then that He bestows blessings, sciences, and perfect knowledge on every level, for this theophany is the nearest since it takes place at the heaven of the here-below. This is why the knowledge of this community is more perfect near its end than it ever was in its middle or in its beginning after the passing of the Messenger of God ﷺ. [. . .]

Our generations are more perfect in knowledge, and the first generations of this community were more perfect in their actions. As for faith, no time is better than the one preceding it.

(*Fut.*, III, p. 188)

141. See M. Lings, *The Eleventh Hour*, London: Archetype, 2002.

Amīr 'Abd al-Qādir

The Predecessors were able to benefit, just as we can, from this "descent" and that which it brings with it. However, in their case, it was a matter of a partial and discontinuous theophany (*tajallin munqaṭi'*). As for the theophany of the last third of the night having started at the death of the Prophet ﷺ and lasting until the Day of Judgement, nobody has a part in it if not us.

(*Mawāqif*, no. 295)

Ḥadīth 124

عن أبي هريرة : "إنَّ ٱللهَ عَزَّ وَجَلَّ يَقُولُ يَوْمَ ٱلقيامة : يا ٱبْنَ آدَمَ مَرِضْتُ فَلَمْ تَعُدْني. قالَ : يا رَبِّ كَيْفَ أَعُودُكَ وَأَنْتَ رَبُّ ٱلعَالَمين ؟ قالَ : أَما عَلِمْتَ أَنَّ عَبْدِي فلاناً مَرِضَ فَلَمْ تَعُدْهُ، أَما عَلِمْتَ أَنَّكَ لَوْ عُدْتَهُ لَوَجَدْتَنِي عِنْدَهُ ؟ يا بْنَ آدَمَ ٱسْتَطْعَمْتُكَ فَلَمْ تُطْعِمْنِي. قالَ : يا رَبِّ وَكَيْفَ أُطْعِمُكَ وَأَنْتَ رَبُّ ٱلعالَمين ؟ قالَ : أَما عَلِمْتَ أَنَّهُ ٱسْتَطْعَمَكَ عَبْدِي فُلانٌ فَلَمْ تُطْعِمْهُ أَما عَلِمْتَ أَنَّكَ لَوْ أَطْعَمْتَهُ لَوَجَدْتَ ذٰلِكَ عِنْدِي ؟ يا بْنَ آدَمَ ٱسْتَسْقَيْتُكَ فَلَمْ تَسْقِنِي. قالَ : يا رَبِّ كَيْفَ أَسْقِيكَ وَأَنْتَ رَبُّ ٱلعالَمين ؟ قالَ : اسْتَسْقاكَ عَبْدِي فُلانٌ فَلَمْ تَسْقِه أَما إِنَّكَ لَوْ سَقَيْتَهُ وَجَدْتَ ذٰلِكَ عِنْدِي ؟"

(رواه مسلم. حديث صحيح)

Narrated Abū Hurayra: "Verily, God, the Exalted and Glorious, will say on the Day of Resurrection: 'O son of Adam, I was sick but you did not visit Me.' He will say: 'O my Lord; how could I visit Thee whereas Thou art the Lord of the worlds?' Thereupon He will say: 'Did you not know that such and such a servant of Mine was sick but you did not visit him and were you not aware that if you had visited him, you would have found Me by him?' [The Lord will again say:] O son of Adam, I asked food of you but you did not feed Me.' He will say: 'My Lord, how could I feed Thee whereas Thou art the Lord of the worlds?' He said: 'Did you not know that such and such a servant of Mine asked food of you but you did not feed him, and were you not aware that if you had fed him you would have found him by My side?' [The Lord will again say:] 'O son of Adam, I asked drink of you but you did not provide Me.' He will say: 'My Lord, how could I provide Thee whereas Thou art the Lord of the worlds?' Thereupon He will say: 'Such and such servant of Mine asked you for a drink but you did not provide for him, and had you provided him drink you would have found it near Me.'"

(Quoted by Muslim. Authenticated *ḥadīth*)

Commentary

This *ḥadīth* not only enjoins empathy and generosity towards those who suffer, it emphasizes that all altruistic action of a believer is not only done *for* God but that it is also, as it were, done *to* God. Nothing masks this reality but the "veil of appearances"—the illusion of multiplicity.

al-Munāwī

In his commentary on this *ḥadīth*, Kalābādhī has written: "God uses for Himself certain attributes belonging to His servants, and says, 'I was sick; I asked food from you; I was thirsty.' When the bonds of love between two beings are profound enough, the soul is necessarily moved. Do you not know that Qays who was madly in love with Layla said, 'Love is the means to achieve union. I have already realized this union and therefore I need no means. I am Laylā, and Laylā is me!'"

(*Fayḍ al-Qadīr*, *ḥadīth* no. 1934)

Ḥadīth 125

عن أنس بن مالك : "الْمُؤْمِنُ مِرْآةُ الْمُؤْمِنِ."

(رواه الترمذي. حديث حسن)

Narrated Anas ibn Mālik: "The Faithful (*al-Mu'min*) is the mirror of the faithful (*mu'min*)."

(Quoted by al-Tirmidhī. Validated *ḥadīth.*)

Commentary

This *ḥadīth* is generally interpreted according to the most immediate meaning: "The believer is the mirror of the believer," thus emphasizing the importance of bonding with others and the aid this bond can provide in the path of the knowledge of the self. However, the spiritual masters emphasize that the Arabic term *mu'min* is also a Divine name, and that, keeping this in mind, the *ḥadīth* sheds light on the importance of the bond with God in knowing oneself. At this point, it is pertinent to mention another *ḥadīth* which, despite not being included in the canonical collections, is often quoted by the spiritual masters: "He who knows his soul, knows his Lord (*man 'arafa nafsahu [fa-qad] 'arafa rabbah*)."

Amīr 'Abd al-Qādir

The *ḥadīth* teaches us: "The Faithful (*al-Mu'min*) is the mirror of the faithful (*al-mu'min*)." This means that the Mu'min, who is none other than God, is the mirror of the saint (*walī*) and *vice versa*. Even if the Real (*al-Ḥaqq*) reflects the entirety of the Creation (*al-khalq*), the believer is mentioned here in an exclusive mode in order to honor him and also because the saint is well nigh the only one to perceive this "play of mirrors" between God and Creation. This is what led our master Muḥyī al-Dīn [Ibn al-'Arabī] to say: "He is your mirror, and you are His mirror." This means that He is your mirror when you contemplate yourself, as well as your "existential receptacle" (*āniya wujūdiyya*). He is equally your mirror when you contemplate someone else, and He is still your mirror when you contemplate your non-manifested "immutable essence" (*ghaybiyya*) which is contained in Divine Knowledge. But you will only be able to realize this if you are amongst the elite of the elite. With regard to your essential being (*wujūd 'aynī*), you are the mirror of His Names which are none other than the affected Essence of certain attributes and which do not really differ from the Essence. And this is how the mirror and the one looking into it are confused. Where, then, is the Real? And where is the creature? At times it is God who is the Mirror in which He sees the servant, and at times it is the servant who is the mirror in which God is both the reflected and the reflection.

(*Mawāqif*, no. 109)

Ḥadīth 126

عن عائشة : "إِنَّ ٱللهَ تَعالَى يُحِبُّ ٱلرِّفْقَ فِي ٱلأَمْرِ كُلِّهِ."

(رواه البخاري. حديث صحيح)

Narrated 'Ā'isha: "Verily, God the Exalted loves kindness in everything."
(Quoted by al-Bukhārī. Authenticated *ḥadīth.*)

Ḥadīth 127.

عن علي : "إِنَّ ٱللهَ رَفِيقٌ يُحِبُّ ٱلرِّفْقَ وَيُعْطِي عَلَيْهِ ما لا يُعْطَى عَلى ٱلعُنْفِ."

(رواه الإمام أحمد. حديث حسن)

Narrated 'Alī: "Verily, God is kind and He loves kindness: He accords to it that which can never be attained through the use of force."
(Quoted by Aḥmad ibn Ḥanbal. Validated *ḥadīth.*)

Commentary

As we have seen in other *ḥadīth*, God loves to see in His creature reflections of the Attributes belonging to Him. On the importance of kindness towards others and refraining from violence, refer to *ḥadīth* 7 and 8.

Ḥadīth 128

عن أبي هريرة :" إِذا أَحَبَّ ٱللهُ عَبْداً نادَى جِبْرِيلَ : إِنَّ ٱللهَ يُحِبُّ فُلاناً فَأَحْبِبْهُ. فَيُحِبُّهُ جِبْرِيلُ فَيُنادِي جِبْرِيلُ فِي أَهْلِ ٱلسَّماءِ : إِنَّ ٱللهَ يُحِبُّ فُلاناً فَأَحِبُّوهُ. فَيُحِبُّهُ أَهْلُ ٱلسَّماءِ ثُمَّ يُوضَعُ لَهُ ٱلقَبُولُ فِي ٱلأَرْضِ."

(رواه البخاري. حديث صحيح)

Narrated Abū Hurayra: "When God loves one of His servants, He calls Gabriel saying, 'God loves so-and-so; O Gabriel! Love him.' Gabriel loves him and makes an announcement amongst the inhabitants of Heaven. 'God loves so-and-so, therefore you should love him also,' and so all the inhabitants of Heaven love him, and then he is granted the acceptance [of the believers] on earth."

(Quoted by al-Bukhārī. Authenticated *ḥadīth*.)

Commentary

This *ḥadīth* mentions the love of God for the creature, as well as some of its consequences. This love radiates and spreads: first to Gabriel, then to the angels, and finally to the inhabitants of the earth. Unlike the angels, not all the inhabitants of the earth will feel love for the one who is loved by God: to be receptive to the love that God bestows upon His servant is already in itself a grace. Be that as it may, it is worth pondering on the nature of God's love for His creatures.

al-Ghazzālī

Know that in numerous passages, the Qur'ān affirms God's love for His servant. We must therefore understand the meaning of this love. The Exalted has said: *He loves them, and they love Him*;[142] *Lo! God loveth them who battle for His cause in ranks, as if they were a solid structure*;[143] *Truly God loves those who turn (unto Him), and He loveth those who purify themselves*.[144]

However, the term "love" cannot be used in the same meaning for God and for His creatures. Indeed, all the terms which are used both for God and His creatures must be of a different mode. Even the term "existence"

142. V: 54.
143. LXIV: 4.
144. II: 222.

(*wujūd*)—which is a most universal one—cannot be applied in the same fashion for both God and the creature because, except for God, the existence of everything is dependent (*mustafād*) on that of God. Unconditioned existence and contingent existence cannot be equivalent . . .

Despite the common denotation, their gap is even more visible in the use of Divine Qualities: Knowledge, Will, Power, etc. The Creator and the creature do not possess them in the same degree! On a lexical level then, these terms denote qualities of a creature, because it is easier to grasp the nature of the latter than that of the Creator. Thus love (*maḥabba*) denotes the inclination of the soul towards that which corresponds to it. And yet, this can only be conceived for an imperfect (*nāqiṣ*) being lacking something it needs in order to perfect itself. Such a love cannot pertain to God because all perfection, all beauty, all splendour, and all majesty can be attributed to Him: in reality, they belong to God eternally without any change or diminution. God cannot have an interest for "another *qua* other": He has no interest except for His Essence (*Dhāt*) and His Actions (*af'āl*). There is nothing in existence except His Essence and His Actions. That is why Shaykh Abū Sa'īd al-Mahaynī[145] has said about the verse *He loves them and they love Him*: "It is by the Truth that He loves them for He loves none other than Himself." He meant that He is the All and that there is no existence outside Him.

It is thus that all the words related to the love of God for His servants must be interpreted: they allude to the lifting of the veils from the heart of the believer so that he can see through his heart, to his achieving the nearness of God, and to the eternal Will which determines that. The love of God for the creature He loves is in fact eternal . . . even if contingent (*ḥādith*) causes are an occasion (*sabab*) for the Action of God to perform the lifting of the veil from the heart, as announced by the Most High in the saying: "My servant ceaseth not to draw near unto Me with added devotions of his free will until I love him." The practice of supererogatory works is the second cause, which enables the servant to realize inner purity, to remove the veil from the heart, and to achieve the nearness of his Lord. All this constitutes the Act of God and testifies to His Grace (*luṭf*). This is the meaning of His love.

(*Iḥyā'*, IV, pp. 318-319)

145. For this shaykh's name we follow Nabhānī's *Karamāt al-awliyā'*, II, p. 439. He was a companion of al-Junayd.

Ḥadīth 129

عن أبي هريرة : "إِنَّ ٱللَّهَ تَعَالَى يُبْغِضُ كُلَّ عَالِمٍ بِٱلدُّنْيَا
جَاهِلٍ بِٱلآخِرَةِ."

(رواه الحاكم. حديث حسن)

Narrated Abū Hurayra: "Verily, God Most High detests one who possesses knowledge related to this world while ignoring the Hereafter."
(Quoted by al-Ḥākim. Validated *ḥadīth*)

Commentary

This *ḥadīth* comprises a condemnation of purely outward knowledge accompanied by forgetting—not to say rejection—of all that transcends the material world. From this viewpoint, the *ḥadīth* complements the Qur'ān:

$$﴿يَعْلَمُونَ ظَاهِراً مِنَ ٱلْحَيَاةِ ٱلدُّنْيَا وَهُمْ عَنِ ٱلآخِرَةِ هُمْ غَافِلُونَ﴾$$

They know the outward nature of this world's life, but of the Hereafter they are heedless.[146]

However, this *ḥadīth* can also refer to the theologians who use their knowledge for worldly goals. al-Ghazzālī devotes a long text to the condemnation of this attitude.

al-Ghazzālī

Heavy condemnations have been related regarding the venal scholars (*'ulamā' al-sū'*): they are the persons whose chastisement will be the severest on the Day of Resurrection. We have to grasp what differentiates the worldly scholars (*'ulamā' al-dunyā*) from the spiritual scholars (*'ulamā' al-ākhira*). By "worldly scholars" we mean the venal scholars whose aim is to acquire the pleasures of the here-below, celebrity, and fame amongst the greats of this world through their knowledge. [. . .]

The spiritual scholars are recognized through certain distinctive signs (*'alāmāt*): they do not seek this world through their knowledge. Even if a scholar does not possess a high degree of knowledge, he must at least perceive the mediocrity, futility, instability, and the ephemeral character of the here-below. Conversely, he must be aware of the supremacy of the Hereafter, of its eternity, of the bliss and majesty of this kingdom. He must know

146. XXX: 7.

that these two worlds are opposed; they are similar to two rivals: when you please one, you anger the other. They are also comparable to the two plates of a balance: when one of them is elevated, the other is abased. Just like East and West: approaching one means getting farther from the other. It is the same as communicating vessels (*qadah*): the content which passes into the second empties the first. Whoever does not perceive the mediocrity of the here-below, its instability, the relation of all its ephemeral pleasures with suffering, is not of a healthy mind for observation and experience sufficient to realize this. How can someone then be amongst the scholars if he has no sane mind?

(*Iḥyā'*, I, pp. 58-60)

Ḥadīth 130

عن أبي الدرداء : "إِنَّ ٱللهَ تَعالَى يُحِبُّ كُلَّ قَلْبٍ حَزِينٍ."

(رواه الطبراني. حديث حسن)

Narrated Abū al-Dardā': "Lo! God Most High loves saddened hearts."
(Quoted by al-Ṭabarānī. Validated *ḥadīth*.)

Commentary

In contrast to the *ḥadīth* presenting sadness as expiation for the sins which are more numerous than the good deeds,[147] this *ḥadīth* emphasizes a sadness which in reality is a nostalgia for the celestial homeland of the soul.

al-Munāwī

"Lo! God Most High loves saddened hearts," meaning [hearts] filled with gentleness, kindness, and mercy. But the saddened hearts are also those which are marked by the fear of God, and who are dedicated to religion, and preoccupied with their shortcomings before God. Regretting these shortcomings is, in fact, the state of the lover towards his beloved.

God Most High looks at the hearts of His servants and loves those who assume the "virtues of gnosis" (*akhlāq al-ma'rifa*) which are fear, hope, sadness, love, modesty, gentleness, and purity . . .

(*Fayḍ al-Qadīr*, *ḥadīth* no. 1888)

Amīr 'Abd al-Qādir

The spiritual states of the traveller to God (*al-sālik al-sā'ir*) change their hue continuously: sometimes contraction (*qabḍ*) and sometimes expansion (*basṭ*), sometimes laughter and sometimes crying. This is due to two considerations taken into account by the traveller:

> The first concerns taking into consideration the benefits and forgiveness that God grants him. He becomes aware that he is a slave of God who is travelling towards His presence. He has a good opinion of his Lord; he expects Him to have mercy on him, to lift the veils separating him from God, to give him the knowledge of the reality of his soul, and to introduce him to the gathering of Bliss with the beloved ones who are gratified by intimacy and honour. This awareness necessarily generates joy, laughter, and inner plenitude (*inbisāṭ*).
>
> The second is the taking into consideration by the traveller of his shortcomings pertaining to spiritual manners (*adab*) and Divine commands, as well as the absence of gratitude for the benefits he receives. To this is added his realizing his present state, his remoteness from the

147. Cf. *ḥadīth* 6.

presence of the beloved ones, the accumulation of veils, the domination of his ego and passion, and the hold on his heart of the love of this world and concupiscent desires. Consideration of these things necessarily generates contraction, sadness, and tears; furthermore, it generates inner collapse in him who possesses a high spiritual aspiration and a soul which has not turned animal.

The traveller cannot escape the alternation of these two spiritual states.

(*Mawāqif*, no. 27)

Ḥadīth 131

عن ابن مسعود : "إِنَّ ٱللَّهَ تَعالَى جَمِيلٌ يُحِبُّ ٱلْجَمالَ."

(رواه مسلم. حديث صحيح)

Narrated Ibn Mas'ūd: "Verily, God Most High is beautiful and He loves beauty."

(Quoted by Muslim. Authenticated *ḥadīth*.)

Commentary

Being linked to God, love of beauty should not be interpreted here in a subjective and individualist sense. It is often forgotten that beauty, far from being a useless luxury, is an integral part of the spiritual means offered by religions, even if in such a domain the emphasis may vary significantly.

Ibn al-'Arabī

There are many things that the Most High loves to see in His servant. Among these, we will mention the embellishment (*tajammul*) for God, as there is in this a fully-fledged act of worship (*'ibāda mustaqilla*). This is particularly true for prayer, because in this instance God commands you to be careful of the beauty of your clothes: *O children of Adam! Attend to your embellishments at every time of prayer . . .*[148] To those who oppose this practice, God says: Say: *Who hath forbidden the embellishment of God which He has brought forth for His servants and the good provisions? Say: These are for the believers in the life of this world, purely (theirs) on the resurrection day; thus do We make the communications clear for a people who know.*[149]

(*Waṣāyā*, no. 14, p. 38)

Frithjof Schuon ('Īsā Nūr al-Dīn)

Beauty, whatever use man may make of it, belongs fundamentally to its Creator, Who through it projects into the world of appearances something of His Being.

(*Echoes*, p. 21)

In the economy of spiritual means, beauty, which is positive and compassionate, stands in a sense opposite of asceticism, which is negative and implacable; nonetheless the one always contains something of the other, for both are derived from truth and express truth, though from different points of view.

The pursuit of the disagreeable is justified in so far as it is a form of

148. VII: 31
149. VII: 32

asceticism. It must not, however, be carried to the point of becoming a cult of ugliness, for that would amount to a denial of one aspect of truth. This question could hardly arise in a civilization still wholly traditional, for in such a civilization ugliness is more or less accidental. Only in the modern world has ugliness become something like a norm or a principle; only here does beauty appear as a specialty, not to say a luxury. Hence the frequent confusion, at all levels, between ugliness and simplicity.

In our times the discerning of forms assumes a quite special importance. Error appears in all the forms that surround us and in which we live. There is a danger of its poisoning our sensibility—even our intellectual sensibility—by introducing into it a kind of false indifference, hardness, and triviality.

(*Perspectives*, p. 31)

The Qur'ān: القرآن الكريم

Ḥadīth 132

عن ابن عمرو : " لَمْ يَفْقَهْهُ مَنْ قَرَأَ ٱلْقُرْآنَ أَقَلَّ مِنْ ثَلاث."

(رواه الترمذي. حديث صحيح)

Narrated Ibn 'Amr: "Whoever reads a passage from the Qur'ān less than three times has not understood it."

(Quoted by al-Tirmidhī. Authenticated *ḥadīth*.)

Commentary

The understanding of the Qur'ān mentioned in this *ḥadīth* is not of the order of a rationalist analysis but of an impregnation of the reader's being by the Divine word. However, this is only realized progressively, and in this sense this *ḥadīth* invites successive readings. Concerning the inexhaustible character of the Qur'ān, Abū Madyan (d. 594/1198) has said: "The Qur'ān is a Divine descent (*nuzūl*) and a progressive revelation (*tanzīl*), and going on until the Resurrection."[150]

al-Ghazzālī

It is related that one day the Prophet ﷺ read the formula *In the Name of God, the All-Merciful, the Compassionate* and that he repeated it twenty times. He repeated this verse in order for the best ones to meditate upon its meanings. Also, Abū Dharr al-Ghifārī relates the following *ḥadīth*: "One night, when the Messenger of God ﷺ stood for prayers with us, he kept repeating the sentence, If Thou chastisest them, they are but your servants; and if Thou pardonest them, Thou art the Mighty, the Wise."

It is reported that Abū Sulaymān al-Dārānī said: "For me reciting a verse means repeating it in my prayers for four or five nights, and if I do not interrupt my meditation on this verse, I cannot continue with another." It has also been related from another of our predecessors (*salaf*) that he would not recite anything except Sura Hūd for six months before grasping its content through meditation.

(*Iḥyā'*, I, p. 283)

Ibn al-'Arabī

The servant whose inner sight (*al-baṣīra*) is enlightened—he who is guided

150. Cf. Vincent J. Cornell, *The Way of Abū Madyan* (Cambridge: Islamic Texts Society, 1996), p. 117.

by a light from his Lord[151]—obtains with each recitation of a verse a new understanding, distinct from that which he had during the preceding recitation, and from that which he will obtain during the succeeding recitation. God has answered the request that was addressed to Him with the words: *O my Lord, increase me in knowledge.*[152] He whose understanding is identical in two successive recitations loses. As for he who recites without understanding anything, may God have mercy on him!

(*Fut.*, III, p. 129; fr. tr. M. Chodkiewicz: *Océan*, p. 47)

151. Reference to XXXIX: 22

152. XX: 114

Ḥadīth 133

عن أنس : "لِكُلِّ شَيْءٍ حِلْيَةٌ، وَحِلْيَةُ ٱلقُرْآنِ ٱلصَّوْتُ ٱلْحَسَنُ."

(رواه عبد الرزاق. حديث صحيح)

Narrated Anas: "There is an ornamentation for everything, and the ornamentation of the Qur'ān is a beautiful voice."

(Quoted by 'Abd al-Razzāq. Authenticated *ḥadīth.*)

Ḥadīth 134

عن البراء : "زَيِّنُوا ٱلقُرْآنَ بِأَصْوَاتِكُمْ فَإِنَّ ٱلصَّوْتَ ٱلْحَسَنَ يَزِيدُ ٱلقُرْآنَ حُسْناً."

(رواه الحاكم. حديث صحيح)

Narrated al-Barrā': "Embellish the Qur'ān with your voice, because a beautiful voice amplifies the beauty of the Qur'ān."

(Quoted by al-Ḥākim. Authenticated *ḥadīth.*)

Commentary

Some rare but virulent critics of chanted recitation of the Qur'ān may be found amongst certain jurists. The following passage is a response of Shaykh al-'Alawī to some criticisms formulated by 'Uthmān ibn al-Makkī, a Salafi theologian from Tunisia, who considered the chanting of the Qur'ān a blameworthy innovation.

Shaykh al-'Alawī

You continue by saying, "Another innovation is to recite the Qur'ān melodiously, which is a reprehensible act, therefore the banning of it is necessary and it is important that the Qur'ān be kept free from such recitation. Nay! Even in poetry, melody is disapproved of. So it is necessary to stay away from listening to it. What then in the case of the verses of God—exalted be He—and His Divine speech?"

I cannot refrain from reacting in the face of such a tirade: what audacity to speak about the religion of God without knowing it! What looseness in the handling of textual references which you do not understand. [. . .]

Jalāl al-Dīn al-Suyūṭī reports several *ḥadīth* of the Prophet ﷺ—which are more than enough to show that he approved the chanting (*al-taghannī*) of the Qur'ān. Thus, according to Anas, the Prophet ﷺ said: "There is a decoration for everything, and the decoration of the Qur'ān is the beautiful voice." He has also said: "Embellish the Qur'ān with your voice, because the beautiful voice increases the Qur'ān in beauty." [. . .]

Perchance you will say that "embellish" here means respecting the rules of psalmody and especially slow recitation (*tartīl*), whereas I say that these *ḥadīth* encourage very clearly the chanted recitation of the Qur'ān. If this is not obvious to you, then look at something even more explicit. Al-Suyūṭī relates from Ibn Mas'ūd the following saying of the Prophet ﷺ: "He who recites the Qur'ān without chanting (*lam yataghanna*) is not of us"; and also, "Nothing is more appreciated by God than the chanted recitation of the Qur'ān in a high voice by a prophet."

(*Qawl*, p. 59)

Ḥadīth 135

عن ابن مسعود : "إِنَّ لِلْقُرْآنِ بَطْناً وَظَهْراً وَحَدّاً وَمَطْلعاً."

(رواه ابن حبان. حديث صحيح)

Narrated Ibn Mas'ūd: "The Qur'ān has an interior (*baṭn*) and an exterior (*ẓahr*), a limit (*ḥadd*) and a point of ascension (*maṭla'* or *maṭli'*)."
(Quoted by Ibn Ḥibbān. Authenticated *ḥadīth*)

Commentary

The multiplicity of the degrees of profundity in the comprehension of the Qur'ān is stated clearly in this *ḥadīth*. However, the inexhaustible richness of the Qur'ān must not lead to whims and purely individual interpretations. On this matter, al-Ghazzālī makes the following distinctions:

al-Ghazzālī

Perhaps you will say that I venture too far in what proceeds concerning the understanding of the secrets of the Qur'ān, which are unveiled to those whose hearts were purified, and you will pose the question: "How can you reconcile this with the word of the Prophet ﷺ, 'Whoever interprets the Qur'ān according to his personal opinion (*ra'y*) prepares himself a place in Hellfire?'"[153]

This misunderstood *ḥadīth* has led some specialists of the outward interpretation (*ẓāhir al-tafsīr*) of the Qur'ān to reject the commentaries of the mystics as well as of those who are attached to Sufism. They reject all the interpretations of the Qur'ān advanced by these mystics on the grounds that they are not contained in what is related through Ibn 'Abbās and other interpreters of the Qur'ān.[154] These specialists go so far as to accuse these mystics of disbelief (*kufr*). If these detractors are right, the comprehension of the Qur'ān will be reduced to the memorization of the contents of the commentaries; and if they are not correct, then what is the meaning of the saying of the Prophet ﷺ, "Whoever interprets the Qur'ān according to his personal opinion (*ra'y*) is preparing himself a place in Hellfire?"

[I therefore say:] Know that whoever claims that the Qur'ān has no other meaning, apart from those held by the outward commentary, only indicates his own limits. In reality, the *ḥadīth* and the sayings of the Companions show that the Qur'ān contains meanings which are only achieved by those gifted with comprehension (*arbāb al-fahm*). On this subject, 'Alī has said: " . . . we now have access only to the comprehension of the Qur'ān

153. Quoted by al-Tirmidhī, narrated by Ibn 'Abbās.

154. Regarding elements of understanding collected by the first generations of Islam such as *ḥadīth*, lexicography, circumstances of revelation, etc.

which only God can grant to His servant." If there were nothing else apart from the interpretations handed down in writing, then which comprehension was 'Alī alluding to? On the other hand, the Prophet ﷺ has said: "The Qur'ān has an interior and an exterior, a limit and a point of ascension." A similar saying has been related by Ibn Mas'ūd, who was an authority on the interpretation of the Qur'ān. What do the terms "interior," "exterior," "limit," and "point of ascension" mean? It is known that 'Alī used to say: "If I wanted, I could load seventy camels just with the commentary of the chapter Fātiḥa!" What do these words mean, knowing that the outward commentary of this chapter is very short? [. . .] Ibn Mas'ūd used to say: "Whoever wishes to know the knowledge of the first people to the last ones, let him meditate upon the Qur'ān." Obviously, this cannot be achieved by being content with the outward commentary.

To summarize, all knowledge derives from the Actions (*af'āl*) of God and of His Attributes (*ṣifāt*). And yet, the Qur'ān displays the Essence, Actions, and Attributes of God: therefore, knowledge derived from the Qur'ān is limitless.

(*Iḥyā'*, I, p. 290)

Ibn al-'Arabī

'Alī ibn Abī Ṭālib used to say: "Revelation ended with the death of the Messenger of God ﷺ and we now have access only to the comprehension of the Qur'ān which God can grant to His servant." The folk of unveiling (*ahl al-kashf*) amongst us recognize unanimously the validity of the *ḥadīth* affirming that every verse has an outward meaning (*ẓāhir*), an interior (*bāṭin*), a limit (*ḥadd*), and a point of ascension. For each of these degrees, there are folks [forming as many spiritual categories]. Each of these groups of folks (*ṭawā'if*) possesses a pole, and around him revolves the "sphere" of the [type of] unveiling [linked to one of the four aspects the Qur'ān mentioned above].

I visited our master Abū Muḥammad 'Abd Allāh al-Shakkāz from Granada in 595/1199. He was amongst the greatest masters I was able to meet along the Path: I have never met his equal in spiritual effort (*al-ijtihād*). During that visit he told me: "There are four types of spiritual men: those who have been faithful to their covenant with God[155] and they are the people of the outward meaning; those whom neither merchandise nor sale beguileth from the invocation of God[156] and they are the folk of the inner meaning who live in the Presence of the Real (*julasā' al-Ḥaqq*) with whom they converse; there also people of *al-A'rāf*,[157] as the Exalted

155. Cf. XXX: 23.

156. Cf. XXIV: 37.

157. Allusion to verse VII: 46. The *a'rāf* are traditionally described as fortifications surrounding Paradise. According to some commentators the folk of *al-A'rāf*

says, "On the Heights are men, who are the possessors of spiritual smell and discernment, and they are free from any qualification; Abū Yazīd al-Baṣṭāmī was amongst them; and finally there are those who, when called by the Real, come to Him on foot, relinquishing any mount in order to hasten to respond to the Divine call, and proclaim unto mankind the pilgrimage. They will come unto thee on foot . . . ,[158] these are the folk of the point of ascension."

(*Fut.*, I, p. 187)

---

are persons who deserve neither Paradise nor Hell. This is a border zone between these two. In the case of the spiritual category mentioned by al-Shakkāz, *al-A'rāf* indicates going beyond the Heaven-Hell alternative.

158. XXII: 27.

Ḥadīth 136

عن عبد الله بن عمرو : "يُقالُ لصاحبِ ٱلقُرْآنِ : اقْرَأْ وَٱرْقَ كَما كُنْتَ تُرَتِّلُ فِي ٱلدُّنْيا فَإِنَّ مَنْزِلَتَكَ عِنْدَ آخرِ آيةٍ تَقْرَؤُها."

(رواه الإمام أحمد. حديث صحيح)

Narrated 'Abd Allāh ibn 'Amr: "The man of the Qur'ān will be told on the Day of Resurrection: 'Read and rise up! Lo!, your position (*manzila*) is to be found in the last verse that you will read.'"

(Quoted by Aḥmad ibn Ḥanbal. Authenticated *ḥadīth*)

Commentary

This *ḥadīth* shows that every verse which is known by the believer will elevate him in the celestial abodes of Paradise; in the same way, each verse can become an opportunity for a spiritual ascension on the path of Knowledge. Without diminishing the meaning of this *ḥadīth* concerning the Hereafter, Ibn al-'Arabī emphasizes the mode in which the spiritual people should read the Qur'ān in this life.

Ibn al-'Arabī

The man of the Qur'ān will be told on the Day of Resurrection: "Read and rise up!" In this world of responsibility towards God (*taklīf*), the elevation of the man of the Qur'ān consists in passing from one type of reading to another: it should be the Real who reads through the tongue of His servant. Just as He must be the Hearing by which the servant hears, and the Sight by which he sees, and the Hand with which he grasps, and the Foot with which he walks, the Real must be the tongue with which he speaks. Thus the servant will not praise God or glorify Him except through what the Qur'ān contains, and he will be aware [that it is God who does this through him]. The servant must therefore rise from a reading of the Qur'ān by himself to a reading by his Lord: then it is the Real Himself who reads His book . . .

(*Waṣāyā*, p. 64)

Ḥadīth 137

عن أنس بن مالك : "إِنَّ لله أَهْلِينَ مِنَ ٱلنَّاسِ. فَقِيلَ يا رَسُولَ ٱللهِ مَنْ أَهْلُ ٱللهِ مِنْهُمْ ؟ قالَ : أَهْلُ ٱلقُرْآنِ أَهْلُ ٱللهِ وَخاصَّتُه."

(رواه الإمام أحمد. حديث صحيح)

Narrated Anas ibn Mālik: "'There are, in truth, folk of God amongst the people.' Someone asked, 'O Messenger of God, who are the folk of God?' He said: 'The folk of the Qur'ān are the folk of God and His elite.'"

(Quoted by Aḥmad ibn Ḥanbal. Authenticated *ḥadīth*)

Commentary

The expression "the folk of the Qur'ān" can be interpreted—as is always the case in this domain—on diverse levels. Taken in its literal meaning, this expression can denote the "specialists" of the Qur'ān, both for the reciter (*muqri'*) and for the exegete (*mufassir*). But for the mystics of Islam, this expression involves a deeper reality. Indeed, for them the meaning pertains to nourishing oneself with the word of God and living through it. Referring to his relationship with the Qur'ān, the Shaykh al-'Alawī affirms in his collection of poems: "It has taken up its dwelling in our hearts and on our tongues and it has mingled with our blood and our flesh and our bones and all that is in us."[159]

Frithjof Schuon ('Īsā Nūr al-Dīn)

One reason why Westerners have difficulty in appreciating the Qur'ān and have even many times questioned whether this book contains the premises of a spiritual life lies in the fact that they look in a text for a meaning that is fully expressed and immediately intelligible, whereas Semites, and Eastern peoples in general, are lovers of verbal symbolism and read "in depth." The revealed phrase is for them an array of symbols from which more and more flashes of light shoot forth the further the reader penetrates into the spiritual geometry of the words: the words are reference points for a doctrine that is inexhaustible; the implicit meaning is everything, and the obscurities of the literal meaning are so many veils marking the majesty of the content.

(*Understanding Islam*, p. 64)

---

159. pp. 44-46. Cf. Martin Lings, *A Sufi Saint of the Twentieth Century* (Cambridge: Islamic Texts Society, 1993), p. 35.

Ibn al-'Arabī

[In his commentary on the *ḥadīth* according to which God descends to the heaven of this world during the last third of the night,[160] Ibn al-'Arabī explains the Divine intention of this descent by the expression "nocturnal discussion" (*musāmara*). This gives him the chance to clarify what the relationship of the "realized gnostic" (*'ārif al-muḥaqqiq*) with the Word of God could be.]

It is I, He says, who recite My Book for him with his tongue whereas he listens to Me; that is my nocturnal conversation with him. This servant is nourished by My word. But if he goes back to its meanings, he leaves My presence through his thought (*fikr*) and his reflection (*ta'ammul*). What is incumbent upon him is only to turn to Me, and render his hearing receptive to My word until I am present in his recitation. And just as it is I who recite, and I who make him hear, it is also I who then explain My word to him and interpret its meanings. That is My nocturnal coversation with him. He thus draws knowledge from Me and not from his thought and his deductions (*i'tibār*). He no longer cares to think of Paradise, of Hell, of the reckoning, of the Judgment, of the here-below or of the Hereafter, for he no longer considers these things through his reason (*'aql*) and no longer analyzes each verse with his thought; he is satisfied with lending an ear to what I tell him. Thus, he becomes a "witness" (*shahīd*), present with Me. It is I who take charge of his instruction.

(*Fut.*, I, p. 239. Fr. tr. *Océan*, p. 48)

160. Cf. *ḥadīth* 123.

Ḥadīth 138

عن عمر بن الخطاب : "إِنَّ ٱلقُرْآنَ أُنْزِلَ عَلَى سَبْعَةِ أَحْرُفٍ فَٱقْرَؤُوا مِنْهُ ما تَيَسَّرَ."

(رواه البخاري. حديث صحيح)

Narrated 'Umar ibn al-Khaṭṭāb: "Verily, the Qur'ān was revealed in seven readings: read therefore the one accessible to you."

(Quted by al-Bukhārī. Authenticated *ḥadīth*.)

Commentary

Amīr 'Abd al-Qādir

The Predecessors and the Companions have commented extensively on this *ḥadīth*. Imam al-Suyūṭī relates forty sayings on this subject, but there are certainly numerous ones which he did not know of. However, the best commentary on the manner of the folk of gnosis (*ahl al-'irfān*) was written by the gnostic 'Abd al-'Azīz al-Dabbāgh of Fez who had no predecessor in what he said. Of all that has been said concerning this *ḥadīth* there are things which are accurate and others which are even more so; true things and even truer things. All this comes from God and His theophanies, because the Word of the Real and that of His Messenger ﷺ is an overflowing ocean without shore . . .

Among the meanings contained in the Word of God and the word of His Messenger are those which have never been reached or perceived by anyone. That which the Real has cast upon me concerning this sublime *ḥadīth* pertains to the metaphysical readings of the Qur'ān (*aḥruf ḥaqīqiyya*). In fact, one must know that for the most elevated spiritual elite, there are eight kinds of reading: the metaphysical, the sublime (*'āliya*), the spiritual (*rūḥāniyya*), the formal (*ṣuwariyya*), the intelligible (*ma'nawiyya*), the imaginal (*khayāliyya*), the literal (*ḥissiyya lafẓiyya*), and the graphical (*khaṭṭiyya*). The metaphysical readings come under seven main attributes or universal principles: Knowledge, Will, Power, Speech, Hearing, Sight, and Life, which is a condition *sine qua non* of the principles mentioned above . . .

We have neglected nothing in the Book.[161] All those which are called "things" are contained in the sublime Qur'ān, both directly and indirectly, both as contents (*ḍimnan*) and as necessary consequence (*iltizāman*). The term "thing" is more general than the terms "existent" and "non-existent,"

161. VI: 38.

and this is why linguists affirm that "thing" is the most undetermined of all, followed by the term "existent." Because it contains an immense collection of things, the Book was called Qur'ān, this term being the collective-plural of *qar'* which means "collection of objects." The noble Qur'ān is but the manifestation of the Knowledge of the Real—exalted be He—and His Knowledge certainly contains the knowledge of the universals and the particulars. Therefore, the Qur'ān contains them too . . .

As for the different readings known [by the common folk], they diverge grammatically depending on an extension or a deletion, a preposition and postposition, a nominative and an accusative, a genitive and an apocope, but these are just minor readings (*al-aḥruf al-ṣighār*) . . .

In His generosity, the Real—exalted be He—works and gives everyone what they deserve in terms of comprehension of the Qur'ān, in accordance with their predispositions.

(*Mawāqif*, no. 85)

Ḥadīth 139

عن أبي سعيد الخدري : "يَقُولُ ٱلرَّبُ عزَّ وَجلّ مَنْ شَغَلَهُ ٱلقُرْآنُ وَذِكْرِي عَنْ مَسْأَلَتِي أَعْطَيْتُهُ أَفْضَلَ ما أُعْطِي ٱلسَّائِلِينَ وَفَضْلُ كَلامِ ٱللهِ عَلَى سائِرِ ٱلكَلامِ كَفَضْلِ ٱللهِ عَلَى خَلْقِه."

(رواه الترمذي. حديث حسن)

Narrated Abū Sa'īd al-Khudrī: "The Lord has said: 'He who is occupied with reading the Qur'ān and invokes Me to the point of not thinking about [addressing] his requests will receive more than the servants who address them to Me. The value of the Word of God in comparison with other words is comparable with the value of God in relation to His creatures."

(Quoted by al-Tirmidhī. Validated *ḥadīth*)

Commentary

This *ḥadīth* confirms the attitude mentioned by Ibn al-'Arabī,[162] according to which it is suitable for the person who really wishes to "hear" the Divine Word to be entirely receptive to the Presence: " . . . [he] no longer cares about thinking of Paradise, Hell, the reckoning, the Judgment, the here-below and the Hereafter, for he no longer considers these things through his reason (*'aql*) and no longer analyzes the verses through his thought: he is content with giving ear to what I say. Thus, he becomes a 'witness' (*shahīd*): he is present with Me. It is I who take charge of his instruction."

162. Cf. *ḥadīth* 137.

The Prophet ﷺ: النبي

Ḥadīth 140

عن قتادة : "كُنْتُ أَوَّلَ ٱلنَّاسِ فِي ٱلْخَلْقِ وَآخِرَهُمْ فِي ٱلبَعْثِ."

(رواه ابن سعد. حديث صحيح)

Narrated Qatāda: "I was the first man to be created and the last to be sent [as a prophet]."

(Quoted by Ibn Sa'd. Authenticated *ḥadīth*.)

Commentary

In this *ḥadīth*, the Prophet ﷺ alludes to his inner reality which prefigures his terrestrial mission. Numerous Muslim spiritual masters have meditated upon the nature of this inner reality (*ḥaqīqa muḥammadiyya*) which has also been called Muḥammadan light (*nūr muḥammadī*). Ja'far al-Ṣādiq (d. 148/765) comments on the letter *nūn* which opens the Chapter al-Qalam (LXVIII), in the following way: "The *nūn* represents the light of Pre-eternity, out of which God created all beings, and which is Muḥammad. That is why He said in the same Chapter: *Truly Thou art of a sublime nature* (4)—that is: you were privileged with that light from pre-eternity."[163]

Concerning the Muḥammadan light, the great saint Abū Yazīd al-Baṣṭāmī (d. 261/874) uttered these monumental words: "If one atom of the light of the Prophet ﷺ appeared to creatures, none would resist except the Throne;" and "That which people know about the Prophet ﷺ is comparable to a drop of water dripping from a closed goatskin flask."[164]

Shaykh 'Alī Jum'a

It has been well established that the Prophet ﷺ is a light, for the Most High has said:

> *O People of the Book! Now hath Our messenger come unto you, expounding unto you much of that which ye used to hide in the Book, and forgiving much. Now hath come unto you a light from God and a plain*

163. Quoted from M. Chodkiewicz: *Le Sceau des Saints*, Gallimard, 1986, p. 85.

164. Cf. Kalābādhī, *Kitāb al-ta'arruf li-madhhab al-taṣawwuf* (Dār al-kutub al-'ilmiyya: 1993), p. 77.

> *Book;*[165] *. . . a summoner unto God by His permission, and a lamp that giveth light.*[166]

The Prophet ﷺ is therefore a "light" (*nūr*) and he is shining (*munīr*). It is completely permissible to say that the Prophet ﷺ is a light since God Himself—exalted be He—described him and named him as such . . .

All of this does not prevent the Prophet ﷺ from being a human being as emphasized by the Qur'ān.

(*Bayān*, pp. 149-150)

René Guénon ('Abd al-Wāḥid Yaḥyā)

"He who sees me sees the Truth" (*man ra'ānī faqad ra'ā al-Ḥaqq*). There, in fact, lies the mystery of "prophetic" manifestation; and it is known that according to Hebrew tradition also, Metatron is both the agent of "theophanies" and the very principle of prophecy, which, explained in Islamic language, amounts to saying that he is none other than *al-rūḥ al-muḥammadiyyah*, within which all the prophets and Divine messengers are one, and which, in the "lower world," finds its ultimate expression in him who is their "seal" (*khātim al-anbiyā'ī wa'l-mursalīn*), that is, the one who reunites them into one final synthesis that is the reflection of their principial unity in the "higher world" (where it is *awwal khalqi 'Llāh*, the last in the manifested order by being analogically the first in the principial order), and who is thus "the Lord of the first and the last" (*sayyid al-awwalīn wa'l-ākhirīn*). It is thus and only thus that all the names and titles of the Prophet ﷺ can be understood in their profundity. These names, in fact, are those of "Universal Man" (*al-insān al-kāmil*), ultimately totalizing in him all the degrees of Existence as they have all been contained in him since the beginning: *'alayhi ṣalātu Rabbi 'l-'arshi dawman*, "May the prayer of the Lord of the Throne be upon him forever!"

(*Ésoterisme islamique*, pp. 60-62)

---

165. V: 15
166. XXXIII: 46

Ḥadīth 141

عن أبي هريرة : "بُعِثْتُ مِنْ خَيْرِ قُرُونِ بَنِي آدَمَ قَرْناً فَقَرْناً، حَتَّى كُنْتُ فِي ٱلْقَرْنِ ٱلَّذِي كُنْتُ فِيهِ."

(رواه البخاري. حديث صحيح)

Narrated Abū Hurayra: "I was kindled from the best of all the generations of the sons of Adam since their Creation, until I appeared in the generation which is mine."

(Quoted by al-Bukhārī. Authenticated *ḥadīth*)

Commentary

Quite obviously, the Prophet ﷺ is not referring to his human identity—which would make no sense here—but to what has been denoted by the expression *nūr muḥammadī*. The distinction between his human identity and his spiritual reality is fundamental for understanding certain aspects of the inner teachings of Islam. However, there is a finer gradation, establishing as it were a sort of continuity between the two poles of this distinction.

Ibn 'Ajība

Uways al-Qaranī has said: "By God, Muḥammad's Companions have only seen of him his outer husk! But his inner (*bāṭin*) none of them knew." By "inner" he meant "the intimate being" (*sirr*) of the Prophet ﷺ. Uways was, however, amongst the Companions who did know the Prophet's spirit. As for the knowledge of the Prophet ﷺ that others can have, it varies depending on their inner orientation (*tawajjuh*) and gnosis (*ma'rifa*). Thus the saints who are firmly established in their spiritual stations possess the inner knowledge of the Prophet ﷺ in different degrees. Among them are those who know certain aspects of his intimate being; others know his spirit; others know his heart; and yet others know his intelligence (*'aql*). And finally others know his soul. The saints who are firmly established in spiritual realization know his intimate being as it manifests itself in all things. That is why they perceive him each instant. Those whose states are still changing know his spirit and contemplate it most of the time. The aspirants travelling on the Path know his heart, which is how they obtain the perfect certainty, and how they are able to see him. As for the veiled ones amongst the common folk of piety, they know his intelligence or his soul; they can see in a dream or in a waking state the physical person of the Prophet, depending on their love for him . . . And God knows best.

(*Silsila*, pp. 43-44)

Ḥadīth 142

عن ميسرة الفخر : "قُلْتُ لِرَسُولِ ٱللهِ : مَتَى كُنْتَ نَبِيًّا ؟ قالَ : وَآدَمُ بَيْنَ ٱلرُّوحِ وَٱلْجَسَد."

(رواه الحاكم. حديث صحيح)

Narrated Maysara al-Fakhr: "I asked the Messenger of God ﷺ: 'When did you become a prophet?' [He said:] 'I was a prophet when Adam was between spirit and body.'"

(Quoted by al-Ḥākim. Authenticated *ḥadīth*)

Commentary

Ibn al-ʿArabī

Compassion (*raḥīm*) is a Divine attribute of the *basmala*[167] and one of the names of the Prophet ﷺ because the Most High has described him as *gentle and compassionate towards the believers*.[168] The creation of the Prophet ﷺ perfected existence just like the Name *al-Raḥīm* completes the *basmala*, and the latter has enabled the perfection of creation. The Prophet ﷺ is the origin (*mubtada'*) of the existence of the world *qua* Intellect and Soul: "Since when have you been a prophet?" "I was a prophet when Adam was between water and clay."

Therefore, it is through the Prophet ﷺ that Existence was initiated—with regard to his inner reality (*bāṭin*)—and it is through him that the station of prophethood was sealed outwardly. This is why the Prophet ﷺ said: "There will be neither prophet nor messenger after me."

The Divine attribute *al-Raḥīm* thus denotes Muḥammad ﷺ and it is through his name that our father Adam was brought into existence, and likewise during the phases of his existentiation. In reality, Adam is the "bearer" of the names, for the Most High has said: . . . We taught Adam all the Names, and Muḥammad is the bearer of the meanings of the names received by Adam. In fact, these names are the words concerning which the Prophet ﷺ has said: "I have received the all-encompassing words . . . "

(*Fut*., I, p. 109)

167. Arabic name for the formula *Bismi-Llāhi l-Raḥmāni l-Raḥīm*.
168. Cf. V: 54. See also III: 159; XV: 88; XXVI: 215.

Ḥadīth 143

عن عمر بن الخطاب : "لَمَّا ٱقْتَرَفَ آدَمُ ٱلْخَطِيئَةَ قالَ : يا رَبِّ أَسْأَلُكَ بِحَقِّ مُحَمَّد لما غَفَرْتَ لِي. فَقالَ ٱللهُ : يا آدَمُ وَكَيْفَ عَرَفْتَ مُحَمَّدًا وَلَمْ أَخْلُقْهُ ؟ قالَ : يا رَبِّ لِأَنَّكَ لَمَّا خَلَقْتَنِي بِيَدِكَ وَنَفَخْتَ فِيَّ مِنْ رُوحِكَ رَفَعْتُ رَأْسِي فَرَأَيْتُ عَلَى قَوائِمِ ٱلعَرْشِ مَكْتُوباً : لا إِلٰـهَ إِلاَّ ٱللهُ مُحَمَّدٌ رَسُولُ ٱللهِ فَعَلِمْتُ أَنَّكَ لَمْ تُضِفْ إِلَى ٱسْمِكَ إِلاَّ أَحَبَّ ٱلْخَلْقِ إِلَيْكَ. فَقالَ ٱللهُ : صَدَقْتَ يا آدَمُ إِنَّهُ لَأَحَبُّ ٱلْخَلْقِ إِلَيَّ ٱدْعُنِي بِحَقِّهِ فَقَدْ غَفَرْتُ لَكَ وَلَوْلا مُحَمَّدٌ ما خَلَقْتُكَ."

(رواه الحاكم. حديث صحيح)

Narrated ‘Umar ibn al-Khaṭṭāb:

After having committed the sin, Adam said to God:

O Lord! By the honor of the Prophet, forgive me.

O Adam. How do you know Muḥammad, since I have not created him yet?

O Lord! When Thou createdst me with Thy Hand, and Thou breathed unto me from Thy Spirit, I raised my head and saw the words, there is no god but God and Muḥammad is the Messenger of God written above the Throne. I then understood that Thou couldst not associate Thy Name except with the name of Thy most beloved creature.

You have spoken the truth, O Adam! This is the creature I love the most. Supplicate Me, therefore, by his honor, for I shall forgive you; if Muḥammad were not, I would not have created you.

(Quoted by al-Ḥākim. Authenticated *ḥadīth*.)

Ḥadīth 144

عن بن عباس : "أَوْحَى ٱللهُ إِلَى عِيسَى ﷺ : يا عِيسَى آمِنْ بِمُحَمَّدٍ وَمُرْ مَنْ أَدْرَكَهُ مِنَ أُمَّتِكَ أَنْ يُؤْمِنُوا بِهِ فَلَوْلا مُحَمَّدٌ ما خَلَقْتُ آدَمَ وَلولا مُحَمَّدٌ ما خَلَقْتُ ٱلْجَنَّةَ وَلا ٱلنَّارَ وَلَقَدْ خَلَقْتُ ٱلعَرْشَ عَلى ٱلْماءِ فَٱضْطَرَبَ فَكَتَبْتُ عَلَيْهِ لا إِلَـٰهَ إِلاَّ ٱللهُ مُحَمَّدٌ رَسُولُ ٱللهِ فَسَكَنَ."

(رواه الحاكم. حديث صحيح)

Narrated Ibn 'Abbās: "God said to 'Īsā (Jesus): O 'Īsā! Believe in the mission of Muḥammad and order those in your community who do not know him to believe in him. Indeed, if Muḥammad were not, I would have created neither Heaven nor Hell. I have created the Throne on the water and it trembled. Then I wrote 'There is no god but God and Muḥammad is the Messenger of God' on it, and it calmed down."

(Quoted by al-Ḥākim. Authenticated *ḥadīth*.)

Commentary

The idea according to which creation would have not taken place without the Prophet ﷺ has sparked heated debates and a lot of ink has been spilled as a consequence. However, it is worth considering the meaning of the expression *lawlā Muḥammad*, which we translate as "if Muḥammad were not." Does this expression really denote the goal of creation? Or does it rather denote the means through which the world was created?

Let us immediately point out that most of the critiques have been put forward in view of an apocryphal (*mawḍū'*) *ḥadīth*: *lawlāka mā khalaqtu l-aflāka*. The two *ḥadīth* authenticated by al-Ḥākim therefore seem little known. On the other hand, these same critics emphasize that the goal of creation is the worship of God: *I have not created the jinn and humankind except that they might worship Me*.[169]

Since the idea that without the Prophet ﷺ creation would not have come to be is supported by authenticated *ḥadīth*, it cannot be rejected by a twisting of the hand as if it were contrary to Muslim orthodoxy. How can one then reconcile this idea with the verse above?

Just as with traditions 140-142, a distinction must be made between

169. LI: 56

the human individual of the Prophet ﷺ and his spiritual reality, *al-nūr al-muḥammadī*. According to the teachings of the spiritual masters, this light is an isthmus (*barzakh*) between the Light of God and that of the creation; without this isthmus no link would be possible between them. Here lies the meaning of the celebrated prayer on the Prophet ﷺ by Ibn Mashīsh (d. 625/1228) which does not mention the qualities embodied by the Mesenger of God but rather the essential aspects of the *nūr muḥammadī*. In the same manner, Būṣīrī[170] composed this verse on the function of the isthmus of the Prophet: If he were not, the world would have not been brought out of inexistence.[171]

Ibn Mashīsh

O my God, bless him from whom derive the secrets and from whom gush forth the lights, and in whom rise up the realities, and into whom descended the sciences of Adam, so that he hath made powerless all creatures, and so that understandings are diminished in his regard, and no one amongst us, neither predecessor nor successor, can grasp him.

The gardens of the spiritual world (*al-malakūt*) are adorned with the flower of his beauty, and the pools of the world of omnipotence (*al-jabarūt*) overflow with the outpouring of his lights.

There existeth nothing that is not linked to him, even as it was said: Were there no mediator (*wāsiṭa*), everything that dependeth on him would disappear! . . .[172]

Amīr ʿAbd al-Qādir

The Prophet ﷺ is the "intermediary" (*waṣl*); indeed he makes the link with the multiplicity of things in order to bring them back to Unity. He is therefore the link between the created and the Uncreated. [. . .]

The Prophet ﷺ is the isthmus of the isthmuses since he unites in himself the reality of necessary being with that of possible being. The proper role of isthmus is indeed to mark a separation between two elements that do not differ in reality; without, however, being identical.

(*Mawāqif*, no. 89)

Shaykh ʿAlī Jumʿa

The meaning of the phrase "if Muḥammad were not, God would not have created the world" is not opposed at all to the foundations of the creed (*uṣūl al-ʿaqīda*) in Islam, or to the basis of the professing of Unity (*tawḥīd*). On the contrary, this sentence confirms them if their meaning is truly understood.

(*Bayān*, p. 148)

---

170. See *ḥadīth* 88.

171. *Burda*, ch. 3.

172. Translated by Titus Burckhardt, *Islamic Quarterly*, 1977, pp. 68-69.

Ḥadīth 145

عن سعد بن هشام : "سَأَلْتُ عائشَةَ فَقُلْتُ أَخْبِرِيني عَنْ خُلُقِ رَسُولِ ٱللهِ ﷺ فقالَتْ : "كانَ خُلُقُهُ ٱلقَرْآن."

(رواه الإمام أحمد. حديث صحيح)

Narrated Sa'd ibn Hishām: "I asked 'Ā'isha about the character of the Prophet ﷺ and she replied: 'His character was the of Qur'ān.'"

(Quoted by Aḥmad ibn Ḥanbal. Authenticated *ḥadīth*)

Commentary

The Arabic term *khuluq*, translated here as "character", may be understood on several levels: in a first meaning, it can denote the characteristic traits of the personality; more profoundly it can denote the set of spiritual virtues manifested in a person; finally, it can denote the nature of a soul that preexists before his terrestrial life. It is precisely on this subject that the Qur'ān addresses the Prophet ﷺ in the following terms: *And lo! thou art of a tremendous nature (khuluq 'aẓīm).*[173]

Ibn 'Ajība

Know that the people who praise the Prophet ﷺ are divided into two categories:

> Those who praise his outward being (*shakhṣahu l-ẓāhir*): they mention that which has been related regarding his beauty, his physical and moral perfections, and the miracles that he performed. These are the folk of the outward (*ahl al-ẓāhir*).
>
> Those who praise his inner secret (*sirrahu l-bāṭin*) and his original light. They mention his preexisting light and the tangible theophanies deriving from it. This is the case of the Pole Ibn Mashīsh[174] and his like. This is also the case of the lordly gnostic (*'ārif rabbānī*), who was gifted with a unique spirituality in his times . . . Muḥyī al-Dīn Ibn al-'Arabī.
>
> (*Silsila*, p. 41)

Frithjof Schuon ('Īsā Nūr al-Dīn)

According to 'Ā'ishah, the "favorite wife," the soul of the Prophet ﷺ is

173. LXVIII: 4

174. 'Abd al-Salām ibn Mashīsh (d. 625/1228) lived all his life in Morocco. It is there that Abū al-Ḥasan al-Shādhilī (d. 656/1258), founder of the *ṭarīqa shādhiliyya*, met him after having searched for the spiritual Pole in the East.

similar to the Qur'ān; in order to understand this comparison, one has to know that this Book possesses, parallel to the literal wording and in an underlying fashion, a supraformal "magic," namely a "soul" extending from the moral qualities to the spiritual mysteries; whence comes the sacramental function of the Text—its mantra nature, if one will—a function independent of its form and contents.

While this magic, for a person receptive to it, can be used as a way of approaching the Muḥammadan Substance, there is nevertheless another way of this kind, more readily accessible because far less demanding, and this is the concrete example of holy men in Islamic countries; certainly not hagiography with its stereotyped moralism and its extravagances, but rather the living men who can communicate the perfume of the *baraka muḥammadiyyah* of which they are the vehicles, witnesses, and proofs. For without the qualities of the Prophet, these men would not exist—neither in his time nor, with all the more reason, a millenium and a half later. [. . .]

In summary, and leaving aside all considerations of the mystical character of Muḥammad, we can say with historical accuracy that the Prophet ﷺ was generous, patient, noble, and profoundly human in the best sense of the word. No doubt, there are those who will point out that this is all very well but hardly significant and the least that could be expected of the founder of a religion. Our reply is that on the contrary, it is something immense if this founder was able to inculcate these qualities into his disciples, both near and distant, if he was able to make of his virtues the roots of a spiritual and social life and to confer upon them a vitality that would carry down through the centuries. Herein lies everything.

(*Face*, pp. 176-177)

Ḥadīth 146

عن ابن مسعود : "أَدَّبَنِي رَبِّي فَأَحْسَنَ تَأْدِيبِي."

(رواه السيوطي. حديث صحيح)

Narrated Ibn Mas'ūd: "My Lord has taught me spiritual courtesy: He has perfected my spiritual comportment."

(Quoted by al-Suyūṭī. Authenticated *ḥadīth*)

Commentary

Numerous verses of the Qur'ān testify to the spiritual refinement that God transmitted to His Messenger. These verses, which were amongst the first to be revealed, would often invite him to contemplation, prayer, and invocation. Thus, for example, Chapter *al-Muzzammil* addresses him in the following terms:

﴿وَٱذْكُرِ ٱسْمَ رَبِّكَ وَتَبَتَّلْ إِلَيْهِ تَبْتِيلاً﴾

And invoke the name of thy Lord and devote thyself with a complete devotion.[175]

Ibn al-'Arabī

The first command that God gave to the Prophet ﷺ was that of assembling (*al-jam'*) which corresponds to spiritual courtesy (*adab*). The term *adab* derives from the same root as *ma'daba* which denotes a gathering around a meal. In the same manner, the word *adab* denotes the assemblage of virtues. This is why when the Prophet ﷺ says: "God has taught me spiritual courtesy . . . ," he means: "God has placed in me all the virtues." In fact, he has said: "He perfected this spiritual refinement," which means "He has made me a being assembling all human perfections."

(*Fut.*, II, p. 640)

175. LXXVIII: 8.

Ḥadīth 147

عن أبي هريرة : "أَنا أَوْلَى ٱلنَّاسِ بِعِيسَى بْنِ مَرْيَمَ فِي ٱلدُّنْيا وَٱلآخِرَةِ، لَيْسَ بَيْنِي وَبَيْنَهُ نَبِيٌّ، وَٱلأَنْبِياءُ أَوْلادُ عَلاَّتٍ : أُمَّهاتُهُمْ شَتَّى وَدِينُهُمْ واحِد."

(رواه البخاري. حديث صحيح)

Narrated Abū Hurayra: "I am the nearest of all the people to Jesus, the son of Mary, both in this world and in the Hereafter. The prophets are paternal brothers; their mothers are different, but their religion is one."

(Quoted by al-Bukhārī. Authenticated *ḥadīth*)

Commentary

Just like other prophetic blessings, the nearness of the Prophet ﷺ to Jesus can be received by certain saints through heritage. Surely, saints can receive a spiritual heritage drawing them to any prophet, but since the Messenger of God had a particular nearness to Jesus, it is normal that the inheritors of the last messenger may sometimes experience some of that nearness. This link is of course experienced within the inner dimension of Islam and does not imply any outward link with another established religion.

Ibn al-'Arabī

I have experienced numerous spiritual encounters (*waqā'i'*) with him [Jesus] and it is beside him that I have returned to God. He prayed to God that I persist in religion in the here-below and the Hereafter, and he called me his beloved. He ordered me to practice detachment (*zuhd*) and purification (*tajrīd*). [. . .]

Jesus was my first spiritual master (*shaykhunā l-awwal*) next to whom I returned to God. He has an immense solicitude for me and he never neglects me for a moment.

(*Fut.*, II, p. 49, and III, p. 341)

Ḥadīth 148

عن عائشة : "ما مِنْكُمْ مِنْ أَحَدٍ إلاّ وَمَعَهُ شَيْطانٌ. قالُوا : وَأَنْتَ يا رَسُولَ ٱللهِ ؟ قالَ : وَأَنا إلاّ أَنَّ ٱللهَ أَعانَنِي عَلَيْهِ فَأَسْلَم."

(رواه مسلم. حديث صحيح)

Narrated 'Ā'isha: " . . . The Messenger of God said: 'There is no one amongst you who is not accompanied by a devil.' I asked him: 'O Messenger of God, is this the case with you as well?' He said: 'Yes, but my Lord has aided me against him and he has been submitted.'"[176]

(Quoted by Muslim. Authenticated *ḥadīth*.)

Commentary

This *ḥadīth* represents a typical description of the Prophet: he is like all human beings—accompanied by a demon—and yet radically different: this demon is benign. There is in this type of paradox an important key for understanding the earthly nature of the Prophet. On this subject, the following sentence of 'Alī is often quoted: "Muḥammad is a man (*bashar*) but not like other men: he is like a precious gem amongst stones (*ka'l yāqūt bayn al-ḥajar*)." This amounts to saying that the inner reality of the Prophet ﷺ cannot be subject to sin; this is the traditional doctrine of *'iṣma* (inerrancy).

Frithjof Schuon ('Īsā Nūr al-Dīn)

Outwardly, the Prophet ﷺ is Legislator, and he can easily be grasped as such; inwardly, in his Substance, he represents esoterism at every level, from whence comes a duality that is at the source of certain antinomies and which in the final analysis has given rise to the schism between Sunnis and Shi'ites. The Legislator points the way and sets the example on the formalistic plane of legality and morality, whereas the Muḥammadan Substance—the soul of the Prophet ﷺ insofar as it is accessible in principle—is a concrete and quasi-sacramental presence that prefigures the state of Salvation or of Deliverance and that invites, not to legality or to the social virtues, but to self-transcendence and transformation, hence to extinction and to a second birth.

(*Face*, p. 161)

176. Or "he converted to Islam."

Ḥadīth 149

عن أبي هريرة : "أُوتِيتُ جَوامِعَ ٱلكَلِمِ وَجُعِلَتْ لِي ٱلأَرْضُ مَسْجِداً وَطَهُوراً."

(رواه الإمام أحمد. حديث صحيح)

Narrated Abū Hurayra: "I have been granted all-encompassing speech, and the entire earth has been rendered for me a mosque and a place of ritual purity."

(Quoted by Aḥmad ibn Ḥanbal. Authenticated *ḥadīth*.)

Commentary

The expression *jawāmi' al-kalim* is often interpreted as denoting the capacity of the Prophet ﷺ to deliver a profound message in few words. But it also signifies that the Prophet ﷺ has received synthetically all knowledge that man can receive. This is what led Amīr 'Abd al-Qādir to say that "all the fountains of Wisdom" were given to the Prophet ﷺ. He unified in himself all the spiritual types that should to be realized in his community.

Amīr 'Abd al-Qādir

The Prophet ﷺ has received the comprehensiveness of word and all the fountains of wisdom have been given to him. Everybody else knows only their own drinking place[177] (*mashrab*) and the walking path (*madhhab*) which has been reserved to them.

(*Mawāqif*, no. 253)

177. II: 60.

Ḥadīth 150

عن أنس بن مالك : "وَدَدْتُ أَنِّي لَقِيتُ إِخْوانِي ٱلَّذِينَ آمَنُوا بِي وَلَمْ يَرَوْنِي."

(رواه الإمام أحمد. حديث حسن)

Narrated Anas ibn Mālik: "How I yearn to meet my brothers, who have believed in me without having seen me!"

(Quoted by Aḥmad ibn Ḥanbal. Validated *ḥadīth*)

al-Munāwī

[When the Prophet ﷺ pronounced these words, the Companions] asked, "Are we not your brothers?" The Prophet ﷺ replied: "Rather you are my Companions! My brothers are those who have believed in me without having seen me." In saying this, the Prophet ﷺ may have wished to pass his Companions from the "knowledge of certainty" (*'ilm al-yaqīn*) to the "eye of certainty" (*'ayn al-yaqīn*); in reality, he sees his brothers and is already in their company. If you ask, "How should one understand the Prophet's yearning to meet his brothers when they only exist in God's knowledge and not in this world?," our reply is the following: The knowledge of the prophets is drawn from the knowledge of God which is not dependent on temporal determinations (*nisab zamāniyya*). The same is therefore true for the knowledge of the prophets [received] during a theophany (*tajallī*) or an unveiling (*kashf*). Since their nature is purity and the absence of any stain, creation is reflected in the mirror of their inner conscience. Creation appears to them as endowed with a profound unity, and they are the polished mirror in which the spiritual realities (*ḥaqā'iq*) and the different aspects of the subtle world (*daqā'iq*) are reflected. But this only comes about at the station of unification (*maqām al-jam'*) through the intervention of a theophany. This intervention might only last for an instant, after which the servant will be returned to his terrestrial condition, his perception assuming again the quality of separateness (*tafriqa*) and the sensory (*ḥiss*). The state of unveiling having passed, the one enjoying it may yearn to perceive again through unveiling . . .

(*Fayḍ al-Qadīr*, *ḥadīth* no. 9617)

Ḥadīth 151

عن عبد الرحمان بن عوف : "إِنِّي لَمَّا رَأَيْتَنِي دَخَلْتُ ٱلنَّخلَ لَقيتُ جِبْرِيلَ عَلَيْهِ ٱلسَّلامُ فقالَ أُبشِّرُكَ أَنَّ ٱللهَ تَعالَى يَقُول : مَنْ سَلَّمَ عَلَيْكَ سَلَّمْتُ عَلَيهِ وَمَنْ صَلَّى عَلَيْكَ صَلَّيْتُ عَلَيْه."

(رواه الإمام أحمد. حديث صحيح)

Narrated 'Abd al-Raḥmān ibn 'Awf: "Verily, when you saw me enter the palm grove, I met the angel Gabriel, and he told me: 'God—exalted be He—has said, He who calls for Peace on you, I call for Peace on him, and he who calls for Blessings on you, I call Blessings on him.'"

(Quoted by Aḥmad ibn Ḥanbal. Authenticated *ḥadīth*.)

Commentary

That which is commonly called the "Prayer on the Prophet" (*ṣalāh 'alā al-nabī*) is in fact a call for blessings on him. God invites the believers to call for Peace and Blessings on the Prophet, specifying that this is what He and His angels do:

﴿إِنَّ ٱللهَ وَمَلائِكَتَهُ يُصَلُّونَ عَلَى ٱلنَّبِيِّ يا أَيُّها ٱلَّذِينَ آمَنُوا صَلُّوا عَلَيْهِ وَسَلِّمُوا تَسْلِيماً﴾

Lo! God and His angels shower blessings on the Prophet. O ye who believe! Ask blessings on him and salute him with a worthy salutation.[178]

This *ḥadīth* specifies that whoever practices the "prayer on the Prophet ﷺ" receives something from the Blessing it manifests. The mystics practice it daily and abundantly, seeking to strengthen their bond of love with the Prophet ﷺ and approach God through His Blessing. The Shaykh al-'Alawī explains, through the notion of theophany, the inner meaning of the "Prayer on the Prophet" in calling for Blessings (*ṣalāh*) and Peace (*salām*).

Shaykhal-'Alawī

By *ṣalāh* the Sufis mean the manifestation of Divine Glory (*al-tajallī al-ilāhī*) as when God poureth forth His Radiance upon one of His slaves, taking him unto Himself and bringing him into His presence . . . The *ṣalāh*

178. XXXIII: 56.

coming from other than God is in fact a supplication (*du'ā'*). [. . .] The Prophet ﷺ has said, "I have a time wherein only my Lord sufficeth to contain me." These are moments wherein God grants him His *ṣalāh*, that is, His theophany . . . In the same way, it is through His *ṣalāh* that God makes the saints escape from the prison of their ego to the contemplation of their Lord. Concerning this, God has said, *He it is Who blesseth you, and His angels (bless you), that He may bring you forth from darkness unto light; and He is ever Merciful to the believers.*[179]

As for *salām*, Peace, when it is conferred by God on His slaves, it denoteth safety (*amān*) and stability (*thabāt*) beneath the Glory that hath come over them. One must therefore not ask God for His Glory alone, but for His Glory together with His Peace, nor must one mention the Peace first, for it refereth back unto the Glory, denoting stability and strength (*tamakkun*) beneath it. Now God may manifest His Glory unto some of His slaves and delay the vouchsafing of His Peace, so that the Glory shaketh them with all manner of agitation and turmoil, and causeth them to cry out, and divulge some teaching unto those who are not qualified to receive it. Thus are they wrongfully accused and unjustly condemned, all by reason of the descending of God's glory upon them. Therefore if God wishes to preserve them and to preserve others through them, He immediately followeth up His Glory with His Peace, whereupon their agitation is stilled and the course of their lives is made straight, so that outwardly they are amongst creatures and inwardly with the Truth, integrating two opposite states and combining the wisdom of each. They are the heirs of the Prophets, and they refer unto this noble station as drunkenness and sobriety, or extinction and subsistence and the like. Thus, by drunkenness, they mean God's manifesting His Glory unto them, whereas sobriety is Peace after being utterly overwhelmed in the direct vision of their Lord.

(*Minaḥ*, pp. 20-21. Part. tr. *A Sufi Saint of the Twentieth Century*, pp. 168-69.)

179. XXXIII: 43.

Ḥadīth 152

عن ابن مسعود : "ما مِنْ أَحَدٍ يُسَلِّمُ عَلَيَّ إِلاَّ رَدَّ ٱللهُ رُوحِي حَتَّى أَرُدَّ ٱلسَّلامَ."

(رواه الحاكم. حديث صحيح)

Narrated Ibn Mas'ūd: "No one calls peace upon me without God restoring my spirit so that I respond to him"

(Quoted by al-Ḥākim. Authenticated *ḥadīth*)

Commentary

We know that the spirits of the prophets are alive, and that their acts of worship do not end with their bodily death (cf. *ḥadīth* 173). Here the Prophet ﷺ emphasizes a particular aspect of the survival of his spirit: he responds to whomever invokes peace on him. One of the aspects of the relationship between the believer and the Prophet ﷺ therefore is that it can be strengthened through the *ṣalāh* and the *salām*. Also, a *ḥadīth* states that the nearest to the Prophet ﷺ on the Day of Resurrection will be the one who has invoked the *ṣalāh* and the *salām* on him the most. When experienced within the spiritual wayfaring (*sulūk*) this nearness allows a veritable "assimilation of the Muḥammadan substance."

Frithjof Schuon ('Īsā Nūr al-Dīn)

The initiatory means of assimilating the Muḥammadan Substance[180] is the recitation of the "Blessing on the Prophet" (*Ṣalāt 'alā'n-Nabī*) whose constituent terms indicate the different modes or qualities of this Substance; these terms are the following: *'Abd, Rasūl, Ṣalāh*, and *Salām*; "Servant," "Messenger," "Blessing," and "Peace." Now the disciple, "he who is poor before his Lord" (*al-faqīr ilā Rabbihi*), must realize the perfection of the *'Abd*, following in the footsteps of the Prophet, by a thorough consciousness of the relation between contingent being and "Necessary Being" (*Wujūd wajīb* or *muṭlaq*) which is ipso facto "Lord" (*Rabb*); correlatively, the perfect and normative man is "messenger," that is to say "transmitter" of the Divine Message, by his radiation, for a perfectly pure mirror necessarily reflects the light. This is expressed precisely by the terms *Salāt* and *Salām*; the latter being the purity of the mirror, and the former, the ray of light. Now purity is also a gift of God; it includes all the receptive,

180. *Barakatu Muḥammad*, the "spiritual aura"—beneficent and protective—of Muḥammad. The terms *Nūr Muḥammadī* and *Haqīqa Muḥammadiyah* refer, with different shades of meaning, to the Logos itself. (FS)

stabilizing, preserving and peace-giving graces; without it, as the Shaykh al-'Alawī pointed out, the soul could not bear either to receive or to carry the "vertical," illuminative and transformative graces offered by the Divine "Blessing" (*Salāt*).

(*Face*, p. 183)

Ḥadīth 153

عن أبي هريرة : "لا تُوَاصِلُوا. قَالُوا : إِنَّكَ تُواصِل. قال : إِنِّي لَسْتُ مِثْلَكُمْ، إِنِّي أَبِيتُ عِنْدَ رَبِّي يُطْعِمُنِي وَيَسْقِينِ."

(رواه البخاري. حديث صحيح)

Narrated Abū Hurayra: "'Do not practice *al-wiṣāl*.'[181] The people said to the Prophet, 'But you practice *al-wiṣāl*?' The Prophet ﷺ replied, 'I am not like any of you, for I spend the night with my Lord who feeds me and provides me drink.'"

(Quoted by al-Bukhārī. Authenticated *ḥadīth*)

Commentary

Although the earthly mission of the Prophet ﷺ implied that he fully embraced the human condition, it is nonetheless true that he could not be an "ordinary man" in the trivial sense of the word. Thus, the intensity of the contemplation of his Lord impregnated him to the extent of nourishing even his body. Let us remark, however, that the confidence he expresses in this *ḥadīth* does not seek to show his spiritual state—something he would only do in the measure of a strict necessity—but rather not to burden the religious practice of his community.

Ibn al-'Arabī

The intensity of the imaginal power (*quwwat al-khayāl*) captivated me to the point that my love was embodied, just like the angel Gabriel could be embodied before the Messenger of God ﷺ. I have reached the point of being unable to look at it when it spoke with me and when I would hear and understand its utterances. For days I could not swallow the least amount of food. Every time the table was spread for me, it stood right in front of me looking at me and making utterances that I could hear with my own ears: "Will you eat while you contemplate me?" It would therefore forbid me to eat and I would feel no hunger. I would be nourished so much by its presence that I would put on weight; my sight was impregnated by it and it held the place of meal for me. My friends were astonished that I could put on weight without eating because I remained like that for days without tasting anything whatsoever, while feeling neither hunger nor thirst. It would remain in my sight ceaselessly in whatever position I would be: standing, sitting, walking, or resting.

Know that love cannot overwhelm the lover when the beloved is the Real (*al-Ḥaqq*)—exalted be He—[considered in Himself] or through a

181. Fasting continuously without breaking fast in the evening or eating before the following dawn.

creature like a young woman or a young man. If this is not the case, the lover will not be overwhelmed by love.

(*Fut.*, II, p. 325)

Ḥadīth 154

عن عبد الله بن عباس : "قَالُوا : يا رَسُولَ ٱللهِ، رَأَيْناكَ تَناوَلْتَ شَيْئاً فِي مَقامِكَ هٰذا، ثُمَّ رَأَيْناكَ تَكَعْكَعْتَ. فَقالَ : إِنِّي رَأَيْتُ ٱلْجَنَّةَ، أَوْ أُرِيتُ ٱلْجَنَّةَ، فَتَناوَلْتُ مِنْها عُنْقُوداً، وَلَوْ أَخَذْتُهُ لأَكَلْتُمْ مِنْهُ ما بَقِيَتِ ٱلدُّنْيا..."

(رواه البخاري. حديث صحيح)

Narrated ʻAbdullāh ibn ʻAbbās: (Once, a solar eclipse occurred during the lifetime of the Messenger of God ﷺ, and he offered the eclipse prayer.) His companions asked, 'O Messenger of God! We saw you trying to take something while standing at your place and then we saw you retreating.' The Prophet ﷺ said, 'I saw, or I was shown, Paradise and wanted to have a bunch of fruit from it. Had I taken it, you would have eaten from it as long as this world remains.'

(Quoted by al-Bukhārī. Authenticated *ḥadīth*)

Commentary

The Prophet ﷺ was indeed an isthmus (*barzakh*) between this world and the Hereafter; not only would the Revelation come to him and he would convey the Word of God to the people, but his contemplativeness also transmitted something from Paradise to the earthly abode.

As in other *ḥadīth*, this confidence of the Prophet ﷺ shows an aspect of his inner life and of the perceptions of the spiritual realities he had. These perceptions are a blessing that can also be received by a saint, albeit of a different nature from those of the Prophet. This difference is introduced in the following commentary.

Ibn ʻAṭā' Allāh

[Abū al-ʻAbbās al-Mursī] has commented on the following saying of the Messenger of God ﷺ: "I was shown Paradise and wanted to have a bunch of fruit from it. Had I taken it, you would have eaten from it as long as this world remains." He has said: "The prophets behold the spiritual realities of things (*ḥaqā'iq al-ashyā'*) whereas the saints perceive their reflected image. This is why the Prophet ﷺ said, 'I was shown Paradise' and not 'It was as if I were shown Paradise.' When the Messenger of God ﷺ asked al-Ḥāritha in what state he had woken up, the latter replied, 'I woke up a true believer.' The Prophet ﷺ asked, 'There is a certain reality behind everything, so what is the reality behind your faith?' al-Ḥāritha said, 'I woke up as if I could see the Throne of God; as if I could see the righteous enjoying Paradise and the wicked screaming in hellfire, so I rose above this worldly life; I stay up at night (praying) and I stay thirsty in the morning (fasting).' The Messenger of God concluded thus, 'From now on you know, O al-Ḥāritha! Persevere in this path; here is a servant whose heart God has illuminated with the light of faith.'"

Note that al-Ḥāritha said, "as if I could see" and not "I see" because this is reserved for the prophets.

(*Laṭā'if*, p. 113)

Ḥadīth 155

عن أبي هريرة : "تَنامُ عَيْنايَ وَلا يَنامُ قَلْبِي."

(رواه ابن خزيمة. حديث صحيح)

Narrated Abū Hurayra: "My eyes sleep but my heart is awake."
(Quoted by Ibn Khuzayma. Authenticated *ḥadīth*)

Commentary

The degree of the contemplation by the Prophet ﷺ was such that he had surpassed the common opposition between the state of wakefulness and that of sleep; he was just as conscious in the former as he was in the latter. This is what the above tradition emphasizes, while confirming that during sleep he had nothing but veridical visions.

al-Munāwī

The Prophet ﷺ said this because the perfect and sanctified souls do not lose their spiritual perception in sleep or the resting of the body. All the prophets possessed this state of spiritual wakefulness because their spirits were equally bonded with the Heavenly Host (*al-mala' al-a'lā*).[182]
(*Fayḍ al-Qadīr*, *ḥadīth* no. 3367)

182. The expression *al-mala' al-a'lā* refers to the angels who are nearest to God (cf. XXXVII: 8 and XXXVIII: 69).

Ḥadīth 156

عن أنس بن مالك : "صَلَّى بِنا ٱلنَّبِيُّ ﷺ صَلاةً، ثُمَّ رَقِيَ ٱلْمِنْبَر، فَقالَ فِي ٱلصَّلاةِ وَفِي ٱلرُّكُوعِ : إِنِّي لأَراكُمْ مِنْ وَرائِي كَما أَراكُمْ."

(رواه البخاري. حديث صحيح)

Narrated Anas ibn Mālik: "The Prophet ﷺ led us in a prayer and then got up on the pulpit and said, 'In your prayer and bowing, I certainly see you from my back as I see you [while facing you].'

(Quoted by al-Bukhārī. Authenticated *ḥadīth*)

Commentary

The spiritual vision of the Prophet ﷺ derives from the sanctity of his body for "when the heart is wholesome, the entire body becomes wholesome," as underlined in *ḥadīth* 36. According to the Sīrah, the heart of the Prophet ﷺ was purified by the angel who opened his breast, while he was still a child. But the sanctity of the body of the Prophet ﷺ follows also from the fact of the ascension (*mi'rāj*) he experienced, which was like a brief anticipation of the Hour for him. During this ascension, the Prophet ﷺ was literally "reabsorbed, body into soul, soul into Spirit, and Spirit into Divine Presence."[183]

'Abd al-'Azīz al-Dabbāgh

The spiritual vision (*baṣīra*) marks the diffusion of understanding (*fahm*) into all the parts of the body just as the senses such as sight, hearing, smelling, touching, and tasting diffuse therein . . .

If the spirit loves the body, and the veil amongst them is lifted, [the spirit] grants [the body] this spiritual vision. The body then becomes capable of seeing, hearing, and smelling in front and behind, above and below, on the right and on the left, with all the elements constituting it. In sum, that which was the prerogative of the spirit is now granted to the body. In the case of the Prophet ﷺ, the veil between his pure body and his noble spirit was lifted from his infancy, on the day when the angel opened his noble breast. Ever since that moment, a symbiosis and harmony were produced between his spirit and his body, which was made to perceive all that his spirit perceived. This explains why the Prophet ﷺ could see from behind as he could see from in front.

(*Ibrīz*, I. pp. 154-55)

---

183. *What is Sufism?*, p. 35.

Ḥadīth 157

عن عبدِ اللهِ بنِ عمرو قال : خَرَجَ عَلَيْنا رَسُولُ ٱللهِ ﷺ وَفي يَدَيْهِ كِتابانِ، فَقالَ : أَتَدْرُونَ ما هٰذانِ ٱلكتابانِ ؟ فَقُلْنا : لا يا رَسولَ ٱللهِ إلاَّ أَنْ تُخْبِرَنا. فَقالَ لِلَّذي في يَدِه ٱليُمْنَى هٰذا كِتابٌ مِنْ رَبِّ ٱلعالَمينَ فيه أَسْماءُ أَهْلِ ٱلْجَنَّة وَأَسْماءُ آبائِهِمْ وَقَبائِلِهِمْ ثُمَّ أُجْمِلَ عَلَى آخِرِهِمْ فَلا يُزادُ فيهِمْ وَلا يُنْقَصُ مِنْهُمْ أَبَداً. ثُمَّ قال لِلَّذي في شِمالِه هٰذا كِتابٌ مِنْ رَبِّ ٱلعالَمينَ فيهِ أَسْماءُ أَهْلِ ٱلنَّارِ وَأَسْماءُ آبائِهِمْ وَقَبائِلِهِم ثُمَّ أُجْمِلَ عَلى آخِرِهِمْ فَلا يُزادُ فيهِمْ وَلا يُنْقَصُ مِنْهُمْ أَبَداً..."

(رواه الترمذي. حديث صحيح)

Narrated ʿAbd Allāh ibn ʿAmr: "The Messenger of God ﷺ came to us while holding two books in his hands, and said: 'Do you know what these two books are?' We replied: 'No, O Messenger of God, unless you inform us.' Regarding the book he held in his right hand he said, 'This is a book coming from the Lord of the worlds; it contains the names of the inhabitants of Paradise as well as those of their forefathers and their tribes. This book contains them all and no one shall be added or removed from this list.' Then, concerning the book he held in his left hand he said, 'This is a book from the Lord of the worlds; it contains the names of the inhabitants of Hell as well as those of their forefathers and their tribes. This book contains them all and no one shall be added or removed from this list . . .'"

(Quoted by al-Tirmidhī. Authenticated *ḥadīth*)

Commentary

Just as the previous one, this *ḥadīth* testifies to a particular type of spiritual perception. This *ḥadīth* has obviously intrigued the commentators a great deal, and it is once again the "infused science" of the *ummī* shaykh ʿAbd al-ʿAzīz al-Dabbāgh who sheds some lights on this puzzling saying.

'Abd al-'Azīz al-Dabbāgh

The writing present in these two books is one of visions (*kitābat naẓar*) and not of ink. In reality, when persons possessing spiritual vision (*baṣīra*)—first and foremost amongst them our master Muḥammad—turn their attention towards a thing, they pierce through the veils separating them from it. This is how they are able to perceive the light of that thing. When the spiritual vision is perfect, that which is perceived is communicated to the physical sight (*baṣar*). Then this sight perceives the object of the spiritual vision on the outside, in whatever he comes across: a wall, his own hand, a sheet of paper . . . And this is what is mentioned in the *ḥadīth*, "Paradise and Hell-fire were imaginalized to me in the breadth of this wall . . . "[184]

184. al-Bukhārī, Adhān 91.

Ḥadīth 158

عن أبي سعيد الخدري : "إِنِّي لَمْ أُومَرْ أَنْ أَنْقُبَ عَلَى قُلُوبِ ٱلنَّاسِ ولا أَشُقَّ بُطُونَهُم."

(رواه البخاري. حديث صحيح)

Narrated Abū Sa'īd al-Khudrī: "I have not been ordered to search the hearts of people nor to cut open their bellies."

(Quoted by al-Bukhārī. Authenticated *ḥadīth.*)

Commentary

Besides possessing a spiritual perception beyond the common, the Prophet ﷺ was called by his function and destiny to fully assume the human condition. This is why in matters pertaining to other people he was content with the words and the good will displayed by them, without seeking to scrutinize the profound motives of those who came to him. This is also the attitude of Khiḍr in the Qur'ān; he accepted the company of Mūsā knowing full well that the commitment of the latter to follow him, without in the meantime being shocked by his actions, could not last.[185]

185. See *ḥadīth* 203 and 204.

Ḥadīth 159

عن أنس : "حُبِّبَ إِلَيَّ مِنْ دُنْيَاكُمْ ثَلاَثٌ : الطِّيبُ وَالنِّسَاءُ وَجُعِلَتْ قُرَّةُ عَيْنِي فِي الصَّلاَةِ."

(رواه الحاكم. حديث حسن)

Narrated Anas ibn Mālik: "Three things of your world were made worthy of love to me: perfume, women, and the coolness of my eyes given to me in prayers."

(Quoted by al-Ḥākim. Validated *ḥadīth*)

Commentary

The things which this *ḥadīth* mentions as having been made worthy of love to the Prophet, can be considered a reminiscence of Paradise, and they enable us to approach the nature of the spirituality of the Prophet.

Ibn al-'Arabī

[The essence] of his wisdom is singularity because he was the most perfect individual of humankind. This is the reason why the creative command (*al-amr*) started with him and was completed with him; for, on the one hand he was a "prophet when Adam was between water and clay," and on the other hand he was, in his terrestrial existence, the seal (*khātim*) of all the prophets. The first singular number from which all the numbers are derived is the ternary. And yet, Muḥammad was the first symbol of his Lord, for he had received the "universal" words which are the contents of the names that God taught to Adam; thus he had the triple nature of the symbol . . . It is due to the fact that the essential reality of the Prophet ﷺ includes primordial singularity—manifested in everything that is naturally triple—that he said concerning love, the source of existence; "Three things of your world, amongst all the things containing three, were made worthy of love to me," namely women, perfumes and prayer, where he found "the coolness of his eyes."

Frithjof Schuon ('Īsā Nūr al-Dīn)

According to a *ḥadīth* as enigmatic as it is famous, "women, perfumes and prayer" were "made lovable" (*ḥubbiba ilayya*) to the Prophet. Since that is so, we have to admit that these three loves, at first sight disparate, necessarily enter into the Muḥammadan Substance and consequently into the spiritual ideal of the Sufis. Every religion necessarily integrates the feminine element—the "eternal feminine" (*das Ewig Weibliche*) if one will—into its system, either directly or indirectly; Christianity in practice deifies the Mother of Christ, despite exoteric reservations, namely the distinction between *latria* and *hyperdulia*. Islam for its part, and beginning with the Prophet, has consecrated femininity, on the basis of a metaphysics of deiformity; the secrecy surrounding woman, symbolized in the veil, basically signifies an intention of consecration. In Muslim eyes, woman, beyond her purely biological and social role, incarnates two poles, unitive "extinction" and "generosity," and these constitute from the spiritual point of view two means of overcoming the profane mentality, made as it is of outwardness, dispersion, egoism, hardness, and boredom. The nobleness of soul that is or can be gained by this interpretation or utilization of the feminine element, far from being an abstract ideal, is perfectly recognizable in representative Muslims, those still rooted in authentic Islam.[186]

As for the love of "perfumes" mentioned by the *ḥadīth*, it symbolizes the sense of the sacred and in a general way the sense for ambiences, emanations, and auras; consequently it has to do with the "discernment of spirits," not to mention the sense of beauty. According to Islam, "God loves beauty" and He hates uncleanness and noise, as is shown by the atmosphere of freshness, harmony, and equilibrium—in short of *baraka*—to be found in Muslim dwellings which have remained traditional, and above all in the mosques; an atmosphere which also is clearly a part of the Muḥammadan Substance.

The *ḥadīth* then mentions prayer, which is none other than "remembrance of God," and this constitutes the fundamental reason for all possible love, since it is love of the source and of the archetypes; it coincides with the love of God, which is the very essence of the Prophetic nature. If prayer is mentioned in third place, it is by way of conclusion: in speaking of women, Muḥammad is essentially speaking of his inward nature; in speaking of perfumes, he has in mind the world around us, the ambience; and in speaking of prayer, he is giving expression to his love of God."

(*Face*, 178-179)

---

186. It is always this we have in view, and not so-called "revivals" which monstrously combine a Muslim formalism with modernist ideologies and tendencies. (FS)

Ḥadīth 160

عن أبي ذر : "هَلْ رَأَيْتَ رَبَّكَ ؟ قالَ : نُورٌ أَنَّى أَراهُ ؟"

(رواه مسلم. حديث صحيح)

Narrated Abū Dharr: I asked the Messenger of God ﷺ, "Did you see thy Lord?" He said: "[He is] Light; how could I see Him?"

(Quoted by Muslim. Authenticated *ḥadīth*)

Amīr 'Abd al-Qādir

The *ḥadīth* relates that a Companion asked the Messenger of God ﷺ one day, "Did you see thy Lord?" He said: "[He is] Light; how could I see Him?" However, when asked the same question by another Companion, he replied: "Indeed, I have seen Him."

According to us, the reality is that he saw Him during the nocturnal ascension in a state of wakefulness and his eye turned not aside nor yet was overbold.[187] The answer of the Prophet ﷺ to the first companion was doubtless motivated by the fact that he knew that his interlocutor, unfamiliar with all the mysteries of the Theophany, envisaged nothing but the vision of only the Essence beyond all manifestation . . . However, the Prophet ﷺ did not respond to this Companion, "I did not see Him" and, in any case, the latter did not know that God can only be seen with the sight of God and not with one's own limited and conditioned sight; does not the *ḥadīth* qudsī say concerning this that, "When I love him, I am the Sight wherewith he seeth and the Hearing wherewith he heareth . . . "

Never do the masters amongst the gnostics pretend to have seen God during their contemplation. Quite the contrary, they affirm to not having seen Him in any way. For they have effectively seen nothing but their own form, their own degree and their own predispositions within the Real, even though the contemplative does in reality contemplate but himself.

(*Mawāqif*, no. 109)

187. LIII: 17.

Ḥadīth 161

عن ابن عباس : "رَأَيْتُ رَبِّي فِي صُورةِ شابٍّ لَهُ وَفْرة."

(رواه الطبراني. حديث صحيح)

Narrated Ibn 'Abbās: "I saw my Lord in the form of an adolescent youth with a thick head of hair."

(Quoted by al-Ṭabarānī. Authenticated *ḥadīth*.)

Commentary

This *ḥadīth* is certainly enigmatic, all the more so if we approach it from the preceding *ḥadīth* which, in effect, affirms that God cannot be seen because He is pure light. Given this, how can one understand the vision of the Lord in a human appearance?

First of all, it must be pointed out that Ḥadīth 160 is an answer to a question posed about the Ascension of the Prophet (*al-mi'rāj*), as Amīr 'Abd al-Qādir reminds us. As for Ḥadīth 161, the commentators emphasize that it refers to a vision in a dream. Now this type of vision comes about in the "imaginal world,"[188] which is a sort of isthmus, an "interworld" (*barzakh*). For spiritual people in Islam, this world is also designated by the expression *'ālam al-mithāl*[189] to insist on the symbolic dimension of what is perceived there. In the imaginal world, supraformal realities take on a formal appearance. It is thus that certain *ḥadīth* lead us to understand that milk seen in a dream symbolizes knowledge. We can understand from this that the imaginal world and authentic dreams can also be means of access to pure Knowledge, for he who possesses a "symbolist spirit" and is able to go beyond the veil of forms.[190] In particular, the imaginal world allows one to unite opposites, such as transcendence and immanence, supraformal and formal, etc. This is why Ibn 'Arabī presents the imaginal faculty (*al-khayāl*) as the only possibility of integral knowledge where opposites are unified.

Ibn al-'Arabī

The visions of God's friends often involve the "embodiment" (*tajassud*) of angels or prophets or even God, though these objects of vision do not in fact possess bodies. In a similar way the cosmos itself consists of nonexistent meanings displayed or "embodied" in Manifest Being, so the cosmos as a whole is nothing but "imagination."

---

188. This term—as well as its Latin equivalent *Mundus imaginalis*—was proposed by Henry Corbin. It is now widely used. See *L'Imagination créatrice dans le soufisme d'Ibn 'Arabī*, Paris, 1958.

189. Lit.: the world of similtude.

190. On this subject, see our chapter Interpretation of Dreams.

The Prophet said, "I saw my Lord in the form of a youth." This is like the meanings that a sleeper sees in his dreams within sensory forms. The reason for this is that the reality of imagination is to embody that which is not properly a body (*jasad*); it does this because its presence (*ḥaḍra*) gives this to it.

None of the strata (*ṭabaqāt*) of the cosmos makes known the situation as it really is except this imaginal presence, for it makes contraries come together, and within it the realities become manifest as they are in themselves. The truth of affairs is that you should say concerning everything that you see or perceive, through whatever faculty perception takes place, "He/not He," just as God said, *You did not throw when you threw.*[191]

You do not doubt in the state of dreaming that the form you see is identical with what it is said to be; and you do not doubt in the interpretation (*ta'bīr*) when you wake up that it was not it. You will not doubt in sound rational consideration that the situation is "He/not He."

It was said to Abū Sa'īd al-Kharrāz,[192] "Through what have you known God?" He replied, "Through the fact that He brings opposites together."

(*Sufi Path of Knowledge,* 116, 120, 396 n3)

---

191. VIII: 17.

192. A spiritual master of Baghdad; died in 277/899.

Ḥadīth 162

عَنْ مُعَاذِ بْنِ جَبَلٍ : "...أَمَا إِنِّي سَأُحَدِّثُكُمْ مَا حَبَسَنِي عَنْكُم الْغَدَاةَ ؟إِنِّي قُمْتُ مِنَ اللَّيْلِ فَتَوَضَّأْتُ فَصَلَّيْتُ مَا قُدِّرَ لِي فَنَعَسْتُ فِي صَلَاتِي حَتَّى ٱسْتَثْقَلْتُ فإِذَا أَنَا بِرَبِّي تَبَارَكَ وَتَعَالَى فِي أَحْسَنِ صُورَةٍ فَقَالَ : يَا مُحَمَّدُ، قُلْتُ لَبَّيْكَ رَبِّ، قَالَ فِيمَ يَخْتَصِمُ الْمَلَأُ الأَعْلَى ؟ قلت : لَا أَدْرِي رَبِّ. قَالَهَا ثَلَاثاً، قَالَ فَرَأَيْتُهُ وَضَعَ كَفَّهُ بَيْنَ كَتِفَيَّ. قَدْ وَجَدْتُ بَرْدَ أَنَامِله بَيْنَ ثَدْيَيَّ فَتَجَلَّى لِي كُلُّ شَيْءٍ وَعَرَفْتُ. فَقَالَ يَا مُحَمَّدُ. قُلْتُ لَبَّيْكَ رَبِّ، قَالَ فِيمَ يَخْتَصِمُ الْمَلَأُ الأَعْلَى؟ قُلْتُ فِي ٱلْكَفَّارَات، قَالَ مَا هُنَّ ؟ قُلْتُ : مَشْيُ ٱلْأَقْدَامِ إِلَى ٱلْجَمَاعَاتِ وَٱلْجُلُوسُ فِي ٱلْمَسَاجد بَعْدَ ٱلصَّلَوات وَإِسْبَاغُ ٱلْوُضُوء حِينَ ٱلْمَكْرُوهَاتِ قَالَ ثُمَّ فِيمَ ؟ قُلْتُ : إِطْعَامُ ٱلطَّعَامِ وَلِينُ ٱلْكَلَامِ وَٱلصَّلَاةُ بِٱللَّيْلِ وَٱلنَّاسُ نِيَامٌ. قَالَ سَلْ، قُلْتُ : اللَّهُمَّ إِنِّي أَسْأَلُكَ فِعْلَ ٱلْخَيْرَات، وَتَرْكَ ٱلْمُنْكَرَات، وَحُبَّ ٱلْمَسَاكِين، وَأَنْ تَغْفِرَ لِي وَتَرْحَمَني، وَإِذَا أَرَدْتَ فِتْنَةً فِي قَوْمٍ فَتَوَفَّنِي غَيْرَ مَفْتُونٍ، وَأَسْأَلُكَ حُبَّكَ وَحُبَّ مَنْ يُحبُّكَ

وَحُبَّ عَمَلٍ يُقَرِّبُ إِلَى حُبِّكَ. قَالَ رَسُولُ اللهِ ﷺ إِنَهَا حَقٌّ فَادْرُسُوهَا ثُمّ تَعَلَّمُوهَا".

(رواه الترمذي. حديث صحيح)

Narrated Mu'ādh ibn Jabal: " . . . Shall I tell you what prevented me from joining you this morning? I got up and did my ablutions, and then I stood in prayer as long as I could. During prayer, I fell into a deep sleep wherein I found myself in front of my Lord—exalted be He—who appeared to me in the best form and asked me over what did the Heavenly Host (*al-mala' al-'alā*) vie. I said I did not know, so He put His hands between my shoulders, and I felt the coldness of His fingertips for a while in my heart, and knowledge of all things between the East and the West came to me.

My Lord then asked again: 'O Muḥammad, do you know what the chiefs on high are disputing about? They are disputing about the things that expiate sins: staying in the mosque after prayers, walking on foot to religious assemblies and performing one's ablutions at times when it is disagreeable. As for excellencies, they consist of feeding the hungry, spreading peace, and performing the *tahajjud* prayer at night when other folk are sleeping.'

'O Muḥammad, state your request!'

Then I said: 'O Lord, I ask Thee to enable me with the performance of good actions, the abandoning of evil actions, and the love of the poor. I ask Thee to forgive me and to have mercy on me; and if Thou seeketh to try Thy servants, make me die without being touched by sedition. Grant me to love Thee, to love those who love Thee, and to love the acts which draw me nigh unto Thy love.'

The Prophet ﷺ then said, 'All of this is true! Learn it and reflect on its meaning!'"

(Quoted by al-Tirmidhī. Authenticated *ḥadīth*)

Commentary

Among the different insights offered by this *ḥadīth*, one must point out the complete receptivity of the Prophet ﷺ before his Lord: it is the recognition of his ignorance that permits him to receive the knowledge which is transmitted directly from God. He recognizes also that only God can possess veritable knowledge and that He alone can grant it.

The knowledge which is directly received from God is called *al-'ilm al-ladunnī*—the knowledge "coming from Me"—in reference to Khiḍr who is described in the Qur'ān as *one from amongst Our servants unto whom We had granted mercy from Us and had taught him knowledge from*

Ourselves (min ladunnā).[193]

Amīr 'Abd al-Qādir

The Most High has said: *God knoweth. Ye know not.*[194] This is quoted numerous times in the Qur'ān. In saying this, God affirms His being the Only One to possess knowledge: *and who can be more truthful than God in utterance?*[195]

There is therefore no Knower except Him. [. . .] Let he who aspires to knowledge seek it through the means by which he can obtain it; only then will he seek to know what he thinks he knows; the person for whom the veil has been removed knows his soul, and he will understand this. As for him who stays veiled, he remains ignorant; his soul hides his ignorance from him, and his ignorance veils him from the ignorance he has about his soul!

We are expressing ourselves in this manner in order to stay close to the current way of speaking, but in reality, just as this person is not knowing, he is no longer ignorant because knowledge and ignorance succeed each other continuously in the being who serves as a support for them.

(*Mawāqif*, no. 213, pp. 476-77)

193. XVIII: 65.
194. III: 66.
195. IV: 122.

Ḥadīth 163

عن عائشة : "إِنَّ ٱللّٰهَ تَعالَى لَمْ يَبْعَثْنِي مُعَنِّتاً وَلا مُتَعَنِّتاً، وَلٰكِنْ بَعَثَنِي مُعَلِّماً مُيَسِّراً."

(رواه مسلم. حديث صحيح)

Narrated ʿĀʾisha: "God Most High has not sent me to make things difficult and cause suffering but He has sent me to teach and render things easy."

(Quoted by Muslim. Authenticated *ḥadīth*)

Commentary

The simplicity of the teachings of the Prophet ﷺ and his constant willingness to facilitate the religious life of his Companions must obviously not be interpreted as an invitation to half-heartedness or an acceptance of superficiality. Quite the contrary, it means turning hearts towards God and insisting on the essential. On this matter, Abū al-Ḥasān al-Shādhilī has said:

"من دلّك على العمل فقد أتعبك ومن دلّك على الله فقد نصحك."

Whoever directs you to performing acts of worship fatigues you, and whoever directs you to God has given you good advice.

Abū al-Ḥasan al-Shādhilī

I asked my master[196]—may God be pleased with him—on the saying of the Prophet ﷺ: "Facilitate and do not make things difficult; encourage and do not make people run away." He replied, "Direct people to God and do not direct them to aught else; Whoever directs you to performing acts of worship fatigues you, and whoever directs you to God has given you good advice."

(Quoted by Ibn ʿAjība, *Silsila*, pp. 11-12)

196. Ibn Mashīsh.

Ḥadīth 164

عن ابن مسعود : "حَياتي خَيْرٌ لَكُمْ تُحْدِثُونَ ويُحْدَثُ لَكُمْ، وَوَفاتي خَيْرٌ لَكُمْ تُعْرَضُ عَلَيَّ أَعْمالُكُمْ فَما رَأَيْتُ مِنْ خَيْرٍ حَمِدْتُ ٱللّٰهَ عَلَيْهِ وَما رَأَيْتُ مِنْ شَرٍّ اسْتَغْفَرْتُ ٱللّٰهَ لَكُمْ."

(رواه السيوطي. حديث صحيح)

Narrated Ibn Mas'ūd: "My life is a good thing for you because you are spoken to and novel legislation and guidance are conveyed to you, and my death shall be a good thing for you because your works will be shown to me; for the good that I shall see I shall praise God, and for the bad that I shall see I shall ask His pardon for you."

(Quoted by al-Suyūṭī. Authenticated *ḥadīth*)

Commentary

This *ḥadīth* clearly states that the spirit of the Prophet ﷺ continues to have a spiritual role within his community. Having accomplished his mission as transmitter of the Divine message and spiritual guide, he continues—after leaving this world—to be a source of mercy and forgiveness for believers.

Shaykh 'Alī Jum'a

The following verse, revealed by God to His Prophet ﷺ in the chapter "The Women," is a general verse (*āya muṭlaqa*): *If, when they had wronged themselves, they had but come unto thee and asked forgiveness of God, and asked forgiveness of the Messenger, they would have found God Forgiving, Merciful.*[197] The meaning of this verse can neither be reduced by other verses (*muqayyid naṣṣī*) nor by a rational argument (*muqayyid 'aqlī*). Nothing therefore justifies limiting its meaning to the earthly life of the Prophet ﷺ. Therefore, what this verse teaches remains valid until the Day of Resurrection. Indeed one must grant a general meaning to the verses of the Qur'ān in most cases. Following this, whoever wishes to reduce the meaning of the above-quoted verse to the earthly life of the Prophet ﷺ must bring textual proof for it. Inversely, affirming the general meaning of a verse does not require a textual proof since this is the normal case; only the affirmation of the restricted meaning of a verse requires a proof.

This is how the commentators of the Qur'ān have assessed the mean-

197. IV: 64.

ing of this verse, especially the majority of them who, like Ibn Kathīr, give great importance to the *Ḥadīth* and the Tradition. The latter relates the following incident regarding this verse:

> Numerous authors—like the Shaykh Abū al-Naṣr al-Ṣabbāgh in his *al-Shāmil*—narrate from 'Utbī the following famous incident: "I was sitting in the Rawḍat al-Nabī[198] when a Bedouin arrived and said: 'God's peace be with you, O Messenger of God! I have heard the word of God saying, "If, when they had wronged themselves, they had but come unto thee and asked forgiveness of God, and asked forgiveness of the messenger, they would have found God Forgiving, Merciful." Here I am therefore begging God's forgiveness for my sins and asking your intercession with my Lord . . . '
>
> "When the Bedouin left, I fell asleep and saw the Prophet ﷺ in my dream who told me: 'O 'Utbī, go find the Bedouin and tell him that God has granted him His forgiveness.'"
>
> (*Bayān*, pp. 153-54)

198. The part of the Prophet's mosque comprising the space between his tomb and his pulpit.

Ḥadīth 165

عن أبي هريرة : "إِنَّما أَنا رَحْمَةٌ مُهْداةٌ."

(رواه الحاكم. حديث صحيح)

Narrated Abū Hurayra: "Lo! I was sent but as a mercy."
(Quoted by al-Ḥākim. Authenticated *ḥadīth.*)

Commentary

'Abd al-'Azīz al-Dabbāgh

The measure of knowledge is contemplation and the former was given to the Prophet ﷺ when he was in the company of his Beloved without there being anybody else present. He is in reality the first created being and it was then that his spirit was drenched in the sacred Divine lights and lordly knowledge. He thus became a source for whomever wanted to drench themselves in them. When his noble spirit entered his pure body, the spirit was fixed therein with satisfaction and love, and started transmitting its secrets to the body slowly and gently, from his infancy to the age of forty, when the veil between the body and the spirit disappeared completely for him. He was then granted a state of contemplation no one else could withstand. He could then contemplate firsthand that the Real—exalted be He—is the Mover of all creatures . . . and they have no power to harm or benefit anyone by themselves. After this contemplation, the Exalted sent him to creatures so that he could be a mercy unto them; by not giving them any power, he could not bear a grudge on them [if they wanted to harm him], and pray to God against them . . .

This is how the words of the Most High, *We sent thee not save as a mercy to the worlds*[199] as well as his own words, "Lo! I was sent but as a mercy" were verified.

(*Ibrīz*, I, pp. 202-203)

199. XXI: 107.

Ḥadīth 166

عن أبي هريرة : "أَحِبُّوا ٱلعَرَبَ لِثلاثٍ : لِأَنِّي عَرَبِيٌّ وَٱلقُرْآنَ عَرَبِيٌّ وَكَلامَ أَهْلِ ٱلْجَنَّةِ عَرَبِيٌّ."

(رواه الحاكم. حديث صحيح)

Narrated Abū Hurayra: "Love the Arabs for three reasons: Because I am an Arab; because the Qur'ān is in Arabic, and because the language of the inhabitants of Paradise is Arabic."

(Quoted by al-Ḥākim. Authenticated *ḥadīth*)

Commentary

This *ḥadīth* invites us to take into account the importance of the "form" in which the Divine message was revealed as well as its providential "receptacle."[200] One can refer to *ḥadīth* 10 in this regard, wherein the Prophet ﷺ summons us to wholehearted love for the Arabs.

200. If the Prophet ﷺ sometimes emphasized his spiritual nature, he nonetheless recognized his anchorage in human kind: his race, his language, and his culture were providential for him.

Ḥadīth 167

عن عائشة : "ما ضَرَبَ رَسُولُ ٱللهِ ﷺ شَيْئاً قَطُّ بِيَدِهِ وَلا ٱمْرَأةً وَلا خادِماً إلاَّ أَنْ يُجاهِدَ في سَبِيلِ ٱللهِ. وَما نِيلَ مِنْهُ شَيْءٌ قَطُّ فَيَنْتَقِمَ مِنْ صاحِبِهِ إلاَّ أَنْ يُنْتَهَكَ شَيْءٌ مِنْ مَحارِمِ ٱللهِ تَعالَى فَيَنْتَقِمَ لِلهِ تَعالَى."

(رواه مسلم. حديث صحيح)

Narrated 'Ā'isha: "The Messenger of God ﷺ never hit anyone with his hand, neither a woman nor a servant; in the case when he was fighting in the cause of God, he never took revenge for anything unless the things made inviolable by God were made violable; he then took revenge for God, the Exalted and Glorious."

(Quoted by Muslim. Authenticated *ḥadīth*)

Commentary

A superficial and purely circumstantial reading of the traditional biographies of the Prophet (*sīrah*) can be misleading and can give a distorted image of his fundamental character. In fact, the literary genre which took the name of *sīrah* was closely related to the account of the [military] expeditions (*kutub al-maghāzī*).

The implacable attitude that the Prophet ﷺ had to demonstrate sometimes was dictated by the situation, but it did not belong to his profound nature, as emphasized by this *ḥadīth*.

Frithjof Schuon ('Īsā Nūr al-Dīn)

Another reproach often leveled at him is that of cruelty; but it is rather implacability that should be spoken of, and it was directed, not at enemies as such, but only at traitors, whatever their origin; if there was hardness here, it was that of God Himself through participation in the Divine Justice which rejects and consumes. To accuse Muḥammad of having a vindictive nature would involve not only a serious misjudgement of his spiritual state and a distortion of the facts, but also by the same token a condemnation of most of the Jewish Prophets and of the Bible itself. In the decisive phase of his earthly mission, at the time of the taking of Mecca, the Messenger of Allāh even showed a superhuman forbearance in the face of a unanimous feeling to the contrary in his victorious army.

(*Understanding Islam*, p. 105)

Ḥadīth 168

عن أنس بن مالك : "ما مَسَسْتُ دِيباجاً وَلا حَريراً أَلْيَنَ مِنْ كَفِّ رَسُولِ ٱللهِ ﷺ وَما شَمَمْتُ رائحةً قَطُّ أَطْيَبَ مِنْ رائحة رَسُولِ ٱللهِ ﷺ. وَلَقَدْ خَدَمْتُ رَسُولَ ٱللهِ ﷺ عَشْرَ سِنينَ فَما قالَ لِي قَطُّ "أُفٍّ" وَلا قالَ لِشَيْءٍ فَعَلْتُهُ : "لِمَ فَعَلْتَهُ ؟" وَلا لِشَيْءٍ لَمْ أَفْعَلْهُ : "أَلا فَعَلْتَ كَذا ؟"

(رواه البخاري. حديث صحيح)

Narrated Anas ibn Mālik: "The hand of the Messenger of God ﷺ was softer than satin or silk and his smell was more agreeable than perfumes. I served the Messenger of God ﷺ for ten years, during which he never reprimanded me, and he never asked me, 'Why did you do such and such and why did you not do such and such?'"

(Quoted by al-Bukhārī. Authenticated *ḥadīth*)

Commentary

For those who knew the Prophet ﷺ directly, he was the embodiment of the perfect model and the personification of virtues. In order to share what it must have been like to experience the Prophet, Anas quotes both his physical and moral mildness and the immense goodness that emanated from him. Behind the "anecdotal manner" of evoking his personality by isolating and accentuating a trait, there lies a very profound description of the spirituality of the Prophet. Thus the softness of his hand and the perfume which he exuded bore witness to the sanctification of the Prophet ﷺ by the Spirit and the Revelation which penetrated not only his soul, but also the smallest particle of his body. As regards the immense goodness mentioned by Anas, this marks the realization of the Divine attributes of mercy and forgiveness, and obviously the total extinction of the ego and its tendencies for dominating others. As P. Nwiya has remarked, the Prophet ﷺ is "the unsurpassable model of all sanctity"[201] in Islam.

Frithjof Schuon ('Īsā Nūr al-Dīn)

"Ye have in the Messenger of God a beautiful example," the Qur'ān says, and not for nothing. The virtue one can observe amongst pious Muslims

201. *Exégèse coranique et langage mystique*, Beirut, 1970, p. 13.

including the heroic modalities that these give rise to amongst the Sufis, are attributed by the *Sunna* to the Prophet; now it is inconceivable that these virtues could have been practiced throughout the centuries all the way to our day without the founder of Islam having personified them in the highest degree; likewise it is inconceivable that the virtues would have been borrowed from elsewhere—one would have wondered from where—since their conditioning and style are specifically Islamic. For Muslims, the moral and spiritual worth of the Prophet ﷺ is not an abstraction or a conjectural matter; it is a living reality, and this is precisely what proves, retrospectively, its authenticity; to deny this amounts to claiming that there can be effects without a cause.

The Muḥammadan character of the virtues explains, moreover, the more or less impersonal bearing of saints: there are no other virtues than those of Muḥammad; thus they can only be repeated by those who imitate his example; it is through them that the Prophet ﷺ lives on in his community.

(*Form*, pp. 91-2)

Ḥadīth 169

عن ابن مسعود : "كَأَنِّي أَنْظُرُ إِلَى رَسُولِ ٱللهِ ﷺ يُحْكِي نَبِيًّا مِنَ ٱلأَنْبِياءِ صَلَواتُ ٱللهِ وَسَلامُهُ عَلَيْهِمْ ضَرَبَهُ قَوْمُهُ فَأَدْمُوهُ, وَهُوَ يَمْسَحُ ٱلدَّمَ مِنْ وَجْهِهِ وَيَقُول :"اللَّهُمَّ ٱغفِرْ لِقَوْمِي فَإِنَّهُمْ لا يَعْلَمُون."

(رواه مسلم. حديث صحيح)

Narrated Ibn Mas'ūd: "I can still see the Messenger of God ﷺ acting like another Prophet ﷺ who had been beaten by his people and had bled. The Messenger of God ﷺ wiped the blood from his face and said: 'My Lord, forgive my people, for they do not know.'"

(Quoted by Muslim. Authenticated *ḥadīth*)

Commentary

If the Prophet ﷺ could react like Jesus in certain situations—which is what Ibn Mas'ūd is stressing in this *ḥadīth*—it is nonetheless true that he led a life radically different from that of Jesus, and that on numerous occasions he showed "another path" to be followed. In fact, his sanctity and his spirituality were, as it were, concealed by his human simplicity; his grandeur remained completely on the inside for, in the message of Islam, God alone should appear with all His grandeur.

Frithjof Schuon ('Īsā Nūr al-Dīn)

This simplicity, or this voluntary smallness of the Prophet, is in fact an unmistakable proof of his sincerity; an impostor coming after Christ would not have failed in declaring himself "Son of God" in his turn; The sincerity is here all the more striking since the Prophet ﷺ admitted the virginal birth of Christ, which was hardly in his interest to do, either humanly or logically; at no time did the Prophet ﷺ endeavor to appear as a superman. Be that as it may, Muḥammad was unquestionably an ascetic; it is well known that he had several wives, though incomparably fewer than David and Solomon who possessed hundreds; but, apart from that situation, which was sacramental from his point of view, he never ate to satiety, spent his nights in prayer, and gave away as alms all that he did not strictly need. As for his political comportment, it is worth recalling that the outward morality of Islam is identical to that of the Old Testament; it is *a priori* practical and not ascetical or mystical; thus it is first of all social. Intrinsic morality, that of the virtues, takes precedence over social morality while belonging to another sector which, though being no doubt parallel, is nonetheless independent . . .

(*Form*, p. 90)

Ḥadīth 170

عن أنس بن مالك : "لا يُؤْمِنُ أَحَدُكُمْ حَتَّى أَكُونَ أَحَبَّ إِلَيْهِ مِنْ وَالِدِهِ وَوَلَدِهِ وَٱلنَّاسِ أَجْمَعِينَ."

(رواه البخاري. حديث صحيح)

Narrated Anas ibn Mālik: "None of you will have faith until he loves me more than his parents, his children and all humankind."

(Quoted by al-Bukhārī. Authenticated *ḥadīth*.)

Ḥadīth 171

عن عبد الله بن هشام : "كَيْفَ أَصْبَحَ حُبُّكَ لِي يا عُمَر ؟ فَقالَ عُمَر : يا رَسُولَ ٱللهِ لأَنْتَ أَحَبُّ إِلَيَّ مِنْ كُلِّ شَـيْءٍ إِلاّ مِنْ نَفْسِي. فَقالَ ٱلنَّبِيُّ ﷺ لَهُ : لا وَالَّذِي نَفْسِي بِيَـدِهِ حَتَّى أَكُونَ أَحَبَّ إِلَيْكَ مِنْ نَفْسِكَ. فَقالَ عُمَر : فَإِنَّهُ ٱلآنَ وَٱللهِ لأَنْتَ أَحَبُّ إِلَيَّ مِنْ نَفْسِي. فَقالَ ٱلنَّبِيُّ ﷺ : الآنَ يا عُمَر."

(رواه البخاري. حديث صحيح)

Narrated 'Abdullah ibn Hishām: "'How is your love for me today, O 'Umar?' 'Umar replied: 'O Messenger of God! You are dearer to me than everything except my own self.' The Prophet ﷺ said, 'Nay, by Him in whose hand my soul is, [you will not have complete faith] till I am dearer to you than your own self.' Then 'Umar said to him, 'However, now, by God, you are dearer to me than my own self.' The Prophet ﷺ said, 'Now, O 'Umar, [you are a believer].'"

(Quoted by al-Bukhārī. Authenticated *ḥadīth*)

Commentary

The Prophet ﷺ was more demanding of 'Umar than he was of the common believers since he added another condition to the love that every believer must have for him; the love of the Prophet ﷺ must lead 'Umar to lose the attachment to his individual existence and therefore to the extinction of his ego. This principle of spiritual life, despite not being a norm imposed on us, is fully affirmed in the following verse: *The Prophet ﷺ has a greater claim on the faithful than they have on themselves, and his spouses are their mothers.*[202]

202. XXXIII: 6.

Ḥadīth 172

عَنْ عمار بن ياسر : "اللَّهُمَّ بِعِلْمِكَ ٱلْغَيْبِ وَقُدْرَتِكَ عَلَى
ٱلْخَلْقِ أَحْيِنِي ما عَلِمْتَ ٱلْحَياةَ خَيْراً لِي، وَتَوَفَّنِي إِذا
عَلِمْتَ ٱلْوَفاةَ خَيْراً لِي. اللَّهُمَّ وَأَسْأَلُكَ خَشْيَتَكَ فِي ٱلْغَيْبِ
وَٱلشَّهادة وَأَسْأَلُكَ كَلِمَةَ ٱلْإِخْلاصِ فِي ٱلرِّضا وَٱلْغَضَبِ
وَأَسْأَلُكَ ٱلْقَصْدَ فِي ٱلْفَقْرِ وَٱلْغِنَى، وَأَسْأَلُكَ نَعِيماً لا يَنْفَذُ،
وَأَسْأَلُكَ قُرَّةَ عَيْنٍ لا تَنْقَطِعُ وَأَسْأَلُكَ ٱلرِّضا بِٱلْقَضاءِ
وَأَسْأَلُكَ بَرْدَ ٱلْعَيْشِ بَعْدَ ٱلْمَوْتِ وَأَسْأَلُكَ لَذَّةَ ٱلنَّظَرِ إِلَى
وَجْهِكَ وَٱلشَّوْقَ إِلَى لِقائِكَ فِي غَيْرِ ضَرَّاءَ مُضِرَّةٍ وَلا فِتْنَةٍ
مُضِلَّةٍ، اللَّهُمَّ زَيِّنَّا بِزِينَةِ ٱلْإِيْمانِ وَٱجْعَلْنا هُداةً مَهْتَدِينَ."

(رواه الحاكم. حديث صحيح)

Narrated 'Ammār ibn Yāsir: "O God, through Thy knowledge of the Unknown and Thy power over creation, give me a life as long as Thou knowest it to be good for me, and make me die if Thou knowest that death is
better for me. I ask Thee to grant me fear of Thee in secret and in public
alike; I ask Thee the veracious word (*kalimat al-ikhlāṣ*) in satisfaction and
in wrath; I ask Thee to grant me restraint in richness as well as poverty; I
ask Thee a blessing which is not exhausted, a coolness of the eyes which
does not lessen; I ask Thee to make me satisfied with destiny; I ask Thee to
grant me a peaceful life after death; I ask from Thee the joy of seeing Thy
face and the aspiration (*shawq*) of meeting Thee; protect me from every
harm and all distraction. O God, adorn us with the embellishment of faith
and make us inspired guides!"

(Quoted by al-Ḥākim. Authenticated *ḥadīth*)

Commentary

All the petitions formulated in this *ḥadīth* indicate the Prophet's strong aspiration towards God (*shawq ilā Llāh*), which culminates in his desire to
behold the Divine Face.

al-Sarrāj

The following has been related from the Prophet ﷺ: "I ask Thee to grant me the joy of seeing Thy face and the aspiration of meeting Thee." The aspiration (*shawq*) consists in a servant's not bearing to live away from his Beloved. A spiritual master was asked about aspiration. He said: "It is the force of love taking hold of the heart when the Beloved is mentioned." Another master has said: "It is a fire that God kindles in the heart of saints in order to burn away the self-propagating thoughts (*khawāṭir*), all individual will, all inner obstacles, and all needs."

(*Luma'*, p. 94)

The Prophets: الأنبياء

Ḥadīth 173

عن أنس بن مالك : "الأَنْبِياءُ أَحْياءٌ فِي قُبُورِهِمْ يُصَلُّونَ."

(رواه أبو يعلى. حديث حسن)

Narrated Anas ibn Mālik: "The Prophets are alive: they pray in their graves."

(Quoted by Abū Ya'lā. Validated *ḥadīth*)

Commentary

Jalāl al-Dīn al-Suyūṭī devoted an entire chapter to the question of whether the Prophets continue to live after having left our world: *Anbā' al-adhkiyā' bi-ḥayāt al-anbiyā'*.[203] In this chapter, he affirms that this question suffers no ambiguity and that the continued life of the Prophets is something well-known and definitely established. However, literalism is not so easy to avoid, and the veneration of the Prophets' tombs always risks being interpreted as a pagan cult by those who prefer to see nothing but this. This is why al-Suyūṭī brings together textual proofs in this chapter in order to convince those who reject the continued life of the Prophets.

al-Suyūṭī

The continued life of the Prophet ﷺ in the grave, as well as that of the other Prophets, is a thing well known and definitely established with regards to textual proofs and facts. Among these proofs, Muslim quotes a *ḥadīth* narrated by Anas according to which the Prophet ﷺ, during the night of his nocturnal ascension, passed by the tomb of Moses and found him praying there. [. . .]

Abū Manṣūr ibn Ṭāhir al-Baghdādī, the jurist and specialist in the principles of jurisprudence (*uṣūl*), has said: "The competent scholars amongst my brothers state that our Prophet ﷺ is alive and that he rejoices in the obedience of the pious believers of the community and is saddened by their sin, and he also receives the prayer of those who send their prayers to him."

(*al-Ḥāwī*, II, p. 149)

203. *Al-Ḥāwī lil-fatāwī* (Beirut: *Dār al-kutub al-'ilmiyya*, 1988), II, pp. 147-155.

Ḥadīth 174

عن أبي الدرداء : "الْعُلَماءُ وَرَثَةُ ٱلأَنْبِياء..."

(رواه الترمذي. حديث صحيح)

Narrated Abū al-Dardā': "The scholars are the heirs of the Prophets . . ."
(Quoted by al-Tirmidhī. Authenticated *ḥadīth.*)

Commentary

The inheritance mentioned by this *ḥadīth* can come from any Prophet. Thus, a true scholar can possess a more or less significant spiritual heritage, of Mosaic (*mūsāwī*), or Christic (*'īsāwī*) nature . . . However, it is commonly accepted amongst the masters of the Path that the highest degrees of spirituality are possessed by the sages of the Muḥammadan heritage.

Ibn al-'Arabī

When Moses returned from his Lord, God covered his face with light so that the truthfulness of his word could be recognized through this sign; and nobody could look at him without being blinded by the intensity of this light, so much so that his face had to be covered by a veil in order for those who beheld it not to be harmed. Our master Abū Ya'zā from the Maghreb was a saint of Mosaic heritage (*mūsāwī al-wirth*) and God had granted him the same miraculous sign. No one could look at his face without losing their sight. Thereupon he would rub one of his garments against that person's face, thus returning his sight. Among those who saw him and were blinded in this way was our Shaykh Abū Madyān, during one of his visits to him. Abū Madyān rubbed his eyes with the garment worn by Abū Ya'zā and gained his sight back. The miracles of Abū Ya'za are famous in the *Maghrib*. He lived during the time when I was there myself but, preoccupied with other things, I could never meet him. Then there were others—amongst those belonging to the Muḥammadan heritage—who were superior to him in knowledge, in spiritual states and in nearness to God, and whom neither Abū Ya'zā nor anyone else knew.

(*Fut.*, IV, pp. 50-51)

Ḥadīth 175

عن أبي هريرة : "كُلُّ بَنِي آدَمَ يَمَسُّهُ ٱلشَّيْطانُ يَوْمَ وَلَدَتْهُ أُمُّهُ، إلاّ مَرْيَمَ وَٱبْنَها."

(رواه مسلم. حديث صحيح)

Narrated Abū Hurayra: "Satan touches every son of Adam on the day when his mother gives birth to him with the exception of Mary and her son."

(Quoted by Muslim. Authenticated *ḥadīth.*)

Commentary

Just as the text of this *ḥadīth*, the Qur'ān associates Mary with her son in order to evoke the blessings they have in common. Thus it declares, *And We made the son of Mary and his mother a Sign, and We gave them refuge on a height, a place of flocks and watersprings.*[204] Another verse specifies the universality of this Sign, and speaking about Jesus, the angel of Annunciation declares to Mary: *And (it will be) that We may make of him a revelation for mankind and a mercy from Us, and it is a thing ordained.*[205]

As for the Prophet, like every human being, he too was touched by Satan at birth but was purified when he was still a child. This purification took place when the angel opened his chest to remove "a black clot" when he was still a child. This event is referred to in Chapter XCIV (*al-Inshirāḥ*) which starts with the following verse: *Have We not caused thy bosom to expand?*

We have explained how a Muslim spiritual person can inherit from any prophet, and this is true of Mary, as is shown by the case of Shaykh 'Abd Allāh al-Yunīnī (d. 617/1220), who was called the "Lion of Syria" for the exceptional courage he showed during the crusades:

> One day he was sitting in his *zāwiya* when a woman introduced herself, riding a mount loaded with copperware and fabric. She thethered it, came to him and greeted him. He asked her:
>
> - Who are you?
> - A Christian from Jubbat al-Qunaytra.
> - What has brought you to me?
> - I saw Lady [Mary] in my dream and she told me: "Go and offer yourself to the service of Shaykh 'Abd Allāh al-Yunīnī until your death."

---

204. XXIII: 50.
205. XIX: 21.

- I told her, "Our Lady, he is a Muslim."
- So what? Indeed, he is a Muslim but his heart is [similar to that of a] Christian.'

The shaykh told her, "Mary is the only one who knows me."
The shaykh gave her a lodge in the *zāwiya* and she stayed in his service for eight months, and then she fell ill. The shaykh asked her:

- What do you want?
- I want to die in the religion of Mary.

The shaykh ordered for a priest to be called . . . and she died in his presence."

(Abū Shāma, *Tarājim*, year 617 H. Fr. tr. Claude Addas, *Ibn Arabî et le voyage sans retour*, Seuil: 1996, p. 121)

The Saints and the Virtuous: الأولياء والصالحون

Ḥadīth 176

عن ابن مسعود : "إذا انْقَلَبَتْ دابَّةُ أَحَدِكُمْ بِأَرْضٍ فَلاةٍ فَلْيُنادِ : يا عِبادَ ٱللهِ احْبِسُوا عَلَيَّ، يا عِبادَ ٱللهِ احْبِسُوا عَلَيَّ، فَإِنَّ لِلهِ فِي ٱلأَرْضِ حاضِراً سَيُحْبِسُهُ عَلَيْكُمْ."

(رواه الطبراني. حديث حسن)

Narrated Ibn Mas'ūd: "When the steed of one of you collapses in a deserted place, he should call out: 'O servants of God come to my aid! O servants of God come to my aid!' For assuredly, God possesses [in every place] a servant He can grant to you."

(Quoted by al-Ṭabarānī. Validated *ḥadīth*)

Yūsuf Khaṭṭār

Upon quoting this *ḥadīth*, Imam al-Ṭabarānī as well as Imam al-Nawawī add that they have put this supplication into practice and used it. The meaning of this *ḥadīth* is clear and needs no interpretation. In a situation like the one described in this *ḥadīth*, it would be natural and spontaneous to supplicate God, as there is no one around. Nevertheless, the Prophet ﷺ taught us to supplicate with the following words: *Yā 'ibād Allāh, iḥbisū 'alayya* (O servants of God, come to my aid), in order to encourage people to use the means that God has put at our disposal in creation (*al-akhdh bi-l-asbāb*).

(*Mawsū'a*, p. 97)

Ḥadīth 177

عن عبادة بن الصامت : "الأَبْدالُ فِي أُمَّتِي ثَلاثُونَ : بِهِمْ تَقُومُ ٱلأَرْضُ وَبِهِمْ تُمْطَرُونَ وَبِهِمْ تُنْصَرُونَ."

(رواه الطبراني. حديث صحيح)

Narrated 'Ubāda ibn al-Ṣāmit: "The *abdāl*[206] of my community are thirty: it is through them that the earth is maintained, the rain comes to you, and you receive God's assistance."

(Quoted by al-Ṭabarānī. Authenticated *ḥadīth*)

Commentary

That God's action takes a certain creature as support does not influence the fact that He is the Unique Agent. However, this "necessitates" taking into account those who are the direct supports of God's action as well as their function.

al-Junayd

God—glorified be He—does not leave the earth deprived of proofs who are His saints, nor devoid of those He loves, for it is through them that He protects those He keeps in life, and it is through them that He protects those whom He has given existence. And I ask Him who is the Ever-benevolent (*al-Mannān*), by His favor and His magnanimity, to grant us, you and me, to be amongst the depositaries of His mystery, the guardians upon whom He has conferred His sublime commandments, and to bestow upon us the grace of the most magnificent spiritual degrees, and to let us observe all that is apparent and all that is hidden.

You were able to admire how God—exalted be He and sanctified are His names—through the adornment of His saints and those who possess knowledge of Him, has embellished the expanse of the earth He spread and the vast space of His kingdom (*al-mulk*: the sensible world). He has made of them the brightest splendor, whose light spreads and whose apparition is manifested in the hearts of the sages. Their embellishment is more beautiful than that of the sky, which glows from the brightness of the stars and the light of the sun and of the moon.

They are like signposts on the road on which God leads men, and on the paths of those who seek to obey Him. They are like beacons illuminating the ways followed by those who exert themselves to conform to Him; [they are] even brighter than the stars which people guide themselves by in the dark, on land and over the sea, and whose trace they follow to find the way to the

206. For the definition of this, see the commentary of *ḥadīth* 179.

inextricable paths. The example of the saints is a manifest source of blessing for creatures, and their beneficial influence in protecting men against evil is evident. The guidance offered by the stars ensures the protection of people's goods and their bodies, whereas the guidance offered by those possessing Divine knowledge ensures the safeguarding of spiritual life, and there is no common measure between succeeding in safeguarding religion and succeeding in safeguarding people's material goods and bodies.

(*Enseignement*, "Lettre à un de ses frères spirituels", pp. 43-44)

Ḥadīth 178

عن عبادة بن الصامت : "الأَبْدالُ فِي هذهِ ٱلأُمَّة ثَلاثُونَ رَجُلاً، قُلُوبُهُمْ عَلَى قَلْبِ إِبْراهِيمَ خَلِيلِ ٱلرَّحْمَان، كُلَّما ماتَ رَجُلٌ أَبْدَلَ ٱللهُ مَكانَهُ رَجُلاً."

(رواه الإمام أحمد. حديث صحيح)

Narrated 'Ubāda ibn al-Ṣāmit: "The *abdāl* in this community are thirty: their hearts are in affinity with that of Abraham, the intimate Friend of the All-Merciful. Each time one of them dies, God replaces him by another."

(Quoted by Aḥmad ibn Ḥanbal. Authenticated *ḥadīth*)

Shaykh al-'Alawī

For every prophet there exists a category of people of Muhammad's ﷺ community whose hearts are in affinity with him. These people who exist in every age are essentially the interlocutors of this Divine representative. In fact, they are the most qualified to accomplish this mission of enjoining good and forbidding evil. Molded for this mission since eternity, they are naturally endowed with the qualities demanded by this function . . . In my opinion, the category of people referred to in the verse are, in most cases, not to be found except amongst the people of the invocation (*dhākirūn*).

(*Qawl*, p. 13)

Ḥadīth 179

عن أبي هريرة : "دَخَلْتُ عَلَى ٱلنَّبِيِّ فَقالَ لِي : يا أَبا هُرَيْرَة يَدْخُلُ عَلَيَّ مِنْ هذا ٱلبابِ ٱلسَّاعَةَ رَجُلٌ مِنْ أَحَدِ ٱلسَّبْعَةِ ٱلَّذِينَ يَدْفَعُ ٱللهُ عَنْ أَهْلِ ٱلأَرْضِ بِهِمْ، فَإِذا حَبَشِيٌّ قَدْ طَلَعَ مِنْ ذٰلِكَ ٱلبابِ أَقْرَعُ أَجْدَعُ عَلَى رَأْسِهِ جَرَّةٌ مِنْ ماءٍ، فَقالَ رَسُولُ ٱللهِ ﷺ : أَبا هُرَيْرَةَ هُوَ هٰذا وَقالَ رَسُولُ ٱللهِ ﷺ ثَلاثَ مَرَّاتٍ : مَرْحَباً بِيسار وَكانَ يَرُشُّ ٱلْمَسْجِدَ وَيَكْنِسُهُ وَكانَ غُلاماً لِلْمُغِيرَةِ بْنِ شُعْبَة."

(رواه السيوطي. حديث حسن)

Narrated Abū Hurayra: "One day I entered upon the Prophet. He told me, 'In a few moments, a man is going to come to me through that door, who is one of the seven through whom God protects the inhabitants of the earth.' An Ethiopian (*ḥabashī*) then entered the door. He was bald and his nose was short. He carried a jar of water on his head. The Messenger of God ﷺ said: 'O Abū Hurayra! It is him.' Then he told him three times: 'Welcome Yasār!' This man used to sprinkle the mosque and sweep it: he was the young servant of Mughīra ibn Shu'ba."

(Quoted by al-Suyūṭī. Validated *ḥadīth*.)

Commentary

The category of spiritual men denoted by the Arabic term *badal* (pl. *abdāl*) is traditionally inserted in the following hierarchical succession: the Pole of the time (*quṭb al-zamān*); the two Assistants (*al-imāmān*); the four Pillars (*al-awtād*); the *abdāl*. This term can be translated literally as "substitutes." Their number varies depending on the sources, and Ibn al-'Arabī has opted for the number seven, thus relating each *badal* to one of the seven domains (*aqālīm*).[207]

Ibn al-'Arabī

Amongst the folk of the esoteric hierarchy, there are seven *abdāl* who are

---

207. This term denotes the division of the known and populated territories into seven regions. Cf. *E.I.* (2): art. IKLĪM.

never more than seven or less than seven. Through them, God preserves each of the seven domains. The first of them is "on the footsteps" of the Intimate friend of God (*Khalīl Allāh*),[208] and he is in charge of the first domain. It is so for each of the seven *abdāl* and the seven domains. The second *badal* is "on the footsteps" of the Mouthpiece of God (*Kalīm Allāh*);[209] the third is "on the footsteps" of Hārūn; the fourth "on the footsteps" of Idrīs; the fifth "on the footsteps" of Yūsuf; the sixth "on the footsteps" of 'Īsā; and the seventh "on the footsteps" of Ādam. These people have knowledge of the secrets that God has placed in the planets, secrets related to their movements and to the different locations they can occupy. Their names derive from Divine attributes: *'Abd al-Ḥayy, 'Abd al-'Alīm, 'Abd al-Wadūd, 'Abd al-Qādir*. These first four names are those of the Pillars (*awtād*). They are followed by *'Abd al-Shakūr, 'Abd al-Samī'* and *'Abd al-Baṣīr*. Each of the seven Divine attributes dominates a *badal*, and it is through the attribute proper to each of them that the Real contemplates them. These men receive the name of Subsitutes (*abdāl*) because when one of them quits a place and wishes to leave a substitute because of a blessing for him or others, he leaves a person (*shakhṣ*) possessing the form of the *abdāl* so that whoever sees the latter cannot doubt that he saw the man himself. In reality, it is not him but a spiritual form (*shakhṣ ruḥānī*) which he has left in his place for a reason related to the knowledge he possesses.

(*Fut*., II, p. 7)

---

208. I.e., Abraham.

209. I.e., Moses.

Ḥadīth 180

عن أبي سعيد الخدري : "اِتَّقُوا فِراسةَ ٱلْمُؤْمِنِ فَإِنَّهُ يَنْظُرُ بِنُورِ ٱللهِ."

(رواه الترمذي. حديث حسن)

Narrated Abū Sa'īd al-Khudrī: "Be wary of the perspicacity of the man of faith for he sees with the light of God."

(Quoted by al-Tirmidhī. Validated *ḥadīth*.)

Commentary

The spiritual masters define perspicacity (*firāsa*) as a synonym of the physiognomy mentioned in *Ḥadīth* 193.

Another *ḥadīth* specifies that this perspicacity is the privilege of the spiritual elite of every religion.

عن عروة بن زبير : "إِنَّ لِكُلِّ قَوْمٍ فِراسةٌ وَإِنَّما يَعْرِفُها ٱلأَشْرافُ."

(رواه الحاكم. حديث صحيح)

Narrated 'Urwa ibn Zubayr: "Verily, perspicacity is present amongst all peoples. Yet, only the noblest in their midst possess it."

(Quoted by al-Ḥākim. Authenticated *ḥadīth*)

al-Munāwī

" . . . Only the noblest amongst them possess it." That is, those who occupy the highest degrees of knowledge of the Path to the Hereafter. We have already seen that perspicacity is a gift that God bestows upon the heart of His friends (*awliyā'*). This is how they know the states of other persons . . . Just as there is an eye for the vision of external things, there exists an eye in the heart [for spiritual vision]. He whose eye of the heart is open and illuminated by the light of God will perceive the realities of things (*ḥaqā'iq al-ashyā'*) and the spiritual world (*al-'alām al-'ulwī*) already in this world: he then sees what no eye has seen, and he hears what no ear has heard, and he knows what no heart has been able to conceive.

The conditions *sine qua non* of true perspicacity are those enumerated by Kirmānī: "He who adopts the Prophetic Sunna in all his conduct realizes the continuous awareness of the Nearness of God (*dawām al-murāqaba*), deprives his soul of its tendencies, turns away his look from what is forbidden, and nourishes himself only with lawful food will be granted an infallible discernment."

(*Fayḍ al-Qadīr*, *ḥadīth* no. 2429)

al-Anṣārī

God—exalted be He—has said: *Lo! therein verily are signs for those who read the physiognomy (mutawwasimīn).*[210] Physiognomy is precisely the spiritual perspicacity which consists in perceiving that which is invisible in something, without a reasoning based on known elements or empirical research of any kind.

Perspicacity consists of three degrees:

- The first is an unexpected and exceptional insight. It is the case of persons who do not really possess it.
- The second degree is an insight coming from the tree of faith; it sprouts from the authenticity of the spiritual state (*ḥāl*) and it scintillates from the light of unveiling (*kashf*).
- The third degree is sublime insight. It is not the fruit of individual understanding, rather it is given but to those elect who are anchored in initiatic knowledge, which is expressed explicitly or implicitly.

(*Manāzil*, no. 55, p. 64 of the Arabic text).

210. XV: 75.

Ḥadīth 181

عن ابن مسعود : "كَانَتِ ٱلأَنْبِياءُ يَسْتَحِبُّونَ أَنْ يَلْبَسُوا ٱلصُّوفَ."

(رواه الحاكم. حديث صحيح)

Narrated Ibn Mas'ūd: "The prophets like to dress in wool."
(Quoted by al-Ḥākim. Authenticated *ḥadīth*)

Ḥadīth 182

عن أبي أمامة : "عَلَيْكُمْ بِلِباسِ ٱلصُّوفِ تَجِدُوا حَلاوَةَ ٱلإِيمانِ فِي قُلُوبِكُمْ."

(رواه الحاكم. حديث صحيح)

Narrated Abū Umāma: "Dress in woolen clothes, and you shall taste the sweetness of faith in your hearts."
(Quoted by al-Ḥākim. Authenticated *ḥadīth*)

Commentary

The Arabic term *ṣūfī* is generally considered to derive from the word *ṣūf* meaning wool. In showing the relation between the sweetness of faith and the wearing of wool, the second *ḥadīth* can be considered a support for this etymology.

al-Junayd

Taṣawwuf is based on eight virtues characterizing eight prophets: generosity (*sakhā'*), contentment (*riḍā*), patience (*ṣabr*), indirect speech (*ishāra*), exile (*ghurba*), wearing of wool (*lubs al-ṣūf*), journeying (*siyāḥā*), and spiritual poverty (*faqr*). Generosity is represented by Abraham, contentment by Ishmael, patience by Job, indirect speech by Zachariah, exile by John, wearing of wool by Moses, journeying by Jesus, and spiritual poverty by Muḥammad.
(*Tāj*, p. 148. Fr. tr.: *Enseignement*, pp. 188-189)

Ḥadīth 183

عن فضالة بن عبيد : "الْمُجاهِدُ مَنْ جاهَدَ نَفْسَهُ فِي ٱللهِ."

(رواه أبن حبان. حديث صحيح)

Narrated Faḍāla ibn 'Ubayd: "The true fighter is he who combats his soul for God."

(Quoted by Ibn Ḥibbān. Authenticated *ḥadīth*)

Commentary

The Arabic term *nafs* which we have translated here as "soul" can denote, depending on the context, both the empirical ego—the psychic tendencies appearing through character traits and behaviour—and the immortal soul which is not separated from the spirit (*rūḥ*). This is why the Qur'ān distinguishes three degrees in the soul forming a hierarchy in the spiritual evolution of an individual. The passing from one degree to the other is contingent upon the sincerity in the *mujāhadat al-nafs*, the combat against the soul.

al-Ghazzālī

The term *nafs* is also susceptible to several meanings, two of which are related to our subject. The first denotes the power of wrath (*ghaḍab*) and of the appetite (*shahwa*) in man, and it constitutes the most frequent use of the term amongst the mystics, who by "soul" denote the blameworthy tendencies in man. They affirm that one has to combat the soul and "shatter" it; this is what the following *ḥadīth* of the Prophet ﷺ alludes to, "Your worst enemy is your soul, which is between your shoulders." The second meaning denotes the subtle element (*laṭīfa*) constituting the reality (*ḥaqīqa*) of man and his essence (*dhāt*). However, this subtle reality is described differently depending on the inner states that may affect it. If it remains under the influence of God and has become exempt from confusion, following the rejection of appetites, it is called "the soul at peace" (*al-nafs al-muṭma'inna*). Regarding this, God the Most High has said: *O thou soul which are at peace, return unto thy Lord, with gladness that is thine in Him and His in thee.*[211] The soul in the first meaning above cannot return to God because its tendency is to distance itself from God, and it is an ally of Satan. If the soul does not obtain a total response and it still has to fight against concupiscence, it is called "the soul which reproaches" itself (*al-nafs al-lawwāma*) because it blames itself for its shortcomings in worshipping God. Regarding this, God the Exalted has said, *I swear by the self-reproaching soul.*[212] If the soul ceases to oppose the appetites and it gives in to the inciting of

211. LXXXIX: 27-28.
212. LXXV: 2.

the desires and the whisperings of Satan, it is called "the soul incited to evil" (*al-nafs al-ammāra bi-l-sū'*). These souls may be said to fit the first meaning of the term.

(*Iḥyā'*, III, p. 3)

Ḥadīth 184

عن أبي هريرة : "لَيْسَ ٱلغِنَى مِنْ كَثْرَةِ ٱلعَرَضِ، وَلَكِن ٱلغِنَى غِنَى ٱلنَّفْسِ."

(رواه الترمذي. حديث صحيح)

Narrated Abū Hurayra: "Wealth is not the accumulation of possessions; true wealth is inner richness."

(Quoted by al-Tirmidhī. Authenticated *ḥadīth*)

Commentary

If wealth is defined as that which enables a life of ease and well-being, then the question arises whether the accumulation of material possessions can really provide this. Although it is obviously desirable to avoid misery—for oneself as well as others—it is also evident that well-being, like unhappiness, is a state of the soul. As emphasized by al-Ghazzālī, detachment (*zuhd*) is an essential virtue for escaping the ego's insatiable thirst for possession.

al-Ghazzālī

Know that detachment is a noble station (*maqām*) amongst those that the travelers to God go through. Like all the spiritual stations, it is related to knowledge, a spiritual state, and worship. Knowledge is the origin of the spiritual state, which in its turn is the origin of worship.

Detachment consists in abandoning something with a view to something superior to it. [. . .] Since detachment supposes abandoning something to which one is attached—otherwise there would be no question of detaching oneself—it can only be conceived in view of a thing, the love of which is even greater. This is why true detachment consists in abandoning everything which is not God, including Paradise, and loving nothing but Him. He who is detached from the things of the here-below for the sake of the delights of the Hereafter—houris, palaces, flowers, fruits . . . is detached, but to a lesser degree.

(*Iḥyā'*, IV, pp. 211-212)

Ḥadīth 185

عن أبي هريرة : "لَيْسَ ٱلشَّدِيدُ بِٱلصُّرْعةِ، إِنَّما ٱلشَّدِيدُ ٱلَّذِي يَمْلِكُ نَفْسَهُ عِنْدَ ٱلغَضَبِ."

(رواه الإمام أحمد. حديث صحيح)

Narrated Abū Hurayra: "He who throws his adversary on the ground is not strong, but he who dominates his soul when angry (is strong)."

(Quoted by Aḥmad ibn Ḥanbal. Authenticated *ḥadīth*)

Commentary

From the spiritual point of view, the only and veritable enemy is the ego, which is very often kept in illusion by the Enemy, namely Satan. Anger and aggressiveness are considered privileged means of access of the Enemy to the heart because they take hold of the ego and make one lose all discernment.

Shaykh al-Darqāwī

One of our brothers complained about an oppressor who had wronged him. We responded to him: "If you want to kill your oppressor, kill your ego! And thus shall you certainly kill your oppressors!"

We said to one of our brothers, "You will be in loss if, when seeing the form of your ego appear, you do not abandon its dwelling place and you do not erase its tracks immediately. However, this consists in making it endure that which is harder for it until you end up killing it. In fact, killing it enables the heart to live, as one of the masters has said: 'The heart cannot live while the ego is alive.'"

Another brother told us that he had struck a Jew for vanity, injustice, and despotism. We told him firmly: "Strike neither Jew, nor Christian, nor Muslim; and if you must absolutely strike—it is inevitable—then strike your ego and do not cease to strike it until it dies. Do not leave it alive!"

This is how I love my brothers to be. The vices, in fact, abound in the disciple whose ego is alive. The disciple whose ego is dead is sheltered from vices (*'uyūb*) and he contemplates the mysteries (*ghuyūb*); he is a master of all people, whether they want this or not, for it is God who grants him this supremacy.

(*Rasā'il*, letter 8)

Ḥadīth 186

عن أبي موسى الأشعري : "مَثَلُ ٱلجَلِيسِ الصّالِحِ وَٱلجَلِيسِ ٱلسُّوءِ كَمَثَلِ صاحِبِ ٱلْمِسْكِ وكِيرِ ٱلْحَدّادِ، لا يَعْدُمُكَ مِنْ صاحِبِ ٱلْمِسْكِ إِمّا أَنْ تَشْتَرِيَهُ أَوْ تَجِدَ رِيْحَهُ، وَكِيْرُ ٱلْحَدّادِ يَحْرِقُ بَيْتَكَ أَوْ ثَوْبَكَ أَوْ تَجِدُ مِنْهُ رِيْحاً خَبِيثاً.

(رواه البخاري. حديث صحيح)

Narrated Abū Mūsā al-Ash'ārī: "The example of a virtuous companion and an unsound one is like that of a musk seller and a blacksmith. You will leave the first carrying a good smell whether you buy some musk from him or not; whereas the blacksmith's [work] can either burn your house or your clothes, [and in the best case] you will receive a bad smell from the forge."

(Quoted by al-Bukhārī. Authenticated *ḥadīth*)

Ibn al-'Arabī

Nothing helps more in the obedience of God than visiting those who obey Him, and nothing pushes more to sinning than associating with sinners. As the Prophet ﷺ has said, "Man has the religion of his friends; therefore everybody should consider whom he befriends."[213] Through an innate tendency, the soul is inclined to imitate its entourage, to take on the attributes of the people it is in contact with, and even to attempt to compete with them in these domains. Associating with the heedless is therefore an invitation to heedlessness, besides which, for the soul, is one of its natural dispositions. What happens when the soul is immersed in the company of the heedless? You will agree with me, brother—may God grant you success—that your soul is not as willing in the same way when you exit from your place, your breast dilated, in resolve to obey your Lord and penetrated by light, except if you go back to self-seclusion. The reasons for this are the stain which associating with the profane brings about, and the darkening of the heart, which lets itself be engrossed by the means of subsistence. Were these secondary causes and the attraction to transgression to disappear from the soul, there would no longer be any insurmountable obstacle for the heart in its journey to God.

(*De l'Abandon de la Volonté propre*, Alif, 1997, p. 131)

213. Quoted by Abū Dāwūd, *ḥadīth* no. 4815. (tr.)

Ḥadīth 187

عن ابن عمرو : "خِيَارُكُمْ مَنْ ذَكَّرَكُمْ بِٱللهِ رُؤْيَتُهُ وَزَادَ فِي عِلْمِكُمْ مَنْطِقُهُ وَرَغَّبَكُمْ فِي ٱلآخِرَةِ عَمَلُهُ."

(رواه الحكيم. حديث صحيح)

Narrated Ibn 'Amr: "The best amongst you are those who evoke the remembrance of God when you see them, whose speech makes your faith increase, and whose actions make you desire the Hereafter."

(Quoted by al-Ḥakīm. Authenticated *ḥadīth*)

Ḥadīth 188

عن ابن عمر : "خِيَارُكُم ٱلَّذِينَ إذا رُؤُوا ذُكِرَ ٱللهُ بِهِمْ، وَشِرَارُكُم ٱلْمَشَّاؤُونَ بِٱلنَّمِيمَةِ، ٱلْمُفَرِّقُونَ بَيْنَ ٱلأَحِبَّةِ، ٱلْبَاغُونَ ٱلْبُرَآءُ ٱلْعَنَتَ."

(رواه البيهقي. حديث حسن)

Narrated Ibn 'Umar: "The best amongst you are those who evoke the remembrance of God in you when they are seen, and the worst amongst you are those who spread calumny, who divide those who love each other and who seek to make others suffer."

(Quoted by al-Bayhaqī. Validated *ḥadīth*)

Commentary

Despite their difference in tone, these *ḥadīth* stress the same essential characteristic of the best people: they bring about the remembrance of God in the hearts of others. In the following text, Ibn al-'Arabī emphasizes the mercy that such persons represent for everyone and their role in the creation:

Ibn al-'Arabī

Certain *ḥadīth* state that when perfect servants are mentioned, Mercy descends. This is so because the invocation of the perfect servants (*dhikr al-ṣāliḥūn*) is part of the invocation of God (*dhikr Allāh*). They are those who, according to a saying of the Prophet ﷺ, "when they are seen, they remind people of God." Thus, when they are mentioned, this is necessarily done by Him, and there can be established regarding them no relation except with Him. They are in fact the chosen servants, those who have worshipped God with sincerity (*ṣidq*) and purity of intention (*ikhlāṣ*). Thereafter, they have no knowledge except through Him, and they are incapable of acting otherwise except for Him. They represent the "recourse" (*al-ghiyāth*), and they maintain the command of the Real (*amr al-Ḥaqq*).

(*Kawkab*, p. 5.)

Ḥadīth 189

عن أنس بن مالك : إِنَّما يَعْرِفُ ٱلفَضْلَ لِأَهْلِ ٱلفَضْلِ أَهْلُ ٱلفَضْلِ.

(رواه ابن عساكر. حديث حسن)

Narrated Anas ibn Mālik: "The eminence of the folk of grace cannot be recognized except by the folk of grace."

(Quoted by Ibn 'Asākir. Validated *ḥadīth*)

Commentary

The expression "folk of grace" (*ahl al-faḍl*) denotes the saints of the Muḥammadan community, and like other *ḥadīth*, this one stresses the fact that they are hidden from those who are unworthy of knowing them, due to their attitude. More precisely, the *ḥadīth* emphasizes that one has to walk on the path of sanctity in order for one to know those who have gone before. Thus, recognizing and knowing a saint is a great favor that God grants to His servant:

> Glory be to Him who has arranged things so that access to His Saints is only possible through seeking access to Him, and who has joined no one to them except him whom God wants to join to Himself.
>
> (Ibn 'Aṭā' Allāh, *Ḥikam*, no. 148)

Ḥadīth 190

عن أبي هريرة : "ما مِنْ صَدَقةٍ أَحَبَّ إِلى ٱللهِ مِنْ قَوْلِ ٱلْحَقِّ."

(رواه البيهقي. حديث حسن)

Narrated Abū Hurayra: "There are no alms more beloved to God than the truthful word."

(Quoted by al-Bayhaqī. Validated *ḥadīth*.)

Commentary

The expression "truthful word" can pertain to every believer when it is understood in the meaning of transmission and sharing of what he knows about the Divine message. The "alms" mentioned by this *ḥadīth* can also denote the function of the spokesperson of wisdom and also of his or her role in the defense of the truth. Emanating from their relation with God, their words are invigorating and revive the faith; they can be an expression of spiritual generosity.

Ḥadīth 191

عن أسير بن جابر : "أَنَّ أَهْلَ ٱلكُوفة وَفَدُوا إِلى عُمَرَ وَفِيهِمْ رَجُلٌ مِمَّنْ كانَ يَسْخَرُ بِأُوَيْس فقالَ عُمَرُ : هَلْ هاهُنا أَحَدٌ مِنَ ٱلقَرَنِيِّينَ ؟ فَجاءَ ذٰلِكَ ٱلرَّجُلُ فَقالَ عُمَرُ إِنَّ رَسُولَ ٱللهِ ﷺ قَدْ قالَ : إِنَّ رَجُلاً يَأْتِيكُمْ مِنَ ٱليَمَنِ يُقالُ لَهُ أُوَيْس لا يَدَعُ بِٱليَمَنِ غَيْرَ أُمٍّ لَهُ قَدْ كانَ بِهِ بَياضٌ فَدَعا ٱللهَ فَأَذْهَبَهُ عَنْهُ إِلاَّ مَوْضِعَ ٱلدِّينارِ أَوْ ٱلدِّرْهَمِ فَمَنْ لَقِيَهُ مِنْكُمْ فَلْيَسْتَغْفِرْ لَكُمْ."

(رواه مسلم. حديث صحيح)

Narrated Usayr ibn Jābir: "A delegation from Kufa came to 'Umar and there was a person amongst them who jeered at Uways. Thereupon 'Umar asked, 'Is there amongst you one from Qaran?' That person came and 'Umar said, 'Verily the Messenger of God ﷺ has said: "There will come to you a person from Yemen called Uways and he will leave none in Yemen except his mother. He had leprosy, so he supplicated God and it was cured except for the size of a dinar or dirham. He amongst you who meets him should ask him to supplicate God for you."'"

(Quoted by Muslim. Authenticated *ḥadīth*)

Ḥadīth 192

عن علي : "خَيْرُ ٱلتَّابِعِينَ أُوَيْس."

(رواه الحاكم. حديث صحيح)

Narrated Alī: "The best of the generation of the Followers (*al-tābi'īn*) is Uways [al-Qarānī]."

(Quoted by al-Ḥākim. Authenticated *ḥadīth*)

Commentary

Uways al-Qaranī (d. 36/657) was a Yemenite contemporary of the Prophet ﷺ whom he never met physically, but whom nevertheless he seemed to know well spiritually. He died at the Battle of Siffīn fighting for 'Alī. The Prophet ﷺ informed his Companions about the existence of this man and advised them to ask him to supplicate God for them if they met him. The peculiar spirituality of Uways has given his name to the spiritual masters who do not have a visible guide. This is notably the case of Khiḍr. Ibn al-'Arabī may be considered an *uwaysī*, for despite having associated with many masters, this was done for reasons other than those of the ordinary disciples. This fact confirms his great spiritual independence from a very young age.

Ibn al-'Arabī

I met him in Seville and he taught me to submit myself to the spiritual masters and to not contradict them. In fact, that day I had contradicted one of my masters on a certain question and I left him. I met Khiḍr at the *Qūs al-ḥaniyya* neighborhood, and he told me, "Accept what the shaykh says!" I immediately returned to the Shaykh. When I entered upon him, before I even started speaking, he said to me: "O Muḥammad, do I have to ask Khiḍr to recommend your submission to the masters every time you contradict me?" I told him, "O master, was the person who advised me to you Khiḍr?" He said, "Yes!" I said: "Praise belongs to God for this blessing! However, the matter [of the dispute] is just as I told you." Some time later, I went to the Shaykh and noticed that he had come round to my opinion. He said: "It is I who was wrong and you were right." I replied, "I understand now why Khiḍr only advised me to submission, and he did not say that you were right on this question. I should not contradict you insofar as the question did not pertain to the rulings laid out by the Law (*aḥkām mashrū'a*), of which it is forbidden to keep silent." I thanked God for this favor and was very happy that the Shaykh knew the truth [about our matter of dispute].

(*Fut.*, III, p. 336)

Ḥadīth 193

عن أنس : "إِنَّ لِلّٰهِ تَعالَى عِباداً يَعْرِفُونَ ٱلنَّاسَ بِٱلتَّوَسُّمِ."

(رواه الحكيم. حديث حسن)

Narrated Anas ibn Mālik: "Verily God—exalted be He—has servants who know people by their physiognomy."

(Quoted by al-Ḥakīm. Validated *ḥadīth*)

Commentary

Physiognomy (*tawassum*) is one of the aspects of perspicacity (*firāsa*).[214]

The spiritual master must possess this knowledge in order to better guide the aspirants who come to him: he will give them spiritual advice according to their diverse predispositions.

al-Munāwī

"Verily God—exalted be He—has servants who know people by their physiognomy." This means that they know their inner states through their spiritual insight (*tafarrus*). This pertains to those who are submerged in the contemplation of God; He has granted them the blessing of removing the veil from their hearts. Then they are capable of perceiving the inner conscience of people. As for the person whose soul is distracted with respect to God, this *ḥadīth* does not concern him . . .

(*Fayḍ al-Qadīr*, *ḥadīth* no. 2349)

---

214. See *ḥadīth* 180.

Ḥadīth 194

عن ابن عمر : "إِنَّ لِلَّهِ تَعالَى عِباداً اخْتَصَّهُمْ بِحَوائِجِ ٱلنَّاسِ، يَفْزَعُ ٱلنَّاسُ إِلَيْهِمْ فِي حَوائِجِهِمْ، أُولئِكَ ٱلآمِنُونَ مِنْ عَذابِ ٱللهِ."

(رواه الطبراني. حديث حسن)

Narrated Ibn ʻUmar: "Verily God—exalted be He—has servants whom he has conferred the task of responding to the needs of the people. The latter find refuge with these servants and they are the persons who have been protected from God's chastisement."

(Quoted by al-Ṭabarānī. Validated *ḥadīth*)

Ibn al-ʻArabī

Abū Muḥammad Makhlūf Qabā'ilī lived in Córdoba and died there with the leave of the Messenger of God ﷺ. One day I went to see him with my father so that he could pray for him. He kept us from the morning until the afternoon prayer and we had lunch with him.

Upon entering his house, one could feel the power of his spiritual presence even before seeing him. And when one saw him, he was wonderful to behold. He always wore wool (*ṣūf*). Besides the other litanies he recited a thousand times a day—the *tasbīh*, the *takbīr*, the *taḥmīd*, and the *tahlīl*—he was always invoking. His prayers extended to all the inhabitants of the heavens and the earth, including the fish in the sea, and he would shed tears readily.

Since he wanted to dig a well in his garden, they gave him a foreign prisoner to help him. The Shaykh then said, "This man has come to serve us, and we shall ask God that he enter Islam." When the night fell, the Shaykh withdrew in order to pray for him. When the man came to work the next morning, he announced that he had become a Muslim. When he was asked about this, he replied: "I saw the Messenger of God in my dream, who ordered me to believe in him, and I believed in him. Then the Messenger of God told me, 'It is thanks to the intercession of Abū Muḥammad Makhlūf that I received you in Islam.'"

(*Soufis*, pp. 114-15)

Ḥadīth 195

عن أبي هريرة : "رُبَّ أَشْعَثَ مَدْفُوعٍ بِٱلأَبْوابِ لَوْ أَقْسَمَ عَلَى ٱللهِ لأَبَرَّهُ."

(رواه مسلم. حديث صحيح)

Narrated Abū Hurayra: "Many a person with disheveled hair and covered with dust is turned away from the doors. They have only to adjure God, and He answers them."

(Quoted by Muslim. Authenticated *ḥadīth*)

Ḥadīth 196

عن أنس : "إِنَّ مِنْ عِبادِ ٱللهِ مَنْ لَوْ أَقْسَمَ عَلى ٱللهِ لأَبَرَّهُ."

(رواه البخاري. حديث صحيح)

Narrated Anas: "There are servants of God who have only to adjure God, and He answers them."

Ibn al-'Arabī

The shaykh Mūsā ibn 'Imrān Mārtulī was the imam of the Mosque of Riḍā in Seville. I paid a visit to him one day, and found him in the company of Abū al-Qāsim ibn Ghafīr, a scholar of the traditions (*muḥaddith*) who denied the charismatic actions of the Friends of God (*karamāt al-awliyā'*). When I arrived, I heard the shaykh refuting a thing that the *muḥaddith* had said to him. The scholar reproached us for two forbidden things which we had not committed, and which we could not even imagine that any of our brothers could have done. I asked the shaykh, towards whom I had a humble attitude, to let me take care of the debate. Then I addressed myself to this Abū al-Qāsim:

> "You are a *muḥaddith*, are you not?" He said, "Yes." "Since the Messenger of God ﷺ knew that his community would include people of your kind, he negated the possibility of charismatic actions in the case of those who limit themselves to the obedience of the Divine injunctions. However, he said a thing or two which could make you reflect." The scholar asked what those could be, and I replied: "Is it not related that the Messenger of God ﷺ has said: Many a person who has disheveled hair, is covered with dust and is turned away from the doors has only but to adjure God, and He answers them? Has he not also said: and

amongst them are those who are granted (their requests). Do you accept these sayings?" When he accepted, I said to him, "Praise belongs to God who has not limited the Prophet ﷺ to one kind of miracle but has given him the possibility to make an oath which could be kept by him. He did not specify the object of this oath, and therefore it contains all possibilities; so that if one of those men [mentioned in the *ḥadīth*] adjured God about lifting something in the air or on water, or the quick covering of long distances, or subsistence without food, perceiving what is in the souls of the others and other things which have been related about this matter, God would grant it to him."

On hearing this, Abū al-Qāsim was confused and kept his silence. Then the shaykh told me: "May God reward you with blessings coming from His saints!"

(*Soufis*, p. 78)

Ḥadīth 197

عن أبي هريرة : "إنَّ ٱللهَ قالَ : "مَنْ عادَى لِي وَلِيّاً فَقَدْ آذَنْتُهُ بِٱلْحَرْبِ، وَما تَقَرَّبَ إِلَيَّ عَبْدِي بِشَيْءٍ أَحَبُّ إِلَيَّ مِمّا ٱفْتَرَضْتُ عَلَيْهِ، وَما يَزالُ عَبْدِي يَتَقَرَّبُ إِلَيَّ بِٱلنَّوافِلِ حَتَّى أُحِبَّهُ، فَإِذا أَحْبَبْتُهُ كُنْتَ سَمْعَهُ ٱلَّذي يَسْمَعُ بِهِ وَبَصَرَهُ ٱلَّذي يُبْصِرُ بِهِ وَيَدَهُ ٱلَّتي يَبْطِشُ بِها، وَرِجْلَهُ ٱلَّتي يَمْشِي بِها وَإِنْ سَأَلَنِي لَأُعْطِيَنَّهُ وَلَئِنِ ٱسْتَعاذَنِي لَأُعيذَنَّهُ."

(رواه البخاري. حديث صحيح)

Narrated Abū Hurayra: "Lo! God has said: 'He who shows enmity to one of My friends, I declare war on him. Nothing is more pleasing to Me, as a means for My slave to draw near unto Me, than worship that which I have made binding upon him; and My slave ceaseth not to draw near unto Me with added devotions of his free will until I love him; and when I love him I am the Hearing wherewith he heareth and the Sight wherewith he seeth and the Hand whereby he graspeth and the Foot whereon he walketh. If he asketh me a thing, I will grant it to him, and if seeketh asylum with Me, I will certainly grant it to him.'"

(Quoted by al-Bukhārī. Authenticated *ḥadīth*)

Commentary

This often-quoted *ḥadīth* by the spiritual masters contains three essential elements: a warning against enmity towards the Friends of God; a mention of the path of sanctity—through the observance of the obligatory acts of worship as well as the voluntary ones; and finally, a description of the spiritual state of the saint who is filled with Divine Presence: his individuality has been extinguished and there remains nothing in him except the action of the One.

Martin Lings (Abū Bakr Sirāj al-Dīn)

The whole of Sufism—its aspirations, its practice, and in a sense also even its doctrine—is summed up in this Holy Tradition, which is quoted by the Sufis perhaps more often than any other text apart from the Qur'ān. As may be inferred from it, their practices are of two kinds: rites which are binding on all Muslims, and additional voluntary rites. When a novice enters an order, one of the first things he or she has to do is to acquire an extra dimension which will confer a depth and a height on rites which (assuming an Islamic upbringing) have been performed more or less exoterically since childhood. The obligations of Islam, often known as "the five pillars," are the Shahāda, the ritual prayer five times a day, the almsgiving, the fast of the month of Ramaḍān, and the pilgrimage to Mecca if circumstances allow, this last obligation being the only one that is conditional.

Of the voluntary rites of Islam as performed by the Sufis, the invocation of the Name Allāh has already been mentioned as by far the most important. There might seem to be a certain contradiction between the opening of the Holy Tradition quoted at the outset of this chapter which sets the obligatory above the voluntary and the Quranic affirmation that *dhikr Allāh*, which is voluntary, is greater even than the ritual prayer, which is obligatory. But it must be remembered that although what is obligatory serves to confer a spiritual rhythm on the flow of the hours, the time that it actually takes is relatively short. The voluntary has therefore a potential precedence over it by being capable of embracing and penetrating the whole of life, and this is what those who practice methodically the invocation aim at making it do. The meaning of the Holy Tradition is clearly that what is a legal obligation cannot be replaced, at the whim of an individual, by something which is not. Thus the Sufis are in agreement that the invocation of the Name, in itself the most powerful of all rites, is only acceptable to God on the basis of the invoker's having performed what is obligatory. It could not be a legal obligation itself for power necessarily means danger; and by no means is every novice allowed to proceed at once to the invocation of the Supreme Name.

(*What is Sufism*, pp. 74; 78-79).

Ḥadīth 198

عن أبي أمامة : "قال ٱللّٰهُ عَزَّ وَجَلَّ : إِنَّ أَغْبَطَ أَوْلِيائِي عِنْدي ٱلْمُؤْمِنُ خَفيفُ ٱلْحاذِ ذُو حَظٍّ مِنْ صَلاةٍ أَحْسَنَ عِبادَةَ رَبِّهِ وَأَطاعَهُ فِي ٱلسِّرِّ وَٱلعَلانيةِ وَكانَ غامِضاً فِي ٱلنَّاسِ لا يُشارُ إِلَيْهِ بِٱلأَصابِعِ وَكانَ رِزْقُهُ كَفافاً فَصَبَرَ عَلى ذٰلِكَ. ثُمَّ نَقَرَ بِيَدِهِ ثُمَّ قالَ : عُجِّلَتْ مَنِيَّتُهُ وَقَلَّتْ بَواكيهِ وَقَلَّ تُراثُهُ."

(رواه الترمذي. حديث صحيح)

Narrated Abū Umāma: "God the Almighty and Majestic has said: 'Verily, for Me, the happiest of My saints is the believer who lives modestly, who finds satisfaction in prayer, worships his Lord in the best manner, and obeys Him in secret as well as in public. He blends in amongst men and is not pointed out. He is content with a meager living and bears this with patience.' Then [the Prophet] snapped his fingers and continued: 'His death is hastened, few people weep for him, and he leaves very few possessions as inheritance.'"

(Quoted by al-Tirmidhī. Authenticated *ḥadīth*.)

Commentary

The saints are often tried in the here-below. Indeed the here-below does not easily tolerate one who vividly and directly manifests the vain and illusory character of all worldliness.

Shaykh al-Darqāwī

No one doubts that the Friends of God (*awliyā'*)—may God be satisfied with them—in general live modestly while ordinary people are only interested in distinctions. How would they know the Friends of God? Apart from those whom God takes by the hand, most are too distanced from them. The noble master Ibn 'Aṭā' Allāh has said in his Ḥikam: "Praise be to Him who has hidden the inner reality of holiness (*sir al-khuṣūṣiyya*) by manifesting the quality of human nature (*bi-ẓuhūr waṣf al-bashariyya*), and who has appeared in the sublimity of Lordship (*'aẓama al-rubūbiyya*) by manifesting servanthood (*al-'ubūdiyya*)!"

If I were asked, "What did you do in order to know the saints and to benefit from their company?" I would say: "I looked from the angle of abasement and not from that of the worldly honor, and I have found therein what I was looking for, praise be to God!" The majority of men look only through the angle of the here-below and those who are successful in it. They are neither interested in poverty, nor in the poor. Some of them run away when they see an indigent saint who possesses nothing of this world, and they do not approach him at all. They say, "If this man were a saint, he would be rich and not poor! He was unable to do anything for himself, how can he be of any use to others?" These people do not know that the saint is one who possesses nothing in this world, and that he is rich with God, who suffices him.

(*Rasā'il*, letter 81, pp. 99-100)

Ḥadīth 199

عن ابن عمرو : "مَنْ أَحْسَنَ فِيما بَيْنَهُ وَبَيْنَ ٱللهِ كَفاهُ ٱللهُ ما بَيْنَهُ وَبَيْنَ ٱلنَّاسِ وَمَنْ أَصْلَحَ سَرِيرَتَهُ أَصْلَحَ ٱللهُ عَلانِيَتَهُ."

(رواه الحاكم. حديث حسن)

Narrated Ibn 'Amr: "God will take care of the human relationships of the person who takes care of his relationship with God, and he will change the external situation of whomever reforms his internal state."

(Quoted by al-Ḥākim. Validated *ḥadīth*)

Commentary

This *ḥadīth* mentions an important key to the spiritual life: the priority of the inward. Man is sunk and dispersed in the outward because he does not see that the latter is but an expression of his inward state. In this sense, this *ḥadīth* explicates the verse,

﴿إِنَّ ٱللهَ لا يُغَيِّرُ ما بِقَوْمٍ حَتَّى يُغَيِّرُوا ما بِأَنْفُسِهِمْ﴾

God will not change what is with a people until they change what is within themselves.[215]

All outward change must proceed from the interior: this is so because "things are hidden in their opposites."

Shaykh al-Darqāwī

Things are hidden in their opposites, it cannot be otherwise; spiritual awareness is hidden in the forgetting of the ego, Divine gifts in privation, grandeur in humility, richness in poverty, strength in the recognition of weakness, plenitude in narrowness, elevation in abasement, life in death, victory in defeat, power in powerlessness, etc. He who wants to realize spiritual awareness must therefore accept losing his ego; he who seeks the Divine gift must accept privation; he who desires grandeur must accept humility; he who desires richness must accept poverty; who desires strength must accept weakness; he who desires plenitude must accept narrowness; he who wants to be elevated must let himself be abased; he who desires life must accept death; he who wants victory must accept defeat, he who wants power must therefore accept powerlessness.

In sum, he who aspires to freedom must accept servitude; he must choose it just as the beloved Prophet ﷺ did, and he must neither be proud

215. XIII: 11

nor rebellious against his condition, for the servant remains a servant and the Lord is Lord.

(*Rasā'il*, letter 31, p. 57)

Ḥadīth 200

عن أبي هريرة : "قالَ ٱللهُ تَعالَى : إذا أَحَبَّ عَبْدي لِقائي أَحْبَبْتُ لِقاءَهُ وَإذا كَرِهَ لِقائي كَرِهْتُ لِقاءه."

(رواه البخاري. حديث صحيح)

Narrated Abū Hurayra: "God Most High has said: 'I love meeting with My servant if he loves meeting with Me, and I detest meeting with My servant if he detests meeting with Me.'"

(Quoted by al-Bukhārī. Authenticated *ḥadīth*)

Commentary

al-Ghazzālī

The Intimacy (*uns*) and love of God belong to states leading to felicity (*al-mus'idāt*) and which bring man to the joys of meeting with God and contemplation (*mushāhada*). This felicity is quickly granted after death and consequently the [spiritual] man reaches the beatific vision in Paradise. Thus, the grave becomes one of the gardens of Paradise. How else could it be in the grave for him who had but one Beloved, but who was prevented by the chains of this world from constant intimacy with God, from His continuous invocation (*dhikr*) and from unceasing contemplation of His beauty? But now that the fetters have been broken and the spiritual man has escaped the prison of the world, he is alone with his Beloved, he turns to Him full of joy, free from obstacles and saved from separation.

As for he who loved this world, how can he not suffer after death, since he has lost forever the lower world which he loved so much?

(*Iḥyā'*, III, p. 215)

Ḥadīth 201

عن أبي قرصافة : "مَنْ أَحَبَّ قَوْماً حَشَرَهُ ٱللهُ فِي زُمْرَتِهِمْ."

(رواه الطبراني. حديث صحيح)

Narrated Abū Qarṣāfa: "Whoever loves some category of being shall be resurrected in their company."

(Quoted by al-Ṭabarānī. Authenticated *ḥadīth*)

Ḥadīth 202

عن ابن مسعود : "جاءَ رَجُلٌ إِلَى رَسُولِ ٱللهِ ﷺ فَقالَ : يا رَسُولَ ٱللهِ كَيْفَ تَقُولُ فِي رَجُلٍ أَحَبَّ قَوْماً وَلَمْ يَلْحق بِهِمْ ؟ فَقالَ رَسُولُ ٱللهِ ﷺ : الْمَرْءُ مَعَ مَنْ أَحَبَّ."

(رواه البخاري. حديث صحيح)

Narrated Ibn Mas'ūd: "A man came to meet the Messenger of God ﷺ and asked him, 'What do you say about someone who loves (pious) people but cannot attain their degree of piety?' The Messenger of God ﷺ said, 'Everyone will be with those whom he has loved.'"

(Quoted by al-Bukhārī. Authenticated *ḥadīth*)

Commentary

The love of a person for a certain category of people bears witness to a profound inner affinity. This remains true even when this person is unable to elevate himself to the spiritual level of those whom he loves, for different reasons which can be both outward and inwaard. In the Hereafter, this affinity will play its full role, as stated in these two *ḥadīth*.

al-Ghazzālī

The Shaykh Abū Ja'far Ṣaydalānī had this [oneiric] vision:

> I saw the Messenger of God ﷺ in my dream. He was with a group of *fuqarā'*. Suddenly, we saw the sky opening and two angels descending therefrom. One held a basin in his hand and the other a jug. The basin

was placed before the Messenger of God ﷺ who washed his hands, then ordered the *fuqarā'* to do the same. After that, the basin was placed in front of me but one of the angels said to the other: "Do not pour water for him, he is not one of them." I protested: "O Messenger of God, is the following saying not from thee: Man shall be with those he loved?" He replied, "That is right." Then I said: "O Messenger of God, in truth I love thee and I love the *fuqarā'*!" The Prophet ﷺ then said to the angel: "Pour water for him, for he is one of the *fuqarā'*."

(*Iḥyā'*, IV, pp. 491-492)

Mediation and Seeking Intercession:
التوسل والاستغاثة

Ḥadīth 203

عن عثمان بن حنيف : "أَنَّ رَجُلاً ضَرِيراً أَتَى ٱلنَّبِيَّ ﷺ فَقالَ : "ٱدْعُ ٱللَّهَ لِي أَنْ يُعافِيَنِي". فَقالَ : "إِنْ شِئْتَ صَبَرْتَ وَهُوَ خَيْرٌ لَكَ". قالَ : "فَٱدْعُهُ". فَأَمَرَهُ أَنْ يَتَوَضَّأَ فَيُحْسِنَ وَضُوءَهُ وَيَدْعُوَ بِهٰذا ٱلدُّعاءِ : "اللَّهُمَّ إِنِّي أَسْأَلُكَ وَأَتَوَجَّهُ إِلَيْكَ بِنَبِيِّكَ مُحَمَّدٍ صَلَّى ٱللهُ عَلَيْهِ وَسَلَّمَ نَبِيِّ ٱلرَّحْمَةِ، يا مُحَمَّدُ إِنِّي تَوَجَّهْتُ بِكَ إِلَى رَبِّي فِي قَضاءِ حاجَتِي لِتُقْضَى لِي، اللَّهُمَّ شَفِّعْهُ فِيَّ". فَقامَ وَقَدْ أَبْصَرَ."

(رواه الحاكم. حديث صحيح)

Narrated ʿUthmān ibn Ḥunayf: "A blind man came to the Prophet ﷺ and said, 'I have been afflicted in my eyesight, please pray to God for me.' The Prophet ﷺ told him, 'If you accept being patient it will be better for you.' But the man insisted, 'Please pray to God . . . ' Then the Prophet ﷺ said: 'Go make ablution, perform two cycles of prayer, and then say, *O God, I ask Thee and turn to Thee through my Prophet Muḥammad ﷺ, the Prophet of Mercy; O Muḥammad, I have turned to you as a means towards my Lord for my need, that it may be fulfilled. O God, grant him intercession (shafāʿa) for me.*' The man stood up and his sight was recovered."

(Quoted by al-Ḥākim. Authenticated *ḥadīth*)[216]

Commentary

Islam emphasizes the worship of the One, rejecting all kinds of association (*shirk*) of other divinities with God, and acknowledging the fact that He

216. In the version quoted by al-Tirmidhī, the Prophet ﷺ is reported to have added, "And if there is some need, do the same."

alone is the Powerful. Thus one of the sacred formulae that accompany the life of a believer and whose recitation is recommended in numerous situations states: "There is no might nor strength save with God" (*lā ḥawla wa lā quwwata illa bi-Llāh*). However, there is a widespread error in certain literalist circles which consists—for reasons which we shall shortly mention—in the rejection of any kind of mediation and intercession, from fear of associating others with God. These rejections, directed mainly to certain manifestations of popular piety which are hardly orthodox, have turned into an extremely rigid doctrinal position.

Conversely, in this *ḥadīth* the Prophet ﷺ teaches the blind man to turn himself to God, not directly but through his mediation (*tawassul*), taking him as an intercessor.

Yūsuf Khaṭṭār

The terms "mediation" (*tawassul*), "seeking intercession" (*istighātha*), and "seeking support" (*isti'āna*) denote the same thing, and in reality, they denote nothing but an action of God. As for the servant's making use of support in his demands, it is but an instrument of God—exalted be He. No one disagrees on the matter of the permissibility of mediation through one's pious acts such as prayer, fasting, reading of the Qur'ān . . . The permissibility of this action is then well established by the *ḥadīth* of three persons locked up in a cave: the first sought mediation to God through his filial piety, the second through his abstention from adultery when the occasion presented itself, and the third through his scrupulous respect for the depositing of trust (*amāna*).[217] These three persons were then saved by God.

(*Mawsū'a*, p. 81)

217. Quoted by al-Bukhārī, narrating from Ibn 'Umar in the Book of Sales and Trade, *ḥadīth* no. 2080.

Ḥadīth 204

عن أنس ابن مالك : "أَنَّ عُمَرَ بْنَ ٱلخَطَّاب رَضِيَ ٱللّٰهُ عَنْهُ كانَ إذا قَحَطُوا اسْتَسْقَى بِٱلعَبَّاسِ بْنِ عَبْدِ الْمُطَّلِبِ فَقالَ : "اللَّهُمَّ إنَّا كُنَّا نَتَوَسَّلُ إلَيْكَ بِنَبِيِّنا فَتَسْقِينا وَإنَّا نَتَوَسَّلُ إلَيْكَ بِعَمِّ نَبِيِّنا فَٱسْقِنا." قالَ أَنَس : "فَيُسْقَوْنَ."

(رواه البخاري. حديث صحيح)

Narrated Anas ibn Mālik: "At times of drought, 'Umar ibn al-Khaṭṭāb used to recite the supplication for rain relying on al-Abbās ibn 'Abd al-Muṭṭalib for his demand, saying: 'O God! We used to seek access to Thee through our Prophet, and Thou would bless us with rain, and now we seek access to Thee through the uncle of our Prophet. O God! Bless us with rain.' And so it would rain."

(Quoted by al-Bukhārī. Authenticated *ḥadīth*)

Commentary

Seeking mediation and asking for intercession is possible not only through the Prophet ﷺ but it extends to the saints of the community as well. In this sense, this *ḥadīth* is part of the textual proofs establishing the permissibility of asking for intercession through the mediation of the saints.

Yūsuf Khaṭṭār

When a Muslim seeks mediation or intercession through the Prophet ﷺ or a saint, he does so only because he knows their charismatic powers (*karamāt*) and their eminence (*jāh*) in the eyes of God—exalted be He. He is therefore convinced that the saint is permitted and supported by God: his eminence derives from the fact that God chooses whom He wants from amongst His servants. Indeed, God is such that: *He selecteth for His mercy whom He will.*[218]

Prophethood and special sanctity (*walāya khāṣṣa*)[219] cannot be acquired through personal effort: they are a pure gift from God. One's selection to sanctity confers a degree in the eyes of God which is called eminence (*jāh*). Regarding this matter, the Most High has said: *Allah chooseth for Himself whom He will, and guideth unto Himself him who turneth (toward Him).*[220]

(*Mawsū'a*, p. 82)

---

218. III: 74.
219. As opposed to general sanctity (*walāya 'āmma*) which derives from *taqwā*.
220. XLII: 13.

Khiḍr: الخضر

Ḥadīth 205

عن أبي هريرة : "إِنَّما سُمِّيَ ٱلْخَضِرُ خضراً لأَنَّهُ جَلَسَ عَلَى فَرْوَةٍ بَيْضاءَ فَإِذا هِيَ تَهْتَزُّ تَحْتَهُ خَضْراء."

(رواه البخاري. حديث صحيح)

Narrated Abū Hurayra: "Al-Khiḍr ('The Verdant') was named so because, having sat one day over a barren white land, it immediately turned green with vegetation."

(Quoted by al-Bukhārī. Authenticated *ḥadīth*)

Commentary

Khiḍr is an enigmatic figure in the sense that he is a man who has been gifted with extraordinary longevity—like that of a long-lived (*mu'ammar*) person—which, amongst other things, enables him to initiate others to supreme knowledge.

Ibn al-'Arabī

The name of Khiḍr is Bālyā son of Mālikān, son of Fāligh, son of Ghābir, son of Shālikh, son of Arfakhshad, son of Sām, son of Nūḥ.[221] Indeed, he was in an army whose commander ordered him to look for water which they were lacking. He found the Fountain of Life from which he drank, and that is why he is still alive, having not known that God had granted longevity to whoever drank from this water. I met him in Seville and he taught me to submit myself to the spiritual masters and to not contradict them. In fact, that day I had contradicted one of my masters on a certain question and I had left him. I met Khiḍr at the *Qūs al-ḥaniyya* neighborhood, and he told me: "Accept what the shaykh says!" I immediately returned to the Shaykh. When I entered upon him, before I even started speaking, he told me: "O Muḥammad, do I have to ask Khiḍr to recommend your submission to the masters every time you contradict me?" I told him, "O master, was the person who recommended me to you Khiḍr?" He said, "Yes!" I said: "Praise belongs to God for this blessing! However, the matter [of the dispute] is just as I told you." Some time later, I went to the Shaykh and noticed that he had

221. He is therefore a descendant of Noah through Shem. Some of the names in this genealogy are found in the Bible: *Genesis*, X-XI; and *Luke*, 3:35-36.

come round to my opinion. He said: "It is I who was wrong and you were right." I replied, "I understand now why Khiḍr only recommended submission for me, and he did not say that you were right on this question. I should not contradict you insofar as the question did not pertain to the rulings laid out by the Law (*aḥkām mashrū'a*), for which it is forbidden to keep silent." I thanked God for this favor and was very happy that the Shaykh knew the truth [about our matter of dispute].

The Fountain of Life contains water through which God grants longevity to whomever drinks from it. When Khiḍr returned to his companions, he informed them about the existence of this water. People then hastened to drink from it but God hid the Fountain from their sight and they could not find it.

(*Fut.*, III, p. 336)

al-Sha'rānī

The folk of unveiling (*ahl al-kashf*) unanimously agree that Khiḍr is always living. This is why we can meet him. Among those who have claimed to have met him, we mention the Commander of the Faithful, 'Umar ibn 'Abd al-'Azīz, who related the following dialogue to us:

> O Prophet of God, give me some advice.
>
> O 'Umar, be cautious against appearing as a saint, while being an enemy of God inwardly.

Among the privileged ones, we also mention:

> Dhu al-Nūn al-Miṣrī who met Khiḍr several times and who was taught the Supreme Name (*Ism al-a'ẓam*) by him.
>
> Abū 'Abd Allāh Bishrī who welcomed Khiḍr into his home.
>
> Shaykh 'Abd al-Razzāq who met Khiḍr several times. He helped the shaykh in his sermons, and recommended him to recite, after the prayer of *ṣubḥ*, the Throne Verse,[222] the end of Chapter al-Baqara,[223] and the following two verses: *God is Witness that there is no god save Him*[224] and *O God, Master of the Kingdom*![225] Khiḍr taught him that God protected his faith through the recitation of these verses, until the meeting with Him in the Hereafter.
>
> People have also mentioned Ibrāhīm al-Khawwāṣ, Abū Yazīd Basṭāmī and Ibrāhīm ibn Adham. As for Ibn al-'Arabī, he met with Khiḍr numerous times, and he said about him: "Khiḍr made me take the oath of not contradicting the spiritual masters, and he invested me with the Sufi mantle (*khirqa ṣūfiyya*) next to the black stone in Mecca." (*Khiḍriyya*, pp. 13-14)

222. II: 255.
223. II: 286-288.
224. III: 18
225. III: 26.

Ḥadīth 206

عن أبي بن كعب : "يَرْحَمِ ٱللهُ مُوسَى، لَوَدَدْتُ أن لَوْ كانَ صَبَرَ حَتَّى يَقُصَّ عَلَيْنا مِنْ أَخْبارِهِما."

(رواه البخاري. حديث صحيح)

Narrated Ubayy ibn Ka'b: "May God have mercy on Moses! Would that he had been more patient [with Khiḍr] so that we could learn more about the story of their meeting."

(Quoted by al-Bukhārī. Authenticated *ḥadīth*)

Commentary

The Chapter *al-Kahf* relates the story of the meeting between Khiḍr and Moses, who had vowed to find the former in order to be taught by him. Unable to understand the meaning of Khidr's actions, Moses ended up questioning him even though he had promised not to do so, and this was the cause of their separation. Many spiritual masters consider that this meeting symbolizes that of the disciple with his master, and they infer from this the principial rules governing this relationship.

Amīr 'Abd al-Qādir

The story of Moses and of Khiḍr tackles several points related to the master-disciple relationship:

> Whatever the degree that may have been reached by a master—both in his own eyes and those of others—he must search for knowledge from whomever is more knowledgeable than him . . .
>
> A master must not push away a disciple who has come to him in search of knowledge even if he knows that the latter is not qualified for it. In fact, Khiḍr knew that Moses could not bear his company, but he still accepted him . . .
>
> The master must impose certain conditions on the disciple and demand commitments from him . . .
>
> If the master sees that the disciple is falling short of his commitments, he has the right to remind him about them. If the disciple offers excuses to him, he will accept them a first time and a second time, just as Khiḍr did with Moses . . .
>
> The disciple must be constant and patient, and he should not allow himself to be disrupted in his commitment to his master if he perceives in him words or actions that [seem to] contradict the truth or the sacred Law, because the Messenger of God ﷺ has said, "May God have mercy on Moses! Would that he had been more patient [with Khiḍr] so

that we could learn more about the story of their meeting."
(*Mawāqif*, no. 195, pp. 425-426)

al-Ghazzālī

Whatever be the method used by the master for teaching, the disciple must put it to practice by giving up his petty personal opinion: If the master is wrong, the disciple will benefit from having had uprightness of mind [in obeying]. [Spiritual] experience is based on peculiar and unexpected realities, but which have a great beneficial effect; how many sick ones caught by fever are sometimes treated by the doctor with an increase in heat until they are cured? He who does not know [this procedure] remains completely stunned. God the Exalted has clearly indicated this in the story of Khiḍr and Moses: *thou canst not bear with me. How canst thou bear with that whereof thou canst not compass any knowledge?*[226]

Then Khiḍr imposed silence and submission (*taslīm*) as conditions, and said: *If thou goest with me, ask me not concerning aught till I myself make mention of it unto thee.*[227]

But Moses could not bear it and his repeated questions were the cause of their separation.

In summary, you may count as going to perdition and ruin those disciples that adhere to their personal opinion and their individual choice.

Perchance you will object [to the story of Moses] that God Most High has said: *Ask the Folk of Remembrance (ahl al-dhikr) if ye know not*[228] and that questioning is an obligation. [I say] know that this is true, but only in the domain in which the master has given his permission, for it is bad to ask questions when one is incapable of grasping their answers. This is why Khiḍr forbade Moses to pose questions.

Avoid, therefore, posing questions before the suitable moment because the master knows better than you what is suitable for you. Avoid questioning about what has not been unveiled to you. At every stage, the question time only starts after the appearance of unveiling (*kashf*).

(*Iḥyā'*, I, pp. 50-51)

226. XVIII: 67-68.
227. XVIII: 70
228. XVI: 43.

The End of Time: آخر الزمان

Ḥadīth 207:

عن عائشة : "خَيْرُ ٱلنَّاسَ ٱلقَرْنُ ٱلَّذِي أَنا فِيهِمْ، ثُمَّ ٱلثَّانِي ثُمَّ ٱلثَّالِث."

(رواه مسلم. حديث صحيح)

Narrated ʻĀʼisha: "The best people are those of my century, then those of the second century, and then those of the third century."

(Quoted by Muslim. Authenticated *ḥadīth*)

Ḥadīth 208

عن جعدة بن هبيرة : "خَيْرُ ٱلنَّاسِ قَرْنِي ٱلَّذِي أَنا فِيهِمْ، ثُمَّ ٱلَّذِينَ يَلُوْنَهُمْ، ثُمَّ ٱلَّذِينَ يَلُوْنَهُمْ وَٱلآخِرُونَ أَراذِل."

(رواه الطبراني. حديث حسن)

Narrated Abū Hurayra: "The best people are those of my century, then those who shall succeed this generation, and thus until the last people, who shall be the worst."

(Quoted by al-Ṭabarānī. Validated *ḥadīth*)

Commentary

The Companions of the Prophet ﷺ had a very clear awareness of their being privileged, not only by the fact that they were the companions of the last messenger from God but also because they were convinced of representing the best generation of Islam. Numerous sayings of the Prophet ﷺ stress the progressive and inevitable decline of humanity. The best manner to preserve, for as long as possible, the legacy of the transmissions they received was, therefore, a constant worry. Hence, all the generations that followed regarded the generation of the Companions as an unsurpassable model. Thus the extraordinary and very rapid expansion of the Muslim world was accompanied, at each period until today, with a firm willingness for faithfulness to the Predecessors.

René Guénon ('Abd al-Wāḥid Yaḥyā)

One question will however naturally spring to mind: what is the reason for the existence of a period such as that in which we are living? Indeed, however abnormal present conditions may be when considered in themselves, they must nevertheless enter into the general order of things, that order which, according to a Far-Eastern formula, is composed of the sum of all disorders; the present phase, however painful and troubled it may be, must also have its appointed place, like any other, in the complete course of human development, and moreover the very fact that it was foreseen by the traditional doctrines is a sufficient indication in that respect. Our opening remarks about the general trend of a cycle of manifestation in the direction of progressive materialization provide the immediate explanation of such a state and clearly show that what is abnormal and disordered from one particular point of view is nevertheless only the consequence of a law relating to a higher and more comprehensive viewpoint. [. . .]

According to tradition it may be said in this connection that what characterizes the final phase of a cycle is the exploitation of everything that has been neglected or rejected during the course of the preceding phase; and indeed this is precisely what is to be observed in modern civilization, which only lives, so to speak, by things which previous civilizations found no use for. To confirm this fact one need but observe how genuine representatives of civilizations that have survived to the present day in the East appraise the Western sciences and their industrial applications. These lower forms of knowledge, so insignificant to anyone possessing knowledge of a different order, had nevertheless to be "realized," and this could only occur at a stage when true intellectuality had disappeared; given that this research, so exclusively practical in the narrowest sense of the word, had to be carried out, it could only be undertaken in an age at the opposite pole to primordial spirituality by men so deeply involved in matter as to be incapable of conceiving of anything outside it, becoming, as they do, the more enslaved to it the more they seek to exploit it, thereby dooming themselves to an ever-increasing agitation, unregulated and aimless, a dispersion in pure multiplicity tending towards final dissolution.

(*Crisis*, pp. 27-28)

Ḥadīth 209

عن مرداس الأسلمي : "يُقْبَضُ ٱلصَّالِحُونَ ٱلأَوَّلُ فَٱلأَوَّلُ وَتَبْقَى حُفالَةٌ كَحُفالَةِ ٱلتَّمْرِ وَٱلشَّعِيرِ، لا يَعْبَأُ ٱللهُ بِهِمْ شَيْئاً."

(رواه البخاري. حديث صحيح)

Narrated Mirdās al-Aslamī: "The virtuous people will depart one after the other, and there will remain useless people like the husk of barley seeds or bad dates: God will pay no heed to them."

(Quoted by al-Bukhārī. Authenticated *ḥadīth*.)

Ḥadīth 210

عن ابن مقرن : "إِنَّ ٱللهَ تَعالَى لَيُؤَيِّدُ ٱلدِّينَ بِٱلرَّجُلِ ٱلفاجِرِ."

(رواه الطبراني. حديث صحيح)

Narrated Ibn Maqran: "Lo! God can strengthen religion through a wicked man."

(Quoted by al-Ṭabarānī. Authenticated *ḥadīth*.)

Commentary

According to the first *ḥadīth*, true virtue will be ever rarer, to the extent of moving away from the origin. Virtuous men therefore risk being replaced by others who, despite a pious appearance and being able to offer some service to religion, are not less wicked in reality. God's action sometimes uses detours which exceed the grasp of human perception. Thus conditions which seem unfavorable can sometimes help bring about a consolidation of religion. Inversely, being—or, as very often happens, imagining being—really useful to religion is not a proof of spiritual guidance; activism, even in its fully laudable forms, is not necessarily accompanied by Divine pleasure (*riḍwān Allāh*). The necessary prudence and the great humility that must be observed in this domain comprise the meaning of the spiritual approach of al-Ghazzālī and of his detachment from his official functions.

Shaykh al-'Alawī

It is reported that after taking up the path of inner purification (*ṣafā bāṭinih*) as the Folk of the Truth understand it, Imam al-Ghazzālī said: "I have wasted my time for nothing! What a bad path I was in!" Somebody then told him, "But what you accomplished earned you the title of the Proof of Islam!" To which al-Ghazzālī replied: "Leave me alone with those frivolities! Have you not heard of the *ḥadīth* of the Prophet ﷺ: Lo! God can strengthen religion through a wicked man?"

Therefore consider, O brother, the humility of this celebrated scholar and his opinion of having squandered his time before meeting the Folk of the Path. Do not think that he said this to deprecate the science of the sacred Law, far from it! On the contrary, he meant to glorify it and to stress that he had ignored it previously. Even though he was an expert in the exterior knowledge he possessed, he was limited in its inner understanding . . . after having met with the Sufis, he started knowing God, whereas before that he had only known the Divine injunctions (*aḥkām Allāh*).

(*Minaḥ*, p. 11)

Ḥadīth 211

عن أنس بن مالك : "لا تَقُومُ ٱلسَّاعةُ حَتَّى لا يُقالُ فِي ٱلأَرْضِ : الله، الله."

(رواه مسلم. حديث صحيح)

Narrated Anas ibn Mālik: "The Hour will not come so long as there are persons on earth saying: Allāh, Allāh . . . "

(Quoted by Muslim. Authenticated *ḥadīth*)

Commentary

According to this *ḥadīth*, the practice of the invocation of the Name is a source of blessing contributing to the safeguarding of the world and maintaining it in existence. The methodical invocation of the Name Allāh requires an initiation (*mubāya'a*) and an authorization (*idhn*), contrary to other forms of invocation, such as the repetition of the formula *lā ilāha illa-'Llāh* which is recommended for every Muslim. Regarding this, one *ḥadīth* invites the believer to renew his faith through this invocation.[229] Knowledge of each type of invocation is the prerogative of the gnostic (*'ārif bi-Llāh*).

Ibn al-'Arabī

All determined invocation (*dhikr muqayyad*) produces a determined effect. God has informed us that He bestows a gift in accordance with the nature of the invocation of this word: "If he mentions me in himself, I will mention him in Myself . . . " This is the reason why a group from amongst the Folk of the Path have given preference to the invocation of the Name Allāh, or the Name Huwa, without any determination. Their intention is not the pronunciation of the word, but the effort of "making present" (*istiḥḍār*) that the Named deserves. In response to the invocation of the Name Allāh, the Real mentions His servant by a Name encompassing (*ism 'āmm*) all the perfections going back to it. The invocation by the servant is done through the efforts of "making present," and the mentioning of the Real is done through Presence itself (*ḥuḍūr*), for we are known and contemplated by Him, whereas He is known but not contemplated by us . . .

God has prescribed the invocation (*dhikr*), stressing its frequent practice, more than any other pious act. He has said: *believing men who invoke God much and believing women who invoke*;[230] *invoke God much*.[231] In these verses, the invocation is that of the Name Allāh without any determination.

229. See *ḥadīth* 95.

230. XXXIII: 35

231. II: 200; XXXIII: 41.

He has also said: *The invocation of God is greater*[232] without specifying the terms of comparison; *Invoke God through the appointed days*[233] without specifying what this invocation should be: *Invoke the Name of God on them without specifying its modes* . . . (XXII: 36).

The Prophet ﷺ has said: "The Hour will not come so long as there are persons on earth saying: Allāh, Allāh . . . " He did not add anything to the invocation of the Name for this is the invocation of the elite amongst His servants, through which He preserves this world and all their dwelling places. When none of these servants remains, this world shall have no reason to exist; it will then be annihilated. Today many people practice the invocation of the Name Allāh without the effort of making present as we have mentioned. The pronunciation of the Name without making present has no value.

(*Fut.*, II, pp. 228-229)

232. XXIX: 45.
233. II: 203.

Ḥadīth 212

عن عياش بن أبي ربيعة : "تَجِيءُ رِيحٌ بَيْنَ يَدَيِ ٱلسَّاعَةِ فَيُقْبَضُ فِيها رُوحُ كُلِّ مُؤْمِن."

(رواه الطبراني. حديث صحيح)

Narrated 'Iyāsh ibn Abī Rabī'a: "When the Hour approaches, a wind shall come to take the spirit of every believer."

(Quoted by al-Ṭabarānī. Authenticated *ḥadīth*)

Ḥadīth 213

عن ابن مسعود : "مِنْ شِرارِ ٱلنَّاسِ مَنْ تُدْرِكُهُمُ ٱلسَّاعَةُ وَهُمْ أَحْياءُ."

(رواه البخاري. حديث صحيح)

Narrated Ibn Mas'ūd: "One from amongst the most wicked people will be living at the time when the Hour is established."

(Quoted by al-Bukhārī. Authenticated *ḥadīth*)

Commentary

These two *ḥadīth* enable us to reconcile two important concepts from the prophetic teachings concerning the end of times: the disappearance of all the believers from the face of the earth and the fact that only the worst people of mankind will suffer the torments of the destruction of this world.

al-Munāwī

"The people who will be living when the Hour comes will be amongst the worst of mankind": this *ḥadīth* is in agreement with that according to which the Hour will not come until there are no more persons saying: *Lā ilāha illa-Llāh*. The people who remain then will be the worst. This *ḥadīth* is not in contradiction with the following one: "A group from my community will not cease fighting for the triumph of the truth and resisting their enemies until the last amongst them will fight the Dajjāl,"[234] for this group will be taken away by a beneficent wind so that only the remaining men shall be surprised by the Hour."

(*Fayḍ al-Qadīr*, *ḥadīth* no. 8254)

---

234. See *ḥadīth* 229 below.

Ḥadīth 214

عن أنس : "ما مِنْ عامٍ إِلاَّ وَٱلَّذِي بَعْدَهُ شَرٌّ مِنْهُ، حَتَّى تَلْقَوْنَ رَبَّكُمْ."

(رواه الترمذي. حديث صحيح)

Narrated Anas: "There is no year except that it is worse than the previous one, and like this until the meeting with your Lord."

(Quoted by al-Tirmidhī. Authenticated *ḥadīth*.)

Ḥadīth 215

عن أبي الدرداء : "ما مِنْ عامٍ إِلاَّ يَنْقُصُ ٱلْخَيْرُ فيهِ وَيَزِيدُ ٱلشَّرُّ."

(رواه الطبراني. حديث حسن)

Narrated Abū al-Dardā': "There is no year that does not see the good decrease and the evil increase."

(Quoted by al-Ṭabarānī. Validated *ḥadīth*.)

Commentary

As these *ḥadīth* affirm, the historical becoming of humanity is seen, not as a continuous progress, but as successive decadences touching upon all aspects of life on earth. All these diverse aspects are summarized by the expressions *yanquṣ al-khayr* (decrease in good) and *yazīd al-sharr* (increase in evil).

Moreover this vision of history is in agreement with the teachings of other great religions and spiritual traditions. This inevitable decline has been exposed in a very explicit manner by the traditional doctrine of the "Four Ages of Humanity" in which each of these four periods takes the name of a metal, from the most precious to the most base.

Martin Lings (Abū Bakr Sirāj al-Dīn)

In particular, the tradition of the four ages of the temporal cycle, Golden, Silver, Bronze, and Iron, which dominated the perspective of classical antiquity, going back in the shadows of prehistory, has also been prevalent from equally ancient times amongst the Hindus and the American Indians.

Or to take one aspect of the evolutionary conjecture, namely that human language evolved from the inarticulate sounds of animals, let it be pointed out that although the origin of language is beyond investigation, linguistic science can none the less take us back to a very remote past, and it teaches us that the oldest languages are the most complex and majestic, while also being the richest in variety of consonantal sounds. All languages in use today have devolved from more elaborate languages which they have simplified and in general mutilated and corrupted. Devolution, not evolution, is also the fate of many word meanings. All students should be made to study the already mentioned degradation of the word "intellect." It is a scientific fact that throughout the ancient world the concept of man's faculties was more exalted and of wider scope than it is today.

(*Eleventh Hour*, pp. 34-35)

Ḥadīth 216

عن أبي هريرة : "يَخرُجُ فِي آخرِ ٱلزَّمانِ رِجالٌ يَخْتِلُونَ ٱلدُّنْيا بِٱلدِّينِ يَلْبَسُونَ لِلنَّاسِ جُلُودَ ٱلضَّأْنِ مِنَ ٱللِّينِ أَلْسِنَتُهُمْ أَحْلَى مِنَ ٱلعَسَلِ وَقُلُوبُهُمْ قُلُوبُ ٱلذِّئابِ. يَقُولُ ٱللّهُ : أَبِي يَغْتَرُّونَ أَمْ عَلَيَّ يَجْتَرِئُون ؟ فَبِي حَلَفْتُ لَأَبْعَثَنَّ عَلَى أُولَـٰئِكَ فِتْنَةً تَدَعُ ٱلْحَلِيمَ مِنْهُمْ حَيْران."

(رواه الترمذي. حديث حسن)

Narrated Abū Hurayra: "At the end of times, there shall appear in people a confusion between profanity and religion; they will look like harmless lambs with speech sweeter than honey but with a heart of a wolf. God will say: 'They want to deceive Me? They want to defy Me? I swear by Myself! I will send a sedition upon them which will cripple the most patient amongst them.'"

(Quoted by al-Tirmidhī. Validated *ḥadīth*.)

Commentary

The confusion between profanity and religion mentioned in this *ḥadīth* alludes to the loss of the "sense of the sacred." Religiosity can put up with a more or less total forgetting of the sense of transcendence, as was the case with pre-Islamic Arab paganism. This loss of the sense of the sacred in a monotheistic climate has been interpreted as an inversion of the priority from belonging to the Hereafter to the here-below.

al-Ghazzālī

He who does not perceive the mediocrity of the here-below, its instability, and the link of all its ephemeral pleasures with a particular suffering, does not have a sane mind, because observation and experience suffice to realize this. How then, can people without sane minds be amongst the scholars? He who does not know the incommensurability of the Hereafter is an infidel without any faith; how can one with no faith be amongst the scholars? He who does not know the fundamental opposition between the Hereafter and the here-below spends his efforts in vain; he ignores the sacred Laws given to all the prophets; furthermore, he is unfaithful to the Qur'ān, from its first verse to the last. How can he be counted amongst the scholars? Finally, he who has understood all this and yet does not give priority to the Hereafter over the here-below is a prisoner of Satan; he is doomed by his concupiscent desires and dominated by his wretched interior. How can such a person have the least authority in religious matters?

(*Iḥyā'*, I. p. 60)

Ḥadīth 217

عن انس بن مالك : "لا تُقومُ ٱلسَّاعةُ حَتَّى يَتَقارَبُ ٱلزَّمانُ فَتَكُونُ ٱلسَّنَةُ كالشَّهْرِ وٱلشَّهْرُ كالْجُمُعَةِ وَتَكُونُ ٱلْجُمُعَةُ كاليَوْمِ وَيَكُونُ ٱليَوْمُ كٱلسَّاعةِ وَتَكُونُ ٱلسَّاعةُ كٱلضَّرْمةِ بِٱلنَّارِ."

(رواه الترمذي. حديث صحيح)

Narrated Anas ibn Mālik: "The Hour will not occur before time has contracted to the point that a year will pass like a month, a month like a week, a week like a day, a day like an hour, and an hour will pass as swiftly as a burning firebrand."

(Quoted by al-Tirmidhī. Authenticated *ḥadīth*.)

Commentary

The contraction of time (*taqārub al-zamān*) mentioned by this *ḥadīth* has been interpreted as one of the different consequences of the lack of grace (*qillat al-baraka*) linked with the end of time.

René Guénon ('Abd al-Wāḥid Yaḥyā)

As stated earlier, in a certain sense time consumes space, and it does so in consequence of the power of contraction contained in it, which tends continuously to reduce the spatial expansion to which it is opposed: but time, in its active opposition to the antagonistic principle, unfolds itself with ever-growing speed, for it is far from being homogenous, as people who consider it solely from a quantitative point of view imagine, but on the contrary it is "qualified" at every moment in a different way by the cyclical conditions of the manifestation to which it belongs. The acceleration of time is becoming more apparent than ever in our day, because it becomes exaggerated in the final periods of a cycle, but it nevertheless actually goes on constantly from the beginning of the cycle to the end: it can therefore be said not only that time compresses space, but also that time is itself subject to a progressive contraction. [. . .] It is sometimes said, doubtless without any understanding of the real reason, that today men live faster than in the past, and this is literally true; the haste with which the moderns characteristically approach everything they do being ultimately only a consequence of the confused impressions they experience. [. . .]

Thus it is that "time the devourer ends by devouring itself," in such a way that, at the "end of the world, that is to say at the extreme limit of cyclical manifestation, "there will be no more time."

(*Règne*, pp. 157-58)

Ḥadīth 218

عن أبي هريرة : "بَدَأَ ٱلإسلامُ غَرِيباً وَسَيَعُودُ كَما بَدَأَ غَرِيباً فَطُوبَى لِلغُرَباءِ."

(رواه مسلم. حديث صحيح)

Narrated Abū Hurayra: "Islam began as a stranger and it shall return as a stranger; therefore, blessed be the estranged."

(Quoted by Muslim. Authenticated *ḥadīth*)

Commentary

Every religion necessarily possesses the tendency to lose its purity and the profundity of the spirituality of its beginnings, the weight of the centuries and worldliness playing their part. However, a spiritual renewal is always possible when contact with Revelation still exists and an uninterrupted transmission of the Baraka through initiation is still ensured, as in the case of *taṣawwuf*. When these two sources are sapped—or become inaccessible in practice—the decline risks being irremediable.

Frithjof Schuon ('Īsā Nūr al-Dīn)

All civilizations are in decline, but in different ways; the decline of the East is passive and that of the West is active.

The fault of the East in decline is that it no longer thinks; that of the West is that it thinks too much and thinks wrongly.

The East is sleeping over truths; the West is living in errors.

(*Perspectives*, p. 26)

Ḥadīth 219

عن أبي موسى الأشعري : "إِنَّ بَيْنَ يَدَيِ ٱلسَّاعة فِتَناً كَقَطْعِ ٱللَّيْلِ ٱلْمُظْلِمِ يُصْبِحُ ٱلرَّجُلُ فِيها مُؤْمِناً وَيُمْسِي كافِراً وَيُمْسِي مُؤْمِناً وَيُصْبِحُ كافِراً. القاعِدُ فِيها خَيْرٌ مِنَ ٱلقائِمِ وَٱلْقائِمُ فِيها خَيْرٌ مِنَ ٱلْماشِي وَٱلْماشِي فِيها خَيْرٌ مِنَ ٱلسَّاعِي. فَكَسِّرُوا قِسِيَّكُمْ وَقَطِّعُوا أَوْتارَكُمْ وَٱضْرِبُوا سُيُوفَكُمْ بِٱلْحِجارةِ فَإِنْ دُخِلَ عَلَى أَحَدٍ مِنكُمْ بَيْتَهُ فَلْيَكُنْ كَخَيْرِ ٱبْنَيْ آدَم."

(رواه الحاكم. حديث صحيح)

Narrated Abū Mūsā al-Ash'arī: "Shortly before the Hour, there will be seditions as dark as the obscurity of the night. Man may have faith in the morning and lose it in the evening; and he may have faith in the evening and lose it next morning. During these unrests, the sitting person shall be in a better position than the one standing; similarly, the walking one shall be in a better position than the one in haste. Therefore, break your bows, pull out their strings and hit the edges of your swords against a rock! And if an aggressor enters your dwellings, behave like the better of the two sons of Adam."

(Quoted by al-Ḥākim. Authenticated *ḥadīth*)

Commentary

The end of times in this *ḥadīth*, as in numerous other ones, is described as a very troubled period wherein the outer disorder corresponds to the inner chaos of souls; hence the image of the man who can lose his faith in the interval of one day or one night. These two moments may be considered as denoting two different modes of the loss of faith: the first case can be interpreted as an "active loss"—wherein action is not motivated by a righteous intention and is not based on true knowledge; the second may be understood as a "passive loss" of faith, wherein man lets himself be determined by the chaotic ambience in which he lives.

The better of the two sons of Adam, mentioned at the end of this *ḥadīth*, is none other than Abel, whose unconditional pacifism towards the open willingness of his brother Cain to take his life is related in the Qur'ān:

﴿لَئِنْ بَسَطتَ إِلَيَّ يَدَكَ لِتَقْتُلَنِي ما أنا بِباسِطٍ يَدِيَ إِلَيْكَ لِأَقْتُلَكَ إِنِّي أَخافُ ٱللهَ رَبَّ ٱلعالَمِينَ﴾

Even if thou stretch out thy hand against me to kill me, I shall not stretch out my hand against thee to kill thee, lo! I fear God, the Lord of the Worlds.[235]

So far as it was possible, the Prophet ﷺ tried to avoid recourse to force.[236] However, since he had to build a state and a community of believers, he was sometimes compelled to resort to force in virtue of social and historical pragmatism. This is what one may call conditional pacifism. But as the end of time is not destined to found anything, the point of view of social realism is no longer plausible: the spiritual approach is the only thing that matters. This is why the Prophet ﷺ recommended unconditional pacifism for this period, taking Abel as an example.

235. V: 28.

236. See *ḥadīth* 123 and 124.

Ḥadīth 220

عَنْ أَبِي سَعِيدٍ الخدريِّ : "بَعَثَ عَلِيُّ بْنُ أَبِي طَالِبٍ رَضِيَ
ٱللَّهُ عَنْهُ إِلَى رَسُولِ اللَّهِ ﷺ مِنَ ٱلْيَمَنِ بِذُهَيْبَةٍ فِي أَدِيمٍ
مَقْرُوظٍ لَمْ تُحَصَّلْ مِنْ تُرَابِهَا. قَالَ فَقَسَمَهَا بَيْنَ أَرْبَعَةِ نَفَرٍ
بَيْنَ عُيَيْنَةَ بْنِ بَدْرٍ وَأَقْرَعَ بْنِ حَابِسٍ وَزَيْدِ ٱلْخَيْلِ وَٱلرَّابِعُ
إِمَّا عَلْقَمَةُ وَإِمَّا عَامِرُ بْنُ ٱلطُّفَيْلِ. فَقَالَ رَجُلٌ مِنْ أَصْحَابِهِ :
كُنَّا نَحْنُ أَحَقَّ بِهٰذَا مِنْ هٰؤُلَاءِ. قَالَ فَبَلَغَ ذَلِكَ ٱلنَّبِيَّ ﷺ
فَقَالَ أَلَا تَأْمَنُونِي وَأَنَا أَمِينُ مَنْ فِي ٱلسَّمَاءِ يَأْتِينِي خَبَرُ
ٱلسَّمَاءِ صَبَاحًا وَمَسَاءً ؟ قَالَ فَقَامَ رَجُلٌ غَائِرُ ٱلْعَيْنَيْنِ
مُشْرِفُ ٱلْوَجْنَتَيْنِ نَاشِزُ ٱلْجَبْهَةِ كَثُّ ٱللِّحْيَةِ مَحْلُوقُ ٱلرَّأْسِ
مُشَمَّرُ ٱلْإِزَارِ فَقَالَ : يَا رَسُولَ اللَّهِ اتَّقِ ٱللَّهَ ! قَالَ : وَيْلَكَ
أَوَلَسْتُ أَحَقَّ أَهْلِ ٱلْأَرْضِ أَنْ يَتَّقِيَ ٱللَّهَ ؟ قَالَ ثُمَّ وَلَّى
ٱلرَّجُلُ. قَالَ خَالِدُ بْنُ الْوَلِيدِ : يَا رَسُولَ ٱللَّهِ أَلَا أَضْرِبُ
عُنُقَهُ ؟ قَالَ : لَا، لَعَلَّهُ أَنْ يَكُونَ يُصَلِّي. فَقَالَ خَالِدٌ وَكَمْ
مِنْ مُصَلٍّ يَقُولُ بِلِسَانِهِ مَا لَيْسَ فِي قَلْبِهِ ؟ قَالَ رَسُولُ اللَّهِ
ﷺ : إِنِّي لَمْ أُومَرْ أَنْ أَنْقُبَ عَنْ قُلُوبِ ٱلنَّاسِ وَلَا أَشُقَّ

بُطُونَهُمْ. قَالَ ثُمَّ نَظَرَ إِلَيْهِ وَهُوَ مُقَفٍّ فَقَالَ : إِنَّهُ يَخْرُجُ مِنْ ضِئْضِئِ هٰذَا قَوْمٌ يَتْلُونَ كِتَابَ ٱللَّهِ رَطْباً لا يُجَاوِزُ حَنَاجِرَهُمْ يَمْرُقُونَ مِنْ ٱلدِّينِ كَمَا يَمْرُقُ ٱلسَّهْمُ مِنْ ٱلرَّمِيَّةِ. وَأَظُنُّهُ قَالَ لَئِنْ أَدْرَكْتُهُمْ لَأَقْتُلَنَّهُمْ قَتْلَ ثَمُودَ."

(رواه البخاري. حديث صحيح)

Narrated Abū Sa'īd al-Khudrī: "'Alī ibn Abī Ṭālib sent a piece of gold not yet taken out of its ore from Yemen, in a tanned leather container to the Messenger of God ﷺ, who distributed it amongst four persons: 'Uyayna ibn Badr, Aqra' ibn Ḥābis, Zayd al-Khaylī, and the fourth was either 'Alqama or 'Āmir ibn al-Ṭufayl. One of the Companions protested, 'We are more deserving of this (gold) than them.' When that news reached the Prophet ﷺ, he said, 'Do you not trust me though I am trusted by the One in the Heavens, and I receive news both in the morning and in the evening?' Then a man who had sunken eyes, raised cheek bones, a raised forehead, a thick beard, a shaven head, and a waist sheet that was tucked up (*mushammar al-izār*) said, 'O Messenger of God, fear God!' The Prophet ﷺ said, 'Woe unto you! Am I not of all the people of the earth the most entitled to fear God?' Then that man went away. Khālid ibn al-Walīd said:

O Messenger of God! Shall I cut his neck?
No, for it may be that he prays.
Numerous are those who offer prayers and say with their tongues what is not in their hearts.
I have not been ordered to delve into the hearts of people or to penetrate their inner beings.

Then the Prophet ﷺ looked at that man while he was leaving, and said: 'Verily, from the offspring of this man there will come out (people) who will recite the Qur'ān continuously and elegantly but it will not go beyond their throats. They will leave Islam faster than an arrow goes to its target.' I think the Prophet ﷺ concluded thus, 'If I meet them I will make them perish as the Thamūd were perished.'"

(Quoted by al-Bukhārī. Authenticated *ḥadīth*.)

Ḥadīth 221

عن علي : "يَأْتِي فِي آخِرِ ٱلزَّمَانِ قَوْمٌ حُدَثَاءُ ٱلأَسْنَانِ سُفَهَاءُ ٱلأَحْلَامِ يَقُولُونَ مِنْ خَيْرِ قَوْلِ ٱلْبَرِيَّةِ يَمْرُقُونَ مِنَ ٱلإِسْلَامِ كَمَا يَمْرُقُ ٱلسَّهْمُ مِنْ ٱلرَّمِيَّةِ لا يُجَاوِزُ إِيْمَانُهُمْ حَنَاجِرَهُمْ فَأَيْنَمَا لَقِيتُمُوهُمْ فَٱقْتُلُوهُمْ فَإِنَّ قَتْلَهُمْ أَجْرٌ لِمَنْ قَتَلَهُمْ يَوْمَ الْقِيَامَةِ."

(رواه البخاري. حديث صحيح)

Narrated ʻAlī: "In the last days of this world there will appear some young foolish people who will express themselves in a seductive way and they will abandon Islam faster than an arrow goes to its target. Their faith will not go beyond their throats, so wherever you meet them, make them perish, for therein is a reward on the Day of Resurrection."

(Quoted by al-Bukhārī. Authenticated *ḥadīth*.)

Commentary

The first *ḥadīth* is often interpreted as a prediction of the Kharijite (*al-khawārij*) movement, as can be seen in the *Ṣaḥīḥ* of al-al-Bukhārī.[237] Originally the Kharijites were a group who revolted against both ʻAlī and Muʻāwiyya after the arbitration following the battle of Ṣiffīn, which took place in 37 A.H. They were part of ʻAlī's army but refused the idea of regulating the succession of the caliphate through negotiation. They left the army and were therefore called *khawārij*, "secessionists."

However, the second *ḥadīth* offers additional details and widens the perspective of the first. Indeed, it is no longer a question of a historical period fixed in time but of a movement which, having started at an undetermined moment, should take its full amplitude at the end of times.

Thus a number of contemporary authorities of Islam see in these *ḥadīth* the anticipation of Wahhabi salafism, a movement founded by Muḥammad ibn ʻAbd al-Wahhāb (1115-1201/1703-87). They consider this very particular form of salafism as the kharijism of our time. What makes this connection plausible is as much the physical description of the man mentioned in the first *ḥadīth*—a thick beard, a shaven head, and a waist sheet that was tucked up—as the disrespectful attitude he showed towards the Prophet. In fact, wanting to push puritanism to absurd limits and seeing "association"

237. Book XCII, ch. 5 and 6.

(*shirk*) everywhere, the Wahhabi salafis go so far as to refuse any sign of respect towards the Prophet ﷺ despite their being in total opposition with even firmly established *ḥadīth*. The preaching of Wahhabi salafism was adopted by a tribal chief from Najd, in central Arabia. This chief belonged to the family of Saud. Let us recall that before the capture of the holy sites of Islam by the Wahhabis, Mecca and especially Medina were filled with tombs of the Companions and of the Followers. Today, the great majority of these cemeteries have been reduced to wastelands. Even the tomb of the Prophet ﷺ was but spared *in extremis* thanks to the protests from representatives of different Muslim nations and also to the fortunate mishandling of canons by the Bedouins. The Wahhabis pulled down the cover of the Kaaba only to replace it with a curtain made of thick cloth on which, instead of the usual formula of the Shahāda, they embroidered a formula of their creed. This is testified by a document taken from the Egyptian archives, dating from 1809:

> 1 *Rabīʿ al-ākhir* 1224 / 16 May 1809.
>
> Informing on the actions of the commander in chief of Hijaz, after it was ascertained that al-Saʿūd had started the Friday sermon (*khuṭba*) with his grievous name.
>
> What has taken place in the holy sites for many years is shameful and disgraceful; what has befallen the people of these two excellent cities and their precincts is marked by treachery and destruction, from the sect (*ṭā'ifa*) of the Kharijites [. . .].
>
> The Kharijites have pulled down the sacred cloth (*kiswa*) which has been covering the pure Kaaba from the time [of the Prophet], and which had been sent by the Ottoman sultans. They have replaced it with a curtain which is woven like a black *'abayya* on which they have written these words: "There is no god but God and Saʿūd is the Caliph of God" instead of "There is no god but God and Muḥammad is the Messenger of God."[238]

A well-known contemporary preacher, originally from Yemen, al-Ḥabīb al-Jifrī summarizes the different attacks on the honor of the Prophet ﷺ committed by the Wahhabis:

- The parents of the Prophet ﷺ are doomed in Hell.
- One must not say *sayyidunā* Muḥammad, but simply Muḥammad.
- There is no blessing (*tabarruk*) whatsoever attached to the ob jects which belonged to him: hair, clothes, sword . . .
- The Prophet ﷺ is dead: "He can neither harm nor be of any use."

It is astonishing, to say the least, that the Wahhabi doctrine, insisting so heavily on the resort to textual proofs, can be in such contradiction with the

238. Quoted by Henry Laurens, *L'Orient arabe: Arabisme et islamisme entre 1798 et 1945*, ed. Armand Colin, pp. 48-49.

ḥadīth which are found in collections like the Ṣaḥīḥ of al-Bukhārī.[239]

Let us specify that the attitude of the Wahhabis towards the Prophet ﷺ is not completely new, since Jalāl al-Dīn al-Suyūṭī (d. 911/1505) issued fatwas in response to the four above-mentioned points.[240] Among these are:

> *Masālik al-ḥunafā fī wāliday al-Muṣṭafā* ("The Attitude of the Monotheists towards the Parents of the Chosen Prophet")
>
> *Inbā' al-adhkiyā' bi hayāt al-anbiyā'* ("Informing Intelligent People that the Prophets Are Alive")

What is truly new in this modern movement is the financial and technical capacity of the Wahhabis to propagate such ideas.

As regards the second *ḥadīth*, it mentions that at the end of times "there will appear some young foolish people who will use seductive speech." It has been noticed that the preaching of F.I.S. in the beginning of the 1990's and that of the Talibans—a term meaning "students"—in Afghanistan, has especially influenced unemployed young adults. It is also known that the salafism preached by these two movements is inspired entirely by Wahhabism.

It has to be noted that in these *ḥadīth* certain expressions come out more strongly, which implies that they characterize in a fundamental way the people described therein:

> They will abandon Islam faster than an arrow going to its target.
>
> The Qur'ān and faith will not go beyond their throats.

The first expression explicitly affirms that they are at odds with Islam because they lack respect for the Prophet ﷺ and, by extension, for the saints amongst the men of faith. The Qur'ān states explicitly that all the actions of those who behave in a similar way towards the Prophet ﷺ are reduced to nothing: *O ye who believe! Lift not up your voices above the voice of the Prophet, nor shout when speaking to him as ye shout one to another, lest your works be rendered vain while ye perceive not.*[241]

In the same way, in speaking about the saints, a *ḥadīth* qudsī affirms that God declares war against whomever shows hostility to a saint.[242] And yet, on the pretext of fighting *shirk*, Wahhabi salafism has developed a veritable "allergy" to anything that is part of sanctity in Islam.

The Najdite[243] origins of salafism lead many authorities of Islam, like the celebrated Sa'īd Ramaḍān al-Būṭī, to assert that the following *ḥadīth*

239. See the *ḥadīth* in the chapter on the Prophet ﷺ in this volume.

240. Included in his *al-Ḥāwī li-l-fatāwī*.

241. XLIX: 2.

242. Cf. *ḥadīth* 197.

243. Najd is a region of present Saudi Arabia, with Ryadh as its capital. Sa'īd Ramaḍān al-Būṭī has written a work denouncing the deviation of Wahhabi salafism, *The Non-conformity to the Four Legal Schools: The Most Dangerous Heresy Threatening the Divine Law*, Damascus: Maktabat al-Fārābī, 1999.

applies to this very political-religious movement:

Narrated al-Zubayr ibn 'Abdī: "O God! Bless our Sham and our Yemen." People said, "Our Najd as well." The Prophet ﷺ again said, "O God! Bless our Sham and Yemen." They said again, "Our Najd as well." On that the Prophet ﷺ said, "It is from there that earthquakes and afflictions will appear, and from there will come out the horn of Satan." (al-Bukhārī)

Let us conclude with the analysis by Seyyed Hossein Nasr, for whom Wahhabi salafism of today is the result of a meeting between a very literalist approach to religion and a certain modern mentality which is much opposed to the spirit of traditional Islam:

> Only during the past few decades has a new phenomenon appeared which necessitates distinguishing rigorously between traditional Islam and, not only modernism, but also the spectrum of feeling, action, and occasionally thought that has been identified by Western scholarship and journalism as "fundamentalist" or revivalist Islam. There were, needless to say, revivalist movements going back to the 12th/18th century. But this earlier "fundamentalism" associated with, let us say, Wahhabism or the Deoband school of India, was more a truncated form of traditional Islam, in opposition to many aspects of the Islamic tradition and highly exoteric but still orthodox, rather than a deviation from the traditional norm.[244]

Aḥmad ibn Zaynī Daḥlān[245]

Numerous sayings of the Prophet ﷺ have foretold the appearance of the Wahhabis as a misfortune for Islam. Thus, the Prophet ﷺ has said: "From the east there shall appear people who read the Qur'ān but this reading will not go beyond their throat. They will move away from Islam faster than an arrow reaches its target: their distinctive sign is that they shave their heads." This *ḥadīth* has many versions, some of which are included in the *Ṣaḥīḥ* of al-Bukhārī, but also in the other collections. It is not necessary to quote all these *ḥadīth*: they are all authentic and well-known. In saying, "their distinctive sign is that they shave their heads," the Prophet ﷺ clearly denotes the Wahhabis. Since their appearance, most of them have indeed had the habit of shaving the head, which was not the case with the kharijites or any other known heresy. This is why 'Abd al-Raḥmān al-Ahdal, mufti of Zabīd, used to say: "There is no need to offer a refutation of the Wahhabi thesis: the saying of the Prophet ﷺ, their distinctive sign is that they shave their head is the best refutation since they are the only ones amongst the people of blameworthy (*mubtadi'a*) innovations to have done it."

(*Fitnat al-wahhābiyya*, p. 14)

---

244. *Traditional Islam in the Modern West* (London: Kegan Paul International, 1987), p. 12.

245. Aḥmad ibn Zaynī Daḥlān (d. 1886) was the Muftī of Mecca for a long time. He was appointed dean of the scholars in 1871.

Ḥadīth 222

عن عبد الله بن عمرو : "إِنَّ ٱللَّهَ تَعالَى لا يَقْبِضُ ٱلعِلْمَ انْتِزاعاً يَنْتَزِعُهُ مِنْ ٱلعِبادِ، وَلٰكِنْ يَقْبِضُ ٱلعِلْمَ بِقَبْضِ ٱلعُلَماءِ، حَتَّى إِذا لَمْ يَبْقَ عالِماً اتَّخذَ ٱلنَّاسُ رُؤَساءَ جُهَّالاً فَسُئِلُوا فَأَفْتَوْا بِغَيْرِ عِلْمٍ، فَضَلُّوا وَأَضَلُّوا."

(رواه البخاري. حديث صحيح)

Narrated ‘Abd Allāh ibn ‘Amr: “Verily, God does not take away knowledge by taking it away from [the hearts of] people, but He takes it away through the death of scholars until, when none of them remains, people will take as their leaders ignorant persons who, when consulted, will give their verdict without knowledge. So they will go astray and will lead the people astray.”

(Quoted by al-Bukhārī. Authenticated *ḥadīth*)

Commentary

In previous *ḥadīth*, we have seen that when speaking about knowledge, one must consider its outward meaning of *sharī‘a* and, above all, its inner meaning of *ḥaqīqa*. Also, the disappearance of the scholars mentioned in this *ḥadīth* is related more than anything else to the disappearing of authentic spiritual masters who are the true inheritors of the Prophet.

Let us add however that it is not sufficient to be a “partisan” of a spiritual master in order to be a true traveller on the Path to God. In an age when masters sometimes accept thousands of disciples for compassion—with consideration for the “spiritual hunger” raging everywhere—the emphasis of certain sages on the humility and discretion the aspirant must observe *vis-à-vis* veritable knowledge is more pertinent than ever. Regarding this point, let us mention a strange but not a rare phenomenon of our times: certain disciples from different spiritual paths pose as authorities and criticize the teachings of great masters who do not fit into the simplicity of their views. According to these critiques, all the spiritual teachings which do not correspond to common theology on matters pertaining to the *sharī‘a* and especially the *‘aqīda* are heretical. They criticize spiritual masters with all the more self-confidence since they do have a spiritual master. In fact, a spiritual master cannot be aware of all deeds of each disciple. With this attitude, they demonstrate their confusing exoterism (*‘ilm al-ẓāhir*)—which is necessary for the Path—with the exoterist mentality (*al-ḥashwiyya*) which is amongst the thickest veils. Thus, one meets pseudo-defenders of Sufism who say that there is no inner knowledge in Islam and that the famous *ḥadīth* of Abū Hurayra[246] pertains solely to the Quraysh families supposedly seeking disorder in the community after the death of the Prophet. This attitude, the spread of which is on the rise, is symptomatic of a certain insidious influence of the Wahhabi salafism on certain insufficiently committed aspirants in the path of inner transformation and the purification of the soul. This is why, just like the deniers of the spiritual Path, they are not prepared to receive from their master the esoteric teachings related to the inner knowledge because it will be extremely harmful to them.

Amīr 'Abd al-Qādir

May God protect us from treachery, for only the hypocrite shows himself unworthy . . .

When the people of our order—may God be content with them—write on spiritual realities and they divulge certain secrets of *tawḥīd*, removing some of the veils covering the Divine domain, they only do it for the sake of their companions and those who follow the Path, for they know their capacities and their firm attachment to the Book and the *Sunna*. They do not write for the common believers and even less so for vulgar or ill-intentioned people. They do not utter these things in public gatherings as is the case today with certain ignorant shaykhs who do not convey a spiritual truth save for boasting, before a crowd more ignorant than themselves, which in its turn hastens to divulge it everywhere, without having the least knowledge thereof. These are the misguided who misguide others too!

The authors of works dealing with spiritual realities wrote them for the folk of their Path, and not for the weak-minded ones, who can only be harmed by such works, and can deviate from religion as quickly as an arrow going towards its target, soiling them more than blood or excrements do.

(*Mawāqif*, no. 158)

246. Cf. *Ḥadīth* 66 and the respective commentaries.

Ḥadīth 223

عن ابن عمرو : "لَيْسَ مِنَّا مَنْ لَمْ يَرْحَمْ صَغِيرَنا، وَيَعْرِفْ شَرَفَ كَبِيرَنا."

(رواه الحاكم. حديث صحيح)

Narrated Ibn 'Umar: "He who is not merciful towards our young ones and who does not recognize the nobility of our elderly is not amongst us."

(Quoted by al-Ḥākim. Authenticated *ḥadīth*.)

Ḥadīth 224

عن عبادة بن الصامت : "لَيْسَ مِنَّا مَنْ لَمْ يُجِلَّ كَبِيرَنا وَيَرْحَمْ صَغِيرَنا وَيَعْرِفْ لِعالِمِنا حَقَّهُ."

(رواه الإمام أحمد. حديث حسن)

Narrated 'Ubāda ibn al-Ṣāmit: "Whoever does not honor our elderly, and is not merciful towards our young ones, and ignores the rights of our scholars, is not one of us."

(Quoted by Aḥmad ibn Ḥanbal. Validated *ḥadīth*)

Commentary

These two *ḥadīth* emphasize the importance of harmonious relations between generations. These relations must be marked by respect and compassion. It is therefore strange to see the way in which certain individuals—seeking to "update" Islam—sport the most artificial and most ignorant youth-adoring attitudes. Obsessed by "progress," they happily reject their parental heritage without even trying to discern what essential and precious elements it may contain. According to a *ḥadīth*, this generation gap will reach its climax at the end of time: "There will come a time when people will no longer follow the scholars and will not respect the sages or the elderly. Children will no longer be an object of [adults'] mercy, and people will compete for the goods of this world."[247]

247. *Ḥadīth* quoted by al-Daylamī.

Ḥadīth 225

عن ابن عباس : "البَرَكةُ مَعَ أَكابِرِكُمْ."

(رواه ابن حبان. حديث صحيح)

Narrated Ibn 'Abbās: "Blessing is found amongst your elderly."
(Quoted by Ibn Ḥibbān. Authenticated *ḥadīth*)

Commentary

In its immediate sense, this *ḥadīth* emphasizes the blessing represented by the elderly as a source of experience and wisdom. Youth is often characterized by lack of lucidity and haste. And yet, according to a *ḥadīth*: "Slowness is from God, and haste from Satan."[248]

But this *ḥadīth* can also be interpreted in a spiritual sense, "the elderly" symbolizing the sages and the spiritual masters whatever their age may be. This is the meaning accorded to it by certain *muḥaddithūn* like al-Munāwī (d. 1031/1621).

al-Munāwī

"The elderly" denotes experienced people and those who work for God's sake. Therefore visit them in order to make the most of their advice and benefit from their guidance. But this expression can also denote the folk of knowledge, even though they might be young. It is therefore appropriate to honor (*ijlāl*) them for what the Real—exalted be He—has granted them . . .

God the Most High has said: *Then the oldest of them said* . . . [249] In the same way, the Prophet ﷺ was once holding a *siwāk* (aromatic tooth-stick) and intended to give it to one of his Companions who were present with him. Then Jibrīl told him: "Offer it to the eldest amongst them." And he did so.

Shaykh al-'Alawī

The expression "the elderly" (*al-kibār*) includes the elect of the community even though they might be young in years because the value of a man depends on his inner reality and not on his physical characteristics.

(*Qawl*, p. 17)

---

248. [1] عن سهل بن سعد الساعدي : "الأَناة مِنَ اللّه والْعَجَلَةُ مِنَ الشَّيْطَانِ"

(رواه الترمذي. حديث حسن)

249. XII: 80, referring to the oldest brother of Yūsuf who was the wisest amongst them.

Ḥadīth 226

عن هشام بن عامر : "ما بَيْنَ خَلْقِ آدَمَ إِلى قِيامِ ٱلسَّاعةِ أَمْرٌ أَكْبَرُ مِنَ الدَّجَّال."

(رواه مسلم. حديث صحيح)

Narrated Hishām ibn 'Āmir: "There would be no creation (creating more trouble and deserving more attention) than the (coming of the) Dajjāl right from the creation of Adam to the Last Hour."

(Quoted by Muslim. Authenticated *ḥadīth*)

Commentary

The Antichrist was announced not only by the Messenger of God but also by the prophets who came before him. According to Amīr 'Abd al-Qādir, all the prophets have anticipated his coming as being near. He takes the opportunity to explain why in the case of the Prophet ﷺ this announcement takes on a different character.

Amīr 'Abd al-Qādir

al-Bukhārī relates in his *Ṣaḥīḥ* the following *ḥadīth* narrated by Ibn 'Umar: "The Messenger of God ﷺ stood amongst the people, glorified and praised God as He deserved, and then mentioned the Dajjāl saying, 'I warn you against him and there was no prophet who did not warn his nation against him. No doubt, Noah warned his nation against him . . . '"[250]

Certain individuals, distressed by the difficulty of understanding this, have said: How could every prophet have warned his people against the Dajjāl[251] when he should only appear close to the Day of Resurrection? It is unthinkable that the totality of the prophets could have missed this!

---

250. The remainder of the *ḥadīth* is: " . . . but I tell you about him something of which no prophet told his nation before me. You should know that he is one-eyed, and God is not one-eyed." Here is the Arabic text of the *ḥadīth*:

قامَ النَّبِيُ صَلّى اللهُ عَلَيْه وَ سَلَّمَ في النّاسِ فَأَثْنَىَ عَلى اللهِ بما هُوَ أَهْلُهُ ثُمَّ ذَكَرَ الدَّجالَ فَقالَ إِنِّي أُنْذِرُكُموهُ وَما مِنْ نَبيٍّ إلاّ قَدْ أَنْذَرَهُ قَوْمَهُ لَقَدْ أَنْذَرَهُ نُوحٌ قَوْمَهُ وَلَكِنْ سَأَقولُ لَكُمْ فيهِ قَوْلاً لَمْ يَقُلْهُ نَبِيٌّ لِقَوْمِهِ تَعْلَمونَ أَنَّهُ أَعْوَرُ وَأَنَّ اللهَ لَيْسَ بِأَعْوَرَ.

251. Literally, "Impostor."

Our response is this: Each prophet is a universal man (*insān kāmil*) who has necessarily realized the degree of Unicity (*martabat al-wāḥidiyya*) which is that of the Divine function (*martabat al-ulūhiyya*) totalizing all the Divine Names.[252] However, the theophany of a particular Divine Name is necessarily predominant in each of them. The Real—exalted be He—manifests Itself to them through revelation and informs them that He has not created anything more precious than them and that everything was created for them. He informs each prophet that He has created all things in view of him; that the Mahdi shall appear in his community; that he (the Mahdi) will exercise his authority in the name of the Law instituted by this prophet and that he will erase the deviations brought about by men. In the same way, He informs (each prophet) that his community will be a contemporary of the Dajjāl. Following this, each prophet informs their people about it. After the disappearance of that prophet and of that community, there comes another prophet and the situation is repeated.

All this derives from the "totalizing degree" (*al-martaba al-jāmi'a*) mentioned above, and from the manifestation of God through the Name *Allāh*. The seditions about which God has informed each prophet have been realized in a symbolic (*ma'āniyan*) and not in a concrete manner (*suwaran qā'imatan*) as is the case with our times regarding the impostors and deviators. These seditions will appear entirely and concretely as the Messenger of God has informed us regarding them in such a way that his mission manifests the totalizing Name *Allāh*, which dominates all the Divine Names. Therefore the seditions in question should necessarily manifest themselves in a concrete manner after having been realized symbolically . . .

(*Mawāqif*, no. 317)

252. This is the degree of the Name *Allāh*.

Ḥadīth 227

عن مجمع بن جابر : "يَقْتُلُ ٱبْنُ مَرْيَمَ ٱلدَّجَّالَ بِبابِ لُدّ."

(رواه الترمذي. حديث صحيح)

Narrated Majma‘ ibn Jābir: "The son of Mary shall kill the Dajjāl at the gate of Ludd."

(Quoted by al-Tirmidhī. Authenticated *ḥadīth*)

Ḥadīth 228

عن أنس بن مالك : "سَيُدْرِكُ رَجُلانِ مِنْ أُمَّتي عِيسىَ ٱبْنِ مَرْيَمَ وَيَشْهَدانِ قِتالَ ٱلدَّجَّال."

(رواه الحاكم. حديث صحيح)

Narrated Anas ibn Mālik: "Two men belonging to my community will join Jesus, son of Mary, and they shall witness the putting to death of the Dajjāl."

(Quoted by al-Ḥākim. Authenticated *ḥadīth*)

Commentary

Numerous *ḥadīth* mention that Jesus will put the Antichrist to death. The precise place of this event is cited in several sources; it is the city of Ludd.

Ludd is the Arabic name of Lydda which is now a town in Israel, south-east of Jaffa. This town is mentioned in the Old Testament under the name of Lod. It is said that its fame comes from the fact that it sheltered the tomb of Saint George, on which a church was erected. Indeed, according to F. Robinson: " . . . the real sanctity of Ludd and its great fame in the Christian world are due to the fact that it is allegedly the birthplace of Saint George, who is probably the most venerated hero of Eastern Christianity and who, despite his obscure origin, has become not only the real patron of Syrian Christianity and an object of respect on the part of the Muslims, but also the patron of most Christian peoples of the West. Saint George of Lydda is the Saint George of England."[253] Let us note in passing that Khiḍr is sometimes identified with Saint George.

According to Muqaddasī, it is at the gate of the church sheltering the tomb of Saint George that Jesus shall kill the Dajjāl. However, according to a *ḥadīth* quoted by Aḥmad ibn Ḥanbal, it is at the eastern gate (*bāb ludd al-sharqī*) of the town that Jesus shall put him to death.

253. *E.I. (2)*, vol. V, p. 804.

Ḥadīth 229

عن جبير بن نفير : "لَيُدْرِكَنَّ ٱلدَّجَّالُ قَوْماً مِثْلَكُمْ أَوْ خَيْراً مِنْكُمْ، وَلَنْ يُخْزِيَ ٱللهُ أُمَّةً أَنا أَوَّلُها وَعِيسَى بِنُ مَرْيَمَ آخِرُها."

(رواه الحاكم. حديث صحيح)

Narrated Jubayr ibn Nafīr: "The Antichrist will have to face a group that resembles you, and is even better than you. Assuredly, God will not debase a community which starts with [the time of] my presence and whose end shall be marked by that of Jesus, son of Mary."

(Quoted by al-Ḥākim. Authenticated *ḥadīth*.)

Commentary

It is obviously difficult to identify the group (*qawm*) mentioned by this *ḥadīth*. However, it can be said that the *ḥadīth* speaks about the allies of the Mahdī since this group is the one which should oppose the Antichrist. Thus another *ḥadīth* affirms:

عن عمران بن حصين : "لا تَزالُ طائِفَةٌ مِنْ أُمَّتِي يُقاتِلونَ عَلى ٱلحَقِّ ظاهِرينَ عَلى مَنْ ناوَأَهُمْ حَتّى يُقاتِلُ آخِرُهُمْ ٱلْمَسيحَ ٱلدَّجالَ."

(رواه أبو داود. حديث صحيح)

Narrated 'Imrān ibn Ḥuṣayn: "A group from my community will not cease fighting for the triumph of the truth and resisting those who are hostile to it until the last ones amongst them fight the Antichrist."

(Quoted by Abū Dāwūd. Authenticated *ḥadīth*.)

Another *ḥadīth* specifies the geographical origins of this group which will resist and make the truth triumph:

عَنْ نافِعِ بنِ عُتَيْبة قالَ : "كُنّا مَعَ رَسولِ اللهِ صَلى اللهُ

عَلَيْهِ وَ سَلَّمَ فِي غَزْوَةٍ. قَالَ : فَأَتَى ٱلنَّبِيَّ صَلَّى الله عَلَيْهِ وَ

سَلَّمَ قَوْمٌ مِنْ قِبَلِ ٱلْمَغْرِبِ عَلَيْهِمْ ثِيَابُ ٱلصُّوفِ فَوَافَقُوهُ

عِنْدَ أَكَمَّةٍ وَإِنَّهُمْ لَقِيَامٌ وَ رَسُولُ اللهِ صَلَّى الله عَلَيْهِ وَ سَلَّمَ

قَاعِدٌ. قَالَ : فَقَالَتْ لِي نَفْسِي ائْتِهِمْ فَقُمْ بَيْنَهُ وَبَيْنَهُمْ لا

يَغْتَالُونَهُ, قَالَ : ثُمَّ قُلْتُ لَعَلَّهُ نَجِيٌّ مَعَهُمْ. فَأَتَيْتُهُمْ فَقُمْتُ

بَيْنَهُمْ وَبَيْنَهُ. حَفِظْتُ مِنْهُ أَرْبَعَ كَلِمَاتٍ أَعُدُّهُنَّ فِي يَدِي :

"تَغْزُونَ جَزِيرَةَ ٱلْعَرَبِ فَيَفْتَحُهَا ٱللهُ ثُمَّ فَارِسَ فَيَفْتَحُهَا ٱللهُ

ثُمَّ تَغْزُونَ ٱلرُّومَ فَيَفْتَحُهَا ٱللهُ ثُمَّ تَغْزُونَ ٱلدَّجَالَ فَيَفْتَحُهُ

ٱللهُ."

(رواه مسلم. حديث صحيح)

Narrated Nāfi' ibn 'Utayba: "We were with the Messenger of God ﷺ in an expedition when there came a people to the Messenger of God ﷺ from the direction of the west. They were dressed in woolen clothes and they stood near a hillock and they approached him as he was sitting. I said to myself: 'Better go to them and stand between him and them that they may not attack him.' Then I thought that perhaps secret negotiations had been going on amongst them. The Prophet ﷺ went to them and stood between them, and I remember four things that he said on that occasion which I can repeat: 'You will combat the Arabian peninsula and God will give you victory, then you will attack Persia and God will give you victory. Then Rome (the West) and God will enable you to conquer it, then you will combat the Antichrist, and God will give you victory.'"

(Quoted by Muslim. Authenticated *ḥadīth*)

Tradition and Innovation: سنة وبدعة

Ḥadīth 230

عن عائشة : "مَنْ أَحْدَثَ فِي أَمْرِنا هٰذا ما لَيْسَ مِنْهُ فَهُوَ رَدٌّ."

(رواه ابن ماجه. حديث صحيح)

Narrated ʻĀ'isha: "Whoever innovates in our religion by introducing to it something which is not part of it will be rejected."

(Quoted by Ibn Mājah. Authenticated *ḥadīth*)

Commentary

The terms innovation (*bid'a*) and tradition (*sunna*) correspond to realities which are more subtle than it may seem. Few subjects have given rise to such fierce debates as the one between the partisans of a static reading and those of a dynamic reading of these terms. Their definitions vary depending on the perspective of the theologians discussing them. The following text attempts to make a synthesis of the different interpretations that have been suggested.

Shaykh 'Alī Jum'a

There are two ways of interpreting the legal meaning of the term innovation (*bid'a*) amongst the scholars. The first is that which is held by al-'Izz ibn 'Abd al-Salām who considers that everything the Prophet ﷺ did not do is an innovation. He distinguishes five types of innovation: innovation is everything which was not practiced during the time of the Prophet ﷺ. It is of several kinds: the necessary (*wājiba*), the prohibited (*muḥarrama*), the recommended (*mandūba*), the discouraged (*makrūha*), and the neutral (*mubāḥa*). In order to know to which category an innovation belongs, the innovation must be measured against the principles of the sacred Law (*qawā'īd al-sharī'a*): if it falls under the category of necessity (*ījāb*), it will be necessary;[254] if it falls under the category of the prohibited, it will be prohibited . . .

The second way of interpreting the legal meaning of the term "innova-

254. Thus the innovation of grammar—to the degree that this learning did not exist at the time of the Prophet—is necessary because from the point of view of the sacred Law, the mastery the language of the Qur'ān is a necessity. (Note of the text)

tion" is more restrictive and has the sense of blameworthy innovation. This is the case of Ibn Rajab Ḥanbalī who explained the meaning of innovation in the following terms: "Innovation denotes all that which is not based on any principle (*aṣl*) of the sacred Law. As for that which is rooted in the sacred Law, it does not constitute an innovation at all, even if it were a novelty . . . "

In reality, the two approaches converge . . . the blameworthy innovation, whose practice is a sin, is that which has no basis in the sacred Law, and this is what the following saying of the Prophet ﷺ indicates: "All innovation is a distraction."

(*Bayān*, pp. 204-206)

Ḥadīth 231

عن جرير بن عبد الله : "مَنْ سَنَّ فِي الإِسْلامِ سُنَّةً حَسَنَةً كانَ لَهُ أَجْرُها وَأَجْرُ مَنْ عَمِلَ بِها مِنْ بَعْدِه."

(رواه الإمام أحمد. حديث صحيح)

Narrated Jarīr ibn ʻAbd Allāh: "He who institutes a praiseworthy tradition (*sunna ḥasana*) in Islam will receive a reward for it and for all those who practice it after him."

(Quoted by Aḥmad ibn Ḥanbal. Authenticated *ḥadīth*.)

Commentary

The most important expression of this *ḥadīth* is obviously that of the "praiseworthy tradition" (*sunna ḥasana*) which does not denote the *Sunna* of the Prophet ﷺ but the institution of a practice by those who succeeded him. This action is denoted by the verb *sanna*.

Shaykh al-ʻAlawī

If we were to say that what the Sufis are following is an innovation, then it is eligible to be called a good innovation. This is also called a *Sunna* in the *ḥadīth* of the Prophet ﷺ, "Whoever institutes a good practice will receive its reward and the reward of the one who practices it until the day of Judgement." So consider carefully how an innovation is called a *Sunna*.

(*Qawl*, pp. 31-32)

Ḥadīth 232

عن عبد الرحمن بن عبد القاري : "خَرَجْتُ مَعَ عُمَرَ بْنِ ٱلْخَطَّابِ رَضِيَ ٱللهُ عَنْهُ لَيْلَةً في رَمَضان إلى ٱلْمَسْجِد، فَإذا ٱلنَّاسُ أَوْزاعٌ مُتَفَرِّقُونَ، يُصَلِّي ٱلرَّجُلُ لِنَفْسِه، وَيُصَلِّي ٱلرَّجُلُ فَيُصَلِّي بِصَلاتِهِ ٱلرَّهْطُ، فَقالَ عُمَر: إِنِّي أَرَى لَوْ جَمَعْتُ هٰؤُلاءِ عَلَى قارِئٍ واحِدٍ لَكانَ أَمْثَلَ. ثُمَّ عَزَمَ فَجَمَعَهُمْ عَلَى أُبَيِّ بْنِ كَعْب، ثُمَّ خَرَجْتُ مَعَهُ لَيْلَةً أُخْرَى وَٱلنَّاسُ يُصَلُّونَ بِصَلاةِ قارِئِهِمْ، قالَ عُمَر : نِعْمَ ٱلبِدْعة هٰذِه، وَٱلَّتي يَنامُونَ عَنْها أَفْضَلُ مِنَ ٱلَّتي يَقُومُونَ، يُرِيدُ آخِرَ ٱللَّيْل، وَكانَ ٱلنَّاسُ يَقُومُونَ أَوَّلَه."

(رواه البخاري. حديث صحيح)

Narrated ‘Abd al-Raḥmān ibn ‘Abd al-Qārī: “I went out in the company of ‘Umar ibn al-Khaṭṭāb one night in Ramadan to the mosque and found the people praying in different groups; a man praying alone, and a man praying with a little group behind him. So, ‘Umar said, ‘In my opinion, I would collect these (people) under the leadership of one *qārī’* (reciter of the Qur’ān in prayer).’ So, he made up his mind to congregate them behind Ubayy ibn Ka‘b. Then on another night I went again in his company and the people were praying behind their reciter. On that, ‘Umar remarked, ‘What an excellent *bid‘a* this is; but the prayer during which they sleep is even better than that during which they are awake.’ He meant that the prayers before sunrise are better than those at the beginning of the night, which were the ones these people were performing.”

(Quoted by al-Bukhārī. Authenticated *ḥadīth*)

Commentary

The spiritual masters have sometimes been reproached for introducing rites, ideas and even simply technical terms (*iṣṭilāḥāt*) which were unknown at the time of the Prophet. As Shaykh al-‘Alawī reminds us, this *ḥadīth* is one of the textual bases for their "excellent innovation."

Shaykh al-'Alawī

Such an example does not need any explanation, not withstanding that it falls under [supplementary] worship. However, Sufism falls under the category of worship from the perspective of being an integral aspect, not from the perspective of being additional or not additional, since most of it relates to the purification of the interior, the improvement of morals, the occupation with *dhikr*, closeness with the One remembered, and the rest that is stipulated. [. . .]

Imam al-Shāfi'ī—may God be pleased with him!—said, "Innovation is that which contradicts the Qur'ān, the *Sunna*, or the Consensus of the Companions, or one of their sayings (*athar*); whatever does not contradict these is praiseworthy."

(*Qawl*, pp. 32-33)

Ḥadīth 233

عن عبيد الله بن أبي رافع : "لا أُلْفِيَنَّ أَحَدَكُمْ مُتَّكِئاً عَلَى أَرِيكَتِهِ يَأْتِيهِ ٱلأَمْرُ مِنْ أَمْرِي مِمَّا أَمَرْتُ بِهِ أَوْ نَهَيْتُ عَنْهُ فَيَقُولُ : لا أَدْرِي ما وَجَدْنا فِي كِتابِ ٱللهِ ٱتَّبَعْناهُ."

(رواه أبو داود. حديث حسن)

Narrated ʻUbayd Allāh ibn Abī Rāfiʻ: "None of you should say, when lying down on a couch and being asked about a fact regarding what I have instituted or prohibited: 'I do not know . . . we only apply what we find in the Book of God!'"

(Quoted by: Abū Dāwūd. Validated *ḥadīth*.)

Commentary

This *ḥadīth* addresses clearly the rejection of the prophetic teachings while retaining only the Qur'ān and warns against such an attitude. In fact, such a rejection would not be faithful even to the Qur'ān itself since the latter reminds us in several places that the prophetic mission is not limited simply to the transmission of the Book:

﴿لَقَدْ مَنَّ ٱللهُ عَلَى ٱلْمُؤْمِنِينَ إِذْ بَعَثَ فِيهِمْ رَسُولاً مِنْ أَنْفُسِهِمْ يَتْلُو عَلَيْهِمْ آياتِهِ وَيُزَكِّيهِمْ وَيُعَلِّمُهُمُ ٱلْكِتابَ وَٱلْحِكْمَةَ وَإِنْ كانُوا مِنْ قَبْلُ لَفِي ضَلالٍ مُبِينٍ﴾

God verily hath shown grace to the believers by sending unto them a messenger of their own who reciteth unto them His revelations, and causeth them to grow, and teacheth them the Book and Wisdom; although before (he came to them) they were in flagrant error.[255]

For the majority of the commentators, the expression the "Book and Wisdom" refers to the Qur'ān and the prophetic teaching: in this perspective, one cannot be grasped without the other. This clarifies the condemnation by the majority of the scholars in Islam of those who claim to be upholders of the Qur'ān to the exclusion of the *Ḥadīth* (*ahl al-Qur'ān* or *qur'āniyyūn*).

255. LXII: 2

al-Ābādī

"I do not know . . . we only apply what we find in the Book of God!" This passage of the *ḥadīth* means: "We know only the Qur'ān and follow nothing but it." This prediction of the Prophet ﷺ was actualized by means of the teaching of a man originating from Punjab in India, who coined the term "Quranist." He was assuredly a denier and an apostate. He taught some abnormalities that no one in Islam had advanced before. He denigrated the Prophet ﷺ at length and rejected all the authenticated *ḥadīth* without exception and dared to say: "These are nothing but lies and fabrications against God. One has to conform only to the Qur'ān and leave aside the *ḥadīth* of the Prophet, even if they are authenticated and from numerous sources (*mutawātira*). Whoever is not content with the Qur'ān is part of the people mentioned in the verse *Whoso judgeth not by that which Allah hath revealed: such are disbelievers*."[256] Many ignorant ones followed this man and took him for their imam. The scholars of our time have confirmed his disbelief, his straying, and his rejection of the community of Islam.

(*'Awn al-Ma'būd*, *ḥadīth* no. 4581)

256. V: 44

Ḥadīth 234

عن أبي هريرة : "إِنَّ ٱللهَ تَعالى يَبْعَثُ لِهٰذِهِ ٱلأُمَّةِ عَلَى رَأْسِ كُلِّ مِئَةِ سَنَةٍ مَنْ يُجَدِّدُ لَها دِينَها."

(رواه الحاكم. حديث صحيح)

Narrated Abū Hurayra: "Verily, God—exalted be He—sends to this community at the beginning of each century a man in charge of reviving the religion."

(Quoted by al-Ḥākim. Authenticated *ḥadīth*)

Commentary

The reviver (*mujaddid*), mentioned in this *ḥadīth*, is in charge of eradicating through his intellectual and spiritual radiation blameworthy innovation (*bid'a ḍalāla*) which destroys religion from the inside. But he will also know how to recognize the validity and usefulness of praiseworthy innovation (*bid'a ḥasana*) made necessary by the change of all (social) orders touching Dār al-Islām. 'Abd al-Ra'ūf al-Munāwī defined the function of the *mujaddid* in these terms: "He announces clearly that which belongs to the Tradition (*sunna*) and that which constitutes a blameworthy innovation (*bid'a*); he revives knowledge (*'ilm*) and recalls the supremacy of gnosis (*ma'rifa*)."[257]

Quite often, the man in charge of reviving the religion is aware of his mission and of the graces he has received in order to lead religion to the good. This, however, does not prevent hesitation, which in the case of a saint, are expressions of the extreme humility attained.

Among those who were considered *mujaddidūn* we mention: al-Ghazzālī (d. 505/1111), al-Suyūṭī (d. 1505), Aḥmad al-Sirhindī (d. 1624), and the Shaykh 'Alāwī (d. 1934).

al-Ghazzālī

I finally realized that, in many venues, faith had become weak for different reasons. And yet, I knew myself to be capable of disclosing their shortcomings; this was easier for me than drinking a cup of water. Indeed, I knew very well the doctrines of all those people: false Sufis, philosophers, ta'limites etc. [. . .]

Then I sought the advice of the folk of contemplation and, having mastered the "realities of the heart" (*arbāb al-qulūb*), they all agreed that I end my retreat, and come out of the zāwiya. Furthermore, virtuous men (*ṣāliḥūn*) came to me in different dreams indicating that good and guidance

257. *Fayḍ al-Qadīr*, *ḥadīth* no. 1845.

followed my return. Such was the will of God Most High at the beginning of the [sixth] century. I was encouraged by these beautiful premonitions, for God has promised to revive His Religion at the beginning of each century.

(*Munqidh*, pp. 48-49)

Biographical Notes

(Biographies are in chronological order)

Ḥasan al-Baṣrī:

Abū Sa'īd al-Khudrī al-Ḥasan ibn Abī al-Ḥasan Yasār al-Baṣrī was born in 21/645. This celebrated preacher of the generation of the Followers (*tābi'īn*) has remained one of the most respected Predecessors for later generations. He is often cited in mystical treatises as a major example of asceticism and piety. He died in 110/728.

al-Junayd:

Abū al-Qāsim al-Junayd al-Baghdādī. Often called master (*sayyid*) and guide (*imām*) of the mystics. Numerous brief and incisive sayings on the spiritual life and the path of *taṣawwuf* have been related from him. He died in 297/911.

al-Sarrāj:

Abū Naṣr al-Sarrāj al-Tūsī is the author of the oldest extant mystical treatise in the Muslim world, *Kitāb al-Luma'*. In this work, he laid out the foundations of Sufism based on five *ḥadith*. He also explained the spiritual meaning given to many other *ḥadīth* by the early Sufis. He died in 378/988.

al-Qushayrī:

'Abd al-Karīm al-Qushayrī was born in 376/986. His *Risāla* remains one of the most studied manuals of Sufism. This work is marked by strong reliance on the science of *Ḥadīth*. He also wrote a great mystical commentary of the Qur'ān, *Laṭā'if al-ishārāt*. He died in Nishapur in 465/1072.

al-Anṣārī:

'Abd Allāh al-Anṣārī was born in 396/1006 in Herat. This great mystic was also a Ḥanbali jurist and a remarkable *muḥaddith*. His most important mystical work is *Manāzil al-sā'irīn* where he expounded on the hundred spiritual states that the traveller goes through in the spiritual Path. He died in 481/1089.

al-Ghazzālī:

Abū Ḥāmid al-Ghazzālī was born in Ṭūs in 450/1058. Called *ḥujjat al-islām* ("Proof of Islam") already in his lifetime, he left a mark on the Muslim religious sciences and spirituality. His major work is *Iḥyā' 'ulūm al-dīn* in which he deals with the entirety of the religious sciences in forty books. He died in his birthplace in 505/1111.

Ibn al-'Arabī:

Muḥyī al-Dīn Muḥammad Ibn al-'Arabī was born in Murcia of Andalusia in 560/1165. Among his immense oeuvre, the two principal works are the great spiritual summa *Futūḥāt al-makkiyya* and *Fuṣūs al-ḥikam*, in which he summarizes all his metaphysical doctrine. Regarded as the *Shaykh al-akbar*—the spiritual master *par excellence*—he has had a great impact on the evolution of mystical doctrines. He died in Damascus in 638/1240.

Ibn 'Aṭā' Allāh:

Ibn 'Aṭā' Allāh al-Askandarī was born near the middle of the 7th/13th century in Alexandria, where he received a solid training in the various religious sciences. At first he was hostile to Sufism due to the great confidence he had in bookish knowledge. It was after meeting with Abū al-'Abbās al-Mursī (d. 686/1287)—who would become his master—that he realized the importance of Sufism. His most celebrated work is the collection of "wise sayings" called *al-Ḥikam al-'aṭā'iyya*. This collection was quickly adopted as a teaching manual in the greatest centers of learning of the Muslim world (Qarawiyyīn, al-Azhar, etc.). He died in Cairo, where he is buried, in 709/1309.

al-Suyūṭī:

Jalāl al-Dīn al-Suyūṭī was born in Cairo in 894/1445. From the age of eighteen he taught *fiqh* and issued *fatwas*. Gifted with remarkable scientific aptitudes in many fields, al-Suyūṭī authored works on nearly all religious sciences: commentary of the Qur'ān, *Ḥadīth*, *uṣūl al-fiqh*, *fiqh*, as well as history, lexicography, pharmacopeia, dietetics, etc. Many of his works are still irreplaceable references as *al-Itqān fī 'ulūm al-qur'ān*. He died in 911/1505.

al-Sha'rānī:

'Abd al-Wahhāb al-Sha'rānī was born in Egypt in 903/1497. When he was twelve, his family moved to Cairo, where he grew up in a Sufi environment. His great attachment to the Book and the Sunna showed through in his way of exposing the mystical doctrines of Islam, both in his numerous written works and in his oral teachings which he transmitted to his disciples. He died in 973/1565.

al-Munāwī:

'Abd al-Ra'ūf al-Ḥaddādī al-Munāwī was born in Cairo in 952/1545. His first spiritual master was al-Sha'rānī, and later on he was initiated into the Shādhiliyya and the Naqshbandiyya orders. He has left a considerable oeuvre; over one hundred books are attributed to him, many of which are lengthy works. Particularly well-versed in the science of *Ḥadīth*, he wrote a commentary on al-Suyūṭī's *al-Jāmi' al-ṣaghīr* entitled *Fayḍ al-Qadīr fī sharḥi'l-Jāmi' al-ṣaghīr*. This commentary devotes a large space to the mystical interpretation of the *ḥadīth*.

His teaching and his personal reasoning drew a large number of disciples, but a lot of jealousy as well. He was poisoned and died in Cairo in 1031/1621.

'Abd al-'Azīz al-Dabbāgh:

This *ummī* shaykh who never received any formal theological training was one of the greatest interpreters of the Sufi doctrines. His oral teachings were gathered by a disciple who was well-versed in Islamic sciences, especially in *Ḥadīth*, Ibn al-Mubārak al-Lamṭī (d. 1156/1743). Al-Dabbāgh died in Fez in 1142/1720 and is buried there.

Shaykh al-Darqāwī:

Al-'Arabī al-Darqāwī al-Ḥasanī lived in Morocco, where he died in 1239/1823, at the age of eighty-four. A reviver of the Shādhiliyya order, he founded the branch which is named after him. He did not write any work, leaving this responsibility to eminent disciples like Ibn 'Ajība. His letters were gathered on the initiative of his disciples and are read, meditated and commented upon by spiritual masters to this day.

Ibn 'Ajība:

Aḥmad ibn Ajība al-Ḥasanī al-Ḥajjūjī was born in 1160/1747 in a village of the Tetouan region of Morocco. This disciple of Shaykh al-Darqāwī was a great sage and an accomplished spiritual master. Among his numerous works, his commentary of the Qur'ān, *al-Baḥr al-madīd* should be mentioned in which he makes use of all his erudition—lexicography, reasons of revelation (*asbāb al-nuzūl*), *fiqh*, etc.—but also his spiritual sensitivity which shows through in the mystical interpretations he gives to the verses. He died in 1224/1809.

Amīr 'Abd al-Qādir:

He was born in Mascara (Algeria) in 1807 to a family of scholars. He led the resistance against the French army in Algeria from 1832 to 1847. In 1856, he settled in Damascus, where his master Ibn al-'Arabī had chosen to spend the end of his life. It is there that the radiance of the spiritual master gained its full splendor. The spiritual teachings he transmitted to his disciples were gathered under the title *Kitāb al-Mawāqif*. He died in Damascus in 1883, surrounded by his family and disciples.

Shaykh al-'Alawī:

Born in Mostaghanem (Algeria) in 1864, Aḥmad ibn 'Aliwa was initiated by Shaykh Būzīdī, who was member of the Darqāwiyya branch of the Shādhiliyya order. His spiritual radiance was enormous; he had over one hundred thousand disciples all over the world. His intellectual radiance was no less considerable: besides the technical works he published, he founded a journal, *al-Balāgh al-jazā'irī* in which he dealt with both spiritual and social issues, always from a strictly traditional perspective. He died in Mostaghanem in 1934.

Shaykh 'Abd al-Wāḥid Yaḥyā (René Guénon):

Born on November 15, 1886, this mathematician by training turned very early to the study of traditional doctrines of the East, and then to Islam, which he embraced in 1912. In 1930 he settled in Egypt, where he lived under the name of 'Abd al-Wāḥid Yaḥyā and wrote his most important books. In his works he tried to show the universal principles that are still preserved by the spiritual traditions of the East, and the decline of the modern West due to the loss of these very principles. On this subject, we mention *The Crisis of the Modern World The Reign of Quantity*, and the *Signs of the Times*. He died in Cairo in 1951, and is buried there.

Shaykh 'Īsā Nūr al-Dīn Aḥmad (Frithjof Schuon):

Born in Basel on June 18, 1907, Frithjof Schuon was the great spokeman of traditional metaphysics following Guénon, and at the same time a spiritual master of great stature. His written oeuvre is considered a "masterpiece of equilibrium and nuances." Among the twenty-odd works which he published in his lifetime, mention must be made of *Spiritual Perspectives and Human Facts*, as well as *Understanding Islam*. Relentlessly emphasizing the importance of invocation of the Name of God (*dhikr Allāh*), Shaykh 'Isā Nūr al-Dīn Aḥmad passed away at dawn, while invoking, on May 5, 1998, in Bloomington (Indiana).

Ibrāhīm 'Izz al-Dīn (Titus Burckhardt):

This German Swiss was born in Florence in 1908. Having been drawn very early on by the wisdom of the East, he went to Fez at the beginning of the 1930's to find a spiritual master. He stayed there several years. He dedicated all his life to the study and exposition of the different aspects of Tradition. In this undertaking, he headed the multidisciplinary team mandated by UNESCO for the safeguarding of the city of Fez, from 1975 to 1978. Among his most important works, we mention *Introduction to Sufi Doctrine*, *Principles and Methods of Sacred Art*, *Alchemy: Science of the Cosmos, Science of the Soul*, and *Fez: City of Islam*. He died in Lausanne in 1984.

Shaykh Abū Bakr Sirāj al-Dīn (Martin Lings):

He was born in England on January 24, 1909 to a Protestant family. After having discovered the works of René Guénon, he met with Frithjof Schuon in 1938 and embraced Islam, taking the name Abū Bakr Sirāj al-Dīn. After working as Keeper of Arabic manuscripts at the British Library, he dedicated himself entirely to the functions of spiritual master and to his written works, amongst which we mention: *A Sufi Saint of the Twentieth Century*, *Muḥammad: His life based on the Earliest Sources*, and *What is Sufism?* He died in England on May 12, 2005.

Shaykh ʻAlī Jumʻa:

Born on March 3, 1951, ʻAli Jumʻa has been the Grand-mufti of Egypt since 2003. This expert in the principles of Islamic jurisprudence (*uṣūl al-fiqh*) is also a spiritual man and a fine connoisseur of Muslim mysticism. Besides his numerous works on the principles of jurisprudence, he has recently published a collection of one hundred *fatwas*, many of which concern subjects related to mysticism: *al-Bayān limā yashgal al-adhhān.*

Yūsuf Khaṭṭār:

Yūsuf Muḥammad Khaṭṭār was born in Ramthaniyya (Golan) in 1963. His family settled in Damascus in 1967. He obtained his Ph.D. in Islamic sciences from the University of al-Azhar in 2002. He has received numerous *ijāzāt* in the transmission of *Ḥadīth.*

Index of Proper Nouns

I

J

K

Index of Main Technical Terms in Arabic